# Let's Get Biblical! Why Doesn't Judaism Accept the Christian Messiah?

## By Rabbi Tovia Singer

*Dedicated to my beloved father, Rabbi Shlomo Zalmen Singer,*
*who reared me with an unyielding love for the God of Israel*
*and an unquenchable thirst for His Torah.*

*With deep gratitude to my inspiring uncle, Meir Yisrael Singer,*
*who filled my heart with a love for Zion, and in my*
*youth, gave me a King James Bible in order to*
*bring home our lost Jewish brethren from the Church.*

*In memory of my precious grandmother who*
*inspired me beyond measure.*
לאה בת ר׳ יעקב ע״ה
*Her soul is bound with the Holy One*
נפ׳ כז אייר תשמ״ז

I thank Dr. Lynn Gimpel and Brenne Meirowitz for their devotion in editing the manuscript,
and Svetlana Raivich for her insightful cover design.

*Let's Get Biblical! Why Doesn't Judaism Accept the Christian Messiah?*


RNBN Publishing
ISBN-10 0-615-34839-4
ISBN-13 978-0-615-34839-1

## New York Office

Outreach Judaism
P.O. Box 789
Monsey, NY 10952
(800) 315-5397

## Jerusalem, Israel Office

Outreach Judaism
P.O. Box 1572
Jerusalem, Israel 91014

*This work is*

*dedicated in loving memory of*

*Otto De Souza Aguiar ז״ל*

*and*

*Lillian Jean Kaplan ע״ה*

*by their children in order to uphold*

*the Fifth Commandment*

Outreach Judaism

Your financial support makes it possible for Outreach Judaism to provide much needed counseling, essential programs, and fascinating lectures throughout the world. The work of bringing the Jewish people back from the Church is an expensive one.

Please support Outreach Judaism – your generous contribution makes it possible to for us to help lost souls in the Church return back to the truth and beauty of the Jewish faith.

Outreach Judaism is a non-profit organization and all contributions are tax-deductible.
Visit us on line to support our work,
or send your contribution to:

Outreach Judaism
P.O. Box 789
Monsey, NY 10952

# Contents

## Part V



## Part VI

# Preface

By Gavriel Aryeh Sanders
*(formerly Rev. Mark W. Sanders)*

The last thing I ever expected to be was a Torah-observant Jew. Growing up poor in a broken home with little religious influence, I embraced the Christian gospel at 16, partly through a Calvary Chapel-related commune for former street people during the early "Jesus movement" in Southern California. We were a rag-tag group – burnt out from the sex, drugs, and rock-and-roll influences of the free love culture. But through faith in a personal lord and savior, hundreds of thousands of us united around the Great Commission in a collective effort to evangelize a lost and dying world before it was too late – before hundreds of millions of believers would be divinely snatched off the planet in the Rapture, the precursor event to the seven year Great Tribulation period in which the world would be ruled – and ultimately tyrannized – by the Antichrist.

I became a member and eventually a minister of the International Church of the Foursquare Gospel, a rapidly growing Pentecostal-charismatic denomination – very similar to the Assemblies of God. I was a close disciple of such leaders as Roy Hicks, Jr. and Dr. Jack Hayford. While my evangelical professors had taught me that the gospel must be proclaimed "to all the world," they placed a premium on reaching Jewish people. (This book will explain why.) My passion for winning Jewish souls led me to living four years in Israel, first as a student of Hebrew and later as an English teacher, using my professional skills as a cover for my missionary activities.

Over time, my studies of Hebrew caused fractures in my faith. As I examined missionary proof texts in Hebrew to share them with spiritually illiterate Israelis, I noted that something seemed "off." The English translations I knew so well appeared either mistranslated or taken out of context when compared with the Hebrew original. How could this be? Wasn't the Bible – the Old and New Testaments – a seamless, divinely inspired work? Wasn't Jesus the fulfillment of some 300 Old Testament prophecies by which we could surely identify the promised Redeemer? Hadn't the Jews rejected their own Messiah and for 2,000 years paid the price of exile for rejecting him? I was less and less sure.

The few friends I spoke to of my doubts diagnosed I was under the influence of demons. But having done graduate studies in linguistics, I couldn't argue with the Hebrew texts; they didn't support the missionary interpretations. Questions tugged at me: Was Christianity true because I believed it – or did I believe it because it was true? Gasping to get back on more solid footing, I left Israel to take up a position in a large California church.

Two years later, I left the ministry. There was no gracious way to leave. I was hurting and I hurt a lot of people. For eight years, I wondered and wandered, spiritually and geographically, including a two and half year stint as an English teacher in Saudi Arabia.

Having dabbled with a veritable stew of spiritual alternatives, I had an intuitive sense that Judaism was unique among the world's faith systems, but I wasn't quite sure why. Curiously, I discovered an article by Rabbi Tovia Singer, which challenged me to objectively examine the textual evidence for the resurrection of Jesus. Jesus' resurrection is the most cardinal doctrine in the New Testament; without it, all else unravels. Rabbi Singer recommended an approach of self-study. I took it. And I let go of Jesus.

Now that I was free to examine Judaism with a clearer eye and a freer heart, I entered the Jewish world through a liberal Jewish movement (which actually reminded me of liberal Protestantism). But within a couple of years, I concluded that if Judaism was a house, I was living on the porch. My experience, while warm and culturally stimulating, was spiritually thin.

Around this time, a former Messianic rabbi told me that Rabbi Tovia Singer was lecturing in our area. I attended and left duly challenged to help other Jews influenced by missionaries. I went through another conversion, a more rigorous and demanding Orthodox process, and on the 23rd of Kislev 5760 – two days before Chanukah in December 1999, I emerged from the waters of the Los Angeles *mikveh* with a new name – Gavriel Aryeh ben Avraham. Now ten years later, I can affirm that it's been a whole new, multi-faceted life – as rewarding as it's been challenging.

I've crossed paths with Rabbi Singer a number of times since. I've been a guest on his broadcasts and he was guest on mine when I was on New York radio. We spent challenging days together as part of a support mission to Gush Katif in the summer of 2005. We've shared in lectures together, and like many former evangelical Christians who've embraced Torah observance, I've attentively absorbed his lectures and study materials.

For a quarter of a century, Rabbi Singer has traveled the world helping Jews discover the richness and beauty hidden in their own spiritual heritage. Many of them had taken a detour into missionary Christianity and the Messianic movement in a quest for spiritual satisfaction. The book you hold now contains compelling biblical truths which brought them out of the Church and back home to the faith of Abraham, Isaac, Jacob, David, Solomon, the Hebrew prophets, and millions of anonymous Jews who dared cling to the Torah despite all efforts to convert them away. If it hadn't been for these brave and faithful souls, those Jews who believe in Jesus today wouldn't even know they are Jewish!

Ironically, missionaries will study this book in an effort to sharpen their counter-arguments. Sincere students of the Bible will pour through it to understand why Jews have said "no" to the overtures of evangelicals for centuries. But earnest seekers will employ this book to connect with the unbroken chain of Torah learning and living.

While an easy book to read, this is a hard book to master. It chiropractically adjusts misaligned beliefs. That's not comfortable. But it's necessary as we proceed into these days our Sages regard as "*ikveseh d'meshicha*" – the footsteps of messiah. As Rabbi Singer indicates in these pages, the ultimate redemption and revelation of the Jewish people as the historical torchbearers of the Almighty is near. May this book serve as a homing beacon for many who, like I did, wondered and wandered, yet never stopped looking for the path.

*B'vracha* – with blessing

Gavriel Aryeh ben Avraham
(formerly Rev. Mark W. Sanders)

# Authors's Introduction

The vast, in-depth study of both Jewish and Christian Scriptures explored in this book is not typical of Jewish literature. Rather, I wrote this work in response to the growing and unyielding effort of numerous fundamentalist Christian organizations which aggressively target Jews for conversion.

This *Let's Get Biblical Study Guide*, therefore, delves into the fundamental reasons why Judaism does not accept the Christian messiah. It illustrates why the core teachings and doctrines of the Church are spiritually incompatible with the cornerstone principles declared by the Prophets of Israel, and are opposed by the most cherished tenets expressed in the Jewish Scriptures.

Moreover, this book demonstrates how, over the course of many centuries, the Church systematically and deliberately altered the Jewish Scriptures in its authorized translations of the Bible in order to persuade its adherents that Jesus is the promised Jewish messiah. To accomplish this task, Christian "translators" manipulated, misquoted, mistranslated, and even fabricated verses in the Hebrew Scriptures so that these texts appear to be speaking about Jesus. Consequently, Jewish people who are most vulnerable to Jewish evangelism are those who know least about the faith they have been asked to abandon.

Over the past two millennia, Christendom's faithful have tragically been unaware of this systematic and odious Bible-tampering because virtually no Christian can read or understand the Hebrew Scriptures in its original language. Since time immemorial, earnest parishioners blindly and utterly depended upon manmade Christian "translations" of the "Old Testament" in order to understand the "Word of God." As a result, Christians have wondered aloud why Jewish people, who are reared since childhood in the Holy Tongue, and are the bearers and protectors of the sacred Oracles of God, do not accept Jesus as their messiah. The central goal of this volume is to thoroughly answer this nagging, age-old question.

Finally, this book was written in a manner that uses Christianity as a foil to reflect back the truth and beauty of the Jewish faith.

Included within this volume (Part II - Part XIV) are the extensive references and charts cited in the *Let's Get Biblical* audio series, which is available online at www.OutreachJudaism.org.

With love of Zion,

Rabbi Tovia Singer

# Part I

# Evangelizing the Jews

## MESSIANIC SOUL-WINNER'S CARD

*"The fruit of the righteous is a tree of life, and he that wins souls is wise!" – Proverbs 11:30*

**A. BECOME "AS A JEW, TO THE JEWS!"** (1 Cor. 9:20)

| DO SAY | DON'T SAY |
|---|---|
| (1) MESSIAH YESHUA, MESSIAH JESUS, THE MESSIAH | (1) JESUS CHRIST |
| (2) MESSIANIC JEW, COMPLETED JEW, FULFILLED JEW | (2) CONVERT |
| (3) A BIBLE BELIEVER | (3) A CHRISTIAN |
| (4) COME TO A MEETING OF BIBLE BELIEVERS | (4) COME TO CHURCH |
| (5) 2ND PART OF BIBLE, NEW COVENANT | (5) NEW TESTAMENT |
| (6) TREE, EXECUTION STAKE | (6) CROSS |

***EXPLANATION***

(1) The term "CHRIST" does NOT have *ANY* Jewish connotation to the average Jew.
(2) "Convert" means to TAKE AWAY Judaism and to become a "goy," a Gentile. "MESSIANIC JEW" means to BUILD UPON OR ADD TO his Jewish heritage by *gaining* the atonement, *gaining* the Messiah and *GAINING A MORE PERSONAL RELATIONSHIP WITH GOD!* He does not have to give up his wonderful Biblical Jewish heritage. Emphasize what he gains!
(3) ALL non-Jews are considered CHRISTIANS, even Hitler.
(4) The term "CHURCH" is too Gentile to be desirable to a Jewish person.
(5) "New Testament" is considered a NON-JEWISH book. *Don't emphasize its name*. USE IT!
(6) The "CROSS" has been a symbol of Jewish persecution for centuries.

(OVER)

**Communications Card used to train missionaries to convert Jews**

---

Though I am free and belong to no man, I make myself a slave to everyone, to win as many as possible. [20]To the Jews I became like a Jew, to win the Jews. To those under the law I became like one under the law (though I myself am not under the law), so as to win those under the law. [21]To those not having the law I became like one not having the law (though I am not free from God's law but am under Christ's law), so as to win those not having the law. [22]To the weak I became weak, to win the weak. I have become all things to all men so that by all possible means I might save some.

I Corinthians 9:19-22

# The Reformers Offe

## *On The Jews and Their Lies*
## By Martin Luther — 1543

What then shall we Christians do with this damned, rejected race of Jews? Since they live among us and we know about their lying and blasphemy and cursing, we can not tolerate them if we do not wish to share in their lies, curses, and blasphemy. In this way we cannot quench the inextinguishable fire of divine rage nor convert the Jews. We must prayerfully and reverentially practice a merciful severity. Perhaps we may save a few from the fire and flames [of hell]. We must not seek vengeance. They are surely being punished a thousand times more than we might wish them. Let me give you my honest advice.

First, their synagogues should be set on fire, and whatever does not burn up should be covered or spread over with dirt so that no one may ever be able to see a cinder or stone of it. And this ought to be done for the honor of God and of Christianity in order that God may see that we are Christians, and that we have not wittingly tolerated or approved of such public lying, cursing, and blaspheming of His Son and His Christians.

Secondly, their homes should likewise be broken down and destroyed. For they perpetrate the same things there that they do in their synagogues. For this reason they ought to be put under one roof or in a stable, like gypsies, in order that they may realize that they are not masters in our land, as they boast, but miserable captives, as they complain of incessantly before God with bitter wailing.

Thirdly, they should be deprived of their prayer-books and Talmuds in which such idolatry, lies, cursing, and blasphemy are taught.

Fourthly, their rabbis must be forbidden under threat of death to teach any more....

Fifthly, passport and traveling privileges should be absolutely forbidden to the Jews. For they have no business in the rural districts since they are not nobles, nor officials, nor merchants, nor the like. Let them stay at home...If you princes and nobles do not close the road legally to such exploiters, then some troop ought to ride against them, for they will learn from this pamphlet what the Jews are and how to handle them and that they ought not to be protected. You ought not, you cannot protect them, unless in the eyes of God you want to share all their abomination...

To sum up, dear princes and nobles who have Jews in your domains, if this advice of mine does not suit you, then find a better one so that you and we may all be free of this insufferable devilish burden - the Jews....

Let the government deal with them in this respect, as I have suggested. But whether the government acts or not, let everyone at least be guided by his own conscience and form for himself a definition or image of a Jew. When you lay eyes on or think of a Jew you must say to yourself: Alas, that mouth which I there behold has cursed and execrated and maligned every Saturday my dear Lord Jesus Christ, who has redeemed me with his precious blood; in addition, it prayed and pleaded before God that I, my wife and children, and all Christians might be stabbed to death and perish miserably. And he himself would gladly do this if he were able, in order to appropriate our goods....

Such a desperate, thoroughly evil, poisonous, and devilish lot are these Jews, who for these fourteen hundred years have been and still are our plague, our pestilence, and our misfortune.

I have read and heard many stories about the Jews which agree with this judgment of Christ, namely, how they have poisoned wells, made assassinations, kidnaped children, as related before. I have heard that one Jew sent another Jew, and this by means of a Christian, a pot of blood, together with a barrel of wine, in which when drunk empty, a dead Jew was found. There are many other similar stories. For their kidnaping of children they have often been burned at the stake or banished (as we already heard). I am well aware that they deny all of this. However, it all coincides with the judgment of Christ which declares that they are venomous, bitter, vindictive, tricky serpents, assassins, and children of the devil, who sting and work harm stealthily wherever they cannot do it openly. For this reason, I would like to see them where there are no Christians. The Turks and other heathen do not tolerate what we Christians endure from these venomous serpents and young devils...next to the devil, a Christian has no more bitter and galling foe than a Jew. There is no other to whom we accord as many benefactions and from whom we suffer as much as we do from these base children of the devil, this brood of vipers.

Translated by Martin H. Bertram, *On The Jews and Their Lies*, Luther's Works, Volume 47; Philadelphia: Fortress Press, 1971.

For the complete text of Luther's *On The Jews and Their Lies*, go to
http://www.outreachjudaism.org/luther1543new.html

# Some Advice on the Jews

## *Of The Unknowable Name and The Generations of Christ*

By Martin Luther — 1543

3ut your [God's] judgement is right, justus es Domine. Yes, so shall Jews, but no one else be punished, who held your word and miracles in contempt and ridiculed, insulted and damned it for such a long time without interruption, so that they will t fall, like other humans, heathens and all the others, into sin and death, not up in Hell, r in the middle of Hell but in the pit of Hell, as one cannot fall deeper....

Even if they were punished in the most gruesome manner that the streets ran with ir blood, that their dead would be counted, not in the hundred thousands, but in the llions, as happened under Vespasian in Jerusalem and for evil under Hadrian, still they ıst insist on being right even if after these 1,500 years they were in misery another 1,500 ırs, still God must be a liar and they must be correct. In sum, they are the devil's ldren, damned to Hell....

The Jews too got what they deserved. They had been called and elected to be d's mouth as Jeremiah says...Open your mouth wide and I will fill it; they however, kept ıtly closed their muzzles, eyes, ears, nose, whole heart and all senses, so he polluted and ırted them so full that it oozes from them in all places and devil's filth comes from m.

Yes, that tastes good to them, into their hearts, they smack their lips like swine. ıt is how they want it. Call more: 'Crucify him, crucify him.' Scream more: 'His blood ne upon us and our children.' (Matthew 27:25) I mean it came and found you...

Perhaps, one of the merciful Saints among us Christians may think I am behaving crudely and disdainfully against the poor, miserable Jews in that I deal with them so castically and insultingly. But, good God, I am much too mild in insulting such devils....

---

## *A Response To Questions and Objections of a Certain Jew*

By John Calvin

Their [the Jews] rotten and unbending stiffneckedness deserves that they be oppressed unendingly and without measure or end and that they die in their misery without the pity of anyone.

rpts from *Vom Schem Hamphoras und vom Geschlecht Christi*, By Martin Luther and an excerpt from *uaestiones et Objecta Judaie Cuiusdam Responsio*, by John Calvin; *The Jew in Christian Theology*; rson, NC and London, 1931: Gerhard Falk, McFarland and Company, Inc.

*Germans in Berlin walk by the broken window of a Jewish shop destroyed during Kristallnacht. November 10, 1938.*

זָכוֹר אֵת אֲשֶׁר
עָשָׂה לְךָ

**Deuteronomy 25:17**

Remember...

**On the night of Martin Luther's birthday, November 9-10, 1938, 191 synagogues throughout Germany were set on fire, and 76 were completely destroyed; 815 Jewish-owned shops were demolished, 29 warehouses and 171 homes were set on fire or likewise destroyed. On that night, infamously known as *Kristallnacht* ("Night of the Broken Glass"), more than 30,000 Jews were sent to concentration camps, and 36 Jews were murdered. This study guide is dedicated to their memory.**

# Founders of Christianity Demonize the Jews

## By Jesus of Nazareth — 30 C.E.

Ye [Jews] are of your father the devil, and the lusts of your father ye will do. He was a murderer from the beginning, and abode not in truth, because there is no truth in him. When he speaketh a lie, he speaketh of his own: for he is a liar, and the father of it. [45]And because I [Jesus] tell you the truth, ye believe me not.

John 8:44-45

---

## By Saint Paul — 51 C.E.

...even as they have of the Jews: [15]Who both killed the Lord Jesus, and their own prophets, and have persecuted us; and they please not God, and are contrary to all men: [16]Forbidding us to speak to the Gentiles that they might be saved, to fill up their sins alway: for the wrath is come upon them to the uttermost.

I Thessalonians 2:14-16

# Preying on the Jews

No Sunday services take place here; this congregation meets only on Friday evenings and Saturday mornings. You will never see a cross or an altar; there is an *Aaron Hakodesh* (holy ark) with a star of David adorning its velvet cover, and a *Bimah* (stage for prayer services) in the center of the sanctuary. The majority of the men who worship here wear *kipot*, and their *tzitzit* hang down the sides of their pants. This congregation's rabbi, among many other functions, reads from the Torah and makes *Kiddush* every *Shabbat*. Most of the women are modestly dressed. Joyous shouts of "*Shabbat Shalom*" and "*Baruch Hashem*" can be heard as young couples greet each other. The sanctuary pulsates to a modern Israeli musical beat.

> Evangelical Christian churches use traditional Jewish symbols to entice vulnerable Jews.

If this sounds like a description of a traditional Jewish house of worship, think again. The above is actually a description of any one of the hundreds of Messianic "synagogues" which flourish throughout the world. Confused? Many are.

**New Testament in Hebrew and Yiddish**

Such congregations are designed to appear Jewish, but they are actually fundamentalist Christian churches which use traditional Jewish symbols to lure the most vulnerable of our Jewish people into their ranks. Messianic "rabbis," many of whom are Jewish by birth, are committed to bringing the Jewish people to know Jesus. Their agenda is to make Christianity more palatable to the uneducated Jew, and to the astonishment and horror of the Jewish community, their marketing ploys are proving to be successful.

A few decades ago, only and handful of Messianic congregations existed in the United States. Today, many hundreds actively attract and recruit Jews who, because they lack a sound Jewish education and support system, are buying the manipulative rhetoric and persuasive techniques of the Hebrew-Christian missionary movement.

די בשורה טובה לויט יוחנן

א אין אנהייב איז געווען דאס ווארט. און דאס ווארט איז
געווען ביי גאט. און דאס ווארט איז געווען גאט. 2 דאס דאזיקע
איז געווען אין אנהייב ביי גאט. 3 אלצדינג איז דורך אים געווארן,
און אן אים איז גארניט געווארן, וואס ס'איז געווארן. 4 אין אים
איז געווען לעבן. און דאס לעבן איז געווען דאס ליכט פון די
מענטשן. 5 און דאס ליכט שיינט אין דער פינצטערניש: און די
פינצטערניש האט עס ניט גובר געווען.
6 עס איז געווען א מענטש, געשיקט פון גאט, וואס האט געהייסן
יוחנן. 7 דער דאזיקער איז געקומען פאר אן עדות, אז ער זאל
עדות־זאגן פונוועגן דעם ליכט, כדי אלע זאלן דורך אים גלויבן.
8 ער איז ניט געווען דאס ליכט, נייערט איז געקומען, אז ער זאל
עדות־זאגן פונוועגן דעם ליכט. 9 דאס אמתע ליכט, וואס באלייכט
איטלעכן מענטשן, איז געקומען אין דער וועלט אריין.
10 ער איז געווען אין דער וועלט, און די וועלט איז דורך אים
געווארן, אבער די וועלט האט אים ניט געקענט. 11 ער איז געקומען
צו דעם זייניקן, און זיינע אייגענע האבן אים ניט אויפגענומען.
12 אבער וויפל סע האבן אים יא אויפגענומען, זיי האט ער געגעבן
מאכט צו ווערן קינדער פון גאט, טאקע די, וואס האבן געגלויבט
אין זיין נאמען: 13 וואס זענען געבוירן געווארן ניט פון בלוט,
אויך ניט פון דעם ווילן פון פלייש, אויך ניט פון דעם ווילן פון
א מאן, נייערט פון גאט.
14 און דאס ווארט איז געווארן פלייש, און האט געוואוינט צווישן
אונדז, און מיר האבן געזען זיין כבוד, א כבוד פון א בן־יחיד
ביי זיין פאטער, פול מיט חסד און אמת. 15 יוחנן האט פונוועגן
אים עדות געזאגט, און גערופן: דאס איז געווען דער, פון וועמען
איך האב געזאגט: דער, וואס קומט נאך מיר.

יוחנן

א בראשית היה הדבר והדבר היה את־האלהים והוא
2 הדבר היה אלהים: הוא היה מראש את־האלהים:
3 כל־המעשים נהיו על־ידו ואין דבר אשר נעשה
4 מבלעדיו: בו נמצא חיים והחיים הם אור האדם:
5 6 והאור זרח בחשך והחשך לא יכילנו: איש היה בארץ
7 יוחנן שמו אשר שלחו אלהים: הוא בא לעדות
8 להעיד על־האור למען יאמינו כלם על־ידו: ולא הוא
היה האור כי אם־בא להעיד על־האור ההוא:
9 הוא אור אמת אשר בא לעולם להאיר לכל־אדם:
10 הוא היה בעולם והעולם נהיה על־ידו והעולם אתו
11 לא ידע: הוא בא אל־עמו שלו ועמו שלו לא
12 החזיקו־בו: ואלה אשר החזיקו־בו נתן־כח בידם
להיות בנים לאלהים הלא הם המאמינים בשמו:
13 אשר לדתם לא מדם ולא מתאות בשר ולא מרוח
14 גבר כי אם־מאלהים: והדבר לבש בשר וישכן
בתוכנו ואת־כבודו ראינו ככבוד בן יחיד לאביו
15 מלא חסד ואמת: ויוחנן העיד עליו ויקרא לאמר
זה הוא אשר אמרתי עליו כי הוא בא אחרי והנה
הוא

**In effort to evangelize the elderly, missionaries distribute this Yiddish-Hebrew New Testament. Above, is the first chapter of the book of John.**

Additionally, there are over 1,000 Christian missions dedicated to converting the Jewish people. It is estimated that there are more than a quarter of a million Hebrew-Christians in North America and Israel.

A TRAINING MANUAL ON...

HOW TO SHARE THE MESSIAH

The Messianic Jewish Movement International

"And unto the Jews I became as a Jew, that I might gain the Jews" - I Corinthians 9:20



CONTENTS



As an exit-counselor who works with families to reclaim their Jewish family members from these churches, I can testify that the cost in terms of Jewish souls is dear.

In order to understand the dynamics of the missionary problem, we must first understand who exactly these missionaries are.

To the Jewish community, the word "missionary" is a charged word, with a multitude of misconceptions attached to it. It is typically associated with those people who stand on street corners, annoyingly and ubiquitously distributing literature, seeking to persuade individuals to believe in Jesus.

## Who are these missionaries?

When we think of missionaries we might think of an organization with members, mailing lists, secretaries, and buildings to which we can point and say, "You see that building on 31st street, between Lexington and Park (New York headquarters of Jews For Jesus)? They are the missionaries."

This is merely one of a variety of misconceptions we have about missionaries and how they operate.

A number of years ago, I lectured at a large university campus in Ohio. In my conversation with a dean, we began to discuss the work I do. He immediately reassured me that there was no missionary activity at his university. He recalled how years earlier there were indeed missionaries on his campus who distributed pamphlets and misused traditional Jewish symbols for the purpose of evangelizing. "But we don't have that here anymore," he insisted.

**I. WHAT IS THE PURPOSE OF THIS TRAINING?**

THE PERPOSE OF THIS TRAINING IS TO SHOW YOU HOW TO HELP YOUR JEWISH FRIEND TO PRAY WITH YOU TO INVITE THE MESSIAH INTO HIS HEART AND LIFE.

**II. HOW CAN YOU HELP YOUR JEWISH FRIEND TO PRAY WITH YOU TO INVITE THE MESSIAH INTO HIS HEART AND LIFE?**

A. YOU MUST KNOW WHO THE REAL SOUL-WINNER IS, *THE HOLY SPIRITY*, (Ru-ach Ha-Kodesh.)
B. You must understand your Jewish friend.
C. You must avoid that which will keep him away from the messiah.
D. You must emphasize that which will draw him to the Messiah.
E. You must create an interest in spiritual things.
F. You must make him want "what you (and others) have."
G. You must clearly explain the plan of atonement in the Messiah.
H. You must ask him to pray to invite the messiah into his heart and life.
I. You must show him how to pray to invite the Messiah into his heart and life.
J. You must pray with him to invite the Messiah into his heart and life.
K. You must follow-up with him.
L. You must be prepared to answer his questions.

**III. HOW CAN YOU UNDERSTAND YOUR JEWISH FRIEND?**

A. WHAT YOUR JEWISH FRIEND DOESN'T WANT AND DOESN'T KNOW...
B. HE HAS NO DESIRE TO BECOME A "CHRISTIAN" ("A *GOY, A GENTILE")
C. Even the very worst Jew, in his "heart-of-hearts" will say, "I was born a Jew, and I'll die a Jew!"
D. Becoming a "Christian to him means converting (changing his religion) and becoming a "**Goy*" (a gentile. It means giving up his wonderful Jewish heritage and no longer being a Jew!
E. So-called "Christians" have always persecuted him.
F. He probably is more moral than most of his "Christian" friends' therefore, his religion must be better than their religion. So, why give up his better religion for something inferior (especially at the risk of being ostracized – cut off – from his Jewish family and friends).

*"*Goy*" comes from the Hebrew word "*Goyim*" and refers to "The non-Jews, the nations, the heathen."

**The opening page of the Messianic Jewish Movement International's "Training Manuel on How to Share the Messiah with a Jew."**

**A serious missionary problem exists on any campus with evangelical, fundamentalist Christians**

"Tell me, are there any fundamentalist born-again Christians on your campus?" I asked.

He quickly snapped, "What? Are you kidding? This is the Midwest! We're packed with them!" I then informed him that in fact he had a serious missionary problem on his campus because, with rare exceptions,[1] fundamentalist, born-again Christians are dedicated to the idea of bringing every Jew to the Cross.

Our second mistake is that Jews have a tendency to view the Christian world as a monolithic group of gentiles who all essentially believe the same thing. In fact, the Christian world – with hundreds of

C. Avoid displaying pictures of Jesus or statues (which Jewish people consider as idolatry. Exodus 20:4)
D. Avoid displaying crosses (which Jewish people consider as symbols of persecution – the Crusades, the Spanish Inquisition, the Holocaust, etc.).
E. Avoid jokes about the Jewish people (their money, etc.). Some Jewish people are very sensitive about this. It's permissible for them to tell jokes on themselves; but, it may be offensive for another to do it. (Ephesians 5:4)
F. Avoid saying "Jews" or "You Jews," which are hard terms. It is better to say "The Jewish People."
G. Avoid using the names of Jewish missionary organizations. The word "Missionary" is interpreted by the Jewish people as "we're out to get you heathen Jews!"
H. Avoid saying "Jesus Christ, the Messiah." The term "Christ" does NOT have any Jewish connotation AT ALL to the average Jewish person and only "turns him off!"

   Since "Christ" means "Messiah," you are only really saying "Jesus the Messiah the Messiah," and are being redundant.

   It is much better to say "The Messiah" or "Messiah Yeshua" (The term "Yeshua" comes from the Hebrew and means "Salvation") or "Messiah Jesus" (in that order of preference).
I. Avoid anti-Semitic (anti-Jewish) term; such as… "Jewing-down"… "kikes"… "Christ-killers"… "dirty-Jew"… "Jew-boy"… etc. (Terms of prejudice and hate of ANY minority do not belong in the vocabulary of a child of God – I John 4:20!).

**V. WHAT CAN YOU EMPHASIZE TO DRAW YOUR JEWISH FRIENDS TO HIS MESSIAH?**

**EMPHASIZE THE FOLLOWING IN YOUR SHARING…**

A. Emphasize that one becomes a MESSIANIC JEW (a completed, fulfilled Jew) when he invites the Messiah into his heart and life.

   One does not give up his wonderful Jewish heritage; rather, he gains the atonement, he gains the Messiah and he gains a MORE personal relationship with the God of Abraham, Isaac and Jacob!

   It's not what he gives up. It's what he gains!!!
B. Emphasize that the Messiah makes one a better Jew and a better Person! There's no need to go home and stir up trouble!

   One should go home and QUIETLY show by his IMPROVED LIFE that GOD has made him a better Jew and a better person.

   Jewish believes are often among the most respected members of their families. Their marriages are happier and they don't have the problems of drug, divorce, etc.

**Page 5 of the Messianic "Training Manual on How to Share the Messiah with a Jew"**

> **Sorting out the complex Christian world – Roman Catholics and liberal Protestants are generally not interested in Jewish evangelism**

variant denominations that differ on numerous fundamental theological issues – is far more diverse than the Jewish world. At a baseball game, it is sometimes difficult to know who the players are without a scorecard. Let's break down the Christian world for a moment so that we know precisely to whom we are referring.

The Roman Catholic Church is by far the largest denomination in Christendom. Yet despite its past bitter relationship with the Jewish people, today Catholics are for the most part not interested in converting Jews. I need not worry that a Catholic priest is going to evangelize any of my patients at a hospital. If anything, he is one of the people who will show me where I can secure a kosher meal.

Another significant segment of the Christian world, especially in North America, is the Protestant community. For our purposes, we will over generalize and divide the Protestant world into two groups.

One group, the mainline or liberal Protestants (Methodist, Episcopalian, Unitarian, etc.), is not at all interested in converting Jews. Liberal-leaning Protestant denominations tend to shy away from any form of Jewish evangelism. It is, however, the other highly motivated and vocal segment within the Protestant community – the fundamentalist, born-again Christians – who are unyielding in their staunch commitment to convert the Jews.

There are two rules about Jewish evangelism that must always be kept in mind.

The first rule is that the Christian who makes the very first critical and successful contact with the Jew is almost never a professional missionary. It will not be a paid staff member of Jews for Jesus or Chosen People Ministries. Rather, it is most likely to be a layperson – perhaps a secretary at the office, a roommate in college or

> **Lay, gentile parishioners are most effective in evangelizing the Jews**

someone on the same swim team – who makes that initial effective connection. Only after the lay evangelical Christian has made this preliminary contact will the professional missionaries step in to the conversion process.

Secondly, the Christian layperson who makes that all-important first contact with the Jew is invariably a gentile. It is extremely rare for a "Hebrew-Christian" to successfully make that initial contact with a Jew. The perceived betrayal of the Jewish people by the Hebrew-Christian's apostasy sullies his message in the mind of a Jew. Non-Jewish Christians do not repel Jews. Only after the lay, gentile born-again Christian has made that first crucial and successful encounter with a Jew will the Hebrew-Christian missionaries step in to finalize the conversion.

In essence, the central role that Christian missions like Jews for Jesus plays is to act as a clearinghouse and support system for evangelical churches around the world. As a result, these Jewish missions spend much of their resources and manpower instructing lay missionaries in gentile churches in the art of Jewish-evangelism.

How serious a problem are these Protestant fundamentalist Christians? How many born-again Christians are there in the United States?

Their numbers are not small – they are the largest voting block in the United States. According to most estimates, there are well over 70 million Americans who identify themselves as born-again Christians. That is, nearly one in five Americans is part of this army of lay people dedicated to share their faith with a Jew. When I spoke in Nashville a number of years ago, an Assemblies of God minister bluntly told me that he would rather convert one Jew than 50,000 gentiles.

**Several reasons why fundamentalist Christians are obsessed with converting the Jews**

A question that naturally comes to mind is: Why the Jews? Why are these fundamentalist Christians so consumed with bringing the Jewish people to know Jesus? Why has the largest Protestant denomination in the United States, the Southern Baptist Convention, passed numerous resolutions

## Christian Bible prioritizes Jews

encouraging more than 15 million American members to target and evangelize the Jewish people?

Firstly, the New Testament specifically priori-tizes Jews for conversion. In the book of Matthew, when Jesus is instructing his apostles, he warns them:

> "Go not into the way of the gentiles ... but only go to the lost sheep of the house of Israel." (Matthew 10:5)

The Apostle Paul echoes the identical sentiment in the first chapter of the book of Romans when he declares:

> "For I am not ashamed of the gospel of Christ, for it is the power of God to salvation for everyone who believes, for the Jew first and also for the Greek [gentile]." (Romans 1:16)

We find a recurrent and unique emphasis on reaching the Jews in the New Testament, especially in the Gospels, almost to the exclusion of the gentiles.

A second reason for this obsession relates to the Church's fascination with eschatology, the study of the End of Times. Fundamentalist Christians are consumed by the prophecies surrounding the end of days. They want to know when the Messiah will come/return. How will this take place? To which nations did the prophet Ezekiel refer when he described how apocalyptic nations would wage war against Jerusalem before the final hour leading to the messianic age (Ezekiel 38-39)? Christian bookstores typically set aside an entire section dedicated to eschatological inquiry.

**Evangelical Christians widely believe that the mass conversion of the Jews will bring about Jesus' "second coming"**

How does all this apocalyptic speculation relate to our subject?

At the end of the book of Matthew (23:39), Jesus is quoted making a very important statement. He says,

> "I will not return until you say, 'Blessed is he who comes in the name of the Lord.'"

Because Jesus was addressing a Jewish audience at the time he made this statement, Christians have often understood this proclamation to have one meaning: Jesus will not make his second coming until large numbers of Jews embrace the Church.

The Jews, in a sense, are holding up the show. These evangelicals believe that Jesus' second coming is immanent and the Jews must be converted posthaste *en masse*, in order to enable Jesus to return.

Finally, the most significant reason for the Church's preoccupation with the Jews stems from the credibility problem that Judaism presents to Christendom.

Jesus was a Jew and Christians claim that he is the promised Messiah about whom all the prophets spoke. The idea of the Messiah – a man who will come at the End of Days to usher in a utopian society of love, peace, and the universal knowledge of God – is exclusively Jewish. Fundamentalist Christians insist that if the Jews would only look in their own Hebrew scriptures they would discover that Jesus is literally bouncing off every page. It stands to reason, therefore, that the Jews should have been the first to embrace Jesus and his teachings, if in fact Jesus was the prophesied Messiah. Jews should have overwhelmingly embraced the claims of the Church, if in fact Jesus was the prophesied Messiah. Strangely, the very people who brought the idea of a Messiah to the world and the only people who can read their Scriptures in its original language are the very people who rejected the Cross.

> Only the conversion of the Jew to Christianity lends credibility to the Church

This has always been a troubling reality to the Christendom since its inception. It is for this reason that only the conversion of a Jew to Christianity can lend credibility to the church – never the conversion of the gentile.

Peering back into world history, it would probably be quite difficult to imagine another program that has been a more miserable failure than the Church's persistent effort to convert the Jews to Christianity.

Bear in mind that Christianity swept through Europe almost overnight. The same is true for Latin America. Yet the Jews, with all the unyielding persecution and forced exile that they endured, would still not convert. Why has it been so difficult for the Church to persuade Jesus' coreligionists to embrace the Cross?

With the approach of the end of the second millennium, evangelicals were faced with a serious dilemma: How were they to finally bring the Jewish people to embrace the Cross?

This quandary presented a considerable challenge to the Church. With the year 2000 in sight, two critical conferences were convened during the mid-1970s. The most significant symposiums were held in Switzerland and the other in Thailand. The mystery they sought to unravel at these gatherings was simple: Why has the Church been so unsuccessful in their past efforts to convert the Jews, and most importantly – what new techniques can be employed to finally attract masses of new Jewish converts to the Church?

> Evangelicals sought to understand why it was so difficult to convert the Jews

It was at these unlikely locations that devout evangelists placed the Jewish people under a microscope. Indeed, it was at these symposiums that those Christians grasped that the Church had a number of serious challenges with respect to converting the Jews.

The first problem they discovered was that the Church had a significant public relations problem to overcome. They concluded that Jewish people historically tend to equate Christianity with persecution. Jewish people often feel somewhat uncomfortable just hearing the words "Jesus Christ," and when they see a cross or a church icon, it rarely conjures up warm, affectionate feelings. On the contrary, whereas Christians tend to feel quite comfortable in synagogues, or observing Jewish ceremonies, Jewish people tend to feel alienated by churches and its icons.

Taking this public relations problem head on, these evangelists initiated a unique approach. It goes something like this, "You're Jewish? We Christians just love the Jewish people! Persecution? Oh, no! Any Christian who persecuted a Jew in the name of Jesus couldn't be a real Christian. A real Christian only loves the Jewish people!"

> Evangelicals recognized that Jews did not want to stop being Jewish

This novel technique enables Christians to freely evangelize Jews by distancing themselves from their Christian forbears. In this way, potential Jewish converts will not feel alienated by Christendom.

Jews would not simply start converting to Christianity because evangelicals condemned anti-Semitism. These evangelists realized, however, that simply smothering us with love could not in itself be totally effective. Jews would not simply start converting to Christianity *en masse* because evangelicals loudly condemned anti-Semitism and were staunch supporters of Israel. They understood that the essential reason why Jews do not convert is because they do not want to stop being Jewish; and Jews view Christianity as antithetical to Judaism.

With this realization, these highly innovative and motivated Christians developed an entirely new and remarkably simple approach to Jewish evangelism. It Sounds like this: "When you're becoming a believer in Jesus, you are not converting to another religion. On the contrary, you're becoming a 'fulfilled Jew' or a 'completed Jew.' After all, Jesus was a Jew and his followers were Jewish; therefore, it stands to reason that believing in Jesus is the most Jewish thing you can do."

Messianic "synagogues" do

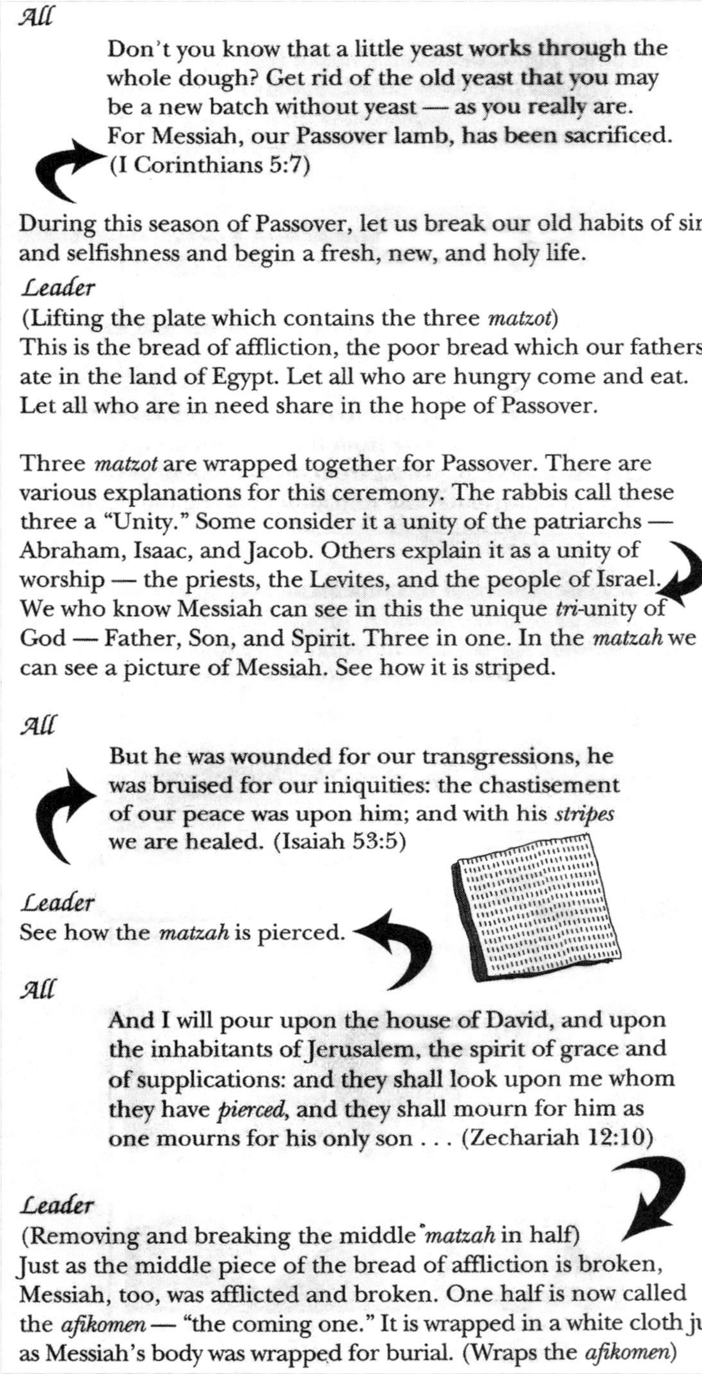

*All*

Don't you know that a little yeast works through the whole dough? Get rid of the old yeast that you may be a new batch without yeast — as you really are. For Messiah, our Passover lamb, has been sacrificed. (I Corinthians 5:7)

During this season of Passover, let us break our old habits of sin and selfishness and begin a fresh, new, and holy life.

*Leader*

(Lifting the plate which contains the three *matzot*)
This is the bread of affliction, the poor bread which our fathers ate in the land of Egypt. Let all who are hungry come and eat. Let all who are in need share in the hope of Passover.

Three *matzot* are wrapped together for Passover. There are various explanations for this ceremony. The rabbis call these three a "Unity." Some consider it a unity of the patriarchs — Abraham, Isaac, and Jacob. Others explain it as a unity of worship — the priests, the Levites, and the people of Israel. We who know Messiah can see in this the unique *tri*-unity of God — Father, Son, and Spirit. Three in one. In the *matzah* we can see a picture of Messiah. See how it is striped.

*All*

But he was wounded for our transgressions, he was bruised for our iniquities: the chastisement of our peace was upon him; and with his *stripes* we are healed. (Isaiah 53:5)

*Leader*

See how the *matzah* is pierced.

*All*

And I will pour upon the house of David, and upon the inhabitants of Jerusalem, the spirit of grace and of supplications: and they shall look upon me whom they have *pierced*, and they shall mourn for him as one mourns for his only son . . . (Zechariah 12:10)

*Leader*

(Removing and breaking the middle *matzah* in half)
Just as the middle piece of the bread of affliction is broken, Messiah, too, was afflicted and broken. One half is now called the *afikomen* — "the coming one." It is wrapped in a white cloth just as Messiah's body was wrapped for burial. (Wraps the *afikomen*)

**Above pages 12-13 in the "Messianic Passover Haggadah" illustrate how missionaries insert Christian theology into Jewish traditions.**

Christianity had to be portrayed as Jewish

not observe Christian holidays. You will never find a Christmas Tree or blinking colored lights around December in a Messianic congregation. Instead, these missionaries celebrate Jewish holidays with a "Christological" spin. Throughout the world, Messianic congregations hold elaborate and well-publicized Passover Seders.

**A MESSIANIC "SEDER"**

**Why is this widely sold "Passover Seder Dinner" set different from all others? Although it is difficult to tell from the packaging, it is a Messianic Seder kit available on online bookstores.**

At first glance, a Messianic Seder table appears quite traditional, with all of the customary essentials: Seder plate, matzah, and wine. Once the ceremony begins to unfold, however, even the most uninitiated will immediately realize that something is askew. Participants are told that the wine at the Seder table represents the blood of Yeshua/Jesus, and the matzah represents his body. Do you know the real reason why Jews have three matzoth at the Seder table? To represent the Holy Trinity: the Father, Son, and Holy Ghost. Do you know why the *matzahs* are perforated? Because Jesus was pierced through when he was crucified. Why does the *matzah* have stripes? Because Jesus had stripes across his back as a result of the beating he endured during his trial. Why is the middle *matzah* broken? Because Jesus was brutally broken on the cross. Why is the *matzah* wrapped in a white towel? Because Jesus was wrapped in a white burial shroud. Why is this middle matzah hidden? Because Jesus was hidden away in the tomb following his crucifixion. Why is the *matzah* brought back at the end of the meal? Because Jesus will return in the Second Coming at the End of Days.

Messianic congregations are rarely listed in the Yellow Pages as "Churches." They try their hardest to be listed with the synagogues. Additionally, the Messianic movement has created a remarkable tool for Jewish evangelism called a "communications card." This card carefully guides evangelicals on how to talk to a Jew in a manner that will not alienate them as potential converts. A two-column card which is usually wallet-sized for easy transport and access reads:

> **"Don't say 'Jesus Christ' – Do say Messiah 'Yeshua,' Don't say 'convert'– do say 'Messianic, completed, fulfilled Jew.' Don't say 'Christian' – do say 'Bible believer'"** (see page 1)

In essence, the Messianic movement's fundamental approach seeks to blur the distinctions between Judaism and Christianity in order to lure Jews who would otherwise resist a straightforward Christian message. To the horror of the Jewish world, it is a tactic that has achieved remarkable success with the most vulnerable segments of our community – the very young, the very old, and our brethren of the former Soviet Union.

Why are these at-risk Jews so desperately susceptible to this current missionary assault? How do evangelicals cull our Jewish youth with relative ease?

The Messianic movement's fundamental approach seeks to blur the distinctions between Judaism and Christianity in order to lure Jews who would otherwise resist a straightforward Christian message.

To the horror of the Jewish world, it is a tactic that has achieved remarkable success with the most vulnerable segments of our community – the very young and old, and our Russian brethren.

Why are these at-risk Jews so susceptible to this current missionary assault? Why do evangelicals cull our Jewish youth with relative ease?

**МЕССИАНСКАЯ КАРТОЧКА ПРИОБРЕТАЮЩЕГО ДУШИ**

*«Плод праведника-дерево жизни, и мудрый привлекает души.»*
*- Притчи 11:30*

с 1963

**А. СТАНЬ «КАК ЕВРЕЙ ДЛЯ ЕВРЕЕВ!»** (1Коринфянам 9:20)

| ***НЕ ГОВОРИ*** | ***ГОВОРИ*** |
|---|---|
| 1. Иисус Христос | 1. Мессия Иешуа, Мессия Иисус, Мессия |
| 2. Обращённый | 2. Мессианский еврей, совершенный еврей, полный иудей |
| 3. Христианин | 3. Верующий в Библию |
| 4. Приходите в церковь | 4. Приходите на собрание библейских верующих |
| 5. Новый Завет | 5. Вторая часть Библии |
| 6. Крест | 6. Дерево, столб для казней |

***ОБЪЯСНЕНИЕ***

1. Само слово «ХРИСТОС» НИЧЕГО НЕ говорит обычному еврею.
2. «Обращённый» означает, что он перестал быть иудеем и стал «гойем», язычником. «МЕССИАНСКИЙ ЕВРЕЙ» означает, что он ДОСТРАИВАЕТ или ДОБАВЛЯЕТ к своему иудейскому наследию через *приобретение* искупления, *приобретение* Мессии и ПРИОБРЕТЕНИЕ БОЛЕЕ БЛИЗКИХ и ЛИЧНЫХ ОТНОШЕНИЙ С БОГОМ! Ему не надо отказываться от замечательного Библейского Еврейского наследия. Делайте ударение на то, что он приобретает!
3. ВСЕ неевреи считаются у евреев ХРИСТИАНАМИ, даже Гитлер.
4. Термин «ЦЕРКОВЬ» слишком нееврейский, чтобы быть привлекательным для еврея.
5. «Новый Завет» считается книгой НЕ ДЛЯ ЕВРЕЯ. *Не делайте упор на названии.* ИСПОЛЬЗУЙТЕ СОДЕРЖАНИЕ!
6. «КРЕСТ» был символом преследования евреев на протяжении всей истории.

(продолжение на обороте)

**"Messianic Soul-winners Card" used to train missionaries how to convert Russian Jews to Christianity**

> Teenagers and college-age youth are seekers by nature – they are wide open to spiritual suggestions

There could be little doubt that the intense and dogmatic obsession that fundamentalist Christians have with Jewish evangelism contributes to the success of groups like Jews for Jesus. If we were doing our job, however, a Christian mission to the Jews – no matter how creative, well staffed, and well funded, would pose little threat to the spiritual integrity of our community. But, a lethal combination of circumstances and factors contribute to the spiritual frailty of Jewish youth.

Young men and women are particularly vulnerable to evangelicals because so often these adolescents are unsure of themselves, the world around them, and the adulthood that awaits them. Teenagers and college-age youth are seekers by nature – they are searching for an identity of their own. They are wide open to spiritual suggestions that controvert and challenge the beliefs of their families. Moreover, adolescents may not be emotionally well-grounded, and they often struggle with a low self-esteem.

For most emerging adults, the university campus is the place where they experience full autonomy for the first time in their lives. A paltry few of our kids are sent off to a university campus armed with a strong Jewish education. Missionaries are well aware of how lethal this combination is for Jewish youth and, as a result, they devote a great deal of their vast energies to Jewish evangelism on campus.

**JEWISH IQ TEST**

Often, when I am lecturing at Hebrew Schools across North America, I give the young students a Jewish IQ test. "Tell me," I ask, "what was Jesus' mother's name and what was Moses' mother's name?" They all know that Mary was the mother of Jesus, yet few know the name of Moses' mother. Asking for the names of any two books in the Talmud, and any two books in the New Testament, will invariably get the same type of response. Typically, the kids

**Typical Messianic jewelry displays the "Jesus fish" with Jewish symbols**

could rattle off the names of all the Gospels in the Christian Bible and are clueless about the names of the Tractates of the Talmud. For the most part, we raised a generation of children who know little about the faith they are being asked to abandon.

A number of years ago, I received a hysterical phone call from a mother living in Long Island. She had just found a New Testament hidden between her daughter's mattress and box spring. There was a terrible confrontation. The daughter stormed out of the house, and the mother knew she desperately needed help.

We spoke for quite a while. It turned out that her daughter was involved in a local Messianic congregation on Long Island called Olive Tree. I explained to her that if I were going to help, I had to meet with her daughter, so we set a date and time to meet. Elizabeth was not happy about meeting with someone like me, but after some well-placed motherly prodding and pressure, an appointment was arranged.

When I first met Elizabeth, she seemed friendly. Within five minutes, she began to tell me all about her new faith. She described how, when she attended Boston University, her roommate gave her a pocket-sized New Testament as a gift. She didn't read it at the time, but just tossed it aside.

She told me how one night she was feeling depressed after an unexpected breakup with her boy friend and decided to look for some solace from her little New Testament. "I began to thumb through it, and I came upon a verse that moved me in a very special way," she said. "It penetrated my soul to the point that I knew that this New Testament had to be the word of God."

> She quoted words of the New Testament that touched her, yet these words were first spoken by Moses!

I asked her to tell me which verse she read that was so inspiring. She picked up the Bible from the table, and her index finger began to flip through the pages. Suddenly she said, "This is it!" She began to read this verse from the Book of Mark, "And you shall love the Lord your God with all your heart, and with all your soul, and with all your might..."

This young woman had no idea that this sacred phrase is the most precious and celebrated creed of the Jewish people and is written in the Five Books of Moses. It wasn't long after this memorable meeting with Elizabeth that she returned back to the faith of her ancestors. Less than a month later, Elizabeth left for Israel to study at a women's college for one year.

## FUNDAMENTALIST RETREATS

Like Elizabeth, many Hebrew-Christians will tell you that the first time they considered believing in Jesus was in college. A university campus is one of the primary places that young people are invited to fundamentalist Christian retreats, prayer meetings, and Bible classes. What they will witness there is like nothing they have ever seen in their synagogue. People stand in their pews, crying to Jesus. Healings take place in the aisles.

Messianic Jews are exceedingly friendly. Visit a Messianic congregation – if you are a new face, members of the congregation, with big smiles and friendly words of introduction, will immediately approach you. They will want to know who you are, what do you do, and if you have a place to eat.

The elderly are also perilously vulnerable to Jewish evangelism. It is little coincidence that there are more Messianic congregations tightly packed into the peninsula of South Florida than any other similarly sized region in North America.

Even more than from physical ailments, the aged suffer from nagging loneliness. The Christian missions volunteers who seek out and witness to the

Jewish elderly in nursing homes are met with little resistance to their aggressive activities by these facilities or their residents.

A pretty smile and a warm touch are priceless commodities to those who are waiting to die. With minds that have slowed down due to the passing of time, and a soul hungry for companionship, our grandparents are falling prey to the Jesus movement.

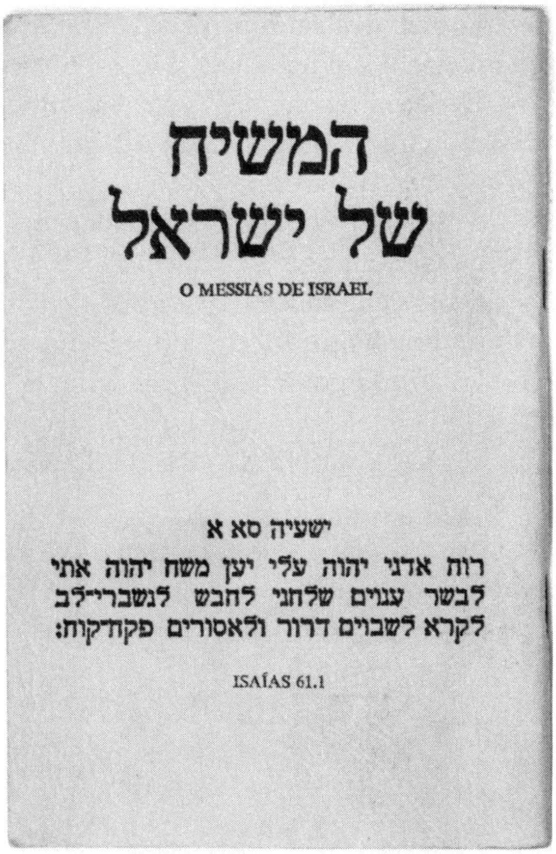


**Messianic training manual designed to evangelize Portuguese-speaking Jews**

It is well known that Russian Jews are a prime target and easy prey for evangelical missionaries. Their upbringing in the former Soviet Union under communism robbed them of any Jewish education or understanding of their rich heritage. Few of these new immigrants are familiar with even the fundamentals of their heritage, such as the Passover Seder or connecting with the State of Israel. This has proven devastating to the Russian Jewish community. As a result, Christian missions have invested extraordinary resources and manpower to large Russian communities in Israel and neighborhoods like Brighton Beach, Brooklyn. It is ironic that although Jews of the former Soviet Union have endured Czarist and communist Russia, yet they rapidly succumb to Christian missionaries in the West.

## A CRY FOR HELP

> Messianic congregations abound in South Florida where many Jewish elderly reside

A number of years ago it became clear to me that although my lectures were being heard by many throughout the nation, and although there have been numerous young men and women like Elizabeth whom I have counseled away from these Christian groups over the years, the vast majority of the Jewish people have not been reached. Many former Hebrew-Christians complained that very few resources were available to them that would have helped them counter the persuasive arguments used by groups like Jews for Jesus.

Something more needs to be done. It is for this reason that our organization, Outreach Judaism, works tirelessly with far-reaching and multifaceted outreach programs specially designed to counter the efforts of fundamentalist Christian groups and cults who specifically target Jews for conversion.

> Estimates are that more than 8,000 Jews will be crossing over to the Hebrew-Christian movement this coming year

Our special Role-Play for teens is regarded as the most effective tool to inoculate adolescents against pernicious evangelicals who seek to rob these youngsters of their faith. For more information on this special program for teens, go to www.outreachjudaism.org/roleplay.html.

If the estimates are correct, more than 8,000 Jews will be crossing over to the Hebrew-Christian movement this coming year.

Christianity is called "the Church;" however, Judaism is never called "the synagogue." The center of Jewish life has always been a Jewish home. This rich source of our heritage, along with a secure Jewish education, must be restored among our people. The place to begin is with our Jewish youth. They are our future.

**Footnote:**

1. There are some conservative Christians who espouse a theology often referred to as "Dual-covenant Theology," which teaches that Jews should not be evangelized but rather remain obedient to the Law of Moses. This belief gained some acceptance among a few fundamentalist Christian leaders who hold that the "covenant" between God and the Jewish people is everlasting, and therefore insist that Jews

should not convert to Christianity. The vast majority of the evangelical Christian world strongly reject this idea.

Kenneth W. Rawson, pastor of the Bible Students Congregation of New Brunswick for over 40 years, is a strong proponent of this theology. Pastor Rawson wants to challenge Jews who are assimilating to embrace their Jewish heritage. Pastor Rawson is an outspoke critic of Jews for Jesus and other such organizations which engage in Jewish evangelism.

It is widely speculated that Reverend John Hagge, senior pastor of Cornerstone Church in San Antonio, Texas, and founder of Christians United for Israel, embraces Dual-covenant Theology.

Fundamentalist Christian organizations strongly criticized Hagee's recent book, *In Defense of Israel* (2007), for apparently arguing that Jesus did not claim to be the Messiah for the Jews, only the Savior for the Christian Church, and therefore attempts should not be made to convert Jews. Hagee issued a statement denying the first of these allegations and revised one chapter in a new edition of his book.

Apparently, as a result of harsh criticism and strong pressure emanating from evangelical leadership over the years, the Christian Zionist pastor has had to retract numerous statements articulating his strong opposition to Jewish evangelism and his apparent support for Dual-covenant Theology.

In a *Houston Chronicle* interview, however, Hagee said:

> "I believe that every Jewish person who lives in the light of the Torah, which is the word of God, has a relationship with God and will come to redemption... In fact, trying to convert Jews is a waste of time."
>
> "The Jewish person who has his roots in Judaism is not going to convert to Christianity. There is

no form of Christian evangelism that has failed so miserably as evangelizing the Jewish people. They (already) have a faith structure. Everyone else, whether Buddhist or Baha'i, needs to believe in Jesus," he says. "But not Jews. Jews already have a covenant with God that has never been replaced by Christianity."

("San Antonio Fundamentalist Battles Anti-Semitism," *Houston Chronicle*, April 30, 1988, sec. 6, pg. 1)

## Part II

# How do Missionaries Paint Jesus into the Jewish Scriptures?

# Taking a Verse Out of Context

### Matthew 2:13-15

And when they were departed, behold, the angel of the Lord appeareth to Joseph in a dream, saying, "Arise, and take the young child and his mother, and flee into Egypt, and be thou there until I bring thee word, for Herod will seek the young child to destroy him." 14 When he arose, he took the young child and his mother by night, and departed into Egypt. 15 And was there until the death of Herod, that it might be fulfilled which was spoken of the Lord by the prophet, saying, ***"Out of Egypt have I called my son."***

### Hosea 11:1

When **Israel** was a child, then I loved him, and called my son out of Egypt.

**The author of the Book of Matthew claims that the last phrase of Hosea 11:1, "Out of Egypt have I called my son," demonstrates that Jesus' childhood escape into Egypt was foretold in the Jewish scriptures. This verse cited by the New Testament author was recklessly torn out of its original context.**

**The opening words of Hosea 11:1 clearly identify the Children of Israel as God's "son," rather than Jesus, as Matthew would have us believe. Moreover, in this famed text, Hosea is recalling the past exodus of the Jewish people from Egypt, not a future child/messiah fleeing into Egypt. The author of the first Gospel boldly ripped this phrase out of its original context in order to apply it to Jesus.**

---

### Zechariah 13:1-6

In that day there shall be a fountain opened to the house of David and to the inhabitants of Jerusalem for sin and for uncleanliness. 2 And it shall come to pass in that day, saith the Lord of hosts, that I will cut off the names of the idols out of the land, and they shall no more be remembered; and also I will cause the prophets and the unclean spirit to pass out of the land. 3 And it shall come to pass, that when any shall yet prophesy, then his father and his mother that begot him shall say unto him, "Thou shalt not live; for thou speakest lies in the name of the Lord." And his father and his mother that begot him shall thrust him through when he prophesies. 4 And it shall come to pass in that day, that the prophets shall be ashamed every one of his vision when he hath prophesied, neither shall they wear a rough garment to deceive. 5 But he shall say, "I am no prophet, I am a husbandman, for man taught me to keep cattle from my youth." 6 **And one shall say unto him, "What are these wounds in thine hands?" Then he shall answer, "Those with which I was wounded in the house of my friends."**

***"I am no prophet"***

בַּיּוֹם הַהוּא יִהְיֶה מָקוֹר נִפְתָּח לְבֵית
דָּוִיד וּלְיֹשְׁבֵי יְרוּשָׁלִָם לְחַטַּאת וּלְנִדָּה׃
ב וְהָיָה בַיּוֹם הַהוּא נְאֻם ה'
צְבָאוֹת אַכְרִית אֶת־שְׁמוֹת הָעֲצַבִּים
מִן־הָאָרֶץ וְלֹא יִזָּכְרוּ עוֹד
וְגַם אֶת־הַנְּבִיאִים וְאֶת־רוּחַ
הַטֻּמְאָה אַעֲבִיר מִן־הָאָרֶץ׃
ג וְהָיָה כִּי־יִנָּבֵא אִישׁ עוֹד וְאָמְרוּ
אֵלָיו אָבִיו וְאִמּוֹ יֹלְדָיו לֹא תִחְיֶה כִּי
שֶׁקֶר דִּבַּרְתָּ בְּשֵׁם ה' וּדְקָרֻהוּ
אָבִיהוּ וְאִמּוֹ יֹלְדָיו בְּהִנָּבְאוֹ׃
ד וְהָיָה בַּיּוֹם הַהוּא יֵבֹשׁוּ הַנְּבִיאִים
אִישׁ מֵחֶזְיֹנוֹ בְּהִנָּבְאֹתוֹ וְלֹא יִלְבְּשׁוּ
אַדֶּרֶת שֵׂעָר לְמַעַן כַּחֵשׁ׃
ה וְאָמַר לֹא נָבִיא אָנֹכִי אִישׁ־עֹבֵד
אֲדָמָה אָנֹכִי כִּי אָדָם הִקְנַנִי מִנְּעוּרָי׃
ו וְאָמַר אֵלָיו מָה הַמַּכּוֹת הָאֵלֶּה בֵּין
יָדֶיךָ וְאָמַר אֲשֶׁר הֻכֵּיתִי בֵּית מְאַהֲבָי׃

# Christian Bibles Mistranslate a Word

| Psalm 22:16 (17) *King James Version* | Psalm 22:17 *Original Hebrew* | Psalm 22:17 *Jewish Translation* |
|---|---|---|
| For dogs have compassed me; the assembly of the wicked have inclosed me; they **pierced** my hands and my feet. | כִּי סְבָבוּנִי כְּלָבִים עֲדַת מְרֵעִים הִקִּיפוּנִי כָּאֲרִי יָדַי וְרַגְלָי׃ | For dogs have encompassed me; a company of evil-doers have inclosed me; like a **lion**, they are at my hands and my feet. |

## The Hebrew word כָּאֲרִי (ka'ari) means "like a lion," not "pierced"

## Examine the Surrounding Verses of Psalm 22:17 (16)

| Psalm 22:12-13 (13-14) *King James Version* | Psalm 22:20-21 (21-22) *King James Version* | Psalm 17:11-12 *King James Version* |
|---|---|---|
| Many **bulls** have compassed me; strong **bulls** of Bashan have beset me around. [13] They gaped upon me with their mouths, as a ravening and a roaring **lion**. | Deliver my soul from the sword; my darling from the power of the **dog**. [21]Save me from the **lion's** mouth; for thou hast heard me from horns of the wild **oxen**. | They have now compassed us in our steps: they have set their eyes bowing down to the earth; [12]Like a **lion** that is greedy of his prey, and as it were a young **lion** lurking.... |

Throughout Psalm 22, King David turns in desperation to God for salvation from his relentless foes and repeatedly uses the imagery of aggressive animals – lions, dogs, and bulls – as metaphors to describe those who sought to destroy him. This violent animal motif appears in the verses immediately before and after Psalm 22:17. Psalm 17:11-12 and 35:17 are almost identical to 22:17, and in those texts Christian translators correctly render the word "lion." The Church deliberately lifted and manipulated numerous verses in Psalm 22 and placed them in the mouth of Jesus. It is for this reason that Christendom refers to Psalm 22 as the "Crucifixion Psalm." (see pages 197-211)

## Why in Isaiah 38:13 does the King James Version correctly translate the exact same word כָּאֲרִי "as a lion"?

| King James Version - Isaiah 38:13 | Original Hebrew - Isaiah 38:13 |
|---|---|
| I reckoned till morning, that ***as a lion***, so will he break all my bones; from day even to night wilt thou make an end of me. | שִׁוִּיתִי עַד־בֹּקֶר כָּאֲרִי כֵּן יְשַׁבֵּר כָּל־עַצְמוֹתָי מִיּוֹם עַד־לַיְלָה תַּשְׁלִימֵנִי׃ |

**Matthew 2:23**

And he came and dwelt in a city called Nazareth; that it might be fulfilled which was spoken by the prophets, ***"He shall be called a Nazarene."***

**Contrary to Matthew's claim, there is no prophecy anywhere in the Jewish scriptures which suggests that the messiah will reside in Nazareth. In fact, the city of Nazareth is never mentioned in the Hebrew Bible.**

# Matthew Claims Jesus' Virgin Birth Was Foretold in the Book of Isaiah

## Matthew 1:20-23

But when he had considered this, behold, an angel of the Lord appeared to him in a dream, saying, "Joseph, thou son of
David, do not be afraid to take Mary as your wife; for that which has been conceived in her is of the Holy Spirit. [21]And
she will bear a son; and you shall call his name Jesus, for it is he who will save his people from their sins." [22]Now all this
took place that what was spoken by the Lord through the prophet might be fulfilled, saying, [23] **Behold, a virgin shall be with
child, and shall bear a son, and they shall call his name Immanuel,**" which translated means, "God is with us."

---

## Isaiah 7:1-7, 10-16

And it came to pass in the days of Ahaz son of Jotham, son of Uzziah, king of Judah, that Rezin, king of Aram, and
Pekah son of Remaliah, king of Israel, marched on Jerusalem to wage war against it, and he could not wage war a-
gainst it. [2]And it was told to the House of David, saying, "Aram has allied itself with Ephraim," and his heart and the heart
of his people trembled as the trees of the forest tremble because of the wind. [3] And the Lord said to Isaiah, "Now go out
toward Ahaz, you and Shar-Yashuv your son to the edge of the conduit of the upper pool, to the road of the washer's field.
[4]And you shall say to him, "Feel secure and calm yourself, do not fear, and let your heart not be faint because of these two
smoking stubs of firebrands, because of the raging anger of Rizin and Aram and the son of Remaliah. [5] Since Aram
planned harm to you, Ephraim and the son of Remaliah, saying: [6]'Let us go up against Judah and provoke it, and annex
it to us; and let us crown a king in its midst, one who is good for us.' [7]So said the Lord God, 'Neither shall it succeed,
nor shall it come to pass....'" [10]And the Lord continued to speak to Ahaz, saying, "Ask for yourself a sign from the Lord,
your God; ask it either in the depths, or in the heights above." [12] And Ahaz said, "I will not ask, and I will not test the
Lord." [13] And he said, "Listen now, O House of David, is it little for you to weary men, that you weary my God as well?
[14] **Therefore the Lord, of His own, shall give you a
sign; behold the young woman is with child, and she
shall bear a son, and she shall call his name
Immanuel.** [15] Cream and honey he shall eat when he
knows to reject bad and choose good. [16]For, when the lad
does not yet know to reject bad and choose good, the land
whose two kings you dread, shall be abandoned."

**Isaiah 7:14 Original Hebrew Text:**
לָכֵן יִתֵּן אֲדֹנָי הוּא לָכֶם אוֹת הִנֵּה הָעַלְמָה
הָרָה וְיֹלֶדֶת בֵּן וְקָרָאת שְׁמוֹ עִמָּנוּאֵל׃

## Isaiah chapter 7 prophecy was fulfilled contemporaneously, not 700 years latter: Pekah and Rezin failed in their war against Ahaz and were assassinated

***Kingdom of Israel and Syria Fail in Their Seige of Jerusalem***

**II Kings 16:5** – Then Rezin the king of Aram and Pekah the son of Remaliah the king of Israel, went up to Jerusalem to wage war, and they besieged Ahaz, **but could not wage war with him**.

***Isaiah's Prophecy Fulfilled: King of the Northern Kingdom and Syria are Killed***

**II Kings 15:29-30** – In the days of Pekah (king of Israel) Hosea the son of Elah plotted a conspiracy against Pekah the son of Ramaliah **and smote him, killed him**, and reigned in his stead in the twentieth year of Jotham, son of Uzziah.

**II Kings 16:9** – And the king of Assyria hearkened to him [Ahaz], for the king of Assyria marched up against Damascus and seized it carrying its people captive to Kir, and **he killed him**.

## God gave Isaiah children as "signs and portents" to the Jewish people

***Names of Isaiah's Sons, Shar-Yashuv and Emmanuel, are Signs to the Jews***

**Isaiah 8:18** – Behold, I and the children the Lord gave me for signs and portents in Israel from the Lord of hosts Who dwells on Mount Zion.

## Many Christian Translators Reject Matthew's Mistranslation of Isaiah 7:14 and Accurately Rendered the Hebrew Word *Almah* as a "Young Woman"

| | |
|---|---|
| **Revised Standard Version**<br>Therefore the Lord himself will give you a sign. Behold, a **young woman** shall conceive and bear a son, and shall call his name Immanuel. | **Revised English Bible**<br>...because you do, the Lord of his own accord will give you a sign; it is this: A **young woman** is with child, and she will give birth to a son and call him Immanuel. |
| **New English Bible**<br>Therefore the Lord himself shall give you a sign: A **young woman** is with child, and she will bear a son, and will call him Immanuel. | **New Revised Standard Version**<br>Therefore the Lord himself will give you a sign. Look, the **young woman** is with child and shall bear a son, and shall name him Immanuel. |
| **The Message of the Bible**<br>He will give you a sign. A **young woman** shall bear a son who shall truly represent the hopes we have inherited from the days of David. His very name, "God-is-with-us," shall express the secret of his power. | **The Layman's Bible Commentary**<br>In reply, Isaiah says that the Lord will provide a sign. It will be a most unusual and remarkable event. A **young woman** shall bear a son and name him "Immanuel," meaning "God is with us." |
| **The Bible: A New Translation**<br>An omen you shall have, and that from the Eternal himself. There is a **young woman** with child, who shall bear a son and call his name "Immanuel" (God is with us); | **The Bible: An American Translation**<br>Therefore the Lord himself will give you a sign: Behold! A **young woman** is with child, and is about to bear a son; and she will call him "God is with us." |
| **The New Jerusalem Bible**<br>The Lord will give you a sign in any case: It is this: The **young woman** is with child and will give birth to a son whom she will call Immanuel. | **International Critical Commentary**<br>Therefore the Lord himself will give you a sign. Behold, a **damsel** is with child, and shall bring forth a son, and call his name Immanuel. |
| **Good News Bible**<br>Well then, the Lord himself will give you a sign: A **young woman** who is pregnant will have a son and will name him "Immanuel." | **World Biblical Commentary**<br>Therefore my Lord himself will give you (pl) a sign. Behold, the **woman** shall conceive and bearing a son — she shall call his name "Immanuel." |

**The Bible in Basic English**

For this cause the Lord himself will give you a sign; a **young woman** is now with child, and she will give birth to a son, and she will give him the name Immanuel.

# Did the Word 'Virgin' Appear in the Original Septuagint?

## *The Oxford Companion to the Bible* Discusses the Definition of the Hebrew Word *Alma*, the Septuagint's Use of the Greek Word *Parthenos*, And Rejects Matthew's Application of Isaiah 7:14 to the Virgin Birth

Isaiah's intent in discussing this child is clearly to set a time frame for the destruction of Israel. There is nothing miraculous about the mother of the conception process. The Hebrew word used *almâ*, means simply "young woman," without any implication of virginity. The Greek word *parthenos* used to translate *alma* can mean either a young woman or a virgin. Matthew used a Greek Bible, so he naturally reinterpreted Isaiah 7:14 as a prophecy referring to the virgin birth of Jesus. For the evangelist, Isaiah's original meaning was superseded by the identification of Jesus as Immanuel (Grk. *Emmanuouēl*).

Daniel N. Schowalter, *The Oxford Companion To The Bible*. Excerpt from "Virgin Birth of Christ," New York: Oxford University Press, 1993, pg. 790.

## An Example of the Word παρθένος (*Parthenos*) in The Septuagint Where it Is Clearly Not Referring to a Virgin

**Genesis 34:2-4** (King James Version)

And when Shechem the son of Hamor the Hivite, prince of the country, saw her, he took her, and lay with her, and defiled her. [3]And his soul clave unto Dinah the daughter of Jacob, and he loved the *damsel* (Septuagint: ðáñèÝíï õ) and spake kindly unto the *damsel* (Septuagint: ðáñèÝíï õ). [4]And Shechem spake unto his father Hamor, saying, Get me this damsel to wife.

## The Anchor Bible Dictionary on the 'Original' Septuagint

The word "Septuagint," (from Lat *septuaginta* = 70; hence the abbreviation LXX) derives from a story that 72 elders translated the Pentateuch into Greek; the term therefore applied originally only to those five books.

*The Anchor Bible Dictionary*. Excerpt from "Septuagint," New York. Vol. V, page 1093.

## Josephus Attests That the Jewish Interpreters of the Septuagint Translated the Law [Of Moses] Alone

I found, therefore, that the second of the Ptolemies was a king who was extraordinarily diligent in what concerned learning and the collection of books; that he was also peculiarly ambitious to procure a translation of our law...into the Greek tongue...for he did not obtain all our writings at that time; but those who were sent to Alexandria as interpreters gave him only the books of the law, while there were a vast number of other matters in our sacred books.[1]

[1] Josephus, *Preface to Antiquities*. For Josephus' detailed description of events surrounding the original authorship of the Septuagint, see Josephus, *Antiquities of the Jews*, XII, ii, 1-4.

## Jerome Affirms Josephus: The Original Septuagint Was Only a Translation of the Five Books of Moses

Add to this that Josephus, who gives the story of the Seventy Translators, reports them as translating only the five books of Moses; and we also acknowledge that these are more in harmony with the Hebrew than the rest.

St. Jerome, *Preface to the Book of Hebrew Questions*, Nicene and Post-Nicene Fathers, Volume 6. Pg. 487. Hendrickson.

**The following related articles can be found in Part XV of this study guide:**

## Part III

# Sin and Atonement

## "It Is the Blood That Atones for a Life"

### Leviticus 17:10-11

If any person, whether of the family of Israel or a proselyte who joins them, eats any blood, I will direct My anger against the person who eats blood and cut him off from his people. [11]This is because the life-force of the flesh is in the blood; and I therefore gave it to you to be placed on the altar to atone for your lives. **It is the blood that atones for a life** (כִּי־הַדָּם הוּא בַּנֶּפֶשׁ יְכַפֵּר).

### Hebrews 9:22

And almost all things are by the law purged with blood; **and without the shedding of blood there is no atonement** (καὶ χωρὶς αἱματεκχυσίας οὐ γίνεται ἄφεσις).

## The Sin Sacrifice Only Atones Unintentional Sins

### Leviticus 4:1-2 — Sin Sacrifice (קָרְבַּן חַטָּאת)

The Lord said to Moses, "Say to the Israelites: [2]'When anyone sins **unintentionally** and does what is forbidden in any of the Lord's commandments...."

## Is Blood Sacrifice the Only Way to Atone for Sin in Tanach?

### Psalms 40:7 (6)

Sacrifice and offerings You did not desire; **but my ears you opened for me** (אָזְנַיִם כָּרִיתָ לִּי). Burnt offerings and sin offerings You have not required.

### Hebrews 10:5

sacrifice and offering thou does not desire, **but a body you have prepared me** (óὢìá .äè êáôçñôßóù ìïé ·).

# ❖Repentance

### II Samuel 12:13

So David Said to Nathan, "I have sinned against the Lord." And Nathan said to David, "The Lord has already forgiven your sin; you shall not die."

### Psalms 51:16-19

Rescue me from blood-guilt, O God, God of my salvation. [17] My Lord, open my lips, that my mouth may declare Your praise. [18]For You desire no offering, else I would give it, a burnt offering You do not favor. [19] The offerings of God are a broken spirit, a heart broken and crushed O God, You will not despise.

**God forgave King David for his sin with Batsheva as a result of his heartfelt confessional prayer (II Sam. 11:2-12:13). He was deeply effected by this profound personal experience, and this epic event shaped his prophetic message in the Book of Psalms.**

**David grasped that a blood sacrifice is far from an efficacious atonement for sin. In Psalm 51 King David vividly describes how humble repentance rather than sacrifice is what the Almighty favors.**

## Devotion to God Is Better than a Sacrifice

### I Samuel 15:22

And Samuel said, "Has the Lord as much desire in burnt offerings and peace-offerings, as in obeying the voice of the Lord? Behold, to obey is better than a peace-offering; to hearken is better than the fat of rams."

### Micah 6:6-8

"With what shall I come before the Lord, bow before the Most High God? Shall I come before Him with burnt offerings, with yearling calves? [7]Will the Lord be pleased with thousands of rams, with myriad streams of oil? Shall I give my firstborn for my transgression, the fruit of my body for the sin of my soul? [8]He has told you, O man, what is good, and what the Lord demands of you: 'Do justice, love loving-kindness, and walk discreetly with your God.'"

**In stark contrast to the teachings of the Jewish scriptures, the New Testament insists that the shedding of blood is the only method for atonement (Heb. 9:22), and animal sacrifices only fore-shadowed the crucifixion (Heb. 10:1). This alien teaching is contradicted by all the prophets of Israel. Both Samuel and Micah declare that obedience to God is far superior to a blood sacrifice for sin.**

## Prayer Replaces the Sacrificial System

### Hosea 14:2-3

Return, O Israel, to the Lord your God, for you have stumbled in your iniquity. [3]Take with you **words** and return to the Lord. Say: You shall forgive all iniquity and teach us the good way, and let us **render for bulls the offering of our lips**.

**Hosea's divine message to the children of Israel is clear: Heartfelt prayer can replace any blood sacrifice. The New International Version Bible (NIV) translators found the theological message contained in the final phrase of Hosea 14:3 ("...let us render for bulls the offering of our lips") so problematic that they altered the last words of the text to instead read, "...that we may offer the fruit of our lips," thereby twisting and concealing the prophet's original message. (see pages 253-261; 437-461)**

## King Solomon Declares at the Inauguration of the First Temple that Future Exiled Generations Will Atone for their Sins with Prayer Alone

**During his inauguration of the first Temple that he built, King Solomon described future troubling events that would befall the Jewish people during their bitter exiles. Anticipating and refuting the eventual claims of Christendom a millennium later, King Solomon assured future Jewish generations that when this Temple no longer stands and they are driven into exile, confessional prayer will atone for all transgressions. Moreover, throughout his entire prophetic declaration, King Solomon never suggests that anyone will believe in a crucified savior for atonement.**

### I Kings 8:46-50

If they sin against You, for there is no man who does not sin, and You will be angry with them, and deliver them to the enemy, and their captors will carry them away captive to the land of the enemy, far or near. [47]And they shall bethink themselves in the land where they were carried captive, and repent, and make supplication to You in the land of their captors, saying, 'We have sinned, and have done perversely, we have committed wickedness.' [48]And they shall return to You with all their heart, and with all their soul, in the land of their enemies, who led them away captive, and **pray to You toward their land**, which You gave to their fathers, the city You have chosen, and the house which I have built for Your name. [49]And **You shall hear their prayer and their supplication in heaven, in Your dwelling place, and maintain their cause.** [50]**And forgive Your people for what they have sinned against You, and all their transgressions that they have transgressed against You....**

(see also Deuteronomy 4:26-31; II Chronicles 6:36-39)

### Ezekiel 18:1-4, 19-23

The word of the Lord came to me, saying: [2]"What do you people mean by quoting this proverb about the land of Israel, saying: 'The fathers eat sour grapes, and the sons' teeth are set on edge?' [3]As I live, declares the Sovereign Lord, you will no longer quote this proverb in Israel. [4]For every living soul belongs to Me, the father as well as the son — they are Mine. Which ever soul sins, it shall die....

**Ezekiel warns Israel that the doctrine of vicarious atonement, which is the foundation of Christian theology, is hostile to the will of God. "The righteous man cannot die for the sins of the wicked," declares the prophet!**

**In addition, the prophet teaches the Jewish people that contrite repentance alone atones for sin. Throughout this epic chapter, which exclusively addresses the doctrine of sin and atonement, Ezekiel does not mention a word about a blood sacrifice or crucified messiah for the expiation of iniquity (see Ezekiel 33:10-11).**

[19]Yet you ask: Why did the son not bear the sin of the father? But the son, justice and righteousness did he do, all My decrees did he safeguard and perform them. He shall surely live. [20]The soul that sins, it shall die! The son shall not bear for the sin of the father, nor the father bear for the sin of the son. The righteousness of the righteous person shall be upon him, and the wickedness of the wicked person shall be upon him. [21]As for the wicked man, if he should turn away from all his sins which he did, and safeguard all My decrees, and do justice and righteousness; he shall surely live. He will not die. [22]All his transgressions which he committed will not be remembered against him. For the righteousness which he did, he shall live. [23]Do I desire at all the death of the wicked man — the words of my Lord, God — is it not rather his return from his ways, that he might live?

# ❖Charity

### Proverbs 10:2

Treasures of wickedness will not avail, but **charity will save from death**.

### Proverbs 11:4

Riches will not avail on the day of wrath, but **charity will save from death**.

### Proverbs 16:6

With loving-kindness and truth will iniquity be expiated, and through fear of the Lord one turns away from evil.

### Proverbs 21:3

Performing charity and justice is preferred by God to a sacrifice.

### Hosea 6:6

For I desire loving-kindness, and not sacrifices, and knowledge of God more than burnt offerings.

### Daniel 4:24 (verse 27 in a Christian Bible)

Nevertheless, O king, let my advice be agreeable to you. Redeem your error with charity, and your sin through kindness to the poor, so that their will be an extension to your tranquility.

### Jeremiah 7:3-7, 21-23

So said the Lord of Hosts, the God of Israel: Improve your ways and your deeds, I then will allow you to dwell in this place.
4Do not rely on false words, saying: The Temple of the Lord, the Temple of the Lord, the Temple of the Lord are they. 5For if you improve your ways and your deeds, if you perform judgment between one man and his fellow man, 6you do not oppress the stranger, an orphan, or a widow, and you do not shed innocent blood in this place, and you do not follow other gods for your detriment. 7I will then allow you to dwell in this place, in the land that I gave your forefathers from days of yore to eternity....
21So says the Lord of Hosts, the God of Israel: Add your burnt offerings upon your sacrifices and eat flesh.
22For neither did I speak with your forefathers nor did I command them on the day I brought them out of the land of Egypt concerning a burnt offering or a sacrifice. 23But this thing did I command them saying: Listen to Me so that I am your God and you are My people, you walk in all the ways that I command you....

***Jeremiah warns against over-reliance on the sacrificial system and berates those who depend on blood-atonement for salvation***

## Church Teaches that the Death of Jesus Was the Final Atonement, and Marked the End of Animal Sacrifices

### Romans 6:10

The death he died, **he died to sin once for all**....

### Hebrews 9:12

He did not enter by means of the blood of goats and calves; but he entered the Most Holy Place **once and for all** by his own blood, having obtained **eternal redemption**.

### Hebrews 10:10, 18

And by that will, we have been made holy through the sacrifice of the body of Jesus Christ **once for all**..... And where these have been forgiven, **there is no longer any sacrifice for sin**.

## The Sacrificial System Will be Restored in the Messianic Age

### Isaiah 56:7

Even them will I bring to My holy mountain, and make them joyful in My house of prayer; their burnt offerings and sacrifices shall be accepted upon My altar: for My house shall be called a house of prayer for all people.

### Jeremiah 33:17-18

For thus saith the Lord: David shall never be without man to sit upon the throne of the House of Israel. 18Neither shall the priests, the Levites, be without man before me to offer burnt offerings, and to kindle meat offerings, and to do sacrifice continually.

**If, as Paul argues, Jesus was the final sacrifice "once and for all" (Heb. 10:10, 18), and the animal sacrificial system was merely a temporary "foreshadowing" of Calvary (Heb. 9-10), why will animal sacrifices be restored in the messianic era? (see Ezekiel 44:27-31, 45:17-25).**

### Zechariah 14:21

Every pot in Jerusalem and Judah will be holy to the Lord Almighty, and all who come to sacrifice will take some of the pots and cook in them....

### Ezekiel 43:22-25

On the second day you are to offer a male goat without defect for a sin offering.... 25For seven days you are to provide a male goat daily for a sin offering....

## The Prophet Hosea Foretold that the Sacrificial System Would be Suspended for 'Many Days' Until its Full Restoration in the Messianic Age. In Hebrew 9-10, however, Paul insists that Jesus' Death Marked the Permanent End of Animal Sacrifices

***(see pages 247-251)***

For the children of Israel shall abide many days without king or prince, without sacrifice or sacred pillar, without *ephod* or *teraphim*. Afterward the children of Israel shall return and seek the Lord their God and David their king. They shall fear the Lord and His goodness in the latter days.

**Hosea 3:4-5**

## Isaiah Declares That the Sinner Is Forgiven Through Heartfelt Repentance Alone. Isaiah's Contradicting Fundamental Christian Doctrine the Churches Claims that Atonement Can be Achieved Only Through the Shedding of Blood

Seek the Lord when He is found, call Him when He is near. The wicked shall give up his way, and the man of iniquity his thoughts, and he shall return to the Lord, Who shall have mercy upon him, and to our God, for He will freely pardon. "For My thoughts are not your thoughts, neither are your ways My ways," says the Lord. "As the heavens are higher than the earth, so are My ways higher than your ways and My thoughts higher than your thoughts."

**Isaiah 55:6-9**

## Why Do Missionaries Continue to Insist that Atonement is Impossible Without the Shedding of Blood? Jonah 3:5-10 Explicitly States that God Forgave the People of Nineveh After they Repented of Their Iniquity (Without Any Blood Sacrifice)!

So the people of Nineveh believed God, proclaimed a fast, and put on sackcloth, from the greatest to the least of them. Then word came to the king of Nineveh; and he arose from his throne and laid aside his robe, covered himself with sackcloth and sat in ashes. And he caused it to be proclaimed and published throughout Nineveh by the decree of the king and his nobles, saying, Let neither man nor beast, herd nor flock, taste anything; do not let them eat, or drink water. But let man and beast be covered with sackcloth, and cry mightily to God; yes, let every one turn from his evil way and from the violence that is in his hands. Who can tell if God will turn and relent, and turn away from His fierce anger, so that we may not perish? **Then God saw their works, that they turned from their evil way; and God relented from the disaster that He had said He would bring upon them, and He did not do it.**

**Jonah 3:5-10**

# The following related articles can be found in Part XV of this study guide:

## Part IV

# Isaiah 53: Who is the Suffering Servant?

## Isaiah 52:13-53:12

13. Behold, My servant shall prosper; he shall be exalted and lifted up, and shall be very high.

14. As many wondered about you, "How marred his appearance is from that of a man, and his features from that of people!"

15. So shall he cast down many nations; kings shall shut their mouths because of him; for what had not been told to them they shall see; and that which they had not heard they shall consider.

1. Who hath believed our report? And to whom is the arm of the Lord revealed?

2. And he came up like a sapling before it, and like a root from dry ground, he had neither form nor comeliness; and we saw him that he had no appearance that we should have desired him.

3. Despised and forsaken by men, a man of pains and accustomed to illness: and as one who hides his face from us; despised, and we esteemed him not.

4. Indeed, he bore our illnesses, and our pains - he carried them, yet we accounted him as plagued, smitten by God and oppressed.

5. But he was pained from our transgressions, crushed from our iniquities; the 'chastisement of our welfare was upon him, and with his wound we were healed.

6. We all went astray like sheep, we have turned, each one on his own way, and the Lord accepted his prayers for the iniquity of all of us.

7. He was oppressed, and he was afflicted, yet he would not open his mouth; like a lamb to the slaughter he would be brought, and like a sheep that is mute before her shearers, and he would not open his mouth.

8. From imprisonment and from judgment he is taken, and his generation who shall tell? For he was cut off from the land of the living; because of the transgression of my people, a plague befell them.

9. And he gave his grave to the wicked, and to the wealthy with his kinds of deaths, because he committed no violence, and there was no deceit in his mouth.

10. And the Lord wished to crush him, He made him ill; if his soul makes itself restitution, he shall see seed, he shall prolong his days, and God's purpose shall prosper in his hand.

11. From the toil of his soul he would see, he would be satisfied; with his knowledge My servant would vindicate the just for many, and their iniquities he would bear.

12. Therefore, I will allot him a portion in public, and with the strong he shall share plunder, because he poured out his soul to death, and with transgressors he was counted; and he bore the sin of many, and interceded for the transgressors.

יג הִנֵּה יַשְׂכִּיל עַבְדִּי יָרוּם וְנִשָּׂא וְגָבַהּ מְאֹד׃
יד כַּאֲשֶׁר שָׁמְמוּ עָלֶיךָ רַבִּים כֵּן־מִשְׁחַת
מֵאִישׁ מַרְאֵהוּ וְתֹאֲרוֹ מִבְּנֵי אָדָם׃
טו כֵּן יַזֶּה גּוֹיִם רַבִּים עָלָיו יִקְפְּצוּ מְלָכִים
פִּיהֶם כִּי אֲשֶׁר לֹא־סֻפַּר לָהֶם רָאוּ וַאֲשֶׁר
לֹא־שָׁמְעוּ הִתְבּוֹנָנוּ׃
א מִי הֶאֱמִין לִשְׁמֻעָתֵנוּ וּזְרוֹעַ ה' עַל־מִי
נִגְלָתָה׃
ב וַיַּעַל כַּיּוֹנֵק לְפָנָיו וְכַשֹּׁרֶשׁ מֵאֶרֶץ צִיָּה
לֹא־תֹאַר לוֹ וְלֹא הָדָר וְנִרְאֵהוּ וְלֹא־מַרְאֶה
וְנֶחְמְדֵהוּ׃
ג נִבְזֶה וַחֲדַל אִישִׁים אִישׁ מַכְאֹבוֹת וִידוּעַ
חֹלִי וּכְמַסְתֵּר פָּנִים מִמֶּנּוּ נִבְזֶה וְלֹא
חֲשַׁבְנֻהוּ׃
ד אָכֵן חֳלָיֵנוּ הוּא נָשָׂא וּמַכְאֹבֵינוּ סְבָלָם
וַאֲנַחְנוּ חֲשַׁבְנֻהוּ נָגוּעַ מֻכֵּה אֱלֹהִים וּמְעֻנֶּה׃
ה וְהוּא מְחֹלָל מִפְּשָׁעֵנוּ מְדֻכָּא מֵעֲוֹנֹתֵינוּ
מוּסַר שְׁלוֹמֵנוּ עָלָיו וּבַחֲבֻרָתוֹ נִרְפָּא־לָנוּ׃
ו כֻּלָּנוּ כַּצֹּאן תָּעִינוּ אִישׁ לְדַרְכּוֹ פָּנִינוּ
וַה' הִפְגִּיעַ בּוֹ אֵת עֲוֹן כֻּלָּנוּ׃
ז נִגַּשׂ וְהוּא נַעֲנֶה וְלֹא יִפְתַּח־פִּיו כַּשֶּׂה
לַטֶּבַח יוּבָל וּכְרָחֵל לִפְנֵי גֹזְזֶיהָ נֶאֱלָמָה וְלֹא
יִפְתַּח פִּיו׃
ח מֵעֹצֶר וּמִמִּשְׁפָּט לֻקָּח וְאֶת־דּוֹרוֹ מִי יְשׂוֹחֵחַ
כִּי נִגְזַר מֵאֶרֶץ חַיִּים מִפֶּשַׁע עַמִּי נֶגַע לָמוֹ׃
ט וַיִּתֵּן אֶת־רְשָׁעִים קִבְרוֹ וְאֶת־עָשִׁיר בְּמֹתָיו
עַל לֹא־חָמָס עָשָׂה וְלֹא מִרְמָה בְּפִיו׃
י וַה' חָפֵץ דַּכְּאוֹ הֶחֱלִי אִם־תָּשִׂים אָשָׁם
נַפְשׁוֹ יִרְאֶה זֶרַע יַאֲרִיךְ יָמִים וְחֵפֶץ ה'
בְּיָדוֹ יִצְלָח׃
יא מֵעֲמַל נַפְשׁוֹ יִרְאֶה יִשְׂבָּע בְּדַעְתּוֹ יַצְדִּיק
צַדִּיק עַבְדִּי לָרַבִּים וַעֲוֹנֹתָם הוּא יִסְבֹּל׃
יב לָכֵן אֲחַלֶּק־לוֹ בָרַבִּים וְאֶת־עֲצוּמִים יְחַלֵּק
שָׁלָל תַּחַת אֲשֶׁר הֶעֱרָה לַמָּוֶת נַפְשׁוֹ וְאֶת־
פֹּשְׁעִים נִמְנָה וְהוּא חֵטְא־רַבִּים נָשָׂא
וְלַפֹּשְׁעִים יַפְגִּיעַ׃ ס

[1]

# Who Is Speaking?

## Isaiah 52:15-53:1

[15]So shall he cast down many nations; the kings shall shut their mouths because of him; for that which had not been told to them they shall see; and that which they had not heard they shall consider.

[1]Who hath believed our report? And to whom is the arm of the Lord revealed?

**Kings of nations are speaking here in numbed astonishment; for what they will witness in the messianic age contradicts everything they had ever heard or considered.**

**"Who would have believed our report?," the astonished and contrite world leaders wonder aloud in their dazed bewilderment (53:1). The humbled kings of nations (52:15) will finally grasp and confess that Jewish suffering occurred as a direct result of "our own iniquity," (53:5) i.e., depraved, reckless Jew-hatred, rather than, as they previously thought, the stubborn blindness of the Jews.**

**They are utterly astounded that the Jewish people, whom all their nations have together despised and molested, are finally vindicated to enjoy the promised salvation of God. The palpable shock that the Israel's neighbors will express at the end of days is a common theme in the Hebrew scriptures.**

**Bear in mind that there is not a single instance in Tanach where prophets foretell that in the messianic age the Jewish people will be surprised or astonished, and never will they seek out the gentiles for spiritual guidance. On the contrary, the Bible clearly testifies that in the End of Days ten gentiles of different languages will grasp the shirt of a Jew and say, "Let us go with you, for we have heard that God is with you." (Zechariah 8:23)**

## Micah 7:15-16

According to the days of thy coming out of the land of Egypt will I show unto them marvelous things. [16]**The nations shall see and be confounded at all of their might; they shall lay their hands upon their mouth**, their ears shall be deaf.

## Isaiah 41:11

Behold all those who were incensed against you shall be **ashamed and confounded**; those who quarreled with you shall be as naught and be lost.

## Jeremiah 16:19-20

O Lord, my strength, my fortress, and my refuge in the day of affliction, the **Gentiles** shall come unto thee from the ends of the earth and say, "Surely our fathers have inherited lies, vanity, and things wherein there is no benefit. [20]Shall a man make gods unto himself, and they are no gods?"

[2]

# Who is the 'Servant' in Isaiah 53?

## Isaiah 41:8-9

But thou, **Israel, art My servant,** Jacob whom I have chosen, the seed of Abraham My friend. [9]Whom I grasped from the ends of the earth, and from it nobles I called you, and I said to you, **"You are My servant"**; I chose you and I did not despise you.

**The identity of the "servant" in Isaiah 53, the prophet's fourth Servant Song, appears christological to those who are unfamiliar with the context of this most-debated chapter. The "servant" is thoroughly established as the nation of Israel throughout the first three Servant Songs, which begin in chapter 41. Moreover, the prophet identifies the "servant" as many people rather than a single individual in 43:10.**

## Isaiah 44:1-2

Yet hear now, O Jacob **My servant** and Israel, whom I have chosen. So said the Lord your Maker, and He who formed you from the womb shall aid you. [2]Fear not, **My servant** Jacob, and *Jeshurun* whom I have chosen.

## Isaiah 44:21

Remember these, O **Jacob and Israel, for thou art My servant**; I have formed thee; thou art **My servant, O Israel**, thou shalt not be forgotten of Me.

## Isaiah 45:4

For the sake of **My servant Jacob, and Israel My chosen one**, and I called to you by your name....

## Isaiah 48:20

Leave Babylon, flee from the Chaldeans; with a voice of singing declare, tell this, publicize it to the end of the earth; say, "The Lord has redeemed His **servant Jacob**."

**Isaiah 49:3**

And said to me, thou art **My servant, O Israel** in whom I will be glorified!

**Psalms 136:22**

Even a heritage unto **Israel His servant**; for His mercy endures forever.

**Jeremiah 30:10**

Therefore fear not, O **My servant Jacob**, says the Lord; neither be dismayed, O Israel, for behold, I will save you from afar....

[3]

## Isaiah Addresses the Jewish People in the Singular Throughout his Servant Songs

**Missionaries contend that the repeated references to the servant in the singular as "he," and "his," in Isaiah 53 proves that this chapter is speaking of a single individual rather than the nation of Israel. This argument collapses when the entire context and surrounding poetic motif of Isaiah 53 is examined. Moreover, in Isaiah 43:10 (see below), the prophet clearly identifies the "servant" (singular) as God's "witnesses" (plural).**

**Additionally, Christians concede that the chapters which immediately surround Isaiah 53 (52 and 54) speak of the Jewish people as a single afflicted individual who is finally vindicated by God. Given that the chapter break between Isaiah 52 and 53 is completely artificial, and the fourth Servant Song begins in 52:13, this missionary argument becomes untenable. Furthermore, as will be discussed below (pages 50-60), the prophet alternately refers to the servant in Isaiah 53 in both the singular and plural.**

**Isaiah 54 continues to speak of the Jewish people as a single tormented individual, pictured as a despised and afflicted barren woman (54:6-11). Following the distinct theme of the previous two chapters, the Almighty assures His tormented people of their final vindication and redemption.**

**Isaiah 43:10**

Ye are My **witnesses** saith the Lord, and My **servant** whom I have chosen, that you may know and believe Me, and understand that I am He: Before Me there was no god formed, neither shall there be after Me.

**Isaiah 52:1-2**

Awaken, awaken, put on your strength, **O Zion**; put on the garments of your beauty, Jerusalem the Holy City, for no longer shall the uncircumcised or the unclean continue to enter you. [2]Shake yourselves from the dust, arise, sit down, O Jerusalem; free yourself of the bands of your neck, **O captive daughter of Zion**.

**These two epic chapters that surround Isaiah 53, repeatedly speak of the gentile nations who oppressed and tormented the Jewish people – not a messiah. In both Isaiah 52 and 54, the nation of Israel is vindicated and redeemed before the eyes of all the world. These references to the afflicted people of Israel are all in the singular, just as in Isaiah 53. In fact, from the first verse of Isaiah 52 through the end of Isaiah 54, Isaiah rarely refers to the Jewish people in the plural.**

**Isaiah 54:1-8**

"Sing you **barren woman** who has not born; burst out into song and jubilate, you who have not experienced birth pangs, for the children of the desolate one are more than the children of the married woman," says the Lord... [4] Fear not, you shall not be shamed; Do not cringe, you shall not be disgraced. For you shall forget The reproach of your youth, And remember no more The shame of your widowhood. [5] For He who made you will espouse you – His name is "Lord of Hosts." The Holy One of Israel will redeem you – He is called "God of all the Earth." [6] The Lord has called you back As a wife forlorn and forsaken. Can one cast off the wife of his youth? – said your God. [7] For a little while I forsook you, But with vast love I will bring you back. [8] In slight anger, for a moment, I hid My face from you; But with kindness everlasting I will take you back in love – said the Lord your Redeemer.

**Hosea 11:1**

When Israel was a child, then I loved **him**, and out of Egypt I called my **son**.

**Exodus 4:22**

Then you shall say to Pharaoh "thus saith the Lord, **Israel is My son**, My first born."

**Matthew misquotes Hosea in the same dubious manner that missionaries misquote Isaiah (see page 6). In Hosea 11:1, the prophet is clearly speaking of the Jewish people in the singular as God's "son." Matthew 2:15 lifts this text out of context and wildly misapplies the "son" to Jesus. Similarly, missionaries rip Isaiah 53 out of its clear context (41:8-9, 43:10, 44:1, 45:4, 21, 48:20, 49:3), where the prophet clearly identifies the "servant" as national Israel in the singular, and misquotes this chapter as if it is speaking about Jesus. Exodus 4:22 declares that it is Israel who is God's "firstborn son."**

[4]

## Isaiah 52:14

As many wondered about you, "How marred his appearance is from that of a man, and his features from that of people!"

Stürmer-Archiv (2)

Im jüdischen Geheimgesetzbuch Talmud steht geschrieben:

„Nur der Jude allein ist Mensch. Die nichtjüdischen Völker werden nicht Menschen genannt; sie werden als Vieh bezeichnet."

(Baba mezia, Fol. 114 b)

Von den „Menschen" — es können nach talmudischer Auffassung also nur die Juden gemeint sein — sagte nun im Jahre 1859 der Gelehrte Darwin, sie würden vom Affen abstammen. Ob das richtig ist oder nicht, wollen wir nicht entscheiden. Vielleicht macht sich der Leser die Mühe, das Gesicht des Affen aus dem Neu-Yorker Zoo (links) und das Gesicht des Trödeljuden aus dem Neu-Yorker Ghetto (oben) zu vergleichen und sich selbst ein Urteil zu bilden.

A typical *Stuermer* feature in the issue of December 29, 1942. The text reads, "In the secret Jewish law book, the Talmud, it is written: 'Only a Jew is a human being. Non-Jewish people should not be called human beings: they should be depicted as animals...' About human beings according to the Talmud this can only mean Jews – the scholar Darwin said in 1859 that man is descended from the ape. Whether is correct or not we do not which to decide. Perhaps the reader will take the trouble to compare the features of the ape from the New York Zoo (left) and the face of the Jewish old-cloths dealer from the New York ghetto (above) and draw his own conclusions."

The Kaftan Jew and the German peasant woman. The text under these two pictures in the *Stuermer* reads, "The racial mixing of Germans of Nordic stock with the Asiatic-oriental-Negroid Jews which is preached and blessed by liberal circles and religious denominations is the greatest cultural disgrace in this world."

[5]

# Kings of Nations Will Be Surprised as They Witness the Final Vindication and Salvation of Israel

### Isaiah 53:1

Who hath believed our report, and to whom is the arm of the Lord revealed?

**The anthropomorphic reference to the "arm of the Lord" appears frequently throughout Tanach and always signifies God's salvation of the Jewish people from its gentile oppressors. Israel's final vindication and redemption in the eyes of the world's nations is the central theme of the last 27 chapters of the Book of Isaiah.**

### Isaiah 52:9-12

Break forth into joy, sing together, ye waste places of Jerusalem, for the Lord hath comforted His people, He hath redeemed Jerusalem. [10]The Lord hath made bare His **Holy Arm** in the eyes of all the nations; and all the ends of the earth shall see the salvation of our God! [11]Turn away, turn away, get out of there, touch no unclean one; get out of its midst, purify yourselves, you who bear the Lord's vessels. [12]For not with haste shall you go forth and not in a flurry of flight shall you go, for the Lord goes before you, and your rear guard is the God of Israel.

**Throughout the chapters that surround Isaiah 53, the prophet carefully describes the salvation of the Jewish nation from the world's nations – their unyielding oppressors.**

### Isaiah 54:7-10

"For a small moment have I forsaken you, and with great mercy will I gather you. [8]With a little wrath did I hide My countenance for a moment from you, and with everlasting kindness will I have compassion on you," said your redeemer, the Lord. [9]"For this is to Me [as] the waters of Noah, as I swore that the waters of Noah shall never again pass over the earth, so have I sworn neither to be wroth with you nor to rebuke you. [10]For the mountains shall depart and the hills totter, but My kindness shall not depart from you, neither shall the covenant of My peace totter," says the Lord, Who has compassion on you.

### Deuteronomy 7:19

...the great miracles that you saw with your own eyes, the signs, the wonders, the mighty hand and the outstretched arm with which God brought you out of Egypt. (see Ex. 14:31; 15:6)

[6]

# Throughout History, the Survival of the Jewish People Seemed as Bleak as a Young Tree Planted in Dry Land

### Isaiah 53:2

And he came up like a sapling before it, and like a root from dry ground, he had neither form nor comeliness; and we saw him that he had no appearance that we should have desired him.

### Hosea 14:6-8

I will be as the dew unto Israel: **he** shall grow as the lily, and cast forth **his** roots as Lebanon. [7]**His** branches shall spread, **his** beauty shall be as the olive tree, and **his** smell as Lebanon. [8]They that dwell under his shadow shall return; they shall revive as the corn and grow as the vine. The scent thereof shall be as the wine of Lebanon.

**A young, vulnerable tree rooted in dry ground has little chance to survive. Such has been the precarious predicament of the Jewish people throughout their dark exile – a nation teetering on the brink of annihilation. This nation who so many sought to destroy will be uplifted in the messianic age to the surprise of the world's nations.**

[7]

# The Nations of the World Despised, Abandoned, and Afflicted the Jewish People

### Isaiah 53:3

Despised and forsaken by men, a man of pains and accustomed to illness. As one who hides his face from us, despised, and we esteemed him not.

**The 49th chapter of Isaiah contains one of the most stirring dialogs in scripture, and continues to set the stage for Isaiah 53. This chapter opens by explicitly identifying the Jewish people as God's 'servant' (49:3), and its verses are filled with a moving conversation between God and his covenant nation. As in all the Servant Songs, Isaiah frequently refers to Israel in the singular, highlighting their singular destiny.**

**The faithful cry out to God throughout the 49th chapter, feeling forsaken, afflicted, and abandoned – the same descriptions of the Servant in Isaiah 53. The reluctant remnant feel unworthy of their divine mission, yet are called upon to be a light to the gentiles, and assigned to restore the rest of the Jewish people who have lost their way (49:6).**

**In response to their agony, the Almighty assures His beleaguered people that His steadfast love for His nation exceeds even the intense bond a new mother feels for her nursing infant (49:15). As in Isaiah 53, the final vindication and salvation of the Jewish people is the chapter's central theme.**

## Isaiah 49:3, 7-8, 13-15

And He said to me, "Thou art **My servant, O Israel** in whom I will be glorified!" 7...for so said the Lord, the redeemer of Israel, his Holy One, about **him** who is despised of men, about him whom the nation abhors, about a slave of rulers, "Kings shall see and rise, princes, and they shall prostrate themselves, for the sake of the Lord Who is faithful, the Holy One of Israel, and He chose you." 8So said the Lord, "In a time of favor I answered you, and on a day of salvation I helped you; and I will watch you, and I will make you for a **people of a covenant**, to establish a land, to cause to inherit the desolate heritages.... 13Sing, O heavens, and rejoice, O earth, and mountains burst out in song, for the Lord has consoled His people, and He shall have mercy on His **afflicted**. 14But Zion said, "The Lord has **forsaken** me, and the Lord has **forgotten** me." 15Shall a woman forget her suckling child, from having mercy on the child of her womb? These too shall forget, but I will not forget you.

## Isaiah 54:4-7, 11, 14, 17

Fear not, for you shall not be ashamed, and not embarrassed, for you shall not be put to shame; for the shame of your youth you shall forget, and for the humiliation of your widowhood you shall no longer be remembered. 5For your maker is your husband; the Lord Hosts is His name; and your redeemer the Holy One of Israel shall be called the God of all the earth. 6For like a wife who is **forsaken** and **afflicted** in spirit has the Lord called you, and a wife of one's youth who was **rejected**, said your God. 7For a small moment have I forsaken you, and with great mercy will I gather you. 11O **thou afflicted**, who was not consoled, behold I will lay thy stones with fair colors, and lay thy foundations with sapphires. 14With righteousness shall you be established, for you will be far from oppression, for you will not fear; and from ruin, for it will not come near you. 17No weapon that is formed against you will prosper, and any tongue that rises against you in judgement, you shall condemn; this is the heritage of the **servants of the Lord** and their righteousness is from Me, says the Lord.

**Bible students who explore the last 27 chapters of Isaiah have little trouble understanding Isaiah 53. These stirring chapters triumphantly declare God's sovereign plan for His "servant Israel." Israel's gentile neighbors will be surprised by the startling events that will unfold in the messianic age. They will together grasp that their age-old assessment of the Jew was wrong. Throughout Israel's long and bitter exile, the nations mistakenly attributed the miserable predicament of the Jew to his stubborn rejection of the world's religions. In the End of Days, however, the gentiles will finally discover what was until then unimaginable: the unwavering Jew was, in fact, all this time faithful to the true God. On the other hand, "We despised and held him of no account" (53:3).**

**In contrast, Christians who only read Isaiah 53 and ignore the contextual significance of the fourth Servant Song, erroneously conclude that Isaiah 53 refers to Jesus.**

## Isaiah 60:14-15

The sons of them who **afflicted you** shall come bending unto you; and all they who **despised** you shall bow themselves down at the soles of your feet; and they shall call you, the city of the Lord, Zion of the Holy One of Israel. 15Whereas **you have been forsaken and despised**, with no passerby, I will make you an everlasting pride, the joy of every generation.

**References to the Jewish people as "afflicted" and "despised" are common to the latter chapters of the Book of Isaiah. The prophet assures his brutalized nation, however, that at the end of days they will be redeemed and vindicated.**

## Isaiah 40:2

Speak to the heart of Jerusalem and call to her, for she has become full from her host, **for her iniquity has been appeased, for she has taken from the hand of the Lord double for all her sins**.

## Zechariah 1:15

And I am very angry with the nations that are at ease, for I was wroth a little, and they helped to do harm.

### Isaiah 52:4-5

For so said the Lord God, "My people first went down to Egypt to sojourn there, but Assyria oppressed **him without cause** (וְאַשּׁוּר בְּאֶפֶס עֲשָׁקוֹ).
[5]And now, what have I here," says the Lord, "that My people have been taken for nothing; **his** rulers (מֹשְׁלָו) boast," says the Lord, "and constantly, all day, My name is blasphemed."

**Christian Bible translators deliberately conceal the pronouns in Isaiah 52 which refer to Israel in the singular, changing them into the plural. (See below)**

### Isaiah 62:2-4, 12

And the gentiles shall see your righteousness, and all kings your glory, and you shall be called a new name, which the mouth of the Lord shall pronounce. [3]And you shall be a crown of glory in the hand of the Lord and a Kingly crown on the land of your God. [4]No longer shall **"Forsaken"** be said of you, and "Desolate" shall no longer be said of your land, for you shall be called "My desire is in her," and your land, "Inhabited," for the Lord desires you, and your land shall be inhabited.... [12]And they shall call them the holy people, those redeemed by the Lord, and you shall be called, **"Sought, a city not forsaken."**

**Isaiah 62 parallels the famed Isaiah 53. When the gentiles "see your righteousness" they will no longer regard you forsaken and smitten by God. In the messianic age, the Jewish people will be vindicated before the world to the astonishment of Israel's neighbors.**

**A number of Christian Bibles tampered with the text of the 52nd chapter Isaiah in order to conceal that the prophet consistently addresses the nation of Israel in the singular as he does in Isaiah 53. These Christian Bible translators seek to completely sever the umbilical relationship between Isaiah 52 and 53, which is otherwise difficult to ignore. The illustrative language of Isaiah 52 and 53 contain a similar theme, poetic structure, and motif. In addition, the chapter break between 52 and 53 is artificial and unwarranted. This parallelism is, of course, impossible to miss when Isaiah 52 is translated correctly.**

**For example, in both Isaiah 52 and 53 the one who suffers is a victim of the unprovoked aggression of the gentile nations. Conspicuously, the sufferer in both of these chapters is referred to in the singular. In Isaiah 52, however, the prophet explicitly identifies the nation of Israel as the one who suffers vicariously. The King James Version (KJV) and the New International Version (NIV) translators were undoubtedly concerned that Bible readers might reject the notion that Isaiah 53 is referring to Jesus, when Isaiah 52 so clearly describes Israel as a single individual, relentlessly persecuted by the world's nations.**

**To solve this problem, Christian Bible translators carefully reconstructed critical segments of Isaiah 52 so as not to appear to resemble Isaiah 53's theme and poetic language. For example, in Isaiah 52:4 the prophet recounts that "Assyria oppressed him [Israel] without cause." As stated above, the concept that the nation of Israel innocently suffered in Isaiah 52 is precisely the underlying theme of Isaiah 53. Moreover, 52:4 speaks of the Jewish people in the singular, as does Isaiah 53. Therefore, the NIV altered this text by removing a most revealing phrase in this verse. The last words of Isaiah 52:4 in an NIV read, "lately, Assyria has oppressed them." The critical words "without cause" were expunged by the NIV. Moreover, the KJV as well as the NIV change the singular pronoun "him" in this verse to the plural "them" (see below).**

**In Isaiah 52:5 the Hebrew word מֹשְׁלָו (*moshlov*) means "his rulers," referring to Israel's rulers. The nation of Israel is once again spoken of in the singular. Therefore, the KJV and NIV translators carefully changed the singular reference, "his rulers," into the plural. The KJV therefore reads, "rule over them." The irony of all this Bible-tampering is that these Christian translators changed the singular references to Israel in Isaiah 52 into the plural, and the plural references to Israel in Isaiah 53 into the singular (see page 59). Although this is a strange way to translate the Bible, it successively perpetuates the erroneous notion that the singular references to the "servant" in Isaiah 53 must not be referring to the Jewish people.**

| Verse | Hebrew | Translation | King James Version | New International Version |
|---|---|---|---|---|
| **52:4** | וְאַשּׁוּר בְּאֶפֶס עֲשָׁקוֹ | Assyria oppressed **him** without cause | the Assyrian oppressed **them** without cause | lately, Assyria has oppressed **them** |
| **52:5** | מֹשְׁלָו יְהֵילִילוּ | **his** rulers boast | they that rule over **them** make them to howl | and those who rule **them** mock |

[8]

## Nations Conclude That Israel Suffered as a Direct Result of Their Own Iniquity

### Isaiah 53:4-5

Indeed, he bore our illnesses, and our pains — he carried them, yet we accounted him as plagued, smitten by God and oppressed. [5]But he was pained because of our transgressions, crushed because of our iniquities; the chastisement of our welfare was upon him, and with his wounds we **were** healed.

> **In order to stress the ongoing and everlasting atonement of Jesus, Christian Bibles incorrectly translate the Hebrew words וּבַחֲבֻרָתוֹ נִרְפָּא־לָנוּ, "with his wounds we *are* healed," in the present tense.**
>
> **Actually, the nations are speaking here of Israel's past suffering, therefore the phrase correctly translated reads,"we *were* healed," in the past tense (see page 59)**

### Ezekiel 36:6-9, 15

Therefore, prophesy about the land of Israel and say to the mountains and to the hills, to the streams and to the valleys: Thus says my Lord, God: Behold! In My jealousy and in My anger I have spoken, because the shame of the nations you have borne. [7]Therefore, thus says my Lord, God: I have lifted My hand in an oath. Surely the nations which surround you — they will bear their shame. [8]But you, O mountains of Israel — you shall shoot forth your branches and bear your fruit for My people Israel, when they are about to come. [9]For behold! I am for you, and I shall turn to you; then you shall be tilled and sown. [15]And I shall no longer cause the ridicule of nations to be heard about you, and the shame of the nations you shall no longer bear, of your nations you shall never again be bereaved - the word of my Lord, God.

### Jeremiah 30:8-13

And it shall be on that day, says the Lord of hosts, [that] I will break his yoke off your neck, and I will break your thongs, and strangers shall no longer enslave them. [9]And they shall serve the Lord their God and David their king, whom I will set up for them. [10]And you, fear not, **My servant Jacob**, says the Lord, and do not be dismayed, O Israel, for behold I save you from afar and your seed from the land of their captivity, and Jacob shall again be silent and at ease, and no one will frighten them. [11]For I am with you, says the Lord , to save you, for I will make an end of all the nations where I dispersed you, but of you I will not make an end, but I will chasten you in measure, and I will not completely destroy you. [12]For so said the Lord: **Your bruise is painful, your wound grievous.** **[13]No one deems your wound to be healed**, you have no healing medicines.

[9]

## The Servant Intercedes For the Gentile Nations

### Isaiah 53:6

We all went astray like sheep, we have turned, each one on his own way, and the Lord accepted his prayers for the iniquity of all of us.

### Jeremiah 29:7

And seek the peace of the city where I have exiled you and pray for it to the Lord, for in its peace you shall have peace.

[10]

## The Remnant of Israel Silently Went to Their Death Like Sheep To the Slaughter

### Isaiah 53:7

He was oppressed, and he was afflicted, yet he would not open his mouth; like a lamb to the slaughter he would be brought, and like a sheep that is mute before her shearers, and he would not open his mouth.

### Psalms 18:28

For you will save the afflicted nation; and you will bring down haughty looks.

> **Although the Bible explicitly and repeatedly describes the Jewish people as afflicted and despised by the gentile nations, there is not even one *clear* reference to the messiah as afflicted or despised anywhere in all of the Jewish scriptures.**

### Psalms 44:12-22

You have delivered us **like sheep for the slaughter**, and among the gentiles you have scattered us. [14]You made us a disgrace to our neighbors, the mockery and scorn of those around us. [15]You made us a byword among the nations to shake their heads. [22]Because for Your sake we are killed all day long, **we are considered as sheep for the slaughter**.

**Psalm 44 describes the desperate plight of the righteous remnant of Israel. Notice how the language used here to describe the condition of the Jewish people parallels that of Isaiah 53.**

**As mentioned above, why isn't there even one *clear* reference to the suffering or death of the messiah anywhere in all of the Jewish scriptures?**

### Ezekiel 34:15-16

I will tend **My sheep**, and lay them down — the words of my Lord, God. [16]The lost, I will seek out; and the banished, I will retrieve; the wounded, I will heal; and the frail, I will strengthen.

### Zechariah 11:4-5, 7

So Said the Lord, my God: Tend the **flock of the slaughter**, [5]whose buyers shall lay them and not be guilty; and whose sellers shall say, "Blessed be the Lord, for I have become wealthy"; and whose shepherds shall not have pity on them. [7]And I tended the **flock of slaughter**; indeed, the poor of the flock.

**Ezekiel and Zechariah vividly describe the Jewish people as a nation who are forsaken for slaughter – like abandoned sheep. There is not a single instance in Tanach where the messiah is described in this fashion.**

[11]

## Gentile Nations Confess That *They* [Israel] Were Stricken as a Result of Their Iniquity

### Isaiah 53:8

From imprisonment and from judgment he is taken, and his generation who shall tell? For he was cut off from the land of the living; because of the transgression of my people, a plague befell **them** (לָמוֹ).

**The prophet's use of the Hebrew word לָמוֹ (*lamo*) "to them" as a pronoun for the servant in 53:8 creates a staggering problem for Christian translators who are committed to casting Jesus as the 'servant' of Isaiah 53.**

**Poetically, the Hebrew Scriptures often addresses the Jewish nation in the singular in order to highlight the nation's singular destiny. The prophets, however, never speak of an individual in the plural. Therefore, the use of the Hebrew word "them" demonstrates that the servant of Isaiah 53 is not a single individual.**

**The KJV, NIV and other Christian Bible translations escape this nagging problem by mistranslating the Hebrew word לָמוֹ as "him" in the singular.**

| Christian Bibles that Mistranslate "מִפֶּשַׁע עַמִּי נֶגַע לָמוֹ" (Isaiah 53:8) | |
|---|---|
| King James Version | for the transgressions of my people was *he* stricken |
| Modern Reader's Bible | for the transgression of my people was *he* stricken |
| New International Version | for the transgression of my people *he* was stricken |
| Living Bible | it was their sins that *he* was dying for — that *he* was suffering their punishment |
| English Standard Version | for the transgression of my people was he stricken. |
| New English Translation | because of the rebellion of his own people he was wounded. |
| New Jerusalem Bible (Catholic) | at his having been struck dead for his people's rebellion? |
| Young's Literal Translation | By the transgression of My people he is plagued. |
| New Living Translation | But he was struck down for the rebellion of my people. |

### Psalms 116:9

I shall walk before the Lord in the **land of the living**.

# Why does the KJV correctly translate the same Hebrew word לָמוֹ as "them" in other places in the Bible?

**Genesis 9:26** (King James Version)
And He said, Blessed be the Lord God of Shem; and Canaan shall be **his** (peoples of Shem) servant (לָמוֹ).

**Deuteronomy 32:35** (King James Version)
...for the day of their calamity *is* at hand, and the things that shall come upon **them** (לָמוֹ) make haste.

**Deuteronomy 33:2** (King James Version)
....He shined forth from Mount Paran, and he came with ten thousands of saints: from His right hand went a fiery law for **them** (לָמוֹ).

**Job 6:19** (King James Version)
The troops of Tema looked, the companies of Sheba waited for **them** (לָמוֹ).

**Job 14:21** (King James Version)
His sons come to honor, and he knoweth it not; and they are brought low, but he perceiveth it not of **them** (לָמוֹ).

**Job 24:17** (King James Version)
For the morning is to **them** (לָמוֹ) even as the shadow of death: if one know them...

**Psalms 2:4** (King James Version)
He that sitteth in the heavens shall laugh: the Lord shall have **them** (לָמוֹ) in derision.

**Psalms 44:4** (King James Version — 44:3)
For they got not the land in possession by their own sword, neither did their own arm save **them** (לָמוֹ)....

**Psalms 78:24** (King James Version)
And had rained down manna upon them to eat, and had given **them** (לָמוֹ) of the corn of heaven.

**Psalm 88:8** (King James Version)
Thou hast put away mine acquaintance far from me; thou hast made me an abomination unto **them** (לָמוֹ): I am shut up, and I cannot come forth.

**Psalms 119:165** (King James Version)
Great peace have they which love Thy law: and nothing shall offend **them** (לָמוֹ).

**Isaiah 16:4** (King James Version)
Let Mine outcasts dwell with thee, Moab; be thou a covert to **them** (לָמוֹ) from the face of the spoiler: for the extortioner is at an end, the spoiler ceaseth, the oppressors are consumed out of the land.

**Isaiah 23:1** (King James Version)
The burden of Tyre. Howl, ye ships of Tarshish; for it is laid waste, so that there is no house, no entering in: from the land of Chittim it is revealed to **them** (לָמוֹ).

**Isaiah 30:5** (King James Version)
They were all ashamed of a people that could not profit **them** (לָמוֹ), nor be an help nor profit, but a shame, and also a reproach.

**Isaiah 44:7** (King James Version)
And who, as I, shall call, and shall declare it, and set it in order for Me, since I appointed the ancient people? And the things that are coming, and shall come, let them show unto **them** (לָמוֹ).

**Isaiah 48:21** (King James Version)
And they thirsted not when he led them through the deserts: He caused waters to flow out of the rock for **them** (לָמוֹ): He calve the rock also, and the waters gushed out.

**Lamentations 1:19** (King James Version)
I called for my lovers, but they deceived me: my priests and mine elders gave up the ghost in the city, while they sought **their** (לָמוֹ) meat to relieve their souls.

**Habakkuk 2:7** (King James Version)
Shall they not rise up suddenly that shall bite thee, and awake that shall vex thee, and thou shalt be for booties unto **them** (לָמוֹ)?

**An expanded word study of (לָמוֹ) continues on the following two pages.**

# Why tamper with

## R. Alcalay
## The Complete Hebrew-English Dictionary



לִמֵּד חוֹבָה (קַטֵּגוֹרְיָה) עַל — to judge unfavourably, to accuse, indict, arraign
מְלַמֵּד שֶׁ־ — from this one may deduce that
לְלַמֵּד שֶׁ־, לְלַמֶּדְךָ שֶׁ־ — in order to explain to you that
לֻמַּד — to be trained, taught, schooled
מִצְוַת אֲנָשִׁים מְלֻמָּדָה ר' מִצְוָה
הִתְלַמֵּד — to learn by oneself, teach, train oneself, practise, be used
לֶמֶד, ז. [לִמְדוֹ] — (poet.) study, knowledge
לָמֵד, ת. [לְמֵדָה, לְמֵדִים, לְמֵדוֹת] — (to be) learned; learning, accustomed, taught; to argue, argumentative
וְלֹא הַבַּיְשָׁן לָמֵד וְלֹא הַקַּפְּדָן מְלַמֵּד (אבות ב, ה) — the shamefast man cannot learn and the impatient man cannot teach (Aboth 2, 5)
מִכָּאן אַתָּה לָמֵד, נִמְצֵאתָ לָמֵד, נִמְצֵאנוּ לְמֵדִים — from this one (we) may deduce (learn)
דָּבָר הַלָּמֵד מֵעִנְיָנוֹ — something deducible from the context
דָּבָר הַלָּמֵד מִסּוֹפוֹ — something deducible from the final context
בָּא לְלַמֵּד וְנִמְצָא לָמֵד — one who comes to teach and ends by learning; teaching others teaches oneself; the best way to learn is to teach
לַמְדָּא, נ. — lambda (Greek letter)
לַמְדִּי, ת. — lambdoid
לְמַדַּי, תה"פ — sufficiently, enough
לַמְדָן, ז. [לַמְדָנִית, לַמְדָנִים, לַמְדָנִיּוֹת] — learned

²לָמָּה, נ. — naught, vanity, nonentity, nothingness
שֶׁהָיָה לְלָמָּה וְלֹא כְלוּם — who was reduced to nought and nothing
אַתֶּם לָמָּה וְדִבְרֵיכֶם לָמָּה! — you are nought and your words are nought
³לָמָה, נ. [לָמוֹת] — llama
⁴לָמָה, ז. — lama (Tibet)
°דָּלַי לָמָה — Dalai Lama
למה"ד – לְמָה הַדָּבָר דּוֹמֶה? — To what can this be likened (compared)?
לָמוֹ, מ"ג = לָהֶם — (poet.) them, to them
לְמוֹ, מ"י — (poet.) to
לָמוּד, ת. [לְמוּדָה, לְמוּדִים, לְמוּדוֹת] — trained, accustomed, experienced, used to, taught
¹לִמּוּד, ז. [לִמּוּדִים, לִמּוּדֵי־] — instruction, learning, study, teaching; custom; disciple, accustomed, trained, taught; Yahrzeit reading in synagogue (so called by Sepharadi Jews)
לִמּוּד עַצְמִי — self-instruction
לִמּוּדִים קְלַסִּיִּים — classics
חֲדַר הַלִּמּוּדִים — schoolroom
חָכְמַת הַלִּמּוּדִים — (obs.) mathematics, astronomy
חֹק לִמּוּדִים — course of study
לְשׁוֹן לִמּוּדִים — academic language
סֵפֶר לִמּוּד — textbook
שְׂכַר לִמּוּד — tuition fee
שְׁנַת הַלִּמּוּדִים — school- (academic) year

The above page appears in the Alcalay Hebrew-English Dictionary.
On page 1,132, the Hebrew word לָמוֹ is translated correctly as "them."

Alcalay, R. *The Complete Hebrew-English Dictionary.* Jerusalem: Chemed Books - Yedioth Ahronoth, 1990.

# an original?

## The Interlinear NIV Hebrew-English Old Testament

**ISAIAH 53:4-12**

אֱלֹהִים וּמְעֻנֶּה: וְהוּא מְחֹלָל מִפְּשָׁעֵנוּ
for-transgressions-of-us being-pierced but-he (5) and-one-being-afflicted God

מְדֻכָּא מֵעֲוֺנֹתֵינוּ מוּסַר שְׁלוֹמֵנוּ עָלָיו
upon-him peace-of-us punishment-of for-iniquities-of-us being-crushed

וּבַחֲבֻרָתוֹ נִרְפָּא־ לָנוּ: כֻּלָּנוּ כַּצֹּאן תָּעִינוּ
we-went-astray like-the-sheep all-of-us (6) to-us he-was-healed and-by-wound-of-him

אִישׁ לְדַרְכּוֹ פָּנִינוּ וַיהוָה הִפְגִּיעַ בּוֹ אֵת עֲוֺן כֻּלָּנוּ:
all-of-us iniquity-of *** on-him he-laid and-Yahweh we-turned to-way-of-him each

נִגַּשׂ וְהוּא נַעֲנֶה וְלֹא יִפְתַּח־ פִּיו
mouth-of-him he-opened yet-not he-was-afflicted and-he he-was-oppressed (7)

כַּשֶּׂה לַטֶּבַח יוּבָל וּכְרָחֵל לִפְנֵי גֹזְזֶיהָ
ones-shearing-her before and-as-sheep he-was-led to-the-slaughter like-the-lamb

נֶאֱלָמָה וְלֹא יִפְתַּח פִּיו: מֵעֹצֶר וּמִמִּשְׁפָּט
and-by-judgment by-oppression (8) mouth-of-him he-opened so-not she-is-silent

לֻקָּח וְאֶת־ דּוֹרוֹ מִי יְשׂוֹחֵחַ כִּי נִגְזַר
he-was-cut-off for he-can-speak who? descendant-of-him and he-was-taken-away

מֵאֶרֶץ חַיִּים מִפֶּשַׁע עַמִּי נֶגַע לָמוֹ:
to-them stroke people-of-me for-transgression-of living-ones from-land-of

וַיִּתֵּן אֶת־ רְשָׁעִים קִבְרוֹ וְאֶת־ עָשִׁיר בְּמֹתָיו
in-deaths-of-him rich and-with grave-of-him wicked-ones with and-he-assigned (9)

עַל לֹא־ חָמָס עָשָׂה וְלֹא מִרְמָה בְּפִיו: וַיהוָה חָפֵץ
he-willed yet-Yahweh (10) in-mouth-of-him deceit or-no he-did violence no though

afflicted
5 But he was pierced for our
transgressions,
he was crushed for our
iniquities;
the punishment that brought
us peace was upon him,
and by his wounds we are
healed.
6 We all, like sheep, have gone
astray,
each of us has turned to his
own way;
and the LORD has laid on him
the iniquity of us all.

7 He was oppressed and
afflicted,
yet he did not open his
mouth;
he was led like a lamb to the
slaughter,
and as a sheep before her
shearers is silent,
so he did not open his
mouth.
8 By oppression and judgment
he was taken away.
And who can speak of his
descendants?
For he was cut off from the
land of the living;
for the transgression of my
people he was stricken.
9 He was assigned a grave with
the wicked,
and with the rich in his
death,
though he had done no
violence,
nor was any deceit in his
mouth.

10 Yet it was the LORD's will to
crush him and cause him
to suffer,
and though the LORD makes
his life a guilt offering,
he will see his offspring and
prolong his days,

This is an extraordinary example of how Christian Bible translators altered the Jewish scriptures in order to sustain a christological reading of Isaiah 53. Because the "servant" of Isaiah 53 is the finally elevated and vindicated nation of Israel in the messianic age, the prophet alternately refers to the servant in both the singular and plural. The prophets often speak of the Jewish people in this poetic fashion. For example, Isaiah identifies the nation of Israel both as God's "witnesses" (plural) and His "servant" (singular) in 43:10. In Isaiah 53, however, the prophet's reference to the Jewish people in the plural creates a significant problem for Christian Bible translators who wish to apply this chapter to Jesus. It would be impossible to translate this chapter precisely as Isaiah wrote it while sustaining a Christological reading of the text. In simple terms, the Hebrew scriptures never refer to a single individual in the plural. Christian translators, however, have found a way around this problem, they alter the meaning of the original words of Isaiah 53.

The above page clearly illustrates how Christian Bible translators revised the text in this crucial chapter. This example comes from *The Interlinear NIV Hebrew-English Old Testament* — a well known word-for-word literal translation of the Old Testament by Christian scholars. Notice how in the interlinear translation of Isaiah 53:8 correctly renders the Hebrew word לָמוֹ as "them" (plural), yet the NIV translation (in the sidebar, on the right) changes the translation to "he" (singular). Of course, the NIV translators had little choice in this matter. Had the NIV Bible properly translated this chapter, it would become clear to the reader that the suffering servant in Isaiah 53 is referring to many people rather than Jesus.

The NIV translators also had no choice with regard to the translation of the next verse (53:9), where the interlinear translation correctly renders בְּמֹתָיו as "deaths" (plural), whereas the NIV deliberately mistranslates this word in the singular as "death."

Kohlenberger III, John R. The Interlinear NIV Hebrew-English Old Testament. Grand Rapids: Zondervan, 1987.

[12]

# The Faithful Remnant of Israel Endured Martyrdom Throughout Their Bitter Exile

## Isaiah 53:9

And he gave his grave to the wicked, and to the wealthy with his kinds of **deaths** (בְּמֹתָיו), because he committed no violence, and there was no deceit in his mouth.

**Isaiah 53:9** (King James Version)

And he made his grave with the wicked, and with the rich in his **death**; because he had done no violence, neither was any deceit in his mouth.

**As had been done to the previous verse, the plural reference to the servant is deliberately changed by Christian translators into the singular. The Hebrew word בְּמֹתָיו (*b'mosov*) is plural, and correctly translated means "deaths." The KJV, NIV and other Christian Bibles translate this word as "death" rather than "deaths" in order to conceal the identity of the servant as the Jewish people. (see page 35)**

### Zephaniah 3:12-17, 19-20

And I will leave over in your midst a humble and poor people, and they shall take shelter in the name of the Lord. [13]The remnant of Israel shall neither commit injustice nor **speak lies; neither shall deceitful speech be found in their mouth**, for they shall graze and lie down, with no one to cause them to shudder. [14]Sing, O daughter of Zion! Shout, O Israel! Rejoice and jubilate wholeheartedly, O daughter of Jerusalem! [15]The Lord has removed your afflictions; He has cast out your enemy. The King of Israel, the Lord, is in your midst - you shall no longer fear evil. [16]On that day it shall be said to Jerusalem, "Have no fear! O Zion, let your hands not be slack. [17]The Lord your God is in your midst — a Mighty One Who will save. He will rejoice over you with joy. He will be silent in His love. [19]He will jubilate over you with song." Behold, I wreak destruction upon all those who have afflicted you at that time. And I will save the one who limps, and I will gather the stray one, and I will make them a praise and a name throughout all the land where they suffered shame. [20]At that time I will bring them, and at that time I will gather you, for I will make you a name and a praise among all the peoples of the earth when I restore your captivities before your eyes, said the Lord.

**Here the prophet Zephaniah vividly describes the righteous remnant of Israel in precisely the same fashion as Isaiah did in the 53rd chapter: "The remnant of Israel shall neither speak lies; neither shall deceitful speech be found in their mouth."**

[13]

# Almighty Promises Servant Biological Children (זֶרַע), Long Life, and Divine Agency

## Isaiah 53:10

And the Lord wished to crush him, He made him ill; **if** (אִם) his soul makes itself restitution, he shall see **seed** (זֶרַע), he shall prolong his days, and God's purpose shall prosper in his hand.

### Deuteronomy 30:8-10, 19-20

You will repent and obey God, keeping all His commandments, as I prescribe them to you today. [9]God will then grant you a good surplus in all the work of your hands, in the fruit of your womb, the fruit of your livestock, and the fruit of your land. God will once again rejoice in you for good, just as He rejoiced in your fathers. [10]All this will happen when you obey God your Lord, keeping all His commandments and decrees, as they are written in this book of the Torah, and when you return to God your Lord with all your heart and soul. [19] I call heaven and earth as witnesses! Before you I have placed life and death, the blessing and the curse. You must choose life, so that you and your seed will survive. [20]If you

**If, as Trinitarian Christians claim, Jesus was God, how can God promise God long life and children? Such a blessing would be absurd; God is eternal. Furthermore, why would God bless Himself and how can He be a servant to Himself?**

**Moreover, the promise of "seed" to the servant is a God-given blessing to the faithful remnant of Israel. The Hebrew word "seed" (זֶרַע) can only mean biological children. According to Church doctrine Jesus had no physical offspring, and thus this blessing could not apply to him.**

choose to love the Lord your God, to obey Him, and to attach yourself to Him. This is the sole means of survival and long life when you dwell in the land that God swore to your fathers, Abraham, Isaac, and Jacob, [promising] that He would give it to them.

### Genesis 15:2-4

And Abram said, "My Lord, God, what can You give to me seeing that I am childless, and the **son** of my house (וּבֶן מֶשֶׁק בֵּיתִי) is the Damascene Eliezer?" [3]Then Abram said, "See, to me You have given no **seed** (זָרַע) and see, the **son** (בֶּן) of my house is my heir." [4]Suddenly, the word of God came to him, saying: That one will not inherit you. None but him that shall come forth from within your bowels shall be your heir.

### Isaiah 45:11, 19

Thus says the Lord, the Holy One of Israel, and His Maker, "Ask Me of things to come concerning My signs; concerning My **children** (עַל בָּנַי). [19] Not in secret did I speak, (or) in a land of darkness; I did not say to the **seed** (לְזֶרַע) of Jacob, seek Me in vain...

[14]

## The Servant Vindicates the World With His Knowledge (Not His Blood)

### Isaiah 53:11

From the toil of his soul he would see, he would be satisfied; with his **knowledge** My servant would vindicate the just for many, and their iniquities he would bear.

**The servant vindicates the world with his "knowledge"? In Christian theology it wasn't Jesus' knowledge that vindicated the world. It was his blood.**

**Isaiah, however, is not speaking of a crucified messiah in his 53rd chapter. The prophet is referring to the faithful of Israel, who, by their knowledge bear witness to the world that there is no Savior other than the God of Israel (Isaiah 43:10-11). The mandate to vindicate the world and be a light to the nations (49:6) is not a task for a common people. The devout remnant of Israel will be righteous (Isaiah 60:21; Zephaniah 3:12-20 ).**

### Exodus 19:5-6

Now if you obey Me and keep My covenant, you shall be **My special treasure among all the nations**, because all the world is Mine. [6]'You will be a **kingdom of priests** and a holy nation to Me.' These are the words that you must relate to the Israelites.

**Immediately before the giving of the Ten Commandments the nation of Israel is given the mandate to be a "Kingdom of priests" (Ex. 19:5-6), as in Isaiah 61:6.**

### Isaiah 61:6-9

And you shall be called **"The Priests of the Lord — Servants of our God"** shall be said of you; the possessions of the nations you shall eat, and with their glory you shall succeed (them). [7]Instead of your **shame**, which was two fold, and your **disgrace**, which they shall inherit two fold; they shall have everlasting joy. [8]For I am the Lord, Who loves justice, hates robbery in a burnt offering; and I gave their wage in truth, and an everlasting covenant I will make for them. [9]And their seed shall be known among the gentiles, and their offspring among the nations; all who see them shall recognize them that they are seed that the Lord blessed.

### Isaiah 42:6

I am the Lord; I called you with righteousness and I will strengthen your hand; and I formed you, and I make you for a people's covenant, for a **light to the nations**.

### Isaiah 49:6

And He said, "Is it too light a thing for you to be **My servant**? To establish the tribes of Jacob and to bring back the besieged of Israel, but I will make you a **light of nations**, so that My salvation shall be until the end of the earth."

### Isaiah 60:3

**And nations shall go by your light** and kings by the brilliance of your shine.

### Proverbs 6:23

For a commandment is a candle, and the **Torah is light**....

### Zechariah 8:13, 23

And it shall come to pass that as you were a **curse among the Gentiles**, O House of Judah and House of Israel, so will I save you - and you shall be a blessing. Fear not; may your hands be strengthened! [23]So said the Lord of Hosts: In those days, when ten men of all the languages of the **gentiles shall take hold of the skirt of a Jewish man, saying, "Let us go with you, for we have heard that God is with you**."

### Numbers 18:1

And God said to Aaron, "You and your sons, and your father's house with you, you must **bear the iniquity** against the sanctuary, and you and your sons must **bear the iniquity** against your priesthood."

### Isaiah 2:2-5

And it shall be at the end of days, that the mountain of the Lord's house shall be firmly established at the top of the mountains, and it shall be raised above the hills, and all the nations shall stream to it. [3]And many **nations shall go, and they shall say, "Come, let us go up to the Lord's mount, to the House of the God of Jacob, and let Him teach us of His ways, and we will go in His paths," for out of Zion shall the Torah come forth, and the word of the Lord from Jerusalem**..." [5]O house of Jacob, come let us go in the light of the Lord."

[15]

## The Servant Is Vindicated

### Isaiah 53:12

Therefore, I will allot him a portion in public, and with the strong he shall share plunder, because he poured out his soul to death, and with transgressors he was counted; and he bore the sin of many, and interceded for the transgressors.

---

### Ezekiel 34:27-30

And the tree on the field will yield its fruit, and the earth will yield its produce, and they shall remain securely upon their ground. Then shall they know that I am God, when I break the bars of their yoke and save them from the hands of those who enslave them... [29]And I shall establish for them a plantation of renown, and they shall no more be gathered in by famine in the land, **and they shall no more bear the shame of the nations.** [30]Then they shall know that I, God their Lord, am with them, and they are My people, the family of Israel — the words of my Lord, God.

***On the Jews***

By John Adams

Second President of the United States

In spite of Bolingbroke and Voltaire, I will insist that the Hebrews have done more to civilize men than any other nation. If I were an atheist and believed in blind eternal fate, I should still believe that fate had ordained the Jews to be the most essential instrument for civilizing the nations. If I were an atheist of the other sect, who believe or pretend to believe that all is ordered by chance, I should believe that chance had ordered the Jews to preserve and propagate to all mankind the doctrine of supreme, intelligent, wise, Almighty Sovereign of the universe, which I believe to be the great essential principle of all morality, and consequently of all civilization.

I have read this last fall half a dozen volumes of this last wonderful Genius' Ribaldry against the Bible. How is it possible this old fellow should represent the Hebrews in such contemptible light. They are the most glorious Nation that ever inhabited this Earth. The Romans and their empire were but a bauble in comparison to the Jews. They have given religion to three quarters of the globe and have influenced the affairs of Mankind more, and more happily than any other nation, ancient or modern.

From a letter to F.A. Van der Kemp (1808), Pennsylvania Historical Society

# ❖How Does the Church Respond?

**For a comprehensive study of the rabbinic interpretation of Isaiah 53, see pages 68-80**

[16]

### Zohar Genesis, *Vayerah*

Come, consider the **congregation of Israel, how it is called a lamb, as it said, "like a lamb to the slaughter he would be brought, like a sheep that is mute before her shearers, and he would not open his mouth."** (Is. 53:7) Why was it mute? Because while other nations ruled over it, it was deprived of speech and made mute.

[17]

### Zohar Genesis, *Vayeshev*

And the Lord wished to crush him, He made him ill; if his soul makes itself restitution, he shall see seed, he shall prolong his days, and God's purpose shall prosper in his hand" (Is. 53:10). That is to say, if the soul desires to be rehabilitated, then he must see seed, for the soul hovers round about and is ready to enter the seed of procreation, and thus 'He will prolong days, and God's purpose...' namely the Torah, "**will prosper in his hand**."

[18]

### Zohar Leviticus *Acharai Mos*

It was taught in the name of Rav Yossi that on this Day of Atonement it has been instituted that this portion should be read to atone for Israel in captivity. Hence we learn that if the chastisements of Lord come upon a man, they are an atonement for his sins, and whoever sorrows for the sufferings of the righteous obtains pardon for his sins. Therefore on this day we read the portion commencing "after the death of the two sons of Aaron," that the people may hear and lament the loss of the righteous and obtain forgiveness for their sins. For whenever a man so laments and sheds tears for them, God proclaims of him, "thine iniquity is taken away and thy sin purged" (Is. 6:7). Also he may be assured that his sons will not die in his lifetime, and of him it is written, **"he shall see seed, he shall prolong his days"** (Is. 53:10).

[19]

### *Midrash Rabbah* Numbers XIII. 2

I have eaten my honeycomb with my honey (Song of Songs 5:1): because the Israelites poured out their soul to die in the captivity, as it is said, **"Because he poured out his soul to death, and with transgressors he was counted; and he bore the sins of many, and interceded for the transgressors"** (Is. 53:12) — and bruised themselves with the Torah which is sweeter than honey, the Holy One, blessed be He, will therefore in the hereafter give them to drink of the wine that is preserved in its grapes since the six days of creation, and let them bathe in rivers of milk.

[20]

### Babylonian Talmud, *Berachoth* 5a

Rabba states in the authority of Rav Shorah that Rav Huna said, "If the Holy One, blessed be He, is pleased with any man, He crushes him with painful sufferings. For it is said, "**And the Lord was pleased with him, hence He crushed him by disease**" (Is. 53:10). Now, you might think that this is so even if he did not accept them with love, therefore it is said, "To see if his soul would offer itself in restitution" (ibid.). Just as the trespass-offering must be brought by consent. And if he does accept them, what is his reward? "**he shall see his seed, he shall prolong his days**" (ibid.). And more than that, his knowledge of the Torah will endure with him. For it is said, "and God's purpose shall prosper in his hand" (ibid.).

[21]

### Babylonian Talmud, Sabbath 105b

Whoever sheds tears for the righteous, all his transgressions will be forgiven of him.

[22]

## Why Was Peter Surprised to Learn That Jesus Would Suffer?

### Matthew 16:21-22

From that time forth began Jesus to shew unto his disciples, how that he must go unto Jerusalem, and suffer many things of the elders and chief priests and scribes, and be killed, and be raised again the third day. Then Peter took him, and began to rebuke him saying, **"Be it far from thee, lord: this shall not be unto thee!"**

[23]

## The Tradition to Read The Haftorah Predated The Christian Era (see page 279)

### Acts 13:14-15, 27

...and went into the synagogue on the Sabbath day, and sat down. And after the **reading of the Law and the prophets** the rulers of the synagogue sent unto them....For they that dwell at Jerusalem, and their rulers, because they knew him not, nor yet the **voices of the prophets** which are read every Sabbath day, they have fulfilled them in condemnation.

[23a]

## *Origen Contra Celsum*, Chadwick, Henry; Cambridge Press, Page 50

# *Origen Contra Celsum*

Chadwick, Henry; Cambridge Press, page 50

**54.** Since Celsus, who professes to know everything about the gospel, reproaches the Savior for his passion, saying that he was not helped by *his father, nor was he able to help himself*, I have to affirm that his passion was that he should die for them and endure the stripe to which he was condemned. It was also foretold that the people of the Gentiles would 'take notice of him,' although the prophets have not lived among them. And it was said that he shall be seen with a form dishonorable as men regard it. The passage reads as follows:

> Behold, my servant shall have understanding, and shall be exalted and glorified and raised very high. Just as many will be astonished at thee (so inglorious will thy form be among men, and thy glory among men), even so many nations shall be amazed at him and kings shall shut their mouths; because those to whom he was not proclaimed shall see him and those who have not heard shall take notice of him. Lord, who has believed our report? And to whom was the arm of the Lord revealed? We proclaimed as a child before him, as a root in a thirsty land; there is no form nor glory in him. And we saw him, and he had not form or beauty, but his form was dishonored and not considered. This man bears our sins and suffers pain for us, and we considered him to be in trouble and in calamity and affliction. But he was wounded for our transgressions, and he was made sick for our iniquities; the chastisement of our peace was upon him; by his stripe we were healed. All we like sheep went astray, a man went astray in his path; and the Lord delivered him for our sins, and because of his affliction he opens not his mouth. As a sheep he was led to the slaughter, and as a lamb before his shearer is dumb, so he opens not his mouth. In his humiliation his judgement was taken away; who shall explain his generation? Because his life is taken away from the earth, because of the iniquities of my people he was led to death.

**55. I remember that once in a discussion with some whom the Jews regard as learned I used these prophecies. At this the Jew said that these prophecies referred to the whole people as though of a single individual,** since they were scattered in the dispersion and smitten, that as a result of the scattering of the Jews among the other nations many might become proselytes. In this way he explained the text: 'Thy form shall be inglorious among men.... and 'those to whom he was not proclaimed shall see

**Why do missionaries argue that the first rabbi to say that Isaiah 53 was speaking of the nation of Israel was 11th century rabbi, Rashi? Here Origen, the 3rd century church father, admits that learned Jews of his time said that Isaiah 53 "referred to the whole [Jewish] people."**

[24] **The New English Bible — Oxford Study Edition**



6 day long, says the LORD. But on that
day my people shall know my name;
they shall know that it is I who speak;
here I am.

7 How lovely on the mountains are
the feet of the herald
who comes to proclaim prosperity
and bring good news,
the news of deliverance,
calling to Zion, 'Your God is king.'
8 Hark, your watchmen raise their
voices
and shout together in triumph;
for with their own eyes they shall
see
the LORD returning in pity to Zion.
9 Break forth together in shouts of
triumph,
you ruins of Jerusalem;
for the LORD has taken pity on his
people
and has ransomed Jerusalem.
10 The LORD has bared his holy arm
in the sight of all nations,
and the whole world from end to end
shall see the deliverance of our God.
11 Away from Babylon; come out,
come out,
touch nothing unclean.
Come out from Babylon, keep
yourselves pure,
you who carry the vessels of the
LORD.
12 But you shall not come out in
urgent haste
nor leave like fugitives;
for the LORD will march at your
head,
your rearguard will be Israel's
God.

Behold, my servant shall prosper, 13
he shall be lifted up, exalted to the
heights.

Time was when many[c] were aghast 14
at you, my people;[d]
so now many nations[e] recoil at 15
sight of him,
and kings curl their lips in disgust.
For they see what they had never
been told
and things unheard before fill their
thoughts.

Who could have believed what we **53**
have heard,
and to whom has the power of the
LORD been revealed?

He grew up before the LORD like a 2
young plant
whose roots are in parched ground;
he had no beauty, no majesty to
draw our eyes,
no grace to make us delight in him;
his form, disfigured, lost all the
likeness of a man,
his beauty changed beyond
human semblance.[f]
He was despised, he shrank from 3
the sight of men,
tormented and humbled by
suffering;
we despised him, we held him of
no account,
a thing from which men turn
away their eyes.
Yet on himself he bore our 4
sufferings,

*c* *Or* the great. *d* *See note on 53. 2.*
*e* *Or* great nations.
*f* his form . . . semblance: *transposed from end of 52. 14.*

of Israel's slavery by the plagues and death of its firstborn, but Babylon *paid no price* when it *carried* them *off* into Exile. **6:** *That day:* see 7.18–25 n. *Know my name:* see 43.1.

**52.7–12: A pilgrim victory hymn.** This is a continuation of the song, interrupted after v. 2, which celebrates the joyful return of the LORD and his people to the holy city. **7:** *God is king:* see 43.15 n. **8–9:** *Watchmen* are the people left in the *ruins of Jerusalem* at the time of its destruction by the Babylonians in 587 B.C. (2 Kgs.25.8–12). They look for the return of *the LORD* who was considered to have gone to Babylon with the captives; compare Ezek.11.22–25; 43.1–7. **12:** The Israelites on their return from Babylon did not ask for an escort of soldiers but trusted that the LORD would be their guard: see Ezra 8.21–23.

**52.13–53.12: Fourth servant song. The suffering servant.** See 42.1–4 n. Israel, the servant of God, has suffered as a humiliated individual. However, the servant endured without complaint because it was vicarious suffering (suffering for others). **13–15:** *Nations* and *kings* will be surprised to see the servant *exalted.* **53.1:** The crowds, pagan nations, among whom the servant (Israel) lived, speak here (through v. 9), saying that the significance of Israel's humiliation and exaltation is hard to believe. **2:** In traditional Hebrew thought, the good man prospers like a tree by water but the wicked is like a *plant* growing in *parched ground;* see Ps.1.3–6. **3:** *Turn away their eyes:* lit. hide their faces, an expression used in relation to lepers, whose sickness, considered a sign of sin, made them *despised.* **4–5:** The vicarious suffering expressed here is in





our torments he endured,
while we counted him smitten by
God,
struck down by disease and
misery;
5 but he was pierced for our
transgressions,
tortured for our iniquities;
the chastisement he bore is health
for us
and by his scourging we are healed.
6 We had all strayed like sheep,
each of us had gone his own way;
but the LORD laid upon him
the guilt of us all.
7 He was afflicted, he submitted to
be struck down
and did not open his mouth;
he was led like a sheep to the
slaughter,
like a ewe that is dumb before the
shearers.[g]
8 Without protection, without justice,[h]
he was taken away;
and who gave a thought to his fate,
how he was cut off from the
world of living men,
stricken to the death for my people's
transgression?
9 He was assigned a grave with the
wicked,
a burial-place among the refuse of
mankind,
though he had done no violence
and spoken no word of treachery.
10 Yet the LORD took thought for his
tortured servant
and healed him who had made
himself[i] a sacrifice for sin;
so shall he enjoy long life and see
his children's children,
and in his hand the LORD's cause
shall prosper.
11 After all his pains he shall be
bathed in light,

after his disgrace he shall be fully
vindicated;
so shall he, my servant, vindicate
many,
himself bearing the penalty of their
guilt.
Therefore I will allot him a portion 12
with the great,
and he shall share the spoil with
the mighty,
because he exposed himself to face
death[j]
and was reckoned among
transgressors,
because he bore the sin of many
and interceded for their
transgressions.

Sing aloud, O barren woman who **54**
never bore a child,
break into cries of joy, you who
have never been in labour;
for the deserted wife has more sons
than she who lives in wedlock,
says the LORD.
Enlarge the limits of your home, 2
spread wide the curtains of your
tent;
let out its ropes to the full
and drive the pegs home;
for you shall break out of your 3
confines right and left,
your descendants shall dispossess
wide regions,[k]
and re-people cities now desolate.
Fear not; you shall not be put to 4
shame,
you shall suffer no insult, have no
cause to blush.

*g* *Prob. rdg.; Heb. adds* and he would not open his mouth.
*h* Without protection, without justice: *or* After arrest and sentence.
*i* healed . . . himself: *prob. rdg.; Heb.* he made sick, if you make.
*j* *Or* because he poured out his life to the death.
*k* wide regions: *or* the nations.

contrast both to the traditional solidarity in guilt of Exod.20.5 and to individual responsibility proposed by the prophets at the time of the Exile; see Jer.31.30; Ezek. ch. 18. **5:** *Health for us:* lit. "our peace," which means "general welfare." **6–7:** The servant is *led like a sheep* in contrast to the peoples going their *own way.* **8:** Although some legal process seems to be involved, the servant does not receive *justice;* see Jer.39.5–6. **9:** The death probably refers to the destruction and Exile of Israel. Compare Ezek. ch. 37. **10–12:** The theme of 52.13 is resumed. Israel, which has suffered for all mankind, will now be granted her rightful place. **10:** *Long life* and *children's children* are the signs of a final vindication before God; see Job 42.16–17. **11:** *Bathed in light:* enjoying God's favor; see Ps.80.3.

**54.1–17: Reassurance to Israel.** A series of metaphors is used to repeat the promise that the nation will be rebuilt and Israel's relationship to the LORD restored. **1:** The *deserted wife* represents Israel in Exile; the one *in wedlock* represents preexilic Israel. **4:** *Shame of your*

name is despised. 6 Therefore my
people shall know my name; there-
fore in that day they shall know that it
is I who speak; here am I."

7 How beautiful upon the mountains
are the feet of him who brings
good tidings,
who publishes peace, who brings
good tidings of good,
who publishes salvation,
who says to Zion, "Your God
reigns."
8 Hark, your watchmen lift up their
voice,
together they sing for joy;
for eye to eye they see
the return of the LORD to Zion.
9 Break forth together into singing,
you waste places of Jerusalem;
for the LORD has comforted his
people,
he has redeemed Jerusalem.
10 The LORD has bared his holy arm
before the eyes of all the nations;
and all the ends of the earth shall
see
the salvation of our God.

11 Depart, depart, go out thence,
touch no unclean thing;
go out from the midst of her, purify
yourselves,
you who bear the vessels of the
LORD.
12 For you shall not go out in haste,
and you shall not go in flight,
for the LORD will go before you,
and the God of Israel will be your
rear guard.

13 Behold, my servant shall prosper,
he shall be exalted and lifted up,
and shall be very high.
14 As many were astonished at him[s]—
his appearance was so marred,
beyond human semblance,
and his form beyond that of the
sons of men—
15 so shall he startle[t] many nations;
kings shall shut their mouths
because of him;
for that which has not been told them
they shall see,
and that which they have not
heard they shall understand.

53 Who has believed what we
have heard?
And to whom has the arm of the
LORD been revealed?
2 For he grew up before him like a
young plant,
and like a root out of dry ground;
he had no form or comeliness that
we should look at him,
and no beauty that we should
desire him.
3 He was despised and rejected[u] by
men;
a man of sorrows,[v] and acquainted
with grief;[w]
and as one from whom men hide
their faces
he was despised, and we esteemed
him not.

4 Surely he has borne our griefs[x]
and carried our sorrows;[y]
yet we esteemed him stricken,
smitten by God, and afflicted.
5 But he was wounded for our
transgressions,

*s* Syr Tg: Heb *you*
*t* The meaning of the Hebrew word is uncertain
*u* Or *forsaken* *v* Or *pains* *w* Or *sickness*
*x* Or *sicknesses* *y* Or *pains*

---

(10.7–11), Babylon (Jer.50.29). **7–8:** Tensely, all creation awaits word of God's decisive victory (Ps.125.2; 2 Sam.18.25–27; Nah.1.15; Rom.10.15). The *watchmen* see the victor returning (40.5). **11–12:** Ritually clean, people and priests return home in peace (Ex.13.21–22).

**52.13–53.12: The fourth Servant Song** (see 42.1–4 n.). **52.13–15:** God will exalt his brutally disfigured Servant (Israel) to the numbed astonishment of the world's rulers (49.7,23). **15:** Rom.15.21. **53.1–3:** A lament (40.12; 50.8–10). The Servant's background and appearance (52.14) are undistinguished; his person, rejected. **1:** Jn.12.38. **2:** *Young plant*, compare 11.1; *root*, 11.10, compare Jer.23.5; these are sometimes considered Messianic allusions. **3:** Like a leper, he suffers painful loneliness and rejection by the community (Job 19.13–19). **4–6:** By the Servant's vicarious suffering, he restores all people to God (Mt.8.17; 1 Pet.2.24–25). *Whole*,

# What is a Jew?

By Leo Nikolaievitch Tolstoy

What is a Jew? This question is not at all so odd as it seems. Let us see what kind of peculiar creature the Jew is, which all the rulers and all the nations have together and separately abused and molested, oppressed and persecuted, trampled and butchered, burned and hanged — and in spite of all this is yet alive. What is a Jew, who has never allowed himself to be led astray by all the earthly possessions which his oppressors and persecutors constantly offered him in order that he should change his faith and forsake his own Jewish religion? The Jew is that sacred being who has brought down from heaven the everlasting fire and has illumined with it the entire world. He is the religious source, spring and fountain out of which all the rest of the peoples have drawn their beliefs and their religions.

The Jew is the pioneer of civilization. Ignorance was condemned in olden Palestine even more than it is today in civilized Europe. Moreover, in those wild and barbarous days, when neither the life nor the death of anyone counted for anything at all, Rabbi Akiba did not refrain from expressing himself openly against capital punishment, a practice which is recognized today as a highly civilized way of punishment.

The Jew is the emblem of civil and religious toleration. "Love the stranger and the sojourner," Moses commands, "because you have been strangers in the land of Egypt." And this was said in those remote and savage times when the principal ambition of the races and nations consisted in crushing and enslaving one another. As concerns religious toleration, the Jewish faith is not only far from the missionary spirit of converting people of other denominations, but on the contrary the Talmud commands the rabbis to inform and explain to everyone who willingly comes to accept the Jewish religion, all the difficulties involved in its acceptance, and to point out to the would-be proselyte that the righteous of all nations have a share in immortality. Of such a lofty and ideal religious toleration not even the moralists of our present day can boast.

The Jew is the emblem of eternity. He whom neither slaughter nor torture of thousands of years could destroy, he whom neither fire nor sword nor inquisition was able to wipe off the face of the earth, he who was the first to produce the oracles of God, he who has been for so long the guardian of prophecy, and who transmitted it to the rest of the world — such a nation cannot be destroyed. The Jew is as everlasting as is eternity itself.

From "Jewish World" London (1908)

# Who is God's Suffering Servant? The Rabbinic Interpretation of Isaiah 53

Despite strong objections from conservative Christian apologists, the prevailing rabbinic interpretation of Isaiah 53 ascribes the "servant" to the nation of Israel who silently endured unimaginable suffering at the hands of its gentile oppressors. The speakers, in this most-debated chapter, are the stunned kings of nations who will bear witness to the messianic age and the final vindication of the Jewish people following their long and bitter exile. "Who would have believed our report?," the astonished and contrite world leaders wonder aloud in dazed bewilderment (53:1).[1]

The stimulus for the world's baffled response contained in this famed cluster of chapters at the end of the Book of Isaiah is the unexpected salvation of Israel. The redemption of God's people is the central theme in the preceding verse (52:12) where the "you" signifies the Jewish people who are sheltered and delivered by God. Moreover, the "afflicted barren woman" in the following chapter is protected and saved by God, and is also universally recognized as the nation of Israel[2] (54:1).

The well-worn claim frequently advanced by Christian apologists who argue that the noted Jewish commentator, Rashi (1040 CE – 1105 CE), was the first to identify the suffering servant of Isaiah 53 with the nation of Israel is inaccurate and misleading. In fact, Origen, a prominent and influential church father, conceded in the year 248 CE – many centuries before Rashi was born – that the consensus among the Jews in his time was that Isaiah 53 "bore reference to the whole [Jewish] people, regarded as one individual, and as being in a state of dispersion and suffering, in order that many proselytes might be gained, on account of the dispersion of the Jews among numerous heathen nations."[3]

The broad consensus among Jewish, and even some Christian commentators, that the "servant" in Isaiah 52-53 refers to the nation of Israel is understandable. Isaiah 53, which is the fourth of four renowned Servant Songs, is umbilically connected to its preceding chapters. The "servant" in each of the three previous Servant Songs is plainly and repeatedly identified as the nation of Israel.

> **Isaiah 41:8-9**
> But you, Israel, my servant, Jacob, whom I have chosen, the offspring of Abraham, my friend; you whom I took from the ends of the earth, and called from its farthest corners, saying to you, "You are my servant, I have chosen you and not cast you off."
>
> **Isaiah 44:1**
> But now hear, O Jacob my servant, Israel whom I have chosen!
>
> **Isaiah 44:21**
> Remember these things, O Jacob, and Israel, for you are my servant; I formed you; you are my servant; O Israel, you will not be forgotten by me.
>
> **Isaiah 45:4**
> For the sake of my servant Jacob, and Israel my chosen, I called you by your name, I name you, though you do not know me.
>
> **Isaiah 48:20**
> Go out from Babylon, flee from *Chaldea*, declare this with a shout of joy, proclaim it, send it out to the end of the earth; say, "The Lord has redeemed his servant Jacob!"
>
> **Isaiah 49:3**
> And he said to me, "You are my servant, Israel, in whom I will be glorified."

According to this widespread rabbinic opinion, Isaiah 53 contains a deeply moving narrative which world leaders will cry aloud in the messianic age. The humbled kings of nations (52: 15) will confess that Jewish suffering occurred as a direct result of "our own iniquity," (53:5) e.g., depraved Jew-hatred, rather than, as they previously thought, the stubborn blindness of the Jews.

The stunned reaction of the world's nations to the unexpected vindication and redemption of the Jewish nation in the messianic age is a recurring theme throughout the Hebrew Scriptures. Israel's neighbors will be amazed when their age-old assessment of the Jew is finally proved wrong. Throughout Israel's long and bitter exile, the nations mistakenly attributed the miserable predicament of the Jew to his stubborn rejection of the world's religions. In the End of Days, however, the gentiles will discover what was until then unimaginable – the unwavering Jew was, in fact, all this time faithful to the one true God. On the other hand, "We despised and held him of no account" (53:3).

In essence, the final and complete redemption of the Jews, to which the stunned nations will bear witness, contradicts everything Israel's gentile neighbors had ever previously anticipated, heard, or considered (52:15). "Who would have believed our report?" the kings will ask with their mouths wide open in amazement (53:1). The curtain of blindness is finally lifted when the "holy Arm of the Lord before the eyes of all the nations, all the ends of the earth will witness the salvation of His people" (52:10).

The unanticipated vindication of the Jews in the End of Days, however, will raise nagging, introspective questions for Israel's neighbors: How then can we explain the Jews' long-enduring suffering at our own hands? After all, the age-old reasons we contrived to explain away Israel's agony are clearly no longer valid. Who is to blame for Israel's miserable existence in exile? In short, why did the servant of God seem to suffer without measure or cause?

Therefore, Isaiah 53:8 concludes with their stunning confession, "for the transgressions of my people [the gentile nations] they [the Jews] were stricken." The fact that the servant is spoken of in the third person, plural לָמוֹ (*lamo*) illustrates beyond doubt that the servant is a nation rather than a single individual.

The rabbinic interpretation of Isaiah 53 fits in seamlessly with its surrounding chapters which all clearly depict the nation of Israel as "despised, afflicted" (54:6-11), and oppressed "without cause" (52:4) at the hands of the gentile nations.

According to the most ancient rabbinic commentaries, the identification of Israel as God's servant is evident throughout the four Servant Songs. As such, rabbinic sources from the Talmudic period identify the servant of Isaiah 53 in the plain sense as the Jewish people, consistent with the previous three Servant Songs.

For example, commenting on Isaiah 53 the Talmud Berachos 5a states:

> Rava said in the name of Rav Sachorah who said it in the name of Rav Huna: Whomever the Holy One, blessed is He, desires, He

> crushes with afflictions as it is stated "And the one whom Hashem desires He crushed with sickness (Isaiah 53:10). Now, one might have thought that this applies even if he does not accept [the afflictions] with love. Scripture therefore states in the continuation of the verse "if his soul acknowledges his guilt" (ibid.)... And if he accepts [the afflictions with love] what is his reward? He will see offspring and live long days. Moreover, he will retain his studies, as it is stated "and the desire of *Hashem* will succeed in his hand" (ibid.).

The ancient Midrash Rabba on Numbers 23 likewise attests that Isaiah 53 refers to the nation of Israel:

> "I have eaten my honeycomb with my honey" (Song of Songs 5:1): because the Israelites poured out their soul to die in captivity, as it is said, "Because he poured out his soul to die" (Isaiah 53:12).

Interestingly, the traditional Church did not completely satisfy the Christian mind with their stock interpretation of Isaiah 53. There is, therefore, a consensus among many modern, liberal Christian commentators which is in accord with this prevailing rabbinic exegesis on this most debated chapter. For example, the commentary of the 11th century Rashi and the 20th century Christian Oxford New English Bible[6] are strikingly similar. Both clearly identify the "suffering servant" in Isaiah 53 as the nation of Israel, who suffered as a humiliated individual at the hands of the gentile nations.

Conservative Christians, on the other hand, strongly argue against the Jewish interpretation of Isaiah 53 for a number of expected reasons. Historically, the Church has relentlessly used Isaiah 53 as its most important proof-text in order to demonstrate the veracity of the Gospels. They argue that this chapter proves that Jesus' death was explicitly prophesized in the Hebrew Scriptures. In fact, the author of the Book of Acts claims that Philip converted an Ethiopian eunuch using Isaiah 53,[7] and the author of Luke,[8] John,[9] and I Peter[10] associate Isaiah 53 with Jesus as well. While evangelicals routinely claim that Jesus is alluded to in several hundred verses throughout the Hebrew Bible, there is only a handful of passages in Tanach that the Church insists irrefutably identify Jesus alone as the messiah; Isaiah 53 is chief among these polemical texts.

Consequently, since time immemorial, missionaries fervently used Isaiah 53 to proclaim that the Hebrew prophet Isaiah predicted the advent of Christianity centuries before the birth of Jesus. Accordingly, the traditional Church recoils at the rabbinic interpretation of the fourth Servant Song. Such a monumental concession would require Christendom to abandon one of its most cherished polemical chapters used to defend its own teachings, and a vital part of its textual arsenal used against its elder rival, Judaism.

Besides, the systemic suffering of the Jews plays no essential role in Christian theology. The suffering of Jesus, on the other hand, is the cornerstone of Church doctrine. In fact, widespread Christian teachings throughout history concluded that the suffering of the Jews illustrates the wrongness of their beliefs, while the suffering of Jesus and his followers illustrates the truth and veracity of the Cross. As a result, conservative Christians are unyielding in their rejection of the Jewish interpretation of Isaiah 53.

Liberal Christian scholars, on the other hand, are frequently in accord with the classic rabbinic commentaries on Isaiah 53. Unlike their conservative coreligionists, liberal Christians do not use or depend on Church dogma or creedal statements to interpret the Bible. In other words, liberal Christian Bible commentators tend to interpret scripture without any preconceived notion of the correctness of Church teaching. Instead, they apply the same modern hermeneutics used to understand any ancient writings to their interpretation of the Bible. Given that Isaiah's first three Servant Songs clearly identify Israel as God's servant, and the surrounding chapters of Isaiah 53 clearly speak of Israel as a suffering and humiliated individual, liberal Christian scholarship frequently ascribes the servant in Isaiah's fourth Servant Song to the nation of Israel.[11]

## Rabbinic commentaries that state Isaiah 53 refers to the messiah

According to rabbinic thought when Isaiah speaks of the "servant," the prophet is not speaking of all the Jewish people. Rather, the "servant" in these uplifting prophetic hymns refers to the righteous remnant of Israel – the most pious of the nation. The faithful members of Israel who willingly suffer for Heaven's sake are identified in Tanach as God's servant. These are the devout that call upon the name of the Lord (43:7), who bear witness to His unity (43:11), and are therefore charged to restore the rest of Jacob (49:5).

"You are my witnesses declares the Lord, and My servant whom I have chosen" (43:10).

In essence, God's "servant" are the cherished few – the faithful who walk in the footsteps of Abraham, whom the Almighty called "My friend."

> "But you, O Israel, My servant, Jacob, whom I have chosen, you, descendants of Abraham My friend" (Isaiah 41:8)

Simply put, the Servant Songs address only the believers of Israel who emulate the first patriarch of the Jewish people. As Abraham endured trials and adversity in his walk with God, so too would His servant, the righteous remnant of Israel, endure ordeals and affliction in its sacred path (Isaiah 49:3; 51:21; 54:11; Psalm 44:11-15).

The Hebrew prophet Zephaniah vividly describes in two seminal verses the cherished remnant of Israel in the following manner:

> "And I will leave in the midst of thee an afflicted and poor people, and they shall take refuge in the name of the Lord. The remnant of Israel shall not do iniquity, nor speak lies, neither shall a deceitful tongue be found in their mouth; for they shall feed and lie down, and none shall make them afraid" (Zephaniah 3:12-13).

In rabbinic thought, all of God's faithful, gentiles included (Zechariah 13:8-9), endure suffering on behalf of God (Isaiah 40:2; Zechariah 1:15). Thus, Jewish leaders of the past, such as Moses[12] and Jeremiah,[13] Rabbi Akiva,[14] as well as future eschatological figures, such as the messiah ben Joseph and the messiah ben David, are held up in rabbinic literature as individuals who exemplify the "servant" who willingly suffers on behalf of Heaven.

Therefore, when the Talmud describes the predicament of the messiah as he is waiting to be summoned by God, the rabbis cast him as

> "sitting among other paupers, all of them afflicted with disease. Yet, while all the rest of them tie and untie their bandages all at once, the messiah changes his bandages one at a time, lest he is summoned for the redemption at a moments notice" (Sanhedrin 98a).

While this story may be understood allegorically, its jarring message is clear: The messiah, like other afflicted members of Israel, endures the agony and trials assigned to the faithful. However, unlike the other suffering saints who completely remove all their bandages before patiently replacing them with a fresh dressing, the messiah must methodically replace each bandage, one at a time. In other words, the messiah does not suffer more or less than other servants of God. Rather, according to the Talmud, the messiah is different from other men of God because he must be ready at a moment's notice to usher in the deliverance of his beleaguered people. Because he is prepared to be summoned for the redemption at all times, he is never in a predicament where his bandages are fully removed.

When Isaiah speaks of the suffering remnant of Israel, the messianic king is, therefore, included. The final heir of David's throne is an integral member of the pious of Israel. This is, according to rabbinic interpretation, the *pshat*, or the plain meaning of the text in Isaiah 52:13 – 53:12. Therefore, when both ancient and modern rabbinic commentators expound on the clear meaning of the text, they ascribe the suffering servant in Isaiah 53 to the nation of Israel.

Moreover, while Ezekiel warned that the righteous can never suffer or die as a sacrificial atonement for the wicked,[15] the Talmud teaches:

> "Whosoever weeps over the [suffering] of the righteous man, all his sins are forgiven." (Talmud, Shabbat 105b)

In order to shed much needed light on the famed Servant Songs, numerous rabbinic commentators hold up Jewish heroes as a paradigm of Isaiah 53's "servant." Accordingly, while on one hand the Talmud, Zohar, and other ancient rabbinic texts state explicitly that the "servant" of Isaiah 53 refers to the faithful of corporate Jewry,[16] the same sources frequently point to renowned saints of Israel as an archetype of the Suffering Servant. These virtuous individuals include saints such as Moses, Elijah, Jeremiah, the messiah the son of Joseph and David – each of them embody perfect examples of God's servant, the righteous remnant of Israel.

Bear in mind that the rabbinic commentary on Isaiah 53 is not dualistic or multilateral. Meaning, the sages of old did **not** suggest that Isaiah 53 refers to **either** the righteous remnant of Israel, Moses, Jeremiah, **or** an anointed leader. Rather, the servant in all four Servant Songs are the faithful descendants of Abraham. Isaiah 53 attests to an unprecedented worldwide repentance of all of mankind – a redemptive achievement accomplished by no other saint in history. Therefore, rabbinic commentators tend to lift up the messiah's name more frequently than the names of other faithful servants of God.

While the bulk of rabbinic commentary seeks to provide the *pshat* – the principal analysis which illuminates the plain meaning of sacred literature – there is, broadly speaking, a second, and distinct stream of rabbinic commentary which explores the *drash*. In general terms, the *drash* delves into the deeply profound, yet often less precise homiletic method of exegesis used to interpret the Hebrew Scriptures. This sacred material is often referred to as *midrashic*, literally "derived from a *drash*."

In Jewish thought, the *pshat* conveys the foundational understanding of any text in Tanach; this is the commentary which elucidates the clear and basic meaning of a verse. As the sages declare in the Talmud, "A verse cannot depart from its plain meaning." (Shabbat 63a; Yev. 11b, 24a). Accordingly, the *midrashic* interpretation of a biblical verse is never intended to nullify, contradict, or injure the natural sense of a text. On the contrary, the *pshat* always supplies the primary meaning of a passage. Moreover, it is impossible to fully grasp the inspirational *midrashic* commentary without first comprehending the simple meaning of a text.

On the other hand, without the sublime illumination of the *Midrash*, seminal, seemingly-disconnected principles throughout various regions of Tanach can be challenging to harmonize and fully comprehend. In other words, with only the *pshat* commentary, Biblical principles when studied independently, can only be understood on a fundamental level. Yet the separate, straightforward commentaries of the *pshat* may appear incompatible and disjointed from other regions of scripture without the *midrashic* commentary. *Midrashic* literature, generally speaking, weaves together and painstakingly merges Judaism's Written and Oral tradition into a transcendent revelation. Because the *Midrash* illuminates rabbinic thought to its fullest, holistic expression, it stands out as a vital tool for the student of sacred literature.

Few chapters in Tanach better illustrate the vital role the *Midrash* plays in expounding Biblical texts than Isaiah 53. The straightforward rabbinic approach to elucidate Isaiah 53 begins by identifying the astonished speakers in Isaiah 53:1-9 and the "Servant" in Isaiah 52:13 and 53:11. The rabbinic commentaries, i.e. the *pshat*, convey in clear and essential commentary how astonished the contrite kings of nations are when they discover that the faithful members of Israel are God's true servant. As mentioned, the identities of the speakers and the servant are evident from the surrounding chapters of Isaiah 53.

The *Midrash*, however, illuminates a most profound, yet often overlooked central theme of Isaiah 53; never before in history has any servant of God brought about the mass repentance of the gentiles. Whereas the patriarch Abraham redeemed only 70 souls in Haran, the future scion of the House of David will usher in an unprecedented epoch, where gentile kings of nations will repent, as vividly described in the fourth

Servant Song. In other words, the messiah will bring about an age when the most important feature of Isaiah 53 will materialize – the worldwide repentance of the gentiles.

Whereas Moses drew only a single nation from Egypt into the service of God, the messianic king will redeem the other nations as well. At this epic, redemptive moment in the future all the nations will perceive that Judaism is the only true faith, as it is written:

> "For then I will make the peoples pure of speech, so that they all invoke the name of the Lord and serve Him with one accord" (Zephaniah 3:9).

Thus, in the messianic age, the gentiles will cry aloud the remorseful and repentant words sketched in Isaiah 53. In essence, the sequence of events outlined in the fourth Servant Song will be an unparalleled occasion in history. Never before throughout the annals of time have "the gentiles come to your light, and kings to the brightness of your rising" (Isaiah 60:3).

Consequently, although various rabbinic literature highlights numerous Biblical saints whose lives exemplify the Suffering Servant of Israel in Isaiah 53, the future messiah is held up more frequently and prominently than any other pious Jew in this startling context; for the future anointed Davidic king will usher in this dramatic epoch in which the gentiles will repent, as outlined in Isaiah 53. In other words, the stunning narrative of the fourth Servant Song will be made possible by the reign of the messiah, the foremost member of God's Suffering Servant Israel. Only the messiah will accomplish this global achievement in the final redemption, which neither Abraham, Moses, or Jeremiah were able to accomplish. Only the messianic age will spawn worldwide repentance of the nations. Therefore, the rabbis teach, "'My servant shall be high, and lifted up, and lofty exceedingly' – he will be higher than Abraham, more exalted than Moses, loftier than the angels '" In short, the messiah will ignite the contrition of Israel's neighbors as outlined in Isaiah's fourth Servant Song.

Because of the deeply esoteric and widely elastic nature of *midrashic* writings, these millennia-old texts are vulnerable to misuse by opponents of the Jewish faith. Isaiah 53 – the chapter in the Bible which has for ages formed one of the principal battlefields between Jews and their Christian opponents – is no exception to this rule.

Under ordinary circumstances, traditional Church apologists regard rabbinic commentaries with sneering derision, casting them at best as damaging to spiritual enlightenment. However, ancient *midrashic* annotations on Isaiah 53 which can be ripped out of context and portrayed as supportive of Christian teachings are wildly quoted and cheerfully paraded by missionaries with the hope of winning more unclaimed souls to the Cross. The fact that the Christian interpretation of Isaiah 53 is not supported by the chapters that surround it, only adds to the Church's desperate feeding frenzy on these ancient rabbinic texts. It is astonishing that missionaries would use rabbinic texts to support Christian doctrines given that each and every one of the rabbis that they zealously quote utterly rejected the teachings of Christianity.

The most frequently quoted rabbinic text in Christian literature is, without doubt, the second-century Targum Yonatan ben Uziel on Isaiah 53. Although the word "*Targum*" literally means a "Translation," the Targum Yonatan ben Uziel is not at all a word-for-word translation of Tanach. Rather, this unique, highly-regarded Aramaic annotation on the Hebrew Scriptures fuses together both *drash* and *pshat* – the homiletic and plain meaning of a text – in its running, dynamic commentary on the Prophets. Accordingly, it is the messiah who is raised up as God's ideal servant in the Targum Yonatan ben Uziel on Isaiah 52:13, yet in the same commentary it is the faithful of the Jewish nation who vicariously suffer in Isaiah 52:14.

As expected, missionaries selectively quote the Targum Yonatan ben Uziel on Isaiah 52:13, which identifies God's servant as the messiah.

The Targum's rendering of Isaiah 52:13 is as follows:

> "Behold my servant Messiah shall prosper; he shall be high, and increase, and be exceedingly strong."

Yet the Targum's commentary on the following verse, Isaiah 52:14, identifies Israel as the long-suffering and humiliated servant:

> "As the house of Israel looked to him during many days, because their countenance was darkened among the peoples, and their complexion (darkened) beyond the sons of men."

As expected, the commentary of Targum Yonatan ben Uziel on Isaiah 52:14 is nowhere to be found in Christian missionary material. There is not a single church apologist who quotes the Targum's elucidation on Isaiah 53:10. For it is upon these words of Isaiah, "He is crushed and made ill," where the Targum identifies the suffering servant as the nation of Israel who suffers unbearable chastisement in the following commentary:

> "But it is the Lord's good pleasure to refine and cleanse the remnant of His people in order to purify their souls from sin; they shall see the kingdom of the messiah, they shall increase their sons and daughters, they shall prolong their days; and those who perform the Law of the Lord shall prosper in good pleasure."

Although the above quotation from Targum Yonatan ben Uziel on Isaiah 53:10 is deliberately ignored by Christendom's missionaries, this two-millennia-old message remains immortal. The nation of Israel, God's servant, suffered unimaginable torment at the hands of her gentile neighbors so that her sins would be washed away.

> "Speak tenderly to Jerusalem, and declare to her: Her term of service is over, her iniquity is expiated; for she has received at the hand of the Lord double for all her sins." (Isaiah 40:2)

Simply put, there are 15 verses in the Targum's annotation on Isaiah 53 (52:13-15 and 53:1-12), yet with surgical precision, missionary conversionist tracts selectively and deliberately ignore almost all of them with the exception of the first verse on Isaiah 52:13. This is a well-worn technique of wielding rabbinic literature as an evangelical sledgehammer, in order to drive home the well-crafted message to unlettered Jews that ancient rabbis concealed the truth that Isaiah 53 is speaking of Jesus, and not the nation of Israel. Nothing, of course, could be further from the truth.

---

**Footnotes:**

1. *Midrash Rabbah* (Numbers XXIII.2), Zohar (Genesis, & Leviticus), Talmud (Brochos 5a), Rashi, Joseph Kara, Ibn Ezra, Joseph Kimchi, David Kimchi, Nachmanadies, Abarbinbanel, et all
2. Ibn Ezra on Isaiah 53
3. *Origen, Contra Celsum*, Chadwick, Henry; Cambridge Press, book 1, chapter 55, page 50
4. Isaiah 41:11; Micah 7:15-16; Jeremiah 16:19-20;
5. Isaiah 41:8-9; 43:10; 44:1; 44:21; 45;4; 48:20; 49:3

6. The New English Bible, Oxford Study Edition, page 788-789. See also the Revised Standard Bible, Oxford Study Edition, page 889.
7. Acts 8:28-34
8. Luke 22:37
9. John 12:38
10. I Peter 2:22
11. *The Christian New English Bible, Oxford Study Edition*, annotation on Isaiah 52:13-53:12 explains:

> The "fourth Servant Song, the Suffering Servant, Israel, the servant of God, has suffered as a humiliated individual. However, the servant endured without complain because it was vicarious suffering (suffering for others). 52:13-15: Nations and kings will be surprised to see the servant exalted. 53:1: The crowds, pagan nations, among whom the servant (Israel) lived, speak here (through verse 9), saying that the significance of Israel's humiliation and exaltation is hard to believe (page 788-789). See also the Revised Standard Bible, Oxford Study Edition, page 889.

Walter Brueggemann Ph.D., *Isaiah 40 – 66* (Louisville: Kentucky, 1998), p. 143, states:

> "There is no doubt that Isaiah 53 is to be understood in the context of the Isaiah tradition. Insofar as the servant is Israel – a common assumption of Jewish interpretation – we see that the theme of humiliation and exaltation serves the Isaiah rendering of Israel, for Israel in this literature is exactly the humiliated (exiled) people who by the powerful intervention of Yahweh is about to become the exalted (restored) people of Zion. Thus the drama is the drama of Israel and more specifically of Jerusalem, the characteristic subject of this poetry.
>
> Second, although it is clear that this poetry does not have Jesus in any first instance on its horizon, it is equally clear that the church, from the outset, has found the poetry a poignant and generative way to consider Jesus, wherein humiliation equals crucifixion and exaltation equals resurrection and ascension."

12. Talmud, Sotah 14a and the Sifri on Deuteronomy 355 applies Isaiah 53:12 to Moses
13. Rabbi Sadyah Gaon (tenth century), Oxford Ms. (Poc 32)
14. Jerusalem Talmud, Shkalim V.I.
15. Ezekiel 18:20-23
16. Midrash Rabbah (Numbers XXIII.2), Zohar (Genesis & Leviticus), Talmud (Brochos 5a),
17. Yalkut, ii, 571 on Zachariah 4:7

# The following related articles can be found in Part XV of this study guide:

## Part V

# The Trinity, Isaiah 9:5-6, and Zechariah 12:10

**Exodus 20:2-3 - The First of the Ten Commandments**

"I am the Lord your God, who brought you out of Egypt, and of the land of slavery. You shall have no other gods before Me." (Deuteronomy 5:7)

**Numbers 23:19**

"God is not a man that He should lie, nor a mortal that He should change His mind."

**Deuteronomy 4:11-12**

"You came near and stood at the foot of the mountain while it blazed with fire to the very heavens, with black clouds and deep darkness. Then the Lord spoke to you out of the fire. You heard the sound of words but saw no image; there was only a voice."

**Deuteronomy 4:35**

"You are the ones who have been shown, so that you will know that God is the Supreme Being, and there is none other besides Him!"

**Deuteronomy 4:39**

"Know therefore today, and take it to you heart, that the Lord, He is God in heaven above and on the earth below; there is no other!

**Deuteronomy 6:14**

"You shall not follow other gods, any of the gods of the peoples who surround you!"

**Deuteronomy 32:39**

"See, now, that I, I am He - and no god is with Me..."

**I Samuel 2:2**

"There is none holy as the Lord: for there is none beside Thee; neither is there any Rock like our God.

**I Samuel 15:29**

"The Eternal One of Israel will not lie nor change His mind: for He is not a man that He should change His mind."

**I Kings 8:27**

"For will God indeed dwell on the earth? Behold the heaven and heaven of heavens cannot contain Thee; how much less this house that I have built?"

**I Kings 8:60**

"So that all the nations of the earth may know that the Lord is God and that there is no other!"

**II Kings 19:19**

"Now, O Lord our God, deliver us from his hand, so that all kingdoms on earth may know that You alone, O Lord, are God." (Psalm 113:5)

**Isaiah 40:18**

"To whom then will you liken God? To what likeness will you compare unto Him?"

**Isaiah 40:25**

"To whom will then will you liken Me, that I should be his equal?" says the Holy One.

**Isaiah 42:8**

"I am the Lord, that is My name, and My glory will I not give to another. Neither My praise to graven images!"

**Isaiah 43:10-11**

"You are My witnesses," declares the Lord, "and My servant whom I have chosen, so that you may know and believe Me and understand that I am He. Before Me no god was formed, nor will there be one after Me. I, even I, am the Lord, and besides Me there is no Savior."

**Isaiah 44:6-8**

This is what the Lord says, Israel's King and Redeemer, the Lord Almighty, "I am the first and I am the last; apart from Me there is no God! Who then is like Me? Let him proclaim it. Let him declare and lay out before Me...Do not tremble, do not be afraid. Did I not proclaim this and foretell it long ago? You are My witnesses. Is there any God besides Me? No, there is no other Rock; I know not one."

**Isaiah 44:24**

So said the Lord, your Redeemer, the One who formed you from the womb, "I am the Lord Who makes everything, Who stretched forth the heavens alone, Who spread out the earth by Myself."

**Isaiah 45:5-6**

"I am the Lord, and there is no other; besides Me there is no God... I will strengthen you...I order that they know from the shining of the sun and from the west that there is no one besides Me; I am the Lord and there is no other!"

**Isaiah 45:18-19**

For this is what the Lord says – he who created the heavens, He is God; He who fashioned and made the earth, He founded it; He did not create it to be empty, but formed it to be inhabited – he says: "I am the Lord, and there is no other. I have not spoken in secret, from somewhere in a land of darkness; I have not said to Jacob's descendants, Seek Me in vain.' I, the Lord, speak the truth; I declare what is right."

**Isaiah 45:21-22**

"...who announced this before, who declared it from the distant past? Is it not I, the Lord, and there is no God apart from Me, a righteous God and Savior; there is none but Me. Turn to Me and be saved all you ends of the earth; for I am God, and there is no other!"

**Isaiah 46:5**

"To whom shall you liken Me and make Me equal and compare Me that we may be alike?"

**Isaiah 46:9**

"Remember the first things of old, that I am God and there is no other; I am God and there is none like Me."

**Isaiah 48:11**

"...And My honor I will not give to another."

**Hosea 13:4**

"And I am the Lord your God, Who brought you out of Egypt. You shall acknowledge no God but Me, no Savior except Me!"

**Joel 2:27**

"And you shall know that I am in the midst of Israel, and I am the Lord your God, there is no other; and My people shall never be ashamed."

**Malachi 2:10**

"Have we not all one Father? Has not one God created us? Why should we betray, each one his brother, to profane the covenant of our forefathers?"

**Psalm 73:25**

"Whom have I in heaven but You? And earth has nothing I desire besides You."

**Psalm 81:8-9**

"Hear, O My people, and I will admonish you; O Israel, if you would listen to Me! Let there be no strange god among you; nor shall you worship any foreign god.

**Psalm 146:3**

"Do not put your trust in princes, nor in the son of man, in whom there is no salvation!"

**Nehemiah 9:6**

"You alone are the Lord; You made the heavens, the heavens of the heavens and all their host, the earth and all that is upon it, the seas and all that is in them, and You give life to them all, and the heavenly host bow down before You."

**I Chronicles 17:20**

"O Lord, there is none like You, neither is there any God beside You, acording to all that we have heard with our ears!"

# Maimonidies Thirteen Fundamental Principles of Faith

1. I believe with perfect faith that God is the Creator and Ruler of all things. He alone has made, does make, and will make all things.

2. I believe with perfect faith that God is One (יָחִד). There is no unity that is in any way like His. He alone is our God He was, He is, and He will be.

3. I believe with perfect faith that God does not have a body – physical concepts do not apply to Him. There is nothing whatsoever that resembles Him at all.

4. I believe with perfect faith that God is first and last.

5. I believe with perfect faith that it is only proper to pray to God. One may not pray to anyone or anything else.

6. I believe with perfect faith that all the words of the prophets are true.

7. I believe with perfect faith that the prophecy of Moses is absolutely true. He was the chief of all prophets, both before and after Him.

8. I believe with perfect faith that the entire Torah that we now have is that which was given to Moses.

9. I believe with perfect faith that this Torah will not be changed, and that there will never be another given by God.

10. I believe with perfect faith that God knows all of man's deeds and thoughts. It is thus written, "He has molded every heart together, He understands what each one does." (Psalm 33:15)

11. I believe with perfect faith that God rewards those who keep His commandments, and punishes those who transgress Him.

12. I believe with perfect faith in the coming of the Messiah. How long it takes, I will await His coming every day.

13. I believe with perfect faith that the dead will be brought back to life when God wills it to happen.

# Genesis 1:26-27

And God said, "Let us make man in our image, after our likeness...." 27So God created man in His image, in the image of God He created him....

### I Kings 22:19

Micah continued, "Therefore hear the word of the Lord: I saw the Lord sitting on His throne with all the host of heaven standing around Him on His right and on His left."

### Isaiah 6:1-2, 8

In the year that king Uzziah died I saw also the Lord sitting upon a throne, high and lifted up, and his train filled the temple. 2Above it stood the seraphims; each one had six wings.... 8Also I heard the voice of the Lord, saying, Whom shall I send, and who will go for us?

### Jeremiah 22:26

But which of them has stood in the council of the Lord to see or to hear His word?

### Jeremiah 23:18, 22

But which of them [false prophets] has stood in the council of the Lord to see or to hear His word?.... 22But if they had stood in My council they would have proclaimed My words to My people and would have turned them from their evil ways....

### Job 1:6

Now there was a day when the sons of God came to present themselves before the Lord, and Satan came also with them.

### Job 15:8

Do you listen in on God's council? Do you limit wisdom to yourself?

## Christian (Trinitarian) Commentators on Genesis 1:26

### G. J. Wenham

Christians have traditionally seen [Genesis 1:26] as adumbrating [foreshadowing] the Trinity. It is now universally admitted that this was not what the plural meant to the original author.

**Word Biblical Commentary on Genesis, Word Books, 1987, p. 27.**

---

### The NIV Study Bible

*us...our...our.* God speaks as the Creator-king, announcing his crowning work to the members of his heavenly court (see 322; 11:7; Isa. 6:8; see also I Ki. 22:19-23; Job 15:8; Jer. 23:18)

**Grand Rapids: Zondervan, 1985, p. 7.**

---

### The Ryrie Study Bible

*Us...Our.* Plurals of majesty.

**Charles Caldwell Ryrie (Dallas Theological Seminary), Chicago: Moody Press, 1978, p. 9.**

---

### Liberty Annotated Study Bible

The plural pronoun us is most likely a majestic plural from the standpoint of Hebrew grammar and syntax.

**Jerry Falwell (Executive Editor), Lynchburg: Liberty Univ., 1988, p. 8.**

---

### Keil and Delitzsch

The plural 'We' was regarded by the fathers and earlier theologians almost unanimously as indicative of the Trinity: modern commentators, on the contrary, regard it either as *pluralis majestatis*....No other explanation is left, therefore, than to regard it as *pluralis majestatis*....

**Keil & Delitzsch Commentary on the Old Test., Peabody: Hendric., 1989, Vol. I, p. 62.**

# Did the Authors of the New Testament Believe in the Doctrine of the Trinity?

**Matthew 20:20-23**

The mother of the sons of Zebedee.... [21]said to him [Jesus], "Command that these two sons of mine may sit, one at your right hand and one at your left, in your kingdom." [22]But Jesus answered and said...., [23] "You will drink my cup, but to sit at my right hand and at my left is not mine to grant, but is for those for whom it has been prepared by my Father."

**If Jesus was fully God, why could only the Father, and not Jesus, grant that the two sons of Zebedee sit at the right and left of Jesus?**

**Matthew 26:39**

Going a little farther, he [Jesus] fell on his face to the ground and prayed, saying, "O my Father, if it is possible, may this cup be taken from me. Yet not as I will, but as you will.

**If the Father and Jesus were of the same substance, such a prayer would have been meaningless. Jesus would have been praying to himself, and his will, out of necessity, would have been that of the Father's.**

**Matthew 26:53**

Do you think I cannot call on my Father, and he will at once put at my disposal more than twelve legions of angels?

**Why would Jesus need to request from God legions of angels?**

**Mark 10:17-20**

And as he [Jesus] was setting out on a journey, a man ran up to him and knelt before him, and began asking him, "Good Teacher, what shall I do to inherit eternal life?" [18] And Jesus said to him, "Why do you call me good? No one is good except God alone." [19] "You know the commandments: 'Do not murder....'" [20] And he said to him, "Teacher, I have kept all these things from my youth up."

**If, as Trinitarians insist, Jesus was God, why does Jesus rebuke the man for addressing him as *"Good Teacher"*? (Jesus believed that the title *"good"* was appropriate for God *alone*, who he considered the *only* standard of goodness).**

**Interestingly, once the man was corrected, thereafter he only referred to Jesus as "Teacher."**

**Mark 13:32**

But of that day and that hour knoweth no man, no, not the angels which are in heaven, neither the son, but the Father.

**If Jesus was coequal with the Father, how could the Father have information that Jesus lacked? Moreover, if, as some Trinitarians suggest, the son was limited by his human nature, why didn't the Holy Spirit know?**

### John 10:30-34

"I, and my Father are **one (ἕν)**." 31 Again the Jews picked up stones to stone him, but Jesus said to them "I have shown you many great miracles from the Father. For which of these do you stone me?" 32 "We are not stoning you for any of these," replied the Jews, "but for blasphemy, because you, a mere man, claim to be God." 34 Jesus answered them, "Is it not written in your Law, 'I have said you are gods?'" *(see Psalm 82:6)*

**Trinitarians maintain that Jesus' statement, "I and my Father are *one*," demonstrates that Jesus was declaring himself to be God. The Greek word ἕv (one), however, does not imply being a part of the same substance. We see this clearly in John 17:11 and 17:21-22. In these verses Jesus prays to God that the disciples may be one (ἕv) as Jesus and God are. Clearly, Jesus is requesting that the disciples be of one *unified purpose*, not of the same substance or part of the Trinity.**

**Moreover, John 10:30-34 is particularly revealing. The fourth Gospel describes how when the Jews heard Jesus proclaim, "I and my Father are one," they immediately wanted to stone him. When Jesus asked why they wanted to kill him, the Jews responded because "you claim to be God." Upon hearing this Jesus asked, "Is it not written in your Law, 'I have said you are gods'?"**

**This response gives us insight into the mind of the author of the book of John, and should at least give Trinitarians pause. The verse is found in Psalm 82:6 where the Bible refers to judges who teach God's divine Law as gods. This title was bestowed on them because they are agents of the Almighty's divine law, not because they were actually God in any way. The Jewish scriptures often refers to agents of God as a god. For example, in Exodus (7:1) Moses is called a god because he was God's representative to Pharaoh. The New Testament never claims that Jesus is God, the Creator of the universe, but rather His representative.**

### John 14:28

"...I [Jesus] go unto the Father, for my father is greater than I."

**This verse speaks for itself.**

### John 17:3

And this is life eternal, that they might know thee the only true God, and Jesus Christ, Whom thou hast sent.

**Here Jesus insists that the Father is the "*only* true God." The Greek word used here for "only" is *monos*, which is meant to exclude all others. Clearly, the Father cannot be "the *only* true God" if there are two others who are God to the same degree as he is.**

### John 20:17

Jesus saith unto her [Mary], "Touch me not; for I am not yet ascended to my Father. But go to my brethren, and say unto them, I ascend unto my Father, and your Father; and to my God, and your God."

**If Jesus was God, why would he tell Mary that he considered her Father as his Father, and her God as his God? In Revelations 3:12, after the crucifixion, we continue to see Jesus calling the Father "my God." But never in the Christian Bible is the Father reported to refer to Jesus as "my God," nor does either the Father or Jesus refer to the Holy Spirit as "my God."**

*Continued on the following page*

# Did Paul Believe In Doctrine of the Trinity?

### I Corinthians 8:4-6

...and that is none other God but one. [5]For though there be that are called gods, whether in heaven or in earth, (as there may be many gods, and many lords,) [6]But to us there is but one God, the Father, of whom are all things, and we in him; and one Lord Jesus Christ, by whom are all things, and we by him.

> **Paul insists that only the Father is declared to be the one and only God. In Ephesians 1:17 Paul is still unaware of the Trinity when he says, "That the God of our Lord Jesus Christ...."**

### I Corinthians 11:3

But I would have you know, that the head of every man is Christ; and the head of the woman is the man; and the head of Christ is God.

> **This verse does not depict Jesus as coequal with God. On the contrary, God is of superior rank to Jesus. Moreover, this statement reveals that the New Testament did not consider Jesus to be equal with God even after the ascension. Paul wrote these words around 55 C.E. — long after the crucifixion.**

### I Peter 1:3

Blessed be the God and Father of our Lord Jesus Christ....

> **As mentioned above, this concept is restated many times throughout the New Testament: the Father is Jesus' God — never the other way around.**

### Colossians 1:15

He [Jesus] is the image of the invisible God, the first-born of all creation.

> **If the earliest Christians believed in the Trinity, why doesn't the New Testament ever refer to the Father or the Holy Spirit as the "firstborn of all creation?" Understandably, the New Testament would never refer to the Father as "firstborn" because primitive Christianity considered the Father alone eternal.**

### I Timothy 2:5

For there is one God and one mediator between God and men, the man Christ Jesus.

> **By Paul clearly distinguishing God and Jesus, this verse places a considerable strain on Trinitarianism.**

### Hebrews 4:15

For we do not have a high priest who cannot sympathize with our weaknesses, but one who has been tempted in all things as we are, yet without sin.

> **James 1:13 states that God cannot be tempted!**

### Hebrews 5:7-8

[Jesus] offered up both prayers and supplications with loud crying and tears to the one who was able to save him from death, and he was heard. [8]Although he was a son, he learned obedience from the things he suffered.

> **Why would God need to beg and cry to God to save him from death? Moreover, if the author of Hebrews considered Jesus God, why does Hebrews 5:8 insist that Jesus learned obedience from suffering? Is there anything God does not know and must learn through experience?**

# Why Do Evangelical Christians Revere and Exalt Martin Luther, a Vulgar Anti-Semite?

## Luther on the Trinity and the Jews

### *On The Jews and Their Lies*

By Martin Luther — 1543

Consequently, if I had power over them [the Jews], I would assemble their scholars and their leaders and order them, on pain of losing their tongues down to the root, to convince us Christians within eight days of the truth of their assertions and prove this blasphemous lie against us, to the effect that we worship more than one true God.

Translated by Martin H. Bertram, *On The Jews and Their Lies*, Luther's Works, Volume 47, page 289; Philadelphia: Fortress Press, 1971.

| Correct Translation | New American Standard | King James Version |
|---|---|---|
| **Isaiah 9:5-6*** For a child **has been born** (יֻלַּד) to us, a son given to us, and the authority **was placed** (וַתְּהִי) upon his shoulder, and his name **was called** (וַיִּקְרָא) Wondrous Adviser, the Mighty God, the Everlasting Father, the Prince of Peace. [6]To him who increases the authority, and for peace without end, on David's throne and on his kingdom, to establish it and to support it with justice and with righteousness; from now and to eternity, **the zeal of the Lord of Hosts shall accomplish this**. | **Isaiah 9:6-7** For a child **will be** born to us, a son **will be** given unto us; and the Government **will** rest on His shoulders; And His name **will be** called Wonderful Counselor, Mighty God, Eternal Father, Prince of Peace. | **Isaiah 9:6-7** For unto us a child is born, unto us a son is given: and the government **shall be** upon his shoulder: and his name **shall be** called Wonderful, Counselor, The Mighty God, The Everlasting Father, The Prince of Peace. |

*Isaiah 9:5-6 in a Jewish Bible appears as 9:6-7 in a Christian Bible.

**Christian Bibles violently twist Isaiah 9:6 so that this text appears to be a prophecy about a divine Jesus in the future. This verse, however, is not describing any future event. Rather, it contains the epic exaltation of Hezekiah and the divine names bestowed upon him because the Jews were miraculously saved from the hands of Assyria 2,700 years ago. The KJV, NAS, and other Christian Bibles meticulously changed all of the past tense verbs in this verse into the future tense. Below are the Hebrew verbs which the KJV clearly mistranslated in Isaiah 9:6, yet correctly rendered in other places in Tanach where these identical words appear. In an effort to further conceal that Isaiah 9:6 is referring to names given to Hezekiah, the New International Version Bible deletes the word "name," causing the verse to read, "and he will be called." For the full record of Hezekiah's salvation from Assyria, read Isaiah 37:32 and II Kings 19:31.**

## Verbs are in the past tense:

and was *called* (וַיִּקְרָא) — and it *was* (וַתְּהִי) — was born (יֻלַּד)

כִּי־יֶלֶד יֻלַּד־לָנוּ בֵּן נִתַּן־לָנוּ וַתְּהִי הַמִּשְׂרָה עַל־שִׁכְמוֹ וַיִּקְרָא שְׁמוֹ פֶּלֶא יוֹעֵץ אֵל גִּבּוֹר אֲבִי עַד שַׂר־שָׁלוֹם׃

| וַיִּקְרָא | וַתְּהִי | יֻלַּד |
|---|---|---|
| **Leviticus 1:1 – (King James)** And the Lord **called** (וַיִּקְרָא) unto Moses.... | **Isaiah 5:25 – (King James)** Their carcasses **were as** (וַתְּהִי) refuse in the streets.... | **Genesis 4:26 – (King James)** And to Seth, to him also there **was born** (יֻלַּד) a son; and he called his name Enos.... |
| **Isaiah 21:8 – (King James)** Then **he cried** (וַיִּקְרָא), "A lion, my Lord!" | **Isaiah 23:3 – (King James)** ...**and she is** (וַתְּהִי) the marketplace for the nations. | **Genesis 10:21 – (King James)** And children **were born** (יֻלַּד) also to Shem.... |
| **Isaiah 36:13 – (King James)** Then the Rabshakeh stood **and called out** (וַיִּקְרָא) with a loud voice in Hebrew.... | **Isaiah 29:11 – (King James)** The whole vision **has become** (וַתְּהִי) to you like the words of a book that is sealed.... | **Genesis 35:26 – (King James)** ...these are the sons of Jacob, which **were born** (יֻלַּד) to him in.... |

## Many Jewish Names Contain the Name of God

**Hezekiah - The Mighty God**
Tovia - Goodness of God
Elienai - God Is My Eyes
Jehoiada - Knowledge of God
Hananiah - Gracious Lord
Elisha - God Is Salvation
Elijah - Yhwh God

Gedalia - Great God
Jesse - the Lord Is
Elihu - God Is He
Eliab - God Is Father
Eli - God Is
Eliezer - Help of God
Netanyahu - God Gives

### *Moses is Called a "God"*

Exodus 7:1

And the Lord said unto Moses, See, I have made thee a ***god*** (אֱלֹהִים) to Pharaoh, and Aaron thy brother shall be thy ***prophet***. *(see also Exodus 4:16)*

### *Jerusalem is Called "Lord"*

Jeremiah 33:16

In those days shall Judah be saved, and Jerusalem shall dwell safely; and this is the name wherewith she shall be called, "***The Lord Our Righteousness***" (יהוה צִדְקֵנוּ).

### *Angels are Called "God"*

Psalms 8:6

For you have made him a little lower than the ***angels*** (מֵאֱלֹהִים)....

### *An Altar is Called "God"*

Genesis 33:20

And he [Jacob] erected there an alter, *and called it* ***El-Elohe-Israel*** (וַיִּקְרָא־לוֹ אֵל אֱלֹהֵי יִשְׂרָאֵל)

### *Judges are Called "God"*

Exodus 21:6, 22:8

Then his master shall bring him to the ***judges*** (הָאֱלֹהִים).... [8]for any kind of lost thing which another claims to be his, the cause of both parties shall come before the ***judges*** (אֱלֹהִים); and whomever the ***judges*** (אֱלֹהִים) condemn shall pay double to his neighbor.

### Isaiah 37:31-35

And the remaining survivors of the house of Judah shall continue to take root below and they shall produce fruit above. [32]For from Jerusalem shall come forth a remnant, and survivors from Mt. Zion; **the zeal of the Lord of hosts shall do this** (קִנְאַת יְהוָה צְבָאוֹת תַּעֲשֶׂה־זֹּאת) [33]Therefore, so has the Lord said concerning the king of Assyria: "He shall not enter this city, neither shall he shoot there an arrow, nor shall he advance upon it with a shield, nor shall he pile up a siege mound against it. [34]By the way he comes he shall return, and this city he shall not enter," says the Lord. [35]I will protect this city to save it, for My sake and *for the sake of My servant David*. *(see also II Kings 19:30-34)*

**(see page 96)**

### Isaiah 10:20-27

And it shall come to pass on that day that the remnant of Israel and the survivors of the house of Jacob shall not continue to lean on him that smote them; but he shall lean on the Lord, the Holy One of Israel, in truth. [21]The remnant shall return, the remnant of Jacob, *to the mighty God*.... [24]Therefore, so said the Lord God of Hosts, "Fear not, My people who dwell in Zion; *Assyria, with a rod may he smite you*, and his staff may he bear over you as he did in Egypt." ... [26]And the Lord of Hosts shall stir up a scourge against him, *like the smiting of Midian* at the Rock of Oreb, and His staff on the sea, and He shall carry him off after the manner of Egypt. [27]And it shall come to pass on that day, that his burden shall be removed from upon your shoulder, and his yoke from upon your neck, and the yoke shall be destroyed....

**(see page 95)**

# Biblical Revisionism

**The chart below illustrates how renowned Christian Bibles deliberately altered the ninth chapter of Isaiah of the book of Isaiah in order to make the prophet's words appear as though he is speaking about a future event – the birth of a divine savior – rather than something that had occurred in the past. Christian translators accomplish this task by changing past-tense verbs in these passages into the future tense.**

**In Isaiah chapter nine, the prophet is recalling the exile of the ten northern tribes by the Assyrian Empire, and the miraculous salvation of Hezekiah's southern kingdom. Isaiah is describing the euphoric reaction of the Kingdom of Judah, who were facing immanent destruction while under a unyielding Assyrian siege, when they awoke to discover that 185,000 enemy solders were lying dead outside of their walls. The nation grasped that it was King Hezekiah who inspired them to rely on God during Assyria's horrifying blockade 2,700 years ago. They understood that the Kingdom of Judah was miraculously saved because of Hezekiah's leadership. Isaiah 37 and II Kings 19 discuses this epic event in greater detail. This simple forensic textual study below reveals how two well-known Christian Bibles carefully misdirect their readers by changing past tense verbs in these verses into the future tense. The sheer volume of ambitious Bible-tampering in which these translators engaged in is astounding. There can be little doubt as to why Christian schools routinely refrain from teaching Christian children the Hebrew language.**

| Christian Translation | Jewish Translation | Original Hebrew |
|---|---|---|
| **Isaiah 9:1**<br>***New International Version*** | **Isaiah 8:23**<br>(Verses in Jewish translation are numbered one verse behind Christian verses) | **Isaiah 8:23**<br>***Messoretic Text*** |
| [1]Nevertheless, there will be no more gloom for those who were in distress. In the past he humbled the land of Zebulun and the land of Naphtali, but in the **future** he **will honor** Galilee of the Gentiles, by the way of the sea, along the Jordan. | [23]For there is no weariness to the one who oppresses her; like the first time, he dealt mildly, [exiling only] the land of Zebulun and the land of Naphtali, and the last one he dealt harshly; the way of the sea, and the other side of the Jordan, the attraction of the nations. | כִּי לֹא מוּעָף לַאֲשֶׁר מוּצָק לָהּ כָּעֵת הָרִאשׁוֹן<br>הֵקַל אַרְצָה זְבֻלוּן וְאַרְצָה נַפְתָּלִי וְהָאַחֲרוֹן<br>הִכְבִּיד דֶּרֶךְ הַיָּם עֵבֶר הַיַּרְדֵּן גְּלִיל הַגּוֹיִם׃ |
| **Isaiah 9:2-4**<br>***New American Standard (NASB)*** | **Isaiah 9:1-3**<br>***Jewish Translation*** | **Isaiah 9:1-3**<br>***Messoretic Text*** |
| [2]The people who **walk** in darkness **will see** a great light; those who live in a dark land, the light **will** shine on them. | [1]The people who **walked** in darkness, **have seen** a great light; those who dwell in the land of the shadow of death, light **has** shone upon them. | הָעָם הַהֹלְכִים בַּחֹשֶׁךְ רָאוּ אוֹר גָּדוֹל<br>יֹשְׁבֵי בְּאֶרֶץ צַלְמָוֶת אוֹר נָגַהּ עֲלֵיהֶם׃ |
| [3]Thou **shalt** multiply the nation, thou **shalt** increase their gladness; they **will** be glad in Thy presence as with the gladness of harvest, as men rejoice when they divide the spoil. | [2]You **have** aggrandized this nation; you **have** magnified the joy for them; they **have** rejoiced over You like the joy of the harvest, as they rejoice when they divide spoils. | הִרְבִּיתָ הַגּוֹי לֹא (לוֹ) הִגְדַּלְתָּ<br>הַשִּׂמְחָה שָׂמְחוּ לְפָנֶיךָ כְּשִׂמְחַת<br>בַּקָּצִיר כַּאֲשֶׁר יָגִילוּ בְּחַלְּקָם שָׁלָל׃ |
| [4]For Thou **shalt** break the yoke of their burden and the staff on their shoulders, the rod of their oppressor, **as at the battle of Midian.** | [3]For, the yoke of his burden and the staff of his shoulder, the rod of the one who oppressed him **have** You broken, **as on the day of Midian**. | כִּי אֶת־עֹל סֻבֳּלוֹ וְאֵת מַטֵּה שִׁכְמוֹ שֵׁבֶט<br>הַנֹּגֵשׂ בּוֹ הַחִתֹּתָ כְּיוֹם מִדְיָן׃ |

# The Critical Context of the Ninth Chapter of Isaiah

**Isaiah's tenth chapter provides the epilogue to the events described in chapter nine. In these two sister chapters, the prophet recounts how God saved King Hezekiah and his people from Sannacherib's enormous military attack.**

**The Assyrian army had successfully carried off nine and a half tribes of the Northern Kingdom of Israel. Now Assyria was poised to exile the remaining Kingdom of Judah with a massive siege of Jerusalem. This remnant of the Jewish people faced an existential threat, and urgently needed divine intervention.**

**In these chapters, Isaiah recounts how the desperate Jewish nation was miraculously delivered from the Assyrian army. Thus, Isaiah begins the ninth chapter declaring, "The people who walked in darkness, have seen a great light; those who dwell in the land of the shadow of death, light has shone upon them."**

**The story of Hezekiah's remarkable salvation from Assyria more than 2,700 years ago is related in the tenth chapter of Isaiah as well. The fact that the tenth chapter continues to speak of Hezekiah's victory and Assyria's remarkable defeat does not bode well for evangelical Christians who insist that the ninth chapter of Isaiah is speaking of a deified Jesus. As can be seen below, Isaiah nine and ten use identical language to convey God's miraculous intervention on Hezekiah's behalf.**

| Isaiah 9 | Isaiah 10 |
|---|---|
| For the **yoke** of his **burden** and the **staff** of his **shoulder**, the **rod** of the one who oppressed him have You broken, **as on the day of Midian**. (9:3) | And it shall come to pass on that day, that his **burden** shall be removed from upon your **shoulder**, and his **yoke** from upon your neck, and the **yoke** shall be destroyed.... (10:27) |
| | Woe to Assyria, the **rod** of My anger And the **staff** in whose hands is My indignation. (10:5)<br><br>Assyria, with a **rod** may he smite you, and his **staff** may he bear over you as he did in Egypt." (10:24) |
| | And the Lord of Hosts shall stir up a scourge against him, like the smiting of **Midian** at the Rock of Oreb.... (10:26) |
| ...and his name was called...the **Mighty God** (9:5) | The remnant shall return, the remnant of Jacob, to the **mighty God**.... (10:21) |

## "The zeal of the Lord of hosts shall do this"

| Isaiah 9:6 | Isaiah 37:32 | II Kings 19:31 |
|---|---|---|
| Of the increase of his government and peace there will be no end, upon the throne of David and over his kingdom, to order it and establish it with judgment and justice From that time forward, even forever. **The zeal of the Lord of hosts will perform this.** | For out of Jerusalem shall go a remnant, and those who escape from Mount Zion. **The zeal of the Lord of hosts will do this.** | For out of Jerusalem shall go a remnant, and those who escape from Mount Zion. **The zeal of the Lord of hosts will do this.** |

## Tanach Use the Expression "The Zeal of the Lord of Hosts Shall Do This" Only When Describing Hezekiah's Miraculous Victory Over Assyria

**The term "the zeal of the Lord of hosts shall do this" (קִנְאַת יְהוָה צְבָאוֹת תַּעֲשֶׂה־זֹּאת) is uncommon in Tanach and appears only three times in the Jewish scriptures (Isaiah 9:6, 37:32, and II Kings 19:31). Moreover, these three verses all recount the same epic event in Jewish history, when God saved Hezekiah from certain defeat at the hands of the Assyrian army.**

**There is a reason why the Hebrew Bible uses this uncommon phrase when retelling this story of the miracle which saved Hezekiah's nation. The king inspired his frightened people to turn back to God. This occurred in spite of the overwhelming threat posed by the Assyrian military campaign against Jerusalem. The petrified nation was warned by Assyria that no other people ever withstood its military might.**

**Hezekiah's trust in God prevailed. He successfully persuaded his people not to loose trust in the Almighty. Because of this national spiritual affirmation, God zealously saved the Jewish people from Sannacherib's powerful army in a supernatural fashion. In one night an angel killed 185,000 soldiers in the military camp of the Assyrians. When King Sannacherib awoke the next morning and grasped that his army was completely destroyed, he fled to his capitol city Nineveh, and was soon assassinated. God had zealously intervened for His faithful people. Thus, "the zeal of the Lord of hosts" miraculously saved Hezekiah's pious nation.**

### John 19:34-37

But one of the soldiers with a spear pierced his side, and forthwith came there out blood and water. [35]And he that saw it bare record, and his record is true: and he knoweth that he saith true, that ye might believe. [36]For these things were done, that the scripture should be fulfilled, A bone of him shall not be broken. [37]And again another scripture saith, "They shall look upon him (ὃν) whom they have pierced."

---

### Obadiah 1:17-18, 21

And on Mount Zion there shall be a remnant, and it shall be holy, and the house of Jacob shall inherit those who inherited them. [18]And the house of Jacob shall be fire and house of Joseph a flame, and the house of Esau shall become stubble, and they shall ignite them and consume them, and the house of Esau shall have no survivors, for the Lord has spoken.... [21]And the saviors shall ascend Mt. Zion to judge the mountain of Esau, and the Lord shall have the kingdom.

### Zechariah 12:8-14 (King James Version)

In that day shall the Lord defend the inhabitants of Jerusalem; and he that is feeble among them at that day shall be as David; and the house of David shall be as God, as the angel of the Lord before them. [9]And it shall come to pass on that day, that I will seek to destroy all the nations that come against Jerusalem. [10]I will pour out upon the house of David and upon the inhabitance of Jerusalem a spirit of grace and supplications. And **they shall look upon me** (וְהִבִּיטוּ אֵלַי) **whom** (אֵת אֲשֶׁר) they have pierced, and they shall mourn for ***him*** as one mourneth for his only son. [11]On that day there shall be great mourning in Jerusalem, like the mourning of Hadadrimmon in the valley of Megiddon. [12]And the land shall mourn, every family apart: The Family of the house of David apart, and their wives apart. [13]The family of the house of Levi apart, and their wives apart; the family of the Shimeites apart, and their wives apart. [14]All the remaining families — every family apart, and their wives apart.

### Zechariah 12:10

And they shall look to Me **because of the one** (אֵת אֲשֶׁר) who was thrust through, and they shall mourn over him as one mourns over an only son....

וְהִבִּיטוּ אֵלַי אֵת אֲשֶׁר דָּקָרוּ וְסָפְדוּ
עָלָיו כְּמִסְפֵּד עַל הַיָּחִיד וְהָמֵר עָלָו
כְּהָמֵר עַל הַבְּכוֹר:

## The Living Bible

*(Christian Translation)*

### Zechariah 12:10

and they will look on ***him*** they pierced, and mourn for him....

### Isaiah 61:3

To place for the mourners of Zion, to give them glory instead of ashes, oil instead of mourning, a mantle of praise instead of feeble spirit, and they shall be called the elms of righteousness, the planting of the Lord.

### Isaiah 66:10

Rejoice with Jerusalem and exalt in her all those who love her; rejoice with her a rejoicing, all who mourn over her.

### II Chronicles 35:22-25

Nevertheless, Josiah would not turn his face from him, but disguised himself, that he might fight with him, and hearkened not unto the words of Necho from the mouth of God, and came to fight in the valley of Megiddo. [23]And the archers shot at King Josiah; and the king said to his servants, "Have me away, for I am sore wounded." [24]His servants therefore took him out of that chariot, and put him in the second chariot that he had, and they brought him to Jerusalem, and he died, and was buried in one of the sepulchers of his fathers. And all Judah and Jerusalem mourned for Josiah. [25]And Jeremiah lamented for Josiah; and all the singing men and singing women spoke of Josiah in their lamentations, unto this day; and they made them an ordinance in Israel; and, behold, they are written in the Lamentations.

# The following related articles can be found in Part XV of this study guide:

## Part VI

# The Law of Moses and the New Covenant

**Ecclesiastes 7:20**

For there is not a just man upon the earth, that doeth good, and **yet sinneth not**.

**Genesis 8:21**

The Lord smelled a sweet aroma, and the Lord said "I will not again curse the ground anymore for man's sake," **for the imagination of man's heart is evil from his youth**; neither will I again smite anymore everything living, as I have done.

**Psalm 51:7**

"Behold, **I was brought forth in iniquity**, and in sin did my mother conceive me."

# Paul on Torah Observance

**Romans 3:20**

"Therefore, by the deeds of the law there shall no flesh be justified in his sight: for by the law is the knowledge of sin."

**Romans chapter 7 is revealing because in these passages Paul is addressing Jews (Rom 7:1), calling on them to abandon the commandments given to them at Mt. Sinai. It is a common misconception that Paul was dismissing the Torah as a "curse" only for Gentiles. Paul is clearly demanding that the Jewish people violate the *mitzvoth as well.***

**Romans 7:4-6**

"Wherefore, my brethren, ye also are becoming dead to the law by the body of Christ....[6]But now we are delivered from the law, that being dead wherein we were held; that we should serve in newness of spirit, and not in the oldness of the letter."

**Romans 10:4**

"For Christ is the end of the law for righteousness to everyone that believeth."

**Galatians 2:16, 21, 3:13**

"For by works of the law shall no flesh be justified. [21]I do not frustrate the grace of God: for if righteousness came by the law, then Christ is dead in vain.... [3:13]Christ has redeemed us from the curse of the law, being made a curse for us...."

**Galatians 5:2-3, 6**

"Behold, I Paul say unto you, that if you are circumcised, Christ shall profit you nothing. [3]For I testify again to every man that is circumcised, that he is a debtor to do the whole Law. [6]For in Jesus Christ neither circumcision availeth anything, nor uncircumcision, but faith which worketh by love."

# Does the Torah Ever State That it Is Too Difficult to Observe the Commandments?

**Deuteronomy 30:10-14**

If thou shalt hearken to the voice of the Lord your God, to keep His commandments and His statutes which are written in this book of the law; if you turn unto the Lord thy God with all your heart and with all your soul. [11]For this commandment which I command you this day is not too hard for you neither is it too far off. [12]It is not in heaven, that you should say: 'Who shall go up for us to heaven, and bring it to us, and make us hear it, that we may do it?' [13]Neither is it beyond the sea, that you should say: 'Who shall go over the sea for us, and bring it unto us, and make us to hear it that we may do it?' [14]But the word is very near to you, in your mouth and in your heart, that **you may do it.**

**Deuteronomy 30:14 deals a serious blow to the cornerstone of Paul's teachings. Consequently, the evangelist deliberately deleted an offending phrase from this end of this verse in Romans 10:8.**

**Paul's theology has no greater foe than the Torah's message at the conclusion of verse 14, "that you may do it [keep the commandments]." Throughout all of 13 letters, Paul argues that man is unable to keep the commandments, for the Law of God "has been made a curse for us" (Gal. 3:13). In Romans 10:8, Paul expunged this offense phrase. In fact, the entire thirtieth chapter of Deuteronomy bears witness that one can keep the *mitzvoth*, a principle that is completely antithetical to the teachings of Paul.**

**Romans 10:4-8**

For Christ is the end of the law for righteousness to everyone who believes. [5]For Moses writes about the righteousness which is of the law, "The man who does those things shall live by them." [6]But the righteousness of faith speaks in this way, "Do not say in your heart, 'Who will ascend into heaven?'" (that is, to bring Christ down from above). [7]Or, "'Who will descend into the abyss?'" (that is, to bring Christ up from the dead). [8] But what does it say? "The word is near you, in your mouth and in your heart."

**The last phrase of Deut. 30:14, "that you may do it," was expunged by Paul in Rom. 10:8.**

## Deuteronomy 30:15-19

See! Today I have set before you the choice between life and good [on one side], and death and evil [on the other]. [16]I have commanded you today to love God your Lord, to walk in His paths, and to keep His commandments, decrees and laws. You will then survive and flourish, and God your Lord will bless you in the land that you are about to occupy. [17]But if your heart turns aside and you do not listen, you will be led astray to bow down to foreign gods and worship them. I am warning you today, that [if you do that] you will be utterly lost.... [19]I call heaven and earth as witnesses! Before you I have placed life and death, the blessing and the curse. You must choose life, so that you and your descendants will survive.

## Deuteronomy 4:5-8

See! I have taught you rules and laws as God my Lord has commanded me, so [that you] will be able to keep them in the land to which you are coming and which you will be occupying. [6]Safe-guard and keep [these commandments], since this is your wisdom and understanding in the eyes of the nations. They will hear all these rules and say, "This great nation is certainly a wise and understanding people." [7]What nation is so great that they have God so close to it, as God our Lord is, whenever we call on him? [8]What nation is so great that they have such righteous statutes and laws, like this entire Torah that I am presenting before you today?

## Deuteronomy 10:12-13

And now, Israel, what does God want of you? Only that you remain in awe of God your Lord, so that you will follow all His paths and love Him, serving God your Lord with all your heart and with all your soul. [13]You must keep God's commandments and decrees that I am prescribing for you today, so that good will be yours.

## Deuteronomy 29:28 (29)

The things that are revealed belong unto us and to our children forever, that we may do all the words of the law.

## Psalm 111:7-8

The works of His hands are truth and justice, all his commandments are sure. [8]They stand fast **forever and ever**, done in truth and uprightness.

## Psalm 19:8-9 (7-8)

**The law of the Lord is perfect**, it restores the soul; the testimony of the Lord is trustworthy, making the simple one wise! [9]The statutes of the Lord are right, rejoicing the heart; the commandments of the Lord are pure, enlightening the eyes!

## Psalm 119:44, 72, 97, 155, 163, 165

So shall I keep Thy Torah continually, forever and ever! [72]The Torah of Thy mouth is better unto me than thousands of gold and silver! [97]O how I love Thy Torah! All day long it is my conversation! [155] Salvation is far from the wicked: for they seek not Thy law. [163]I hate and abhor falsehood, but Thy Torah do I love! [165]Great peace have they that love Thy Torah; there is no stumbling block for them!

# The Jewish People will Perform the *Mitzvos* (the Commandments) in the Messianic age

## Ezekiel 11:19-20

And I will give them one heart, and I will put a new spirit within you; and I will take the stony heart out of their flesh, and will give them a heart of flesh. [20]That they may walk in My statutes, and keep My ordinances, and do them; and they shall be My people, and I will be their God.

## Ezekiel 37:24

And David My servant shall be king over them; and they all shall have one shepherd. They shall also walk in My judgments, and observe My statutes, and do them.

## Ezekiel 44:9

Thus saith the Lord God: No stranger, uncircumcised in the heart, nor uncircumcised in the flesh, shall enter into My sanctuary...

**Why does Paul claim that Jesus' death marked the end of the sacrificial system (Heb 10:18), when Ezekiel prophesies that the sacrificial system will be restored in the messianic age?**

## Isaiah 2:3

And many nations shall go, and they shall say, "Come, let us go up to the Lord's mount, to the House of the God of Jacob, and let Him teach us of His ways, and we will go in His paths," for out of Zion shall the Torah come forth, and the word of the Lord from Jerusalem.

## Zachariah 14:16

It shall come to pass that everyone that is left of all the nations who came against Jerusalem shall go up from year to year to the King, the Lord of hosts, and to keep the Feast of Tabernacles.

## Malachi 3:22 (4:4)

Remember ye the Torah of Moses My servant, which I commanded unto him in Horeb, for all Israel, with all statutes and judgments!

# Paul's Christian Message on Torah Observance

A reoccurring theme advanced throughout the New Testament is Paul's principle message that faithfulness and obedience to the Torah's commandments is to be thoroughly abandoned and replaced with an unflinching belief in Jesus.

For example, according to the book of Mark, Jesus insists that although what leaves the mouth defiles man, what enters the mouth does not (7:18-19). The author of the second Gospel stridently concludes that, "Thus he [Jesus] declared all foods clean." The message is clear; man's salvation is determined by belief in Jesus alone; the Law of Moses must be discarded as a temporal, decaying relic of the past.

To support this driving theology, a story in the book of Acts (10:11-16, 11:5-10) is told where Peter has a repeating, jarring dream. He beholds a variety of unclean animals on a sheet falling from heaven. A voice calls out to Peter calling upon him to kill and eat these unkosher animals. Peter at first refuses, pointing out that these animals are unclean. At once the heavenly voice rebukes Peter for refusing to eat what God has cleansed.

This christological transition from the Mosaic Law of the "old covenant" to the law of believing in Jesus alone of the "new covenant," without the observance of commandments, is clearly reflected by the structure of the book of Acts as well.

The Church regards the book of Acts as an essential "bridge" in the New Testament which links the itinerant ministry of Jesus in the Gospels and the ministry of the church once the apostles received the Holy Spirit on the festival of Pentecost.

For Christendom, however, the book of Acts plays far more important role than an outline conveying the transition between epochs of the emerging Church. The book of Acts transfers the guiding leadership of the church from the Peter to Paul, from a movement that emerged from the Jewish world to a religion that sought to supercede its elder rival.

Until the 11th chapter of the Book of Acts, Peter is cast as a Jew grappling with the Jew within him, unsure how to conduct himself with others who don't share his birthright. He is concerned about meeting and eating with gentiles and is determined to resist unkosher food. Every step along the way, Peter is encouraged to abandon his old Jewish ways, and is prodded along toward the Pauline way of assimilation. Paul sternly rebukes Peter for acting in this stubborn manner (Gal. 2:11-14) and he is consistently portrayed in the New Testament as someone who blunders and flounders in his walk as a new Christian.

In contrast, once Paul embraces Christianity, he is virtually infallible throughout the New Testament. Moreover, following Saul's conversion (Acts 9), Saul takes on the name Paul and is regarded as the father of Christen doctrine. To this day, Paul's teachings remains the foundation of Christian theology.

Changing his Jewish name from Saul to the Roman name Paul is an important model and illustration of his assimilationist Christian message. Following the narratives in the book of Acts, Paul is never again called to by his former Jewish name Saul. His conversion is complete.

**Jeremiah 31:30-36 (31-37 in a Christian Bible)**

[30]Behold, days are coming, says the Lord, and I will form a covenant with the House of Israel and with the house of Judah, a new **covenant** (בְּרִית). [31] Not like the covenant that I formed with their forefathers on the day I took them by the hand to take them out of the land of Egypt, that they broke My covenant, although **I was a husband unto them** (וְאָנֹכִי בָּעַלְתִּי בָם), says the Lord. [32]For this is the covenant that I will form with the house of Israel after those days, says the Lord; I will place My law (תּוֹרָתִי) in their midst and I will inscribe it in their hearts, and I will be their God and they shall be My people. [33]And no longer shall one teach his neighbor or shall one teach his brother, saying, "Know the Lord," for they shall all know Me, from their smallest to their greatest, says the Lord, for I will forgive their iniquity and their sin I will no longer remember. [34] So said the Lord, Who gives the sun to illuminate by day, the laws of the moon and the stars to illuminate at night, Who stirs up the sea and its waves roar, the Lord of Hosts is His name. [35] If these laws depart from before Me, says the Lord, so will the **seed** (זֶרַע) of Israel cease being a nation before Me for all time. [36] So said the Lord: If the heavens above will be measured and the foundations of the earth below will be fathomed, I too will reject all the **seed** (זֶרַע) of Israel because of all they did, says the Lord.

# A Covenant is a promise. In the past, the Almighty Forged other Covenants with Abraham, Isaac, Jacob, and Pinchas.

**Leviticus 26:42**

I will remember My covenant with Jacob as well as My covenant with Isaac and My covenant with Abraham. I will remember the land.

**Numbers 25:12**

Therefore, tell him [Pinchas] that I have given **him My covenant** of peace.

**Hebrews 8:7-13**

[7] For if that first covenant had been faultless, then should no place have been sought for the second. [8] For finding fault with them, He saith, "Behold the days come, saith the Lord, when I will make a new covenant with the house of Israel, and with the house of Judah: [9] Not according to the covenant that I made with their fathers in the day when I took them by the hand to lead them out of the land of Egypt; because they continued not in my covenant, and I regarded them not (κἀγὼ ἠμέλησα αὐτῶν - *literally: although I disregarded them*), saith the Lord. [10] For this is the covenant that I will make with the house of Israel after those days, saith the Lord; I will put my laws unto their mind, and write them in their hearts: and I will be to them a God, and they shall be to me a people: [11] And they shall not teach every man his neighbor, and every man his brother, saying, "Know the Lord," for all shall know me, from the least to the greatest. [12] For I will be merciful to their unrighteousness, and their sins and their iniquities will I remember no more." [13] In that he saith, "A new covenant," He hath made the first old. **Now that which decayeth and waxeth old is ready to vanish away.**

**The book of Hebrews twisted the words of the prophet whom it claims to be quoting. Whereas Jeremiah 31:31 states "I was a husband unto them [the Jews]," Paul reverses Jeremiah's prophecy to read, "I disregarded them." How can Paul disregard the words of Jeremiah? How could he so flagrantly change the word of God?**

**God's bond with Israel in Jeremiah 31:31 is intimately portrayed as a betrothed woman, which is precisely the opposite relationship contained in Hebrews 8:9, where the Jews are cast as a rejected people.**

# The final Ingathering of Israel will Eclipse the Exodus from Egypt

**Jeremiah 23:7-8**

Therefore, behold days are coming, says the Lord, when they shall no longer say, "As the Lord lives, Who brought up the children of Israel from the land of Egypt." But, "As the Lord lives, Who brought us up and Who brought the seed of the House of Israel from the North Land and from all the lands where I have driven them, and they shall dwell on their land."

***(See also Jeremiah 16:14-15)***

## Can So Few Be So Right? Israel's Faithful Remnant Will Remain "Few in Number"

### Deuteronomy 4:27

And the Lord shall scatter you among the nations, and you shall be left few in number among the heathen, where the Lord will lead you.

## The Covenant Bestowed Upon Faithful of Israel

### Deuteronomy 7:6-9, 12

For you are a holy nation unto the Lord your God. The Lord your God has chosen you to be a special nation unto Himself, above all people are upon the face of the earth. [7]The Lord did not set His love upon you, nor choose you, because you were more in number than any people, for you were the fewest of all the people. [8]But because the Lord loved you, and because He would keep the oath which He had sworn unto your fathers, has the Lord brought you out with a mighty hand, and redeemed you out of the house of bondmen, from the hand of Pharaoh king of Egypt. [9]Know therefore that the Lord your God, He is God, the faithful God, **which keeps His covenant and mercy with them that love Him and keep His commandments** to a thousand generations. [12]Wherefore it shall come to pass, **if you hearken to these judgments, and keep and do them, that the Lord your God shall keep unto you the covenant** and the mercy which He swore to your fathers.

## Concerning the Jews
by Mark Twain

If the statistics are right, the Jews constitute but one percent of the human race. It suggests a nebulous dim puff of star dust lost in the blaze of the Milky Way. Properly the Jew ought hardly to be heard of; but he is heard of, has always been heard of. He is as prominent on the planet as any other people, and his commercial importance is extravagantly out of proportion to the smallness of his bulk. His contributions to the world's list of great names in literature, science, art, music, finance, medicine, and abstruse learning, are also away out of proportion to the weakness of his numbers. He has made a marvelous fight in this world, in all the ages; and has done it with his hands tied behind him. He could be vain of himself, and be excused for it. The Egyptian, the Babylonian, and the Persian rose, filled the planet with sound and splendor, then faded to dream-stuff and passed away; the Greek and the Roman followed, and made a vast noise, and they are gone; other peoples have spring up and held their torch high for a time, but it burned out, and they sit in twilight now, or have vanished. The Jew saw them all, beat them all, and is now what he always was, exhibiting no decadence, no infirmities of age, no weakening of his parts, no slowing of his energies, no dulling of his alert and aggressive mind. All things are mortal but the Jew; all other forces pass, but he remains. What is the secret of his immortality?

**From the article "Concerning the Jews";** *Harpers* (1899). See "*The Complete Essays of Mark Twain*"; Doubleday (1963), page 249.

# If the entire human race is infected with the "Original Sin" and mankind is "totally depraved," why does the Bible testify that there were many righteous people?

**Genesis 26:5**

Because that Abraham obeyed My voice, and kept My charge, My commandments, My statutes, and My laws.

**Numbers 14:24**

But My servant Calev, because he had another spirit with him, and has followed Me fully, him will I bring into the land which he went, and he will leave it to his descendants.

**I Kings 15:11**

And Asa did that which was just in the eyes of the Lord, as had done David his father.

**II Kings 22:2**

And he [Josiah] did that which was right in the sight of the Lord, and walked in all the ways of David his father, and turned not aside to the right hand or the left.

**II Chronicles 29:2**

And he [Hezekiah] did what was right in the sight of the Lord, according to all that David his father had done.

In one village, a certain soldier on this occasion found a copy of the sacred Law, tore the book to pieces and threw it into the fire. The Jews, as if their whole country were in flames, flocked together, religious fervor drawing them together like an instrument.

On the first announcement of the news, they hurried together with united clamor to Cumanus in Caesarea, where they besought him not to leave unpunished the author of such an outrage to God and their Law, but punish him for what he had done. Cumanus, seeing that the multitude could not be appeased unless amends were made, agreed to send for the soldier and ordered him to be led between the lines of his accusers to his execution. Then the Jews withdrew.

Josephus, "The Jewish Wars" Book II, 12:2
ed. Cornfeld, Mazar, and Mazar, Zondervan, Michigan 1982

# The following related articles can be found in Part XV of this study guide:

## Part VII

# Daniel 9's 70 Weeks, Psalm 110 and 2:12

## Psalm 110:1

| Jewish Translation | King James Version |
|---|---|
| Of David a Psalm. The **Lord** (יהוה) said to y **master** (לַאדֹנִי), "Sit thou at My right hand, ıtil I make your enemies a footstool at your feet." | A Psalm of David. The **Lord** said to my **Lord**, "Sit thou at my right hand, until I make thine enemies thy footstool." |

**Iatthew 22:41-46**

While the Pharisees were gathered together, Jesus asked them, Saying, "What think ye of Christ? Whose son is he? ıey say unto him, "The son of David." He saith unto them, "How then doth David in spirit call him Lord, saying, The Lord id unto my Lord, `Sit thou on my right hand, till I make thine enemies thy footstool?' If David then called him Lord, how he his son?" And no man was able to answer him a word, neither was any man from that day forth ask him any more ıestions.

## Psalm 2:12

| Jewish Translation | King James Version |
|---|---|
| **Desire purity** (נַשְּׁקוּ בַר) lest He become angry ınd you perish in the way, for in a moment His wrath will be kindled; the praises of all who take refuge in Him. | Kiss the Son (בַר), lest he be angry, and ye perish from the way, when his wrath is kindled but a little. Blessed are all they that put their trust in Him. |

**Why does the King James Version translate the Hebrew word בַר as "son" in Psalm 2:12, yet correctly translates the exact same word as "pure" or "clean" in every other place where this word appears in the Book of Psalms?**

**Psalms 18:20 (21) — King James Version**

The Lord rewarded me according to my righteousness; according to the ***cleanness*** (כְּבֹר) of my hands hath He recompensed me...

**Psalm 18:24 (25) — King James Version**

Therefore hath the Lord recompensed me according to my righteousness, according to the ***cleanness*** (כְּבֹר) of my hands in His eyesight.

**Psalm 19: 9 — King James Version**

The statutes of the Lord are right, rejoicing the heart: the commandment of the Lord is pure (בָּרָה) enlightening the eyes.

**Psalms 24:4 — King James Version**

He that hath clean hands, and a **pure** (וּבַר) heart...

**Psalm 73:1 — King James Version**

Truly God is good to Israel, even to such as are of a **clean** לְבָרֵי Heart.

**The word בַר means "son" in Aramaic, not Hebrew. The Book of Psalms does not contain any Aramaic words! If King David wished to use the word "son," he would have written the Hebrew word בני, as he did six verses earlier in Psalm 2:7.**

**Psalm 2:7 — King James Version —** I will declare the decree: the Lord hath said unto me, "Thou art My son (בְּנִי) This day have I begotten thee."

## Daniel 9:1-3, 13-27

In the first year of Darius, son of Ahasuerus, of the seed of Media, who was made king over the kingdom of the
Chaldeans: 2 In the first year of his reign, I Daniel, contemplated with books the calculation, the number of years about
which the **word** (דְבַר) of Hashem had come to the prophet Jeremiah, to complete the seventy years from the ruins of
Jerusalem. 3 And I set my face toward my Lord, God, to request prayer and supplication, with fasting, sackcloth, and
ashes. 13 As is written in the Law of Moses, all this evil has come upon us, and we did not entreat the countenance of the
Lord our God to repent of our iniquities and to contemplate Your truth.... 14 And the Lord hastened with the evil and
brought it upon us, for the Lord our God is righteous with all His deeds which He performs, and we did not hearken to
His voice. 15 And now, O Lord our God, Who took Your people out of the land of Egypt with a strong hand, and You
have made for Yourself a Name as of this day; we have sinned, we have dealt wickedly. 16 My Lord, in keeping with all
Your righteousness, please let Your anger and Your fury turn away from Your city Jerusalem, Your holy mountain; for
because of our sins and the sins of our ancestors, Jerusalem and Your people have become the scorn of all those around
us. 17 And now, pay heed, our God, to the prayer of Your servant and to his supplications, and let Your countenance shine
upon Your desolate Sanctuary for my Lord's sake. 18 Incline, my God, Your ear, and listen, open Your eyes and see the
desolation of ourselves and of the city upon which Your Name is proclaimed; for not because of our righteousness do
we cast down our supplications before You, rather because of Your great compassion. 19 O my Lord, heed; O my Lord,
forgive; O my Lord, be attentive and act, do not delay; for Your sake, my God, for Your Name is proclaimed upon Your
city and Your people.' 20 And more I was speaking, praying, and confessing my sin and the sin of my people, Israel, and
casting my supplication before Hashem, my God, for the mountain of the Sanctuary of my God. 21 Still I was speaking
in prayer, and the man Gabriel, whom I saw in the beginning vision, was lifted in flight and approached me about the
time of the afternoon offering. 22 He made me understand and spoke to me. And he said, `Daniel, I have just gone to
make you skillful in understanding. 23 At the beginning of your supplications a word went forth, and I have come to relate
it, for beloved are you. Contemplate the matter and gain understanding in the vision. **24 Seventy weeks have been**
**decreed upon your people and your holy city to terminate transgression, to end sin, to wipe away iniquity, to bring everlasting righteousness, to seal vision and prophet, and to anoint the Holy of Holies.**

# Daniel 9:25-27

### King James Version

Know therefore and understand, that from the going forth of the commandment to restore and to build Jerusalem unto **the Messiah the Prince shall be seven weeks, and threescore and two weeks;** the street shall be built again, and the wall, even in troublous times.

26 And **after threescore and two weeks** shall Messiah be cut off, but not for himself: and the people of the prince that shall come shall destroy the city and the sanctuary; and the end thereof shall be with a flood, and unto the end of the war desolations are determined.

27 And he shall confirm the covenant with many for one week: and in the midst of the week he shall cause the sacrifice and the oblation to cease, and for the overspreading of abominations he shall make it desolate, even until the consummation, and that determined shall be poured upon the desolate.

### Jewish Translation

And you should know and comprehend: From the emergence of the **word** (דְבַר) to return and build Jerusalem until **an anointed prince** (עַד מָשִׁיחַ נָגִיד) will be seven weeks (שָׁבֻעִים שִׁבְעָה); and for sixty two weeks (וְשָׁבֻעִים שִׁשִּׁים וּשְׁנַיִם) it will be rebuilt, street and moat, but in troubled times.

26 And after the sixty two weeks **an anointed one will be cut off** (יִכָּרֵת מָשִׁיחַ) **and will be no more** (וְאֵין לוֹ); the people of the prince who comes will destroy the city and the Sanctuary, but his end shall come like a flood. Until the end of a war, desolation is decreed!

27 He will strengthen a covenant with the great ones one week; and for half of the week he will abolish the sacrifice and offering, and upon soaring heights will the mute abominations be, until extermination as decreed will pour down upon the abomination.

## Isaiah 44:28-45:1, 13

Who says of Cyrus, "He is My shepherd, and all My desire he shall fulfill," and to say of Jerusalem, "It shall be built, and the Temple shall be founded." [1]So said the Lord to **His anointed one** (לִמְשִׁיחוֹ לְכוֹרֶשׁ) to **Cyrus**, whose right hand I held, to flatten nations before him, and the loins of kings I will loosen, to open portals before him, and gates shall not be closed. [13]"I aroused him with righteousness, and all his ways I will straighten out. He shall build My city and free My exiles, neither for a price nor for a bribe," said the Lord of Hosts.

## Ezra 1:1-3

And in the first year of **Cyrus**, the king of Persia, at the completion of the **word** (דְּבַר) of the Lord from the mouth of Jeremiah, the Lord aroused the spirit of Cyrus, the king of Persia, and he issued a proclamation throughout his kingdom, and also in writing, saying: [2]"So said Cyrus, the king of Persia, 'All the kingdoms of the earth to Lord God of the heavens delivered to me, and He commanded me to build Him a House in Jerusalem, which is in Judah. [3]Who is among you of all His people, may his God be with him, and he may ascend to Jerusalem, which is Judea, and let him build the House of the Lord, God of Israel; He is the God Who is in Jerusalem."

## Jeremiah's Two 70-Year Prophecies

### Jeremiah 25:12

And it shall be at the completion of **seventy years**, I will visit upon the king of Babylon and upon that nation, says the Lord, their iniquity, and upon the land of the Chaldeans, and I will make it for everlasting desolations.

### Jeremiah 29:10

For so said the Lord: for at the completion of **seventy years** of Babylon I will remember you, and I will fulfil My good **word** (דְּבָרִי) toward you, **to restore you to this place.**

## II Chronicles 36:21-23

To fulfil the **word** (דְּבַר) **of the Lord in the mouth of Jeremiah**, until the land was **appeased for its Sabbaths**; [for] all the days of its desolation it rested until the completion of seventy years. [22]And in the first year of Cyrus, king of Persia, at the completion of the **word** (דְּבַר) of the Lord in the mouth of Jeremiah, the Lord aroused the spirit of Cyrus the king of Persia, and he issued a proclamation throughout all his kingdom, and put it also in writing, saying: [23]"So said Cyrus the king of Persia: all the kingdoms of the earth has the Lord God of the heavens delivered to me, and He commanded me to build Him a House in Jerusalem, which is in Judah. Who among you is of all His people, may the Lord his God be with him, and he may ascend."

## Leviticus 26:18

If despite this you do not heed Me, then I shall punish you seven times for your sins **(7 X 70 years = 490 years)**.

## Leviticus 25:1-22 — *Shmittah* — The Sabbatical Year

God spoke to Moses at Mount Sinai, telling him to speak to the Israelites and say to them: When you come to the land that I am giving you, the land must be given a rest period, a Sabbath to God. For six years you may plant your fields, prune your vineyards, and harvest your crops, but the seventh year is a Sabbath of Sabbaths for the land. It is God's Sabbath during which you may not plant your fields, nor prune your vineyards. Do not harvest crops that grow on their own and do not gather the grapes on your unpruned vines, since it is a year of rest for the land. What grows while the land is resting may be eaten by you....Keep My decrees and safeguard My laws. If you keep them, you will live in the land securely. The land will produce its fruit, and you will eat your fill, thus living securely in the land. **If you ask, "What will we eat in the seventh year? We have not planted nor have we harvested crops." I will direct My blessing to you in the sixth year, and the land will produce enough crops for three years.** You will therefore be eating your old crops when you plant in the eighth year. You will still be eating your old crops until the crops of the ninth year are ripe.

**Notice how none of these *Christian* translations of Daniel 9:25 (below) compress the seven week period with the 62 week period into one period of 69 weeks. By correctly designating an anointed prince who comes after seven weeks, or 49 years, and another anointed one (9:26) who is cut off after a subsequent 62 weeks (434 years), these translators are accurately rendering Gabriel's message that there are *two* anointed ones spoken of in Daniel 9:25-26.**

**King James Version — 1611 Edition**
Know therefore and vunderstand, *that* from the going foorth of the commandement to restore and to build Ierusalem, vnto the Messiah the Prince, *shall be* seuen weekes; and threescore and two weekes, the street shall be built againe, and the wall, euen in troublous times.

**1885 Revision of the King James Version — 1611 Edition**
Know therefore and discern, that from the going forth of the commandment to restore and to build Jerusalem unto the anointed one, the prince, shall be seven weeks: and threescore and two weeks, it shall be built again, with street and moat, even in troublous times.

**The Bible: An American Translation**
Learn, therefore, and understand: `from the going forth of the word to restore and rebuild Jerusalem, Till there comes a prince, an anointed one, there shall be seven weeks; Then for sixty-two weeks it shall stay rebuilt, with its squares and streets;

**The Modern Readers Bible**
Know therefore and discern, that from the going forth of the commandment to restore and to build Jerusalem unto the anointed one, the prince, shall be seven weeks: and threescore and two weeks, it shall be built again, with street and moat, even in troublous times.

**The Bible: A New Translation**
Know then, understand, that between the issue of the prophetic command to re-people and rebuild Jerusalem and the consecrating of a supreme high priest, seven weeks of years shall elapse; in the course of sixty-two weeks of years it shall be rebuilt, with its squares and streets.

**The Anchor Bible**
Know then, and understand this: from the utterance of the word regarding the rebuilding of Jerusalem to the coming of an anointed leader there will be seven weeks. Then during sixty-two weeks it will be rebuilt, with its streets and moat, but in a time of distress.

**Revised Standard Version**
Know therefore and understand that from the going forth of the word to restore and build Jerusalem to the coming of an anointed one, a prince, there shall be seven weeks. Then for sixty-two weeks it shall be built again with squares and moat, but in a troubled time.

**New Revised Standard Version**
Know therefore and understand: from the time that the word went out to restore and rebuild Jerusalem until the time of an anointed prince, there shall be seven weeks; and for sixty-two weeks it shall be built again with streets and moat, but in a troubled time.

**New English Bible**
Know then and understand: from the time that the word went forth that Jerusalem should be restored and rebuilt, seven weeks shall pass till the appearance of one anointed, a prince; then for sixty-two weeks it shall remain restored, rebuilt with streets and conduits.

**Revised English Bible**
Know, then, and understand: from the time that the decree went forth that Jerusalem should be restored and rebuilt, seven of those seventy will pass till the appearance of one anointed, a prince; then for sixty-two it will remain restored, rebuilt with streets and conduits. At the critical time....

**New American Bible (Catholic)**
Know and understand this: From the utterance of the word that Jerusalem was to rebuilt until one who is anointed and a leader, there shall be seven weeks. During sixty-two weeks it shall be rebuilt, with streets and trenches, in time of affliction.

**The Expositor's Bible**
From the decree to restore Jerusalem unto the Anointed One (or "the Messiah"), the Prince, shall be seven weeks. For sixty-two weeks Jerusalem shall be built again with street and moat, though in troublous times.

**The Good News Bible: Today's English Version**
Note this and understand it: From the time the command is given to rebuild Jerusalem until God's chosen leader comes, seven times seven years will pass. Jerusalem will be rebuilt with streets and strong defenses, and will stand for seven times sixty-two years, but this will be a time of troubles.

**A New Commentary on Holy Scriptures**
The first period lasts seven weeks, and runs from the prophesy of the restoration to the coming of the anointed prince; the second period of sixty-two weeks is that during which the restoration is duly carried out:

**The International Critical Commentary**
And thou art to know and understand. From the issue of the word to build again Jerusalem unto an Anointed-Prince seven weeks. And for sixty-two weeks it shall be built again, street and moat, but in distress of times.

**The Abington Bible Commentary**
From the day when Jeremiah announced the future restoration of Jerusalem, i.e., from 586 B.C., to an anointed one, a prince, i.e., Cyrus the Great (538 B.C.), would be seven weeks, i.e., forty-nine years. This was the data of the formal close of the exile by the decree of Cyrus, forty-eight years from the destruction of the holy city. There would follow sixty-two weeks (434 years) during which Jerusalem was to be rebuilt with streets and open spaces, but not without experiencing many troubles.

## Daniel 9:26 (RSV):

And after the sixty-two weeks, an anointed one shall be cut off, and shall have nothing....

# Who Tampered with the KJV?

## King James Version
## 1611 Edition

**Daniels viſion. Chap.x. He is dumbe.**

> † Heb. a man of desires.

art † greatly beloued: therefore vnderstand the matter, & consider the vision.

> ‖ Or, to restraine.
> ‖ Or, to seale vp.
> † Heb. prophet.

24 Seuentie weekes are determined vpon thy people, and vpon thy holy
citie, ‖ to finish the transgression, and to ‖ make an ende of sinnes, and to make reconciliation for iniquitie, and to bring in euerlasting righteousnes, and to seale vp the vision and † prophecie, and to anoynt the most Holy.

> † Heb. shall returne and be built.
> ‖ Or, breach or ditch.
> † Hebr. in strait of times.

25 Know therefore and vnderstand,
*that* from the going foorth of the commandement to restore and to build Ierusalem, vnto the Messiah the Prince, *shall be* seuen weekes; and threescore and two weekes, the street † shall be built againe, and the ‖ wall, euen † in troublous times.

> ‖ Or, shall haue nothing.
> ‖ Or, it shall be cut off by desolations.

26 And after threescore and two
weekes, shall Messiah be cut off, ‖ but not for himselfe, and the people of the Prince that shall come, shall destroy the citie, and the Sanctuarie, and the ende thereof *shall be* with a flood, and vnto the ende of the warre ‖ desolations are determined.

> ‖ Or, with the abominable armies.
> * Mat. 24. 15. marke 13. 14. luke

27 And hee shall confirme the coue-
nant with many for one weeke: and in the midst of the weeke he shall cause the sacrifice and the oblation to cease, and ‖ for the ouerspreading of * abominations hee shall make *it* desolate, euen vntill the consummation, & that determined, shalbe powred vpon the desolate.

ded with fine gold of Vphaz.

6 His body also *was* like the Berill,
and his face as the appearance of lightning, and his eyes as lampes of fire, and his armes, and his feete like in colour to polished brasse, and the voice of his words like the voice of a multitude.

7 And I Daniel alone saw the vi-
sion: for the men that were with mee saw not the vision: but a great quaking fell vpon them, so that they fled to hide themselues.

> ‖ Or, vigor.
> * Dan. 7. 28.

8 Therefore I was left alone, and
saw this great vision, and there remained no strength in me: for my ‖ * comelinesse was turned in me into corruption, and I retained no strength.

9 Yet heard I the voice of his
words: and when I heard the voice of his wordes, then was I in a deepe sleepe on my face, and my face toward the ground.

> † Heb. mooued.

10 ¶ And behold, an hand touched
me, which † set me vpon my knees, and *vpon* the palmes of my hands.

> † Heb. a man of desires.
> † Heb. stand vpon thy standing.

11 And hee said vnto me, O Daniel,
† a man greatly beloued, vnderstand the wordes that I speake vnto thee, and † stand vpright: for vnto thee am I now sent; and when he had spoken this word vnto me, I stood trembling.

12 Then sayd hee vnto me; Feare
not, Daniel: for from the first day that thou diddest set thine heart to vnder-

**Who tampered with the King James Version (KJV)? The original 1611 edition of the KJV (above) correctly separates the seven weeks from the sixty two weeks in Daniel 9:25 with a semicolon. The current KJV, however, deceptively compresses these two separate time periods into one period of 483 years. It reads, "Know therefore and understand that from the going forth of the commandment to restore and build Jerusalem unto the Messiah the Prince shall be seven weeks, and threescore and two weeks."**

**Those who revised the KJV altered the punctuation of Daniel 9:25 in order the change the message of Gabriel's prophecy. By combining "seven weeks" with "sixty two weeks" into one period of sixty nine weeks, Christian translators create the notion in the mind of their readers that there is only on "messiah" spoken of the the ninth chapter of Daniel rather than two.**

**Until 1885, however, the KJV correctly separated these two time frames, so that it was clear that the angel Gabriel spoke of two different anointed ones. The first anointed ruler (Cyrus) who arises after 49 years, and a second who is anointed and removed after a subsequent 434 years (the high priest).**

# Chronological Chart of Daniel Chapter Nine

| Kings of Judah: Name of King | Kings of Judah: Years of Kingship | Year From Creation | Kings of Babylon and Persia: Years of Kingship | Kings of Babylon and Persia: Name Of King |
|---|---|---|---|---|
| | | 3319 | | |
| Jehoiakim | 4 | 3320 | 1 | Nebuchadnezzar |
| | 5 | 3321 | 2 | |
| | 6 | 3322 | 3 | |
| | 7 | 3323 | 4 | |
| | 8 | 3324 | 5 | |
| | 9 | 3325 | 6 | |
| | 10 | 3326 | 7 | |
| | 11 | | | |
| Jehiachin | 3-month reign | 3327 | 8 | |
| Zedekiah | 1 | 3328 | 9 | |
| | 2 | 3329 | 10 | |
| | 3 | 3330 | 11 | |
| | 4 | 3331 | 12 | |
| | 5 | 3332 | 13 | |
| | 6 | 3333 | 14, 15 | |
| | 7 | 3334 | 16 | |
| | 8 | 3335 | 17 | |
| | 9 | 3336 | 18 | |
| | 10 | 3337 | 19 | |
| | 11 | 3338 | 20 | |
| | | 3339 | 21 | |
| | | 3340 | 22 | |
| | | 3341 | 23 | |
| | | 3342 | 24 | |
| | | 3343 | 25 | |
| | | 3344 | 26 | |
| | | 3345 | 27 | |
| | | 3346 | 28 | |
| | | 3347 | 29 | |
| | | 3348 | 30 | |
| | | 3349 | 31 | |
| | | 3350 | 32 | |
| | | 3351 | 33 | |
| | | 3352 | 34 | |
| | | 3353 | 35 | |
| | | 3354 | 36 | |
| | | 3355 | 37 | |
| | | 3356 | 38 | |
| | | 3357 | 39 | |
| | | 3358 | 40 | |
| | | 3359 | 41 | |
| | | 3360 | 42 | |
| | | 3361 | 43 | |
| | | 3362 | 44 | |
| | | 3363 | 45 | |
| | | 3364 | 1 | |
| | | 3365 | 2 | |
| | | 3366 | 3 | |
| | | 3367 | 4 | |

**Jeremiah's Prophecies Of Seventy Years**

Jeremiah 25:12 - "And it shall be at the completion of **seventy years**, I will visit upon the king of Ba their iniquity, and upon the Chaldeans, and I will make it for everlasting desolati

Jeremiah 29:10 - "For so said the Lord: `For at the completion דְּבָרִי toward you, **to restore you to this pla**

Beginning of the Kingdom of Babylon - 3319

Babylon's subjugation of Jerusalem - 3320

Destruction of the first temple - 3338

***The prophet Jeremiah envisioned (25:12) the termination of Babylon following a period of 70 years. This prophecy began with Babylon's subjugation of Jerusalem in the year 3320, and ended when Cyrus called for the rebuilding of Jerusalem and a temple (Isa. 44:28-45:1) in the year 3390.**

**Nebuchadnezzer, king of Babylon, destroyed the first temple in the year 3338, 18 years after he subjugated Jerusalem in the year 3320.**

****70 WEEKS (of years) - Gabriel begins his prophecy to Daniel (9:24) with the revelation that "70 weeks" (490 years) have been decreed upon the Jewish people and Jerusalem, after which the Messianic Age can commence. The verses that follow contain a detailed description of what would transpire during this time, which spanned from the destruction of the First Temple until the destruction of the Second (3338-3829).**

**"Seven weeks" (of years) - Gabriel**

*In the year 3390, Daniel contemplated two critical prophecies in which Jeremiah spoke of Babylon's demise following 70 years (Jer. 25:12 and 29:10). Although both of these 70-year visions foretold the termination of the Babylon Empire, it was only the second prophecy (Jer. 29:10) that spoke of the restoration of the Jewish people to the Promised Land. When Daniel examined these two texts, however, he mistakenly thought that Jeremiah's two 70-year prophecies were speaking of an identical period of time. This misunderstanding caused him to draw three flawed conclusions. First, that the point to begin counting the 70 years for both prophecies was the year 3320, when Babylon conquered Jerusalem. Second, these prophecies must therefore end 70 years after Jerusalem's subjugation, in the year 3390, when Darius the Mede succeeded the throne. Third, because Jeremiah's second prophecy (Jer. 29:10) spoke of God restoring Israel after the completion of 70 years, Daniel concluded that the second temple would certainly be built in the year 3390, in the first year of Darius the Mede.

When Daniel realized that the year 3390 was at hand, and there was no sign of the impending redemption, he became deeply agitated. He thought that the sins of Jewry had caused the date to be delayed, or worse - canceled. This terrifying thought compelled Daniel to fast are in fact not identical, and each one of them referred to a separate, but overlapping, 70-year period of time. Whereas the prophecy of Jeremiah 25:12 was in fact referring to the 70-year time span that began in the year 3320, when Jerusalem was subjugated, the prophecy that promised the restoration of the Jewish people to their land (29:10) was not to begin for another 18 years.

Accordingly, Gabriel here relates to Daniel that in order to correctly ascertain when the Second Temple would be built, he must begin counting the 70 years "from the going forth of the WORD [דבר] (9:25)," which is "the WORD [דבר] of Jeremiah" that begins at "the destruction of Jerusalem (9:2)," in the year 3338. In fact, Jeremiah's prophecy of restoration (29:10) was fulfilled in the year 3408, 18 years later than Daniel had originally thought.

---

**The angel Gabriel responds to Daniel's prayerful inquiry of God by carefully outlining the course of events which was to unfold over a crucial period of time that spanned 490 years, or "70 weeks" (the Babylonian exile lasted 70 years, plus the 420 years which the Second Temple stood). Thus, the angel was not only revealing to Daniel when the Second Temple would be restored, but when it would be destroyed as well.

Gabriel also reveals that once these "70 weeks" were completed, the Messianic Age could begin. Thus, in verse 24, the angel describes six elements that will characterize the world in the Messianic Age: 1) termination of transgression 2) end of sin 3) removal of all iniquity 4) ushering in of everlasting righteousness 5) sealing of vision and prophet 6) anointing of the Holy of Holies. And once these 490 years are completed, it would indeed be up to each subsequent generation to turn back to God in order to bring about the glorious arrival of the messiah.

| | | |
|---|---|---|
| | 9 | |
| 3373 | 10 | Evil-meridach |
| 3374 | 11 | |
| 3375 | 12 | |
| 3376 | 13 | |
| 3377 | 14 | |
| 3378 | 15 | |
| 3379 | 16 | |
| 3380 | 17 | |
| 3381 | 18 | |
| 3382 | 19 | |
| 3383 | 20 | |
| 3384 | 21 | |
| 3385 | 22 | |
| 3386 | 23 | |
| 3387 | 1 | Belshazzar |
| 3388 | 2 | |
| 3389 | 3 | |
| 3390 | 1 | Darius the Mede |
| 3391 | 1 | Cyrus |
| 3392 | 2 | |
| 3393 | 3 / 1 | Ahasuerus |
| 3394 | 2 | |
| 3395 | 3 | |
| 3396 | 4 | |
| 3397 | 5 | |
| 3398 | 6 | |
| 3399 | 7 | |
| 3400 | 8 | |
| 3401 | 9 | |
| 3402 | 10 | |
| 3403 | 11 | |
| 3404 | 12 | |
| 3405 | 13 | |
| 3406 | 14 | |
| 3407 | 1 | Darius II (Persian) |
| 3408 | 2 | |

...upon that nation, says the Lord,

...**venty years** of Babylon I will remember you, and I will fulfil My good **WORD**

**Final events of Purim - 3405**

Building of the second temple - 3408

415 Years

| Emperor of Rome | | |
|---|---|---|
| Nero | 3823 | 10 |
| | 3824 | 11 |
| | 3825 | 12 |
| | 3826 | 13 |
| | 3827 | 14 |
| Galba; Otho; Vitellius | 3828 | Year of Three Emperors |
| Vespasian | 3829 | 1 |

Messianic Age

**...destroyed (9:2), an anointed ruler would command the Jewish people to return and rebuild Jerusalem (9:25). Indeed, after a half century passed, Cyrus, who God declared as His "anointed one," (Isaiah 45:1), ordered the Jews to return and rebuild Jerusalem and the holy sanctuary (Isaiah 44:28-45:1, 13; Ezra 1:2-3; II Chronicles 36:22-23).**

Cyrus calls for the city and temple to be rebuilt - 3391

5

**"Sixty two weeks" (of years) - In verse 9:25, the angel reveals to Daniel how, for a nearly four and a half centuries, Jerusalem would be "rebuilt, street and moat." Gabriel adds, however, that throughout these "62 weeks," the Holy City would endure "troubled times." Accordingly, the Second Temple period was filled with spiritual and political turbulence. In verse 9:26, the angel reveals that the "62 weeks" would tragically conclude with two watershed events. First, an anointed one (the high priest) would be cut off, and would cease his ecclesiastical functions. Second, the "people of the prince" (the legions of Vespasian and Titus) would come to destroy the Holy City and its sanctuary. Both of these tragic events occurred simultaneously, shortly after the 434 years, or "62 weeks" were completed.**

6

Sacrifice Ends

**Seven years before the Second Temple was destroyed, Rome permitted the Jews to offer sacrifices. This agreement, however, was broken 3½ years before Titus razed Herod's Temple in the year 3829 (Daniel 9:27).**

Destruction of the second temple 3829

# The following related article can be found in Part XV of this study guide:

# Part VIII

# Confused Texts and Testimonies

# Messianic Prophecies

## World Peace

**Isaiah 2:4**

And he shall judge among the nations, and shall rebuke many people; and they shall beat their swords into plowshares, and their spears into pruning hooks. Nation shall not lift up sword against nation, neither shall they learn war any more.

**Isaiah 11:6-8**

The wolf also shall dwell with the lamb, and the leopard shall lie down with the kid; [7]and the calf and the young lion and the fatling together....[8]And the sucking child shall play on the hole of the cobra....

**Micah 4:3-7**

He shall judge between many peoples, And rebuke strong nations afar off; They shall beat their swords into plowshares, And their spears into pruning hooks; Nation shall not lift up sword against nation, Neither shall they learn war any more. [4] But everyone shall sit under his vine and under his fig tree, And no one shall make *them* afraid; For the mouth of the Lord of hosts has spoken. [5] For all people walk each in the name of his god, But we will walk in the name of the Lord our God Forever and ever. [6] "In that day," says the Lord, "I will assemble the lame, I will gather the outcast And those whom I have afflicted; [7] I will make the lame a remnant, And the outcast a strong nation; So the Lord will reign over them in Mount Zion From now on, even forever.

**Zephaniah 3:12-16**

I will leave in your midst A meek and humble people, And they shall trust in the name of the Lord.
[13] The remnant of Israel shall do no unrighteousness And speak no lies, Nor shall a deceitful tongue be found in their mouth; For they shall feed *their* flocks and lie down, And no one shall make *them* afraid." [14] Sing, O daughter of Zion! Shout, O Israel! Be glad and rejoice with all *your* heart, O daughter of Jerusalem! [15] The Lord has taken away your judgments, He has cast out your enemy. The King of Israel, the Lord, *is* in your midst; You shall see[1] disaster no more. [16] In that day it shall be said to Jerusalem: "Do not fear; Zion, let not your hands be weak.

**Zechariah 8:3-6**

Thus said the Lord: I have returned to Zion, and I will dwell in Jerusalem. Jerusalem will be called the City of Faithfulness, and the mount of the Lord of Hosts the Holy Mount. [4] Thus said the Lord of Hosts: There shall yet be old men and women in the squares of Jerusalem, each with staff in hand because of their great age. [5] And the squares of the city shall be crowded with boys and girls playing in the squares. [6] Thus said the Lord of Hosts: Though it will seem impossible to the remnant of this people in those days, shall it also be impossible to Me? -- declares the Lord of Hosts.

## Universal Knowledge of God

**Isaiah 11:9**

For the earth shall be full of the knowledge of the Lord, as the waters cover the sea.

**Jeremiah 31:33**

No longer shall one teach his neighbor or shall one teach his brother, saying, "Know the Lord," for they shall all know Me, from their smallest to their greatest, says the Lord....

**Zechariah 8:20-23**

Thus said the Lord of Hosts: Peoples and the inhabitants of many cities shall yet come – [21] the inhabitants of on shall go to the other and say, "Let us go and entreat the favor of the Lord, let us seek the Lord of Hosts; I will go, too." [22] The many peoples and the multitude of nations shall come to seek the Lord of Hosts in Jerusalem and to entreat the favor of the Lord. [23] Thus said the Lord of Hosts: In those days, ten men from nations of every tongue will take hold -- they will take hold of every Jew by a corner of his cloak and say, "Let us go with you, for we have heard that God is with you."

**Zechariah 14:9**

And the Lord shall be king over all the earth: in that day shall there be one Lord, and His name one.

**Zephaniah 3:9**

For then I will make the peoples pure of speech, So that they all invoke the Lord by name And serve Him with one accord.

## Resurrection of the Dead

**Isaiah 26:19**

Thy dead men shall live, together with my dead body shall they arise. Awake and sing, ye that dwell in dust, for thy dew is as the dew of herbs, and the earth shall cast out the dead.

**Daniel 12:2**

And many of them that sleep in the dust of the earth shall awake, some to everlasting life, and some to shame and everlasting contempt.

**Ezekiel 37:12-13**

Therefore, prophesy and say to them, "So says the Lord God: Lo! I open your graves and cause you to come up out of your graves as My people, and bring you home to the land of Israel. [13]Then you shall know that I am the Lord, when I open your graves and lead you up out of your graves as My people.

# *Ingathering of Israel*

**Isaiah 11:12**

He will hold up a signal to the nations And assemble the banished of Israel, And gather the dispersed of Judah From the four corners of the earth.

**Isaiah 43:5-6**

I will bring thy seed from the east, and gather you from the west. I will say to the north, "Give up," and to the south, "Keep not back, bring My sons from far, and My daughter from the ends of the earth.

**Jeremiah 16:15**

But rather, "As the Lord lives who brought the Israelites out of the northland, and out of all the lands to which He had banished them." For I will bring them back to their land, which I gave to their fathers.

**Jeremiah 23:3**

And I Myself will gather the remnant of My flock from all the lands to which I have banished them, and I will bring them back to their pasture, where they shall be fertile and increase.

**Ezekiel 37:21-22**

And you shall declare to them: Thus said the Lord God: I am going to take the Israelite people from among the nations they have gone to, and gather them from every quarter, and bring them to their own land. [22] I will make them a single nation in the land, on the hills of Israel, and one king shall be king of them all. Never again shall they be two nations, and never again shall they be divided into two kingdoms.

(*see also Zech. 10:6*)

# *Building of the Third Temple*

**Ezekiel 37:26-28**

And I will set My sanctuary in the midst of them for evermore. [27]My temple also shall be with them. Yes, I will be their God and they shall be My people. And the heathen shall know that I the Lord do sanctify Israel, when My sanctuary shall be in the midst of them for evermore. *(see also Ez. 40-48; Is. 33:20)*

# *Elijah the Prophet Ushers in the Messianic Age*

**Malachi 3:23-24 (4:5-6)**

Behold, I will send you Elijah the prophet before the coming of the great and dreadful day of the Lord. And he shall turn the heart of the fathers to the children, and the heart of the children to their fathers....

## *John the Baptist Denies that He is Elijah*

**John 1:21**

And they asked him [John], "What then? Are you Elijah?" And he said, "I am not." "Are you that prophet?" And he answered, "No."

**Matthew 11:11-14**

"I tell you the truth: Among those born of woman there has not risen anyone greater than John the Baptist....[14]And if you are will to accept it, he is the Elijah who is to come."

## *Jesus Demands Alienation Within the Family*

"Think not that I have come to send peace on earth. I came not to bring peace on earth, but a sword. For I am come to set man at variance against his father, and the daughter against her mother, and the daughter in law against her mother in law. And a man's foes shall be they of his own household." ***Matthew 10:34-36***

# 70 = 75?

Now Stephen, ***a man full of God's Grace and power***, did great wonders and miraculous signs among the people. Opposition arose, however, from members of the Synagogue...These men began to argue with Stephen, but they could not stand up against ***his wisdom or the spirit*** by whom he spoke.

**Acts 6:8-10**

## The Septuagint On Genesis 46:27, Exodus 1:5, and Deuteronomy 10:22 (notice that in Deuteronomy 10:22, the original verse was left in tact, and, as a result, the text reads "seventy souls")

**Genesis 46:27**
And the sons of Joseph, who were born to him in the land of Egypt, were nine souls; all the souls of the house of Jacob who came with Joseph into Egypt, were **seventy-five (ἑβδομηκονταπέντε)** souls.

**Exodus 1:5**
But Joseph was in Egypt. And all the souls born of Jacob were **seventy-five (πέντε καὶ ἑβδομήκοντα** lit. five and seventy).

**Deuteronomy 10:22**
With **seventy** souls (ἑβδομήκοντα) your fathers went down into Egypt....

## *Christian Bible Says 75 People Went to Egypt*

**Acts 7:14-15**

Then sent Joseph, and called his father Jacob to him, and all his kindred, **threescore and fifteen** souls. [15]So Jacob went down into Egypt, and died, he, and our fathers.

## *Christian Bible says that the Tomb of the Patriarchs is in Shechem*

### Acts 7:16

And were carried over into **Shechem**, and laid in the sepulchre that Abraham bought for a sum of money of the sons of **Emmor**, the father of Shechem.

## *Torah States Only 70 People Went to Egypt*

### Genesis 46:27

And the sons of Joseph, which were born him in Egypt, were two souls: all the souls of the house of Jacob, which came into Egypt, were **threescore and ten**.

### Exodus 1:5

And all the souls that came out of the loins of Jacob were **seventy** souls: for Joseph was in Egypt already.

### Deuteronomy 10:22

Thy fathers went down into Egypt with **threescore and ten** persons; and now the Lord thy God hath made thee as the stars of heaven for multitude.

## *Torah States that the Tomb of the Patriarchs is located in Hebron, not Shechem*

### Genesis 23:17-19

And the field of Ephron, which was in Machpelah, which was before Mamre, the field, and the cave which was therein, and all the trees that were in the field, that were in all the borders round about, were made sure....And after this, Abraham buried Sarah his wife in the cave of the field of Machpelah before Mamre: the same is **Hebron** in the land of Canaan.

### Genesis 50:13

For his sons carried him into the land of Canaan, and buried him in the cave of the field of Machpelah, which Abraham bought with the field for a possession of a burying-place of Ephron the Hittite, before Mamre.

| I Chronicles Chapter 1-3 | Matthew Chapter 1 | Luke Chapter 3 |
|---|---|---|
| 1 Abraham | 1 Abraham | 1 Abraham |
| 2 Isaac | 2 Isaac | 2 Isaac |
| 3 Jacob | 3 Jacob | 3 Jacob |
| 4 Judah | 4 Judah | 4 Judah |
| 5 Perez | 5 Perez | 5 Perez |
| 6 Hezron | 6 Hezron | 6 Hezron |
| 7 Ram | 7 Ram | 7 Ram |
| 8 Amminadab | 8 Amminadab | 8 Amminadab |
| 9 Nahshon | 9 Nahshon | 9 Nahshon |
| 10 Salma | 10 Salma | 10 Salma |
| 11 Boaz | 11 Boaz | 11 Boaz |
| 12 Obed | 12 Obed | 12 Obed |
| 13 Jesse | 13 Jesse | 13 Jesse |
| 14 David | 14 David | 14 David |
| 15 Solomon | 15 Solomon | 15 Nathan |
| 16 Rehoboam | 16 Rehoboam | 16 Mattatha |
| 17 Abijah | 17 Abijah | 17 Menna |
| 18 Asa | 18 Asa | 18 Melea |
| 19 Jehoshaphat | 19 Jehoshaphat | 19 Eliakim |
| 20 Jehoram | 20 Jehoram | 20 Jonam |
| 21 Ahaziah | * | 21 Joseph |
| 22 Jehoash | | 22 Judas |
| 23 Amaziah | | 23 Symeon |
| 24 Azariah | 21 Uzziah | 24 Levi |
| 25 Jotham | 22 Jotham | 25 Matthat |
| 26 Ahaz | 23 Ahaz | 26 Jorim |
| 27 Hezekiah | 24 Hezekiah | 27 Eleizer |
| 28 Manasseh | 25 Manasseh | 28 Jesus |
| 29 Amon | 26 Amon | 29 Er |
| 30 Josiah | 27 Josiah | 30 Elmadam |
| 31 Jehoiakim | ** | 31 Cosam |
| 32 Jeconiah | 28 Jeconiah*** | 32 Addi |
| 33 Shealtiel | 29 Shealtiel | 33 Melchi |
| 34 Zerubbabel | 30 Zerubbabel | 34 Ner**** |
| 35 Hananiah | 31 Abiud | 35 Shealtiel |
| 36 Jeshaiah | 32 Eliakim | 36 Zeribbabel |
| 37 Rephaiah | 33 Azor | 37 Rhesa |
| 38 Arnan | 34 Zadok | 38 Joanan |
| 39 Obadiah | 35 Achim | 39 Joda |
| 40 Shecaniah | 36 Eliud | 40 Josech |
| 41 Shemaiah | 37 Eleazar | 41 Semein |
| 42 Neariah | 38 Matthan | 42 Mattathias |
| 43 Elioenai | 39 Jacob | 43 Maath |
| | 40 Joseph | 44 Naggai |
| | 41 Jesus | 45 Esli |
| | | 46 Nahum |
| | | 47 Amos |
| | | 48 Mattathias |
| | | 49 Joseph |
| | | 50 Jannai |
| | | 51 Melchi |
| | | 52 Levi |
| | | 53 Matthat |
| | | 54 Heli |
| | | 55 Joseph |
| | | 56 Jesus |

**Matthew 1:17**
So all the generations from Abraham to David are fourteen generations; and from David until the carrying away into Babylon are fourteen generations; and from the carrying away into Babylon unto Christ are fourteen generations.

**Luke 1:27**
To a virgin betrothed to a man whose name was Joseph, of the house of David.

## I Chronicles 3:11-12*, 15**, 16-17***

Joram his son, Ahaziah his son, Joash his son,
12 Amaziah his son,* Azariah his son, Jotham his son, 15 And
the sons of Josiah** were, the firstborn Johanan, the secon
Jehoiakim, the third Zedekiah, the fourth Shallum. 16 And th
sons of Jehoiakim: Jeconiah his son, Zedekiah his son. 17 A
the sons of Jeconiah;**** Assir, Shealtiel his son,

## Patrilineal Descent For Tribe Affiliation

### Numbers 1:18

And they assembled all the congregation togeth on the first day of the second month, and they declared the pedigrees after their families, **by their fathers' house** according to the number of names, from twenty years o and upward, by their polls.

## The Davidic Covenant Passes Exclusively Through King Solomon

### II Samuel 7:12-16

I [God] will set up your [David's] seed after you, tha
shall proceed out of your body, and I will establish **hi**
**[Solomon's] kingdom**. 13 He shall build a house for M
name, and I will establish the throne of **his kingdo**
**forever**. 14 I will be to him for a father, and he shall be to M
for a son; if he commits iniquity, I will chasten him with th
rod of men, and with the stripes of the children of men; 15 bu
My mercy shall not depart from him, as I took it from Sau
whom I put away before you. 16 And your house and you
kingdom shall be made sure forever before you; your thron
shall be established forever.

*(See also I Chr. 17:11-14, 22:9-10, 28:6-7; Ps. 89:29-3*

## The Curse on Jeconiah and His Descendants****

### Jeremiah 22:30

Thus saith the Lord, "Write ye this man [Jeconia childless, a man that shall not prosper in his days: for **n man of his seed shall prosper, sitting upon the thone c David, and ruling anymore in Judah."**

## I Timothy 1:4

Neither give heed to fables and endless genealogi minister questions, rather than godly edifying which is in fa so do.

## "A Ready Defense" by Josh McDowell, page 188



**And Mary said to the angel, "How can this be, since I am a virgin?"**

**And the angel answered and said to her, "The Holy Spirit, will come upon you, and the power of the Most High will overshadow you; and for that reason the holy offspring shall be called the Son of God . . . For nothing will be impossible with God" (Luke 1:27-37, NASB).**

**The virgin birth is set down in the Bible as an historical fact. The writers who recorded the story were Matthew–an eyewitness to the events in the life of Jesus–and Luke, the doctor, who presents many things in the life of Christ from Mary's viewpoint. The passages in both Matthew and Luke are authentic, with no evidence at all that they were later additions to the text.**

**The doctrine of the virgin birth has been believed by the church from its inception. Ignatius, who lived at the start of the second century, wrote to the Ephesians: "For our God, Jesus the Christ, was conceived in the womb by Mary, according to a dispensation, of the seed of David but also of the Holy Ghost."**

### A Necessary Fact of History

**There are several reasons the virgin birth was a necessity. The Bible teaches that the Word who became flesh was with God from the very beginning (John 1:1). The fact of the pre-existence of Christ is confirmed many times in the New Testament (John 8:58; Philippians 2:5-11; Colossians 1:15,16).**

**When Jesus came into the world, He was not a newly created individual such as we are, but was rather the eternal Son of God. To be born into this world, of the virgin Mary, required divine intervention, and this is exactly what the Gospels record.**

**Another reason Jesus needed to be virgin-born was His sinless nature. A basic New Testament teaching is that from the day He was born until the day He died, Jesus was without sin. To be a perfect sacrifice, He must Himself be perfect–without sin. Since our race is contaminated with sin, a miraculous entrance into the world would be required, hence the virgin birth.**

**Moreover, if Jesus had been sired by Joseph, He would not have been able to claim the legal rights to the throne of David. According to the prophecy of Jeremiah 22:28-30, there could be no king in Israel who was a descendant of King Jeconiah, and Matthew 1:12 relates that Joseph was from the line of Jeconiah. Jesus would have been of the cursed lineage.**

**The virgin birth of Christ is not only an historical fact, but it was also a *necessary* historical fact when one considers all the data.**

## "The Ryrie Study Bible (NIV)", page 1,315



### THE GOSPEL ACCORDING TO MATTHEW

**I THE PERSON OF THE KING, 1:1–4:25**

**A His Background, 1:1–17**

1 [a]A record of the genealogy of Jesus Christ the son of David,[b] the son of Abraham:[c]

2 Abraham was the father of Isaac,[d]
Isaac the father of Jacob,[e]
Jacob the father of Judah and his brothers,[f]
3 Judah the father of Perez and Zerah, whose mother was Tamar,[g]
Perez the father of Hezron,
Hezron the father of Ram,
4 Ram the father of Amminadab,
Amminadab the father of Nahshon,
Nahshon the father of Salmon,
5 Salmon the father of Boaz, whose mother was Rahab,[h]
Boaz the father of Obed, whose mother was Ruth,
Obed the father of Jesse,
6 and Jesse the father of King David.[i]

David was the father of Solomon, whose mother had been Uriah's wife,[j]
7 Solomon the father of Rehoboam,
Rehoboam the father of Abijah,
Abijah the father of Asa,
8 Asa the father of Jehoshaphat,
Jehoshaphat the father of Jehoram,
Jehoram the father of Uzziah,
9 Uzziah the father of Jotham,
Jotham the father of Ahaz,
Ahaz the father of Hezekiah,
10 Hezekiah the father of Manasseh,[k]
Manasseh the father of Amon,
Amon the father of Josiah,
11 and Josiah the father of Jeconiah[a] and his brothers at the time of the exile to Babylon.[l]

12 After the exile to Babylon:
Jeconiah was the father of Shealtiel,[m]
Shealtiel the father of Zerubbabel,[n]
13 Zerubbabel the father of Abiud,
Abiud the father of Eliakim,
Eliakim the father of Azor,
14 Azor the father of Zadok,
Zadok the father of Akim,
Akim the father of Eliud,
15 Eliud the father of Eleazar,
Eleazar the father of Matthan,
Matthan the father of Jacob,
16 and Jacob the father of Joseph, the husband of

*1:1 [a] *1:1-17pp — Lk 3:23-38; 1:3-6pp — Ru 4:18-22; 1:7-11pp — 1Ch 3:10-17* [b] 2Sa 7:12-16; Isa 9:6,7; 11:1; Jer 23:5,6; S Mt 9:27; Lk 1:32,69; Rev 22:16 [c] Ge 22:18; S Gal 3:16
1:2 [d] Ge 21:3,12 [e] Ge 25:26 [f] Ge 29:35; 49:10
1:3 [g] Ge 38:27-30
1:5 [h] S Heb 11:31
1:6 [i] 1Sa 16:1; 17:12 [j] 2Sa 12:24
1:10 [k] 2Ki 20:21
*1:11 [l] 2Ki 24:14-16; Jer 27:20; 40:1; Da 1:1, 2
1:12 [m] 1Ch 3:17 [n] 1Ch 3:19; Ezr 3:2
*1:16

[a]11 That is, Jehoiachin; also in verse 12

**1:1** *Jesus Christ.* The name "Jesus" is from the Greek (and Latin) for the Hebrew "Jeshua" (Joshua), which means "the Lord is salvation." "Christ" is from the Greek for the Hebrew *Meshiah* (Messiah), meaning "anointed one." S[illegible] *of David* was a highly popular messianic ti[illegible] the times. The genealogy is here traced th[illegible]gh Joseph, Jesus' legal (though not natural) [illegible]ther, and it establishes His claim and right to the throne of David (1:6). The genealogy in Luke 3:23–38 is evidently that of Mary, though some believe it is also Joseph's, by assuming that Matthan (Matt. 1:15) and Matthat (Luke 3:24) were the same person and Jacob (Matt. 1:16) and Heli (Luke 3:23) were brothers (one being Joseph's father and the other his uncle). See note at Luke 3:23.

**1:11** *Jeconiah.* Jehoiachin, king of Judah, who was taken into captivity by Nebuchadnezzar in 597 B.C. In the Heb., Jeremiah contracted "Jeconiah" to "Coniah" (Jer. 22:24, 28; 37:1). A curse was pronounced on Coniah that none of his descendants would prosper sitting on the throne of David. Had our Lord been the natural son of Joseph, He could not have been successful on the throne of David because of this curse. But since He came through Mary's lineage, He was not affected by this curse.

**1:16** *of whom.* The word is feminine singular, indicating clearly that Jesus was born of Mary

| | Matthew | Mark | Luke | John |
|---|---|---|---|---|
| Who carried the cross? | Simon of Cyrene (27:32) | Simon of Cyrene (15:21) | Simon of Cyrene (23:26) | Jesus alone (19: |
| A) At what time was Jesus crucified?<br><br>B) On which day was Jesus crucified? | A) Not mentioned in Matthew<br><br>B) The first day of Passover, 15th day of Nissan.* (26:20-30) *(See* below, left)* | A) 9:00 am — "It was the THIRD hour when they crucified him." (15:25)<br>B) The first day of Passover, 15th day of Nissan.* (14:17-25) *(see* below, left)* | A) Not mentioned in Luke<br><br>B) The first day of Passover, 15th day of Nissan.* (22:14-23) *(see* below, left)* | A) 12:00 pm noon — Jesus not crucified until after SIXTH hour! (19:14<br>B) The day before Passo 14th day of Nissan.* (13:1 18:28, 19:14) *(see* below,* |
| A) Did Jesus drink?<br>B) What was in the drink? | A) YES<br>B) Wine mixed with gall. (27:34) | A) NO<br>B) Jesus was offered wine mixed with myrrh (15:23) | A) Not mentioned in Luke<br>B) Vinegar (sour wine) (23:36) | A) YES<br>B) Vinegar (sour wine) (19:29 |
| Did either one of the two thieves believe in Jesus? | Neither one of the thieves believed in Jesus. (27:44) | Neither one of the thieves believed in Jesus. (15:32) | In Luke's story, only one thief does not believe, but ONE DOES! (23:39-41) | Not mentioned in John |
| What were Jesus' last dying words on the cross? | "*Eli, Eli, lama sabachthani*?" That is, "My God, my God, why hast thou forsaken me?" (27:46) | "*Eloi, Eloi, lama sabachthani?*" Meaning, "My God, my God, why hast thou forsaken me?" (15:34) | "Father, into thy hands I commend my spirit." (23:46) | "It is finished" (19 |
| When did Mary prepare the spices? | Not mentioned in Matthew | Mary prepared the spices after the Sabbath was over. (16:1) | Mary prepared the spices before the Sabbath started. (23:56) | Nicodemus, not Mary, pared the spices before Sabbath. (19 |
| Had the sun yet risen when the women came to the tomb? | It was toward dawn of the first day of the week. (28:1) | YES — They came to the tomb when the sun had risen. (16:2) | At early dawn they went to the tomb (24:1) | NO—-Mary came early t tomb, while it was ST DARK. (2 |
| How many days, and how many nights, was Jesus in the tomb? | 3 days and 2 nights** (28:1) | 3 days & 2 nights** (16:2) | 3 days and 2 nights** (24:1) | 2 days and 2 nights** (2 |
| A) How many people came to the tomb?<br>B) Who were they? | A) TWO<br>B) Mary Magdalene and the other Mary (28:1) | A) THREE<br>B) Mary Magdalene, Mary the mother of James and Salome (16:1) | A) FOUR+<br>B) Mary Magdalene, Mary mother of James, Joanna and other women (24:10) | A) ONE<br>B) Only Mary Magdalene c to the tomb. (2 |
| Was the stone removed when the women arrived at the tomb? | NO — After the women arrive at the tomb, an angel rolls back the stone. (28:1-2) | YES — When they arrived, the stone had already been rolled away. (16:4) | YES — When they arrived, the stone had already been taken away. (24:2) | YES — When Mary arr the stone had already taken away. (2 |
| A) How many angels were at the tomb?<br>B) What were they (was he) doing?<br>C) Where were they (was he)? | A) One angel<br><br>B) Sitting (28:2)<br><br>C) On the stone, which he rolled away from the tomb | A) One young man<br><br>B) Sitting (16:5)<br><br>C) On the right side, inside the tomb | A) Two men<br><br>B) Standing (24:4)<br><br>C) By them, inside the tomb | The angels are completely sent when Mary comes to tomb. When Mary arrive second time, she finds angels sitting; one at the and one at the feet (20:1-2 |
| What are the angels' instructions to Mary and the others at the tomb? (No other people in the Book of John; Mary was alone – 20:1-2.) | "He is not here; for he has risen...go quickly and tell his disciples he is going before you to the Galilee!"*** (28:6-7) | "Do not be amazed...he has risen...But go tell his disciples and Peter he is going before you to Galilee!"*** (16:6-7) | In Luke's story (24:5-7), the women are specifically not instructed to go to the Galilee, but to "Stay in Jerusalem!"*** (24:49) See also — "He commanded them that they should not leave Jerusalem!" (Acts 1:4)<br>Luke's post-resurrection tale does not permit any of his followers to leave Jerusalem because Luke must have the apostles stay in Jerusalem for the Pentecost (Acts 2:1). | The angels only ask "Wh you weeping woman?" As M responds, she turns around sees Jesus standing there.<br>Completely contradicting three Synoptic Gospels, Jo story (20:2) has Mary cluele to what happened to Jesus' when she returns to the disc from the empty tomb. Ther no angels giving instructio the women in John's story. the contrary, in the fo Gospel, it is Jesus, not the tw gels, who instructs Mary a the resurrection! (20:1. |

*Because all three synoptic Gospels insist that the Last Supper was a Passover Seder, they must therefore maintain that the crucifixion occurred on the first day of Passover, rather than the eve of Passover as the Book of John claims (see pages 365-370).

**Although Jesus had claimed that he would be in the tomb for "three days and three nights"! (Matthew 12:40)

***Matthew (28:16) and Mark's (16:7) post-resurrection story has the apostles immediately depart Jerusalem, and go to the Galilee, which is about an 80-90 mile journey. Luke's narrative, on the other hand, insists that the apostles were never told to go to the Galilee and never did depart Jerusalem! Because the anonymous person who wrote the Book of Luke authored the Book of Acts as well, his story was written in a manner that would keep the disciples gathered in Jerusalem after the crucifixion in order to form the new Jerusalem church (Luke 24:5-7, 49; Acts 1:4).

| | Matthew/Paul | Mark | Luke | John |
|---|---|---|---|---|
| s Mary wish to he disciples what happened? | YES—- "They departed quickly...and ran to tell the disciples." (28:8) | NO— "They said nothing to anyone; for they were afraid." (16:8) | YES — "Returning from the tomb, they told all this to the eleven..." (24:9) | YES— Mary Magdalene tells the disciples, "I have seen the Lord." (20:18) |
| r seeing the ls, whom does y meet first, Jesus e disciples? | Jesus* (28:9) | Jesus* (16:9) | the Disciples* (24:4-9) | Jesus* (20:14) |
| To whom does s make his first arance? Where does this earance take e? | A) The two Marys<br>B) On the way to Jerusalem, after leaving the tomb (28:9)<br>**Paul — 1 Corinthians**<br>A) Cephas (Peter) 15:5 B) ? | A) Only Mary Magdalene<br>B) Mark's story does not indicate where this appearance takes place. It is quite clear, however, that it occurs sometime after Mary fled the tomb. (16:8-9) | A) Cleopas and another**<br>B) Emmaus** (24:13, 18) | A) Only Mary Magdalene<br>B) At the tomb (20:1, 11-14) |
| ary permitted to h Jesus after the rrection? | YES — ".they came and held him by his feet, and worshiped him." (28:9) | Not mentioned in Mark | YES — "Behold my hands and my feet...handle me and see...." (24:39; 1 John 1:1) | No — Jesus said to her, "Touch me not; for I am not yet ascended to my Father...." (20:17) |
| many times does s appear after the rrection? | <u>Two Times</u><br>1st) 28:9-10 2nd) 28:17-20<br>**Paul — 1 Corinthians**<br><u>Six Times</u><br>1st and 2nd) 1 Cor. 15:5<br>3rd) 1 Cor. 15:6<br>4th and 5th) 1 Cor. 15:7<br>6th) 1 Cor. 15:8 | <u>Three Times</u><br>1st) 16:9<br>2nd) 16:12** (see** above, right)<br>3rd) 16:14-18 | <u>Two Times</u><br>1st) 24:13-31<br>2nd) 24:36-51 | <u>Four Times</u><br>1st) 20:14-17 3rd) 20:26-29<br>2nd) 20:19-23*** 4th) 21:1-23 |
| re whom, and in t chronological r, do these appeaes take place? | 1st) Mary Magdalene and the other Mary. (28:9)<br>2nd) 11 disciples**** (28:16)<br>**Paul**<br><u>1 Corinthians</u><br>1st) Cephas (Peter) 15:5<br>2nd) All 12 apostles**** 15:5<br>3rd) 500 people 15:6<br>4th) James 15:7<br>5th) All 12 apostles 15:7<br>6th) Paul 15:8 | 1st) Mary Magdalene (16:9)<br>2nd) Two strolling followers** (16:12) (see** above, right)<br>3rd) 11 disciples**** (16:14) | 1st) Cloepas and another unknown follower. (24:13)<br>2nd) Eleven disciples**** "...and them that were with them." (24:33) | 1st) Mary Magdalene (20:14)<br>2nd) Ten disciples**** (Thomas was not there) (20:24)<br>3rd) Eleven disciples (20:26)<br>4th) Peter, Thomas, the two sons of Zebedee (James and John), Nathanael and two other disciples. (21:2) |
| ere do these earances take e? | 1st) Leaving the tomb, going to the disciples. (28:8)<br>2nd) On a mountain in the Galilee. (28:16)<br>(But some doubted it! —28:17) | 1st) After fleeing the tomb (16:8-9)<br>2nd) As they walked to the country (16:12)<br>3rd) At a meal (16:14) | 1st) Emmaus (24:13)<br>2nd) Jerusalem (24:33, 49), <u>NOT</u> in the Galilee, as Matthew would have us believe (Mt. 28:6-7, 16) | 1st) At the tomb (20:14)<br>2nd & 3rd) In Jerusalem, behind closed doors. (20:18-29)<br>4th) The Sea of Tiberias (21:1) |

***Entirely contradicting Luke's post-resurrection story, Matthew, Mark and John all insist that Mary met Jesus before she was able to tell any of the disciples what had happened (Matthew 28:8; Mark 16:9; John 20:14), whereas Luke asserts that Mary revealed all to the disciples before ever encountering Jesus! — Luke 24:4-10**

****Contradicting Mark's story, Luke asserts (24:34) that when the two followers who met Jesus on the road to Emmaus returned to Jerusalem and told the eleven about their encounter, the disciples declared "It is true!," whereas Mark insists that when the two reported their encounter, the disciples did not believe! —Mark 16:13**

*****Contradicting Luke's post-resurrection story entirely, John has the apostles receive the Holy Spirit on the first Easter Sunday (John 20:22), whereas Luke insists that the Holy Spirit was bestowed on the Pentecost, fifty days latter! — Acts 1:5, 8; 2:1-4**

******According to Matthew, Mark and Luke, Jesus made this appearance to all the eleven surviving disciples. Paul has this event take place in the presence of all twelve apostles (1 Corinthians 15:5), although Judas had long since died (Matthew 27:5; Acts 1:18). Contrary to all this, John's story places only ten disciples at the scene, Thomas being absent! — John 20:24**

# Luther on Jesus' Genealogy (and the Jews)

## Of the Unknowable Name and The Generations of Christ

By Martin Luther — 1543

From the beginning of the gospel, as St. Luke and St. Mark wrote it, the question has arisen: why the two apostles have told the story of the origins of the family of our Lord Jesus Christ so differently (or, as many have explained it, so contradicted by one another?) and it is peculiar that both agree upon the lineage or origins of these persons and end with Joseph and not with Mary and Christ; from this the wise sought to conclude it is not proved with that that Christ is of the family of David, because he does not come from Joseph, whom the apostles trace as coming directly from the line of David, and then suddenly abandon the same Joseph and substitute Mary....

First, to answer the Jews, if anyone even wants to get into an argument with them. Since the Jew moved me the last time to write about the Jews and touched upon this point: it cannot be proved that Jesus is of the tribe of Judah, because the apostle Matthew traces the tribe of Judah to Joseph and not to Mary; therefore he could not be Messiah as proved by the tribe of Judah and David. Prickly and poisonous are the snakes and make every effort to make our books appear wrong. For they do not ask because they wish to learn from us and know the truth, but to bother and heckle us with such questions — with scorn and derision of our beliefs as if we could not prove it.

Therefore one should step on the heads of these poisonous snakes and answer in the coarsest and rawest manner, defying the Devil, that Mary, the mother of Jesus, is of the tribe of Judah and the House of David says not only the apostle Matthew, (about whom they laugh) but even Moses, the first to say it after whom all the prophets agreed together. And if we Christians otherwise had nothing of the Old Testament, other than Moses, then we would have enough, easily enough, to prove that Mary must be of the tribe of Judah and the House of David so that all devils and the whole world cannot overthrow. (Keep quiet the miserable, screaming Jews.)....

Yes, here one encounters resistance from the Jews: they don't want to have Jesus as the Messiah, therefore they bother us with their poisonous, slanderous goads about Joseph, Mary; for they are hardly concerned as to whether Mary is of the House of David or not. And even if they had seen it themselves, that she was born of David, like Solomon and his other Children, still they would not believe that Jesus, her son, was the Messiah. They are concerned with the son, whom they do not want; they know, the knaves and lying mouths, that if Jesus is the Messiah, then there is no question that Maria is of the house of David.

Excerpts from "Vom Schem Hamphoras Und Vom Geschlecht Christi," By Martin Luther; *The Jew in Christian Theology,* Gerhard Falk, McFarland and Company, Inc., Jefferson, NC andLondon, 1931.

# Deuteronomy 4:32-40

You might inquire about times long past, going
back to the time that God created man on earth,
[exploring] one end of the heavens to the other, see if
anything as great as this has ever happened, or if the like
has ever been heard. 33 Has any nation ever heard God
speaking out of fire, as you have, and still survived?
34 Has God ever done miracles, bringing one nation out of
another nation, with tremendous miracles, signs, wonders,
war, a mighty hand and outstretched arm, and terrifying
phenomena, as God did for you in Egypt before you very
eyes? 35 **You are the ones who have been shown, so that
you will know** that God is the Supreme Being, and there
is none besides Him. 36 From the heavens, He let you hear
His voice admonishing you, and on earth He showed you
His great fire, so that you heard His words from the fire.
37 It was because He loved your fathers, and chose their
children after them, that [God] Himself brought you out
of Egypt with His great power. 38 He will drive away
before you nations that are greater and stronger than you,
so as to bring you to their lands, and give them to you as
a heritage, as [He is doing] today. 39 Realize it today and
ponder it in you heart: God is the Supreme Being in
heaven above and on earth beneath — there is no other.
40 Keep His decrees and commandments that I am prese-
nting to you today, so that He will be good to you and
your children after you. Then you will endure for a long
time in the land that God your Lord is giving you for all
time.

No ancient people of the East has had a stranger history than the Jews...The history of no ancient people should be so valuable, if we could only recover it and understand it.... Stranger still, the ancient religion of the Jews survives, when all the religions of every ancient race of the pre-Christian world have disappeared....

*Again it is strange that the living religions of the world all build on religious ideas derived from the Jews*...This then is the problem offered by the Jews to the historian. The great matter is not, "What happened?" but "Why did it happen?" Why does this race continue? Why does Judaism live? How did it really begin? These questions will not be answered here.... There lay the uniqueness of the Jews.

Glover, T.R., Professor at Queen's University Kingston, Ontario, *The Ancient World*. Penguin Books: Baltimore, 1964. Pages 184-191.

# The following related articles can be found in Part XV of this study guide:

## Part IX

# The Oral Law

**Leviticus 26:46**

These are the decrees, the ordinances, and the ***Torahs*** that the Lord gave, between Himself and the Children of Israel, at Mount Sinai, through Moses.

**Hebrew Text**

(*plural*) אֵלֶּה הַחֻקִּים וְהַמִּשְׁפָּטִים וְהַתּוֹרֹת
בֵּינוֹ וּבֵין בְּנֵי אֲשֶׁר נָתַן ה' יִשְׂרָאֵל בְּהַר
סִינַי בְּיַד מֹשֶׁה:

## Rosh Hashanah

*(A Day of Blowing?)*

**Numbers 29:1**

And in the seventh month, on the first day of the month, you shall have a holy convocation, you shall do no manner of work, it is a **day of blowing** for you.

---

## Yom Kippur

*(You Shall Afflict Your Souls?)*

**Leviticus 16:31**

It is a Sabbath of solemn rest for you, and *you shall afflict your souls*, it is a statute forever.

---

## Zechariah Enumerates Four Jewish Fast Days

**Zechariah 8:19**

So said the Lord of Hosts: The fast of the fourth [month][1], and the fast of the fifth [month][2], the fast of the seventh [month][3], and the fast of the tenth [month][4] shall be for the house of Judah for joy and happiness and for happy holidays; so love truth and peace.

[1] The fast of Tammuz, which commemorates the breaching of the wall of Jerusalem. [2] The fast of Av, when both Temples were destroyed. [3] The fast of the assassination of Gedaliah. [4] The fast of Teveth, which commemorates the siege of Jerusalem by the king of Babylon.

## Sabbath Observance

*(Do Not Do Any Work?)*

**Exodus 20:8-11**

Remember the Sabbath day to sanctify it. Six days shall you work and accomplish all your work; but the seventh day is Sabbath to the Lord, your God; you shall not do any work...for in six days the Lord made the heavens and the earth, the sea and all that is in them, and He rested on the seventh day. Therefore, the Lord blessed the Sabbath day and sanctified it.
*(see Exodus 31:12-17)*

*(Do Not Leave Your Place?)*

**Exodus 16:29-30**

Let every man remain in his place; let no man leave his place on the seventh day. The people rested on the seventh day.

*(Restrain Your Foot?)*

**Isaiah 58:13-14**

If you restrain your foot because of the Sabbath, from performing your affairs on My holy day, and you call the Sabbath a delight, the holy of the Lord honored, and you honor it by not doing your wonted ways, by not pursuing your affairs and speaking words. Then you shall delight with the Lord...for the mouth of the Lord has spoken.

## The Almighty Declares That His Testimonies Were Clearly Transmitted to the Jewish People

**Isaiah 45:19**

**I [God] have not spoken in secret**, or in a place of the land of darkness. I did not say to the seed of Jacob "seek me in vain." I, Hashem, speak righteousness, I declare things that are upright.

## Prohibition of Consuming Food and Wine Prepared a Gentile

**Daniel 1:3-16**

The king [Nebuchadnessar] told Ashpenaz, the chief of his officers, to bring from the children of Israel, from the royal seed, and from the nobles, youths in whom there was no blemish; good-looking, skillful in all wisdom, discriminating in knowledge, perceptive in learning, and who had the stamina to stand in the king's palace; and to teach them the script and language of the Chaldeans.

And the king provided for them a daily portion from the king's food and from his wine to nurture them for three years, after which they should stand before the king. Among them, from the children of Judah, were Daniel, Chanayah, Mishael, and Azaryah....

Daniel resolved not to be defiled by the king's food nor by his wine, and he asked the chief officer that he not be defiled. God granted Daniel favor and mercy before the chief officer, and the chief officer said to Daniel, "I fear my lord the king, who has provided you food and your drinks. For why should he see your faces more depressed than the youths like yourselves, and you will forfeit my head to the king?" So Daniel said to the steward whom the chief officer had assigned to Daniel, Chananyah, Mishael, and Azaryah, "Please test your servants for ten days, and let them give us pulse [raw seeds, peas, beans, etc.] to eat and water to drink. Then let our appearance and the appearance of the youths who eat the king's food be seen by you; in accord with what you will see, act toward your servants."

He heeded them in this matter and tested them for ten days. At the end of ten days they looked better and fatter than all the youths eating the king's food. The stew-ard would take their food and wine, and give them pulse.

## Obligation to Pray Three Times A Day

**Daniel 6:3-13**

Now Daniel so distinguished himself among the administrators and the satraps by his exceptional qualities that the king planned to set him over the whole kingdom. At this, the administrators and the satraps tried to find grounds for charges against Daniel in his conduct of government affairs, but thy were unable to do so. They could find no corruption in him, because he was trustworthy and neither corrupt nor negligent. Finally these men said, "We will never find any basis for charges against this man Daniel unless it has something to do with the law of his God...."

The advisors and the governors have conferred that the king should issue an edict and enforce the decree that anyone who prays to any god or man during the next thirty days, except to you, O king, shall be thrown into the lions' den. Now, O king, issue the decree and put it in writing so that it cannot be altered.... So King Darius put the decree in writing. Now when Daniel learned that the decree had been published, he went home to his upstairs room where the windows opened toward Jerusalem. **Three times a day he got down on his knees and prayed**, giving thanks to God, just as he had done before. Then these men went as a group and found Daniel praying and asking God for help. So they went to the king and spoke to him about his royal decree: "Did you not publish a decree that during the next thirty days anyone who prays to any god or man except to you, O king, would be thrown into the lions' den?"....

Then they said to the king, "Daniel, who is one of the exiles from Judah, pays no attention to you, O king, or to the decree you put in writing. **He still prays three times a day**."

## The Torah Admonishes the Jewish People To Follow the Decrees of the Sages of Israel

**Deuteronomy 17:8-11**

If a matter arises that is too hard for you to judge, between degrees of guilt of bloodshed, between one judgement or another, or between one punishment or another, matters of controversy within your gates, then you shall arise and go up to the place which the Lord your God chooses. And you shall come to the priests, the Levites, and to the judge in those days, and inquire of them; they shall pronounce the word of judgement. You shall do according to the sentence which they pronounce upon you in that place which the Lord chooses. And you shall be careful to do according to all that they order you. According to the teaching that they will teach you and according to the judgement that they will say to you, shall you do; do not deviate from the word that they will tell you, right or left.

## *Shechitah* — Ritual Slaughtering

**Deuteronomy 12:21**

If the place that the Lord, your God, will choose to place His Name will be far from you, you may slaughter from your cattle and your flocks that the Lord has given you as I have commanded you, and you may eat in your cities according to your heart's entire desire.

**The special method of slaughtering animals, called *Shehitah*, consists of an incision made across the neck of the animal or fowl by a qualified person especially trained for ritual slaughter, with a special knife that is razor-sharp and has a smooth edge with absolutely no nicks. The cutting must be made by moving the knife in a single swift and uninterrupted sweep, and not by pressure or by stabbing. The cut severs the main arteries, rendering the animal unconscious and permitting the blood to drain from the body. The slaughterer (shohet) recites a prayer before the act of shehitah.**

**Objection has sometimes been raised to this method of slaughter on grounds of cruelty. The sight of the struggling animal aroused the concern of humane societies, and in some European countries this resulted in legislation forbidding shehitah. Scientific opinion indicates, however, that severance of the carotid arteries and Jugular vein by one swift movement results in almost immediate loss of consciousness, and the afterstruggle is reflex muscular action.**

***Britannica Encyclopedia, "Kosher," 1990, vol 6, page 969.***

## *Tefillin*

**Exodus 13:9**

And it shall be for you a **sign** (לְאוֹת) on your arm and a reminder between your eyes — so that the Lord's Torah may be in your mouth — for with a strong hand the Lord removed you from Egypt.

**Exodus 13:16**

And it shall be a *sign* (לְאוֹת) upon your arm, and an **ornament** (לְטוֹטָפֹת) between your eyes, for with a strong hand the Lord removed us from Egypt.

**Deuteronomy 6:8**

Bind them as a *sign* (לְאוֹת) upon your arm and let them be **ornaments** (לְטוֹטָפֹת) between your eyes.

**Deuteronomy 11:18**

You shall place these words of Mine upon your heart and upon your soul; you shall bind them for a **sign** (לְאוֹת) upon your arm and let them be an **ornament** (לְטוֹטָפֹת) between your eyes.

# First Century Christianity Did Not Question the Authority of The Oral Law

**Matthew 23:1-3**

Then Jesus spoke to the multitudes and to his disciples, saying, "**The scribes and the Pharisees sit in Moses' seat**: therefore all that they tell you, do and observe...."

**Mark 2:23-26**

And it came about that he [Jesus] was passing through the grainfields on the Sabbath, and his disciples began to make their way alone while picking the heads of grain. And the Pharisees were saying to him, "See here, why are they doing what is not lawful on the Sabbath?" And he said to them, "Have you never read what David did when he was in need and became hungry, he and his companions: how he entered the house of God in the time of **Abiathar** the high priest, and ate the consecrated bread, which is not lawful for anyone to eat except the priests, and he gave it also to those who were with him?"

**I Samuel 21:1-4**

Then David came to Nob to *Ahimelech the priest*; and Ahimelech came trembling to meet David, and said to him, "Why are you alone and no one with you?" And David said to **Ahimelech** the priest, "The king has commissioned me with a matter, and said to me, 'Let no one know anything about the matter on which I am sending you and with which I have commissioned you; and I have directed the young men to a certain place.' Now therefore, what do you have on hand? Give me five loaves of bread, or whatever can be found." And the priest answered David and said, "There is no ordinary bread on hand, but there is consecrated bread...."

## "Salvation is of the Jews"

**John 4:19-22**

The [Samaritan] woman said to him, "Sir, I perceive that you are a prophet. Our fathers worshiped on this mountain [Mount Gerizim], and you Jews say that in Jerusalem is the place where one ought to worship." Jesus said to her, "....You worship what you do not know; we know what we worship, for salvation is of the Jews."

# The Prophets Warn the Jewish People To Keep the Oral Law

## The Prohibition of Purchasing and Selling on the Sabbath Day

**Nehemiah 10:30-32**

They held with their brethren, their noblemen, and entered the curse and the oath to follow the Law of God, which was given through Moses, the servant of God, and to keep and perform all the commandments of the Lord our God, and His ordinances and His statutes. And that we shall not give our daughters to the peoples of the land, and we shall not take their daughters for our sons. And as for the peoples of the land who bring merchandise and all grains on the Sabbath day to sell — we shall not purchase from them on the Sabbath or on holy days, and we shall abandon [the land] during the seventh year [and] the loan given by every hand.

---

## The Prohibition of Treading Winepresses, Carrying, and Selling on the Sabbath Day

**Nehemiah 13:15-18**

In those days, I saw in Judea [people] treading winepresses on the Sabbath and bringing stacks [of grain] and loading them on donkeys, and also wine, grapes, figs, and all types of loads and bringing them to Jerusalem on the Sabbath day, and I warned them on the day they sold provisions. The Tyrians [who] sojourned there were bringing fish and all [types of] merchandise and selling on the Sabbath to the people of Judea and Jerusalem. I quarreled with the dignitaries of Judea, and I said to them, "What is this bad thing that you are doing — profaning the Sabbath day? Did not your ancestors do this, and our God brought upon us all this calamity, and upon this city, and you are increasing the wrath upon Israel by profaning the Sabbath?"

## Jewish Identity Passes Exclusively Through the Mother

**Ezra 10:2-3**

"We have betrayed our God, and we have taken in foreign wives of the peoples of the land, but now there is hope for Israel concerning this. Now, let us make a covenant with God to cast out all the wives and their offspring, by the counsel of the Lord, those who hasten to [perform] the commandment of our God, and according the Law it shall be done."

## The Prohibition of Carrying on the Sabbath Day

**Jeremiah 17:19-24**

So said the Lord to me. "Go and stand in the gate of the children of the people, in which the kings of Judah come, and out of which they go, and in all the gates of Jerusalem. And you shall say to them: 'Hearken to the word of the Lord, O kings of Judah and and all the inhabitants of Jerusalem, who come into these gates. So said the Lord: Beware for your souls and carry no burden on the sabbath day, nor bring into the gates of Jerusalem. Neither shall you take a burden out of your houses on the Sabbath day nor shall you perform any labor, and you shall hallow the Sabbath day as I commanded your fore-fathers.' But they did not listen, neither did they bend their ears, and they hardened their nape not to listen and not to receive instruction. And it shall be if you listen to Me, says the Lord, not to bring any burden unto the gates of this city on the Sabbath day and to hallow the Sabbath day not to perform any labor thereon, then shall there enter into the gates of this city kings and princes sitting on David's throne...."

# Identifying Signs of Clean Animals

**Leviticus 11:1-8**

God spoke to Moses and Aaron, telling them: [2]Speak to the children of Israel, saying : These are the creatures that you may eat from among all the animals that are upon the earth. [3]Everything among the animals that has a split hoof, which is completely separated into double hooves, and brings up its cud - that one you may eat. [4]But this is what you shall not eat from among those that bring up their cud or that have split hooves: The *camel*, for it brings up its cud, but its hoof is not split - it is unclean to you; [5]and the *shafan*, for it brings up its cud, but its hoof is not split - it is unclean to you; [6]and the *arnevet*, for it brings up its cud, but its hoof is not split - it is unclean to you; [7]and the *pig*, for its hoof is split and its hoof is completely separated, but it does not chew its cud - it is unclean to you.

# Was Moses a Zoologist?

Was Moses a hunter or an archer? This refutes those who maintain that the Torah was not divinely revealed.

*Talmud Hulin 60b*

---

## Maimonides Laws of Forbidden Foods Chapter 1:2-3

2. The identifying signs of the clean animals are specified in the Torah as two: the true cloven hoof and the chewing of the cud (rumination). Both must be present. In addition, all ruminators have no incisor teeth in the upper jaw. All ruminators have cloven hoofs, with the sole exception of the camel. And all cloven hoofed animals ruminate, with the exception of the pig.

3. Consequently, if a person finds an animal in the wilderness whose species he cannot identify, he should examine its hoofs. If, however, the hoofs are missing (mutilated), he should examine the mouth. If it has no incisor teeth in its upper jaw he may be certain that it is a clean animal provided he can recognize a camel. If he finds an animal whose muzzle had been mutilated, he should examine the hoofs. If they are cloven, the animal is clean provided he can recognize a pig.

# Identifying Signs of Clean Fish

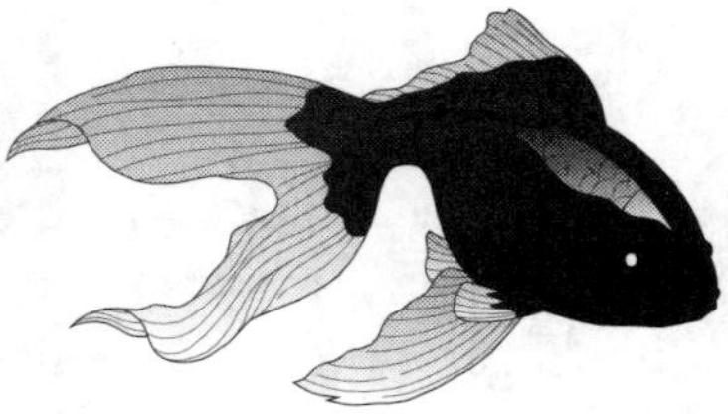

**Leviticus 11:9-12**

This may you eat from everything that is in the water: everything
that has fins and scales in the water, in the seas, and in the streams, those
may you eat. 10 And everything that does
not have fins and scales in the seas and in the streams — from all that
teems in the water, and from all living creatures in the water — they are an
abomination to you. 11 And they shall remain an abomination to you; you
shall not eat of their flesh and you shall abominate their carcass.
12 Everything that does not have fins and scales in the water — it is an
abomination to you.

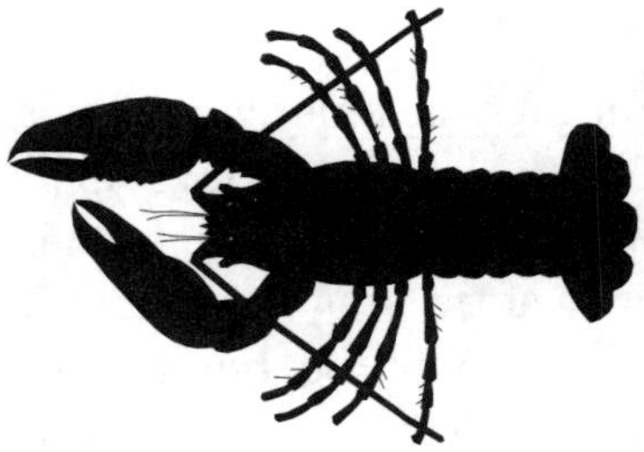

## Was Moses a deep sea diver?

*Mishnah:* <u>Whatsoever has scales has fins</u>, but there are some that have fins and no scales. *Mishnah — Nida 6:9*

*Talmud:* Then why did not the All Merciful write scales and there would be no need for the mention of fins? Rebbe Abbahu replied and so it was also taught at the school of Rebbe Yeshmael: *"To make the teaching great and glorious* (Isaiah 42:21 — יַגְדִּיל תּוֹרָה וְיַאְדִּיר)."

*Talmud Nida 51b*

---

### Maimonides Laws of Proscribed Foods 1:24

24. With fish there are but two tokens, fins and scales. The fin is the organ with which it swims, and the scales form the covering over its whole body. *Every fish which has scales necessarily has also fins.* If it possesses none at the moment, but is known to possess them when fully grown, or if it has scales while it is in the sea, but sheds them when out of the water, it is deemed permitted. If its scales do not cover its whole body, it is still permitted. Even if it has only one scale or only one fin, it is deemed permitted.

# The Jewish Calender

## Passover Must Occur in the Spring Time

You shall observe the month of springtime and perform the pesach-offering for the Lord, your God, for in the month of springtime the Lord, your God, took you out of Egypt at night. ***(Deuteronomy 16:1)***

## Pesach-offering Must Occur On 14th Day of the 1st Month (Nissan)

The Lord spoke to Moses, in the Wilderness of Sinai, in the second year from their exodus from the land of Egypt, in the first month, saying: "The Children of Israel shall make the Pesach-offering in its *appointed time*. On the fourteenth day of this month in the afternoon shall you make it, in its *appointed time*; according to all its decrees and laws shall you make it." ***(Numbers 9:1-3)***

---

## Instructions for Calculating Month Were Transmitted as *a Secret*

My hand will be against the prophets who see vanity and who devine falsehood. *They shall not share the secret of My people*, and in the roll of the Family of Israel shall they not be written, and to the land of Israel shall they not enter. Then you shall know that I am the Lord God. ***(Ezekiel 13:9)***

**"They Shall not be in the council of My people," which refers to the council for intercalation.** ***Talmud Ketubot 112a***

> Hashem said to Moshe and Aaron..."This month shall mark for you the beginning of the months..." (Ex. 12:1-2) At the moment when Moshe received this commandment, the Holy One blessed be He, transmitted to him the precise rules of calculating the new moon. He made known to him the way to intercalate the year and establish the months, in order to fulfill the verse "Observe the spring month and offer a Passover sacrifice..." ***Midrash Sod Ha'Ibbur (see Tal. Rosh Hash. 25a)***

## Maimonides Laws of Sanctifying the Moon Chapter 6:2-3

2. The day and the night consist of 24 hours, 12 for the day and 12 for the night, in any season. The hour is divided into 1,080 parts. The reason for dividing the hour into this number of parts is that this number may be divided without a remainder by two, four, eight, three, six, nine, five, and ten, and with these denominators the fractions may again be divided into many other parts.
3. By these figures, the interval between two conjunctions of moon and sun according to their mean motion is 29 days and 12 hours of the 30th day, beginning with the night of this day, and 793 parts of the 13th hour. That is the time which elapses between one (mean) conjunction and the other, and that is the duration of the lunar month.

***According to the Oral Torah which was handed down by the sages of blessed memory, the time between one new moon and the next is 29 days 12 hours and 793 parts of an hour (the hour is divided into 1080 parts, see Maimonides).***

$$\frac{793}{1080} = \underset{\text{Hours}}{(0.734529)} = \underset{\text{Days}}{(0.03059)}$$

***If we add 29.5 days, we receive a total of 29.53059 days.***

# How does the figure 29.53059 compare with scientific calculations today?

"Facts of File Dictionary of Astronomy"

241 **moon**

| *month* | *reference point* | *length (days)* |
|---|---|---|
| tropical | equinox to equinox | 27.32158 |
| sidereal | fixed star to fixed star | 27.32166 |
| anomalistic | apse to apse | 27.55455 |
| draconic | node to node | 27.21222 |
| synodic | new moon to new moon | 29.53059 |

sky (see table). the differences in the monthly periods result from the complicated motion of the moon.

**moon** (or **Moon**). The only natural satellite of the earth, visible by virtue of reflected sunlight. It has a diameter of 3476 km, lies at a mean distance from the earth of 384 400 km, and completes one orbit around the earth in 27.322 days (*see* sidereal month; month). Its mass in relation to that of the earth is 1 : 81.3, i.e. 0.0123. It is in *synchronous rotation, i.e. it keeps the dame face — the *nearside — toward the earth, although more than 50% of the moon's surface can be seen as a result of *libration. The same face is not however always turned towards the sun, the length of the solar day on the moon being equal to the moon's *synodic period, i.e. 29.53059 days. During this period - the *synodic month - the moon exhibits a cycle of *phases, reaching an apparent magnitude of -12.7 at full moon. It can also undergo *eclipses and produce *occultations.

The moon's mean orbital velocity is 10 km $s^{-1}$.Its orbital mo-

Ellingsworth, "*Facts of File Dictionary of Astronomy*," New York: 1985.

# The New Encyclopedia Britannica

Volume 2, Micropeadia, 1990, Page 740

**Calendar,** any system for dividing time over extended periods, such as days, months, or years, and arranging such divisions in a definite order. A calendric system is essential for regulating the basic affairs of civil life - *e.g.,* agricultural, business, and domestic - and for reckoning time for religious observances and scientific purposes.

A brief treatment of calendars follows. For full treatment, *see* MACROPAEDIA: Calendar.

There are several standard units common to virtually all calendric systems. The day is the fundamental unit of computation in any calendar. It is to some extent a natural division of time, but its subdivision into a number of equal intervals of, for example, 24 hours is purely artificial.

The week, too, is an artificial division of time and cannot be correlated with any astronomical or natural phenomena except insofar as it is a closed cycle of days. The seven-day week that is now universally used may have been derived from the mystical significance attached to the number seven. Support of this view may perhaps be derived from the use of the names of gods and goddesses for each of the days (*see* week).

The month is a calendric period derived from lunation, the time interval in which the Moon completes a full cycle of its phases. This period, known as the synodic month, consists of 29.53059 days. As the earliest adopted of the longer calendar periods, it had a significance in religious observance. The age-old Jewish calendar, for instance, is a lunar one, as are the calendric systems still used by Islam and the Christian Church.

The year is based on the length of time it takes the Earth to orbit the Sun. There are several ways to measure this period, but the most common is the tropical year, which is the interval between successive passages of the Sun through the vernal equinox. The year thus computed consists of 365.242199 mean solar days, each of which is 24 hours 3 minutes 56.55 seconds long. The mean solar day is the average time it takes the Sun to cross the meridian twice.

Unfortunately, the tropical year and the synodic month are incommensurable: 12 lunations come to 254.36706 days, almost 11 days less than a tropical year. In addition, neither the tropical year nor the synodic month is evenly divisible by the length of the day. Therefore, to compile or maintain any calendar that keeps in step with the Moon's phases or with the seasons, it is necessary to insert days at appropriate intervals. These extra days are know as intercalations. The most familiar example of an intercalation is the additional day given to February every fourth year - *i.e.,* leap year.

The origin of the calendric system in general use today - the Gregorian calendar - can be traced back to the Roman republican calendar, which is thought to have been introduced by the fifth king of Rome, Tarquinius Priscus (616-579 BC). Although somewhat similar in style to the dating system of the ancient Greeks, this calendar was more likely derived from an earlier Roman calendar - a lunar calendric system of 10 months - that supposedly was devised around 738 BC by Romulus, traditionally the founder of Rome. The Roman republican calendar consisted of 12 months with a total of 355 days. Like its model, it was basically a lunar system, short by 10¼ days of the 365¼-day tropical year. To keep it in step with the seasons, a special month was supposed to be intercalated between February 23 and 24 once every two years; but because of negligence and political interference, the intercalations were made irregularly. As a result, by 46 BC the calendar had become so hopelessly confused that Julius Caesar was forced to initiate a reform of the entire system. Caesar invited the Alexandrian astronomer Sosigenes to undertake this task. Sosigenes suggested abandoning the lunar system altogether and replacing it with a tropical year of 365¼ days. Further, to correct the accumulation of previous errors, a total of 90 intercalary days had to be added to 46 BC, meaning that January 1, 45 BC, occurred in what would have been the middle of March. To prevent the problem from recurring, Sosigenes suggested that an extra day be added to every fourth February. The adoption of such reformatory measures resulted in the establishment of the Julian calendar, which was used for roughly the next 1,600 years.

During that time, however, the disagreement between the Julian year of 365.25 days and the tropical year of 365.242199 gradually produced significant errors. The discrepancy mounted at the rate of 11 minutes 14 seconds per year until it was a full 10 days in 1545, when the Council of Trent authorized Pope Paul III to take corrective action. No solution was found for many years. In 1572 Pope Gregory III agreed to issue a papal bull drawn up by the Jesuit astronomer Christopher Clavius. Ten years later, when the edict was finally proclaimed, 10 days in October were skipped to bring the calendar back in line. The length of the year was redefined was 365.2422 days, a difference of 0.0078 days per year from the Julian count, which produced a discrepancy between them amounting to 3.12 days every 400 years. Clavius had allowed for such a discrepancy in his suggestion that three out of every four centennial years, which would ordinarily be leap years, should be regarded as common years instead. This led to the practice that no centennial year could be a leap year unless it was divisible by 400. Following this rule, 1700, 1800, and 1900 were common years, but 2000 would be a leap year. These reform measures gave rise to an extremely accurate calendric system; the difference between the Gregorian calendar year and the solar year was less than half a minute. The Gregorian calendar, firmly establishing January 1 as the beginning of its year, was widely referred to as the new style calendar, with the Julian known as the old style calendar.

Although the Gregorian calendar is used throughout much of the world today, it was not immediately accepted everywhere. Most of the Roman Catholic states adopted the improved dating system by 1587. Some Protestant states embraced it around the beginning of the 18th century, but a number of others, such as Great Britain and its colonies, did not do so until the 1750s. Japan, China, and the Soviet Union, to name only a few, adopted the Gregorian rules much later. A few dating systems besides the Gregorian calendar still remain in use. The Muslim calendar, for example, has been retained by most Arab countries, while the traditional Hindu and Jewish calendars continue to be used for religious purposes.

# God's Covenant With the Nation of Israel Is Eternal

**Genesis 17:7**

And I will establish My covenant between Me and you and your descendants after you throughout their generations, an *eternal covenant*; to be your God and the God of your descendants after you.

**Leviticus 26:44-45**

Yet even so, even while they are in the land of their enemies, I will not reject or spurn them, lest I break My covenant with them by destroying them, for I am their God. I will remember them because of the covenant I made with their forefathers, whom I brought out of the land of Egypt under the very eyes of the nations, so that I might be their God.

**Isaiah 59:21**

As for Me, **this is My covenant with them, says God. My spirit, which rests upon you, and *My words which I have put in your mouth*, shall not depart from your mouth nor from the mouths of your children, nor from the mouths of your children's children, says God, from now on to all eternity.**

**Isaiah 54:10**

For the mountains may move and the hills be shaken, but My love shall never move from you, nor My covenant of peace be shaken, said God, Who has compassion on you.

**Jeremiah 31:34-35**

Thus says God, Who establishes the sun to light the day, and the laws of the moon and stars to light the night; Who stirs up the sea into roaring waves, Whose name is the Lord of hosts: If these natural laws should ever give way before Me, says God, only then will the offspring of Israel cease to be a nation before Me for all time.

**Jeremiah 46:27-28**

But fear not O Jacob My servant, neither be dismayed, O Israel, because I shall redeem you from afar, and your children from the land of their captivity; and Jacob will again be quiet and at ease and none shall make him afraid. Fear not, O Jacob My servant, said God, for I am with you. For I will topple all the nations to which I have driven you. But of you I will not make a full end. I will correct you in just measure, but I will not utterly destroy you.

**Malachi 3:6**

For I am God, I do not change; you are the children of Jacob, *you will not cease to be.*

**Isaiah 54:17**

No weapon fashioned against you shall prevail; and every tongue that launches an accusation against you, you shall prove false. This is the heritage of the servants of God, their vindication from me, says God.

**Deuteronomy 4:27**

And the Lord shall scatter you among the nations, and you shall be left few in number among the heathen, where the Lord will lead you.

**Deuteronomy 7:6-9, 12**

For you are a holy nation unto the Lord your God. The Lord your God has chosen you to be a special nation unto Himself, above all people that are upon the face of the earth. The Lord did not set His love upon you, nor choose you, because you were more in number than any people, for you were the fewest of all the people. But because the Lord loved you, and because He would keep the oath which He had sworn unto your fathers, has the Lord brought you out with a mighty hand, and redeemed you out of the house of bondmen, from the hand of Pharaoh king of Egypt. Know therefore that the Lord your God, He is God, the faithful God, which keeps His covenant and mercy with them that love Him and keep His commandments to a thousand generations... Wherefore it shall come to pass, if you hearken to these judgments, and keep and do them, that the Lord your God shall keep unto you the covenant and the mercy which He swore to your fathers.

---

***The Passover Haggadah***

***"Blessed is He who keeps His promise to Israel!"***

*This is what has stood up for our fathers and for us! Not one alone has stood up against us, but in every generation they rise up to finish us - and the Blessed Holy One saves us from their hand!*

# The Eternal Jew

This people are not eminent solely by their antiquity, but are also singular by their duration, which has always continued from their origin till now. For, whereas the nations of Greece and of Italy, of Lacedaemon, of Athens and of Rome, and others who came long after, have long since perished, these ever remain, and in spite of the endeavors of many powerful kings who have a hundred times tried to destroy them, as their historians testify, and as it is easy to conjecture from the natural order of things during so long a space of years, they have nevertheless been preserved (and this preservation has been foretold); and extending from the earliest times to the latest, their history comprehends in its duration all our histories (which it preceded by a long time).

Blaise Pascal, *Pensées*. Paragraph 620, page 285, Encyclopedia Britannica, 1952.

The Jews have played an all-important role in history. They are preeminently an historical people and their destiny reflects the indestructibility of the devine decrees. Their destiny is too imbued with the 'metaphysical' to be explained either in material or positive-historical terms.

I remember how the materialist interpretation of history, when I attempted in my youth to verify it by applying it to the destinies of peoples, broke down in the case of the Jews, where destiny seemed absolutely inexplicable from the materialistic and positivist criterion, this people ought long ago to have perished. Its survival is a mysterious and wonderful phenomenon demonstrating that the life of this people is governed by a special predetermination, transcending the processes of adaptation expounded by the materialistic interpretation of history; all these point to the particular and mysterious foundations of their destiny.

The history of the Jews is not only a phenomenon; it is also a noumenon in that special sense of the word to which I drew attention when speaking of the phenomenal-noumenal historical antithesis. I said that the historical not only represented man's external relations, but that it might also reveal the very noumenon and essence of his being. The peculiarity of Jewish destiny consists in its incommensurability with either the pre-Christian or the Christian era. Scientific criticism applied to traditional Biblical history can neither discredit the universal role played by the Jews nor offer a satisfactory explanation of their mysterious destiny. Nor does this criticism grapple with the absolutely peculiar tie existing between the Jews and the 'historical', and their extraordinarily intense feeling for history.

Professor Nicholai Berdyaev, *The Meaning of History*.
London: Moscow Academy of Spiritual

# The Eternal Nation of Israel Throughout History

The history of Jews and Judaism is a unique phenomenon. It is the most long-lived historical continuum in the emergence, development and spread of western civilization. Since its appearance as a differentiated entity in the ancient Near East about four thousand years ago, Jews and Judaism have been active participants in every phase of the development of the civilizations of Egypt, Babylonia, Assyria, and Persia. They are tightly interconnected with the rise and fall of the Hellenistic monarchies and the waxing and waning of Roman hegemony. They gave birth to Christianity and successfully warded off the rivalry of their offspring. They sustained a creative and differentiated identity under the Sassanians despite the challenge of Zoroastrianism.

They played a vital role in the launching of Islam, even as they spawned a variety of novel forms to cope with the creative expansiveness of this world-girdling religion. And most remarkably, this history not only did not remain confined to either Palestine or the Near East, but spread throughout the western world forming viable and significant communities in Africa, Asia Minor, the Balkans, Greece, Italy, Spain, France, Germany, England, the Slavic lands, even reaching as far east as India and China. This diaspora history is all the more remarkable, because it represents the bulk of the history of the Jews and Judaism during the past two thousand years and because it demanded adaptive powers that border on the phenomenal. In any given century Jews would be living simultaneously in as many as three or four radically different societies, each of which demanded a distinctive form of Jewish adaption if survival was to be sustained. Not only was this challenge met, but it was met without annulling a distinctive Jewish identity.

But this variety by no means fully exposes the uniqueness of Jewish history. Not only did it successfully traverse the ancient and medieval worlds, but it preserved itself as a viable strand within the modern world — a strand so viable as to (1) excite the wish to annihilate it - as Hitler did indeed attempt to do — (2) give birth to the modern nation state of Israel, (3) sustain flourishing communities and multiple Jewish identities throughout the western world, (4) be deemed worthy of sharing with Christianity the responsibility for the highest values of western civilization.

This is the empirical record. The facts as stated are not open to refutation. The uniqueness is there for all to verify. It is not a projection of some religious or ethnic wish.

Ellis Rivkin, *The dynamics of Jewish History.* H.U.C. New College 1970, pp.1-2.

# Six Hundred and Twenty Letters which Comprise the Ten Commandments Represent Six Hundred and Thirteen Scriptural and Seven Rabbinic Commandments

## Exodus 20:2-17
## The Ten Commandments

| | 20 | 19 | 18 | 17 | 16 | 15 | 14 | 13 | 12 | 11 | 10 | 9 | 8 | 7 | 6 | 5 | 4 | 3 | 2 | 1 |
|---|---|---|---|---|---|---|---|---|---|---|---|---|---|---|---|---|---|---|---|---|
| 1 | א | צ | ו | ה | ר | ש | א | ך | י | ה | ל | א | ה | ו | ה | י | י | כ | נ | א |
| 2 | י | ד | ב | ע | ת | י | ב | מ | ם | י | ר | צ | מ | ץ | ר | א | מ | ך | י | ת |
| 3 | ע | ם | י | ר | ח | א | ם | י | ה | ל | א | ך | ל | ה | י | ה | י | א | ל | ם |
| 4 | מ | ת | ל | כ | ו | ל | ס | פ | ך | ל | ה | ש | ע | ת | א | ל | י | נ | פ | ל |
| 5 | ב | ר | ש | א | ו | ל | ע | מ | מ | ם | י | מ | ש | ב | ר | ש | א | ה | נ | ו |
| 6 | ל | ת | ח | ת | מ | ם | י | מ | ב | ר | ש | א | ו | ת | ח | ת | מ | ץ | ר | א |
| 7 | ב | ע | ת | א | ל | ו | ם | ה | ל | ה | ו | ח | ת | ש | ת | א | ל | ץ | ר | א |
| 8 | ק | ל | א | ך | י | ה | ל | א | ה | ו | ה | י | י | כ | נ | א | י | כ | ם | ד |
| 9 | ש | ל | ע | ם | י | נ | ב | ל | ע | ת | ב | א | ן | ו | ע | ד | ק | פ | א | נ |
| 10 | ש | ע | ו | י | א | נ | ש | ל | ם | י | ע | ב | ר | ל | ע | ו | ם | י | ש | ל |
| 11 | ר | מ | ש | ל | ו | י | ב | ה | א | ל | ם | י | פ | ל | א | ל | ד | ס | ח | ה |
| 12 | א | ה | ו | ה | י | ם | ש | ת | א | א | ש | ת | א | ל | ו | ת | ו | צ | מ | י |
| 13 | ה | ו | ה | י | ה | ק | נ | י | א | ל | י | כ | א | ו | ש | ל | ך | י | ה | ל |
| 14 | ו | כ | ז | א | ו | ש | ל | ו | מ | ש | ת | א | א | ש | י | ר | ש | א | ת | א |
| 15 | מ | י | ת | ש | ש | ו | ש | ד | ק | ל | ת | ב | ש | ה | ם | ו | י | ת | א | ר |
| 16 | ו | ך | ת | כ | א | ל | מ | ל | כ | ת | י | ש | ע | ו | ד | ב | ע | ת | ם | י |
| 17 | ה | ל | א | ה | ו | ה | י | ל | ת | ב | ש | י | ע | י | ב | ש | ה | ם | ו | י |
| 18 | ב | ו | ה | ת | א | ה | כ | א | ל | מ | ל | כ | ה | ש | ע | ת | א | ל | ך | י |
| 19 | ת | מ | ה | ב | ו | ך | ת | מ | א | ו | ך | ד | ב | ע | ך | ת | ב | ו | ך | נ |
| 20 | י | ת | ש | ש | י | כ | ך | י | ר | ע | ש | ב | ר | ש | א | ך | ר | ג | ו | ך |
| 21 | ת | א | ו | ם | י | מ | ש | ה | ת | א | ה | ו | ה | י | ה | ש | ע | ם | י | מ |
| 22 | ו | ם | ב | ר | ש | א | ל | כ | ת | א | ו | ם | י | ה | ת | א | ץ | ר | א | ה |
| 23 | ך | ר | ב | ן | כ | ל | ע | י | ע | י | ב | ש | ה | ם | ו | י | ב | ח | נ | י |
| 24 | ו | ה | ש | ד | ק | י | ו | ת | ב | ש | ה | ם | ו | י | ת | א | ה | ו | ה | י |
| 25 | י | ן | ע | מ | ל | ך | מ | א | ת | א | ו | ך | י | ב | א | ת | א | ד | ב | כ |
| 26 | י | ר | ש | א | ה | מ | ד | א | ה | ל | ע | ך | י | מ | י | ן | ו | כ | ר | א |
| 27 | ל | ח | צ | ר | ת | א | ל | ך | ל | ן | ת | נ | ך | י | ה | ל | א | ה | ו | ה |
| 28 | ע | ר | ב | ה | נ | ע | ת | א | ל | ב | נ | ג | ת | א | ל | ף | א | נ | ת | א |
| 29 | א | ל | ך | ע | ר | ת | י | ב | ד | מ | ח | ת | א | ל | ר | ק | ש | ד | ע | ך |
| 30 | ו | ת | מ | א | ו | ו | ד | ב | ע | ו | ך | ע | ר | ת | ש | א | ד | מ | ח | ת |
| 31 | ך | ע | ר | ל | ר | ש | א | ל | כ | ו | ו | ר | מ | ח | ו | ו | ר | ו | ש | ו |

**"Although it may appear that that God only gave Ten Commandments on Mount Sinai, those who know the truth realize that these Ten included all the Commandments."**

Yalkut Me'am Lo'ez, quoting from BeMidbar Rabbah, Nasso, Chapter 13

Scriptural commandments = 613
Rabbinic commandments = 7
620

**7 Rabbinic Commandments**

1. Washing hands for bread
2. Hanukkah candles
3. Megillah reading
4. Sabbath Candles
5. Blessing before eating
6. Reciting Hallel
7. Eruv (Sabbath enclosure)

**"Rabbi Meir (who was a scribe) was cautioned by Rebbi Yeshmael: 'My son, be careful in your work as a scribe, for it is a sacred task. Perhaps you will delete on single letter or add one single letter and thereby destroy the entire world.'"**

Talmud, Ervin, 23b

## Part X

# Bethlehem and The Messiah: What's the Connection?

# The New Jerusalem Bible

(Christian)



↗Mt 2:6 ↗Jn 7:42 **5** But you (Bethlehem) Ephrathah,
the least[a] of the clans of Judah,
from you will come for me
a future ruler of Israel
whose origins go back to the distant past,
to the days of old.[b]
Hence Yahweh[c] will abandon them
Is 7:14 only until she who is in labour gives birth,[d]
and then those who survive of his race
will be reunited to the Israelites.
Is 40:11 He will take his stand and he will shepherd them
with the power of Yahweh,
with the majesty of the name of his God,
and they will be secure, for his greatness will extend
henceforth to the most distant parts of the country.

**5** **a.** 'the least' Gk; 'little' Hebr.

**b.** Ephrathah (to which Micah apparently attaches the etymological meaning of 'fruitful', connecting it with the birth of the liberator) originally indicated a clan related to Caleb, 1 Ch 2:19,24,50, and settled in the district of Bethlehem, Rt 1:2; 1 S 17:12; the name later came to be used of the town itself, Gn 35:19; 48:7; Jos 15:59; Rt 4:11, hence the gloss in the text. Micah is thinking of the ancient origin of the dynasty of David, Rt 4:11,17,18–22; 1 S 17:12. The evangelists later interpreted this passage as a prophecy of Christ's birthplace.

**c.** lit. 'he'.

**d.** Reference to the mother of the Messiah. Micah is perhaps thinking of the famous prophecy of the *'alma*, delivered by Isaiah some 30 years previously, Is 7:14g.

**e.** This fragment announces a future victory over Assyria. It is attributed to the descendant of David (beginning of v. 4, end of v. 5) and to the chieftains of Judah (vv. $4^b$–$5^a$, an old fragment re-used).

**f.** 'in our land' Gk, Syr.; 'in our palaces' Hebr.

**g.** 'with naked blade' one Gk MS and Lat.; 'in its entrances' Hebr.

**h.** This saying, in two symmetrical strophes, announces the function of the 'remnant' in the salvation of the peoples (cf. vv. 1–4; 7:12) and in their punishment (4:13; 5:8,14). The first theme, occurring only at the end of the Exile, suggests a date later than Micah.

**i.** Hebr. adds 'among the nations'.

**j.** The prophecy of vv. 9–13 declares that Yahweh will tear (lit. 'cut off') from his people all their spurious human supports (cf. Is 2:7–8; 30:1–3,15–16; 31:1–3; Ho 3:4; 8:14; 14:4): military power, apparatus of divination and of the cult on the 'high places'. But the threat also implies an era of peace and of true faith. This prophecy is applied by vv. 8 and 14, to the nations, enemies of Yahweh; it is a subsequent adjustment.

**6** **a.** After Yahweh's indictment in which he recalls his goodness to Israel, vv. 3–5, his repentant worshipper enquires what his God demands of him, vv. 6–7. The prophet replies, v. 8.

**b.** The mountains are God's favourite place of meeting with his people (Sinai, Nebo, Ebal and Gerizim, Zion, Carmel). They are changeless witnesses and often personified, Gn 49:26; 2 S 1:21; Ps 68:15–16; Ezk 35–36.

**c.** 'give ear' *weha'azinu* conj.; Hebr. *weha'etanim* 'you solid ones'.

**d.** 'have I been a burden to you' (*hele'etika*) and 'I brought you up' (*he'elitika*) are similar in sound. • In response to Israel's complaint that God has abandoned them, Yahweh recalls his past kindnesses.

**e.** There is a lacuna in the Hebr. text. The reference is to the crossing of the Jordan. • 'you to know' versions; 'knowledge of' Hebr. Yahweh's 'saving justice' are those great events of sacred history by which Yahweh demonstrated his loyalty to the covenantal promises. Since the covenant itself was the issue of a divine initiative, God's 'saving justice' is freely bestowed, not in any sense deserved.

## Micah 5:1 (2)

And you, Bethlehem Ephrathah, you should have been the lowest of the clans of Judah, from you shall emerge for Me, to be a ruler over Israel; and his origin is from old, *from ancient days* (מִימֵי עוֹלָם).

## Part A

וְאַתָּה בֵּית לֶחֶם אֶפְרָתָה צָעִיר לִהְיאת בְּאַלְפֵי יְהוּדָה מִמְּךָ לִי יֵצֵא לִהְיוֹת מוֹשֵׁל בְּיִשְׂרָאֵל

And you, Bethlehem Ephrathah, you should have been the lowest of the clans of Judah, from you shall emerge for Me, to be a ruler over Israel;

## Part B

וּמוֹצָאֹתָיו מִקֶּדֶם מִימֵי עוֹלָם׃

and his origin is from old, **from ancient days**.

### Interlinear:

| וּמוֹצָאֹתָיו | מִקֶּדֶם | מִימֵי עוֹלָם׃ |
|---|---|---|
| and his origin | from old | from ancient days |

| King David Was a Bethlehemite | Ruth Was the Great Grandmother of King David | Ruth Was a Moabite, A Condemned Nation |
|---|---|---|
| **I Samuel 17:58**<br>And Saul said to him, "Whose son are you, young man?" And David said, "The son of your bondsman, Jesse the **Bethlehemite**."<br>*(see also I Sam. 16:1-3)* | **Ruth 4:13-22**<br>And so, Boaz took Ruth and she became his wife; and he came to her. Hashem let her conceive, and she bore a son....and **Boaz begot Oved; and Oved begot Jesse, and Jesse begot David**. | **Ruth 1:4**<br>**Moabite** women, one named Orpah, and the other Ruth...<br><br>**Deuteronomy 23:3**<br>No Ammonite or **Moabite** shall enter the assembly of the Lord... |

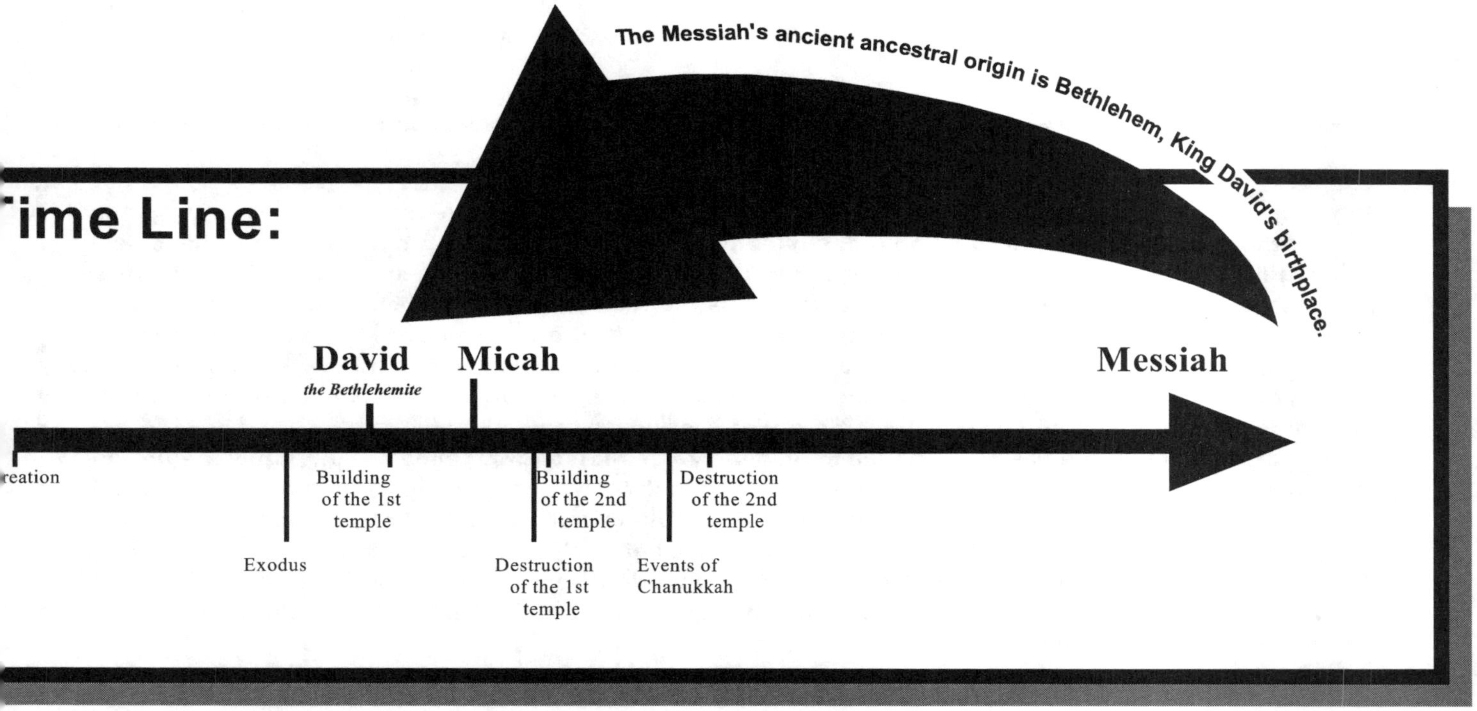

## Matthew 2:6

But you, Bethlehem, in the land of Judah, are **not** the least among the rulers of Judah; for out of you shall come a ruler who will shepherd my people Israel.

## Luke 2:4, 11

Joseph also went up from Galilee, out of the city of Nazareth, into Judea, to the city of David, which is called Bethlehem, because he was of the house and lineage of David....For there is born to you this day in the city of David a Savior, who is Christ the Lord.

## Matthew 2:13-15

And when they were departed, behold, the angel of the Lord appeareth to Joseph in a dream, saying, Arise, and take the young child and his mother, and flee into Egypt, and be thou there until I bring thee word, for Herod will seek the young child to destroy him. When he arose, he took the young child and his mother by night, and departed into Egypt. And was there until the death of Herod, that it might be fulfilled which was spoken of the Lord by the prophet, saying, **Out of Egypt have I called my son.**

## Hosea 11:1

When **Israel** was a child, then I loved him, and called my son out of Egypt.

**Zechariah 9:9-10**

Be exceedingly happy, O daughter of Zion; Shout, O daughter of Jerusalem. Behold, your king shall come to you. He is just and victorious; humble, **riding a donkey, the foal of an ass.** [10]And I will remove the chariots from Ephraim, and the horses from Jerusalem; and the bow of war shall be removed. And he shall speak peace to the nations, and his rule shall be from the sea to the west and from the river to the ends of the earth.

**Matthew 21:1-7**

Then Jesus sent two disciples, saying to them, "Go into the village opposite you, and immediately you will find a **donkey tied and a colt** with her. Loose **them** and bring **them** to me. And if anyone says anything to you, you shall say, 'The lord has need of **them**,' and immediately he will send **them**....So the disciples went and did as Jesus commanded them. They brought the donkey and the colt, laid their c-lothes on **them**, and set him on **them**.

*(also compare Matthew 20:29-34 with Luke 18:35-43.)*

**Luke 19:29-35**

He sent two of his disciples, saying, "Go into the village opposite you, in which as you enter you will find **a colt** tied, on which no one yet has ever sat; untie **it**, and bring *it* here. And if anyone asks you, 'Why are you untying **it**?' thus shall you speak, 'The lord has need of **it**'" And those who were sent went away found **it** just as he had told them. And as they were untying the colt, its owners said to them, "Why are you untying the colt?" And they said the lord has need of *it*." And they brought *it* to Jesus, and they threw their garments on the colt, and put Jesus on **it**.

**The above narratives contain an eye-opening contradiction, and reveal precisely how the Gospel authors created their stories about Jesus. The author of Matthew and Luke sought to have Jesus fulfill Zechariah's notable prophecy of the messiah entering Jerusalem on a donkey. Matthew, however, possessed little knowledge of the Hebrew language and therefore misconstrued Zechariah 9:9. He assumed that the prophet foretold that the messiah will ride into Jerusalem on two animals, rather than one ("a donkey, the foal of an ass"). As a result of this misunderstanding, Matthew claims that Jesus straddled two animals riding into Jerusalem in his Palm Sunday narrative. Luke, on the other hand, tells this same story more carefully with Jesus riding into Jerusalem on a single animal.**

**Unfortunately, many Christians fail to read the verse that follows Zechariah 9:9, which begins with the word "And." This conjunction indicates that Zechariah 9:10 is umbilically connected to the previous verse. In Zechariah 9:10, the prophet continues this prophecy and declares that, "he [the messiah] shall speak peace to the nations, and his rule shall be from the sea to the west and from the river to the ends of the earth." Jesus, of course, brought no peace to the world (see Matthew 10:34-35; Luke 12:51-53) and ruled over no one. It is therefore no coincidence that Christian "Old Testament Fulfilment Charts" always quote Zechariah 9:9 but never 9:10.**

## Why does the King James Version correctly translate the phrase יְמֵי עוֹלָם in every other place in the Bible as "days of old," yet....

| Isaiah 63:9 (King James) | Isaiah 63:11 (King James) | Amos 9:11 (King James) | Micah 7:14 (King James) | Malachi 3:4 (King James) |
|---|---|---|---|---|
| In all their affliction he was afflicted, and the angel of his presence saved them: in his love and in his pity he redeemed them; and he bare them, and carried them all the ***days of old*** (יְמֵי עוֹלָם). | Then he remembered the ***days of old*** (יְמֵי עוֹלָם), Moses and his people, saying, where is he that brought them up out of the sea with the shepherd of his flock? Where is he that put his holy Spirit within him? | In that day will I raise up the tabernacle of David that is fallen, and close up the breaches thereof; and I will raise up his ruins, and I will build it as in ***days of old*** (כִּימֵי עוֹלָם). | Feed thy people with thy rod, the flock of thine heritage, which dwell solitarily in the wood, in the midst of Carmel: let them feed in Bashan and Gilead, as in the ***days of old*** (כִּימֵי עוֹלָם). | Then shall the offering of Judah and Jerusalem be pleasant unto the Lord, as in the ***days of old*** (כִּימֵי עוֹלָם), and as in former years. |

## Here in Micah 5:2 it and other Christian translators render יְמֵי עוֹלָם as "eternity"?

| King James Version | New American Standard | Living Bible | Amplified Bible | Modern Language |
|---|---|---|---|---|
| But thou, Bethlehem Eph ratah, though thou be little among the thousands of Judah, yet out of thee shall he come forth unto me that is to be ruler in Israel; whose goings forth have been from old, from ***everlasting***. | But as for you, Bethlehem Ephrathah, too little to be among the clans of Judah, from you One will go forth for Me to be a ruler in Israel. His goings forth are from long ago, from the **days of *eternity***. | O Bethlehem Ephrathah, you are but a small Judean village, yet you will be the birthplace of my King who is alive from ***everlasting*** | But you, Bethlehem Ephratah, you are little to be among the clans of Judah; [yet] out of you shall one come forth for Me who is to be ruler in Israel, Whose goings forth have been from of old, from ancient days ***(eternity)***. | As for you, Bethlehem Ephrathah, little as you are among the thousands of Judah, from you shall He come forth to Me, who is to be ruler over Israel, His goings forth are from of old, from days of ***eternity***. |

## All Christian translations below render the Hebrew words מִימֵי עוֹלָם in Micah 5:2 correctly.

| | |
|---|---|
| **Revised Standard Version**<br>But you, O Bethlehem Ephrathah, who are little to be among the clans of Judah, from you shall come forth for me one who is to be ruler in Israel, whose origin is from old, **from ancient days**. | **New International Version**<br>But you, Bethlehem Ephrathah, though you are small among the clans of Judah, out of you will come for me one who will be ruler over Israel, whose origins are from of old, **from ancient times**. |
| **Modern Reader's Bible**<br>But thou, Bethlehem Ephrathah, which art little to be among the thousands of Judah, out of thee shall one come forth unto me that is to ruler in Israel; whose goings forth are from of old, **from ancient days**. | **New English Bible**<br>But you, Bethlehem in Ephrathah, small as you are to be among Judah's clans, out of you shall come forth a governor for Israel, one whose roots are far back in the past, in **days gone by**. |
| **The Bible: An American Translation**<br>And you, O Bethlehem Ephrathah, too little to be among the clans of Judah, from you , one shall come forth for me, who shall be ruler over Israel, whose origins are from old, **from ancient days**. | **A New Translation of the Bible — James Moffatt**<br>O Bethlehem Ephrathah, tiniest of townships in all Judah, out of you a king shall come to govern Israel, one whose origin is of old, **of long descent**. |
| **Good News Bible**<br>The Lord says, "Bethlehem Ephrathah, you are one of the smallest towns in Judah, but out of you I will bring a ruler for Israel, **whose family line goes back to ancient times**. | **The Revised English Bible**<br>But from you, Bethlehem in Ephrathah, small as you are among Judah's clans, from you will come a king for me over Israel, one whose origins are far back in the past, **in ancient times**. |
| **The New American Bible (Catholic)**<br>But you, Bethlehem-Ephrathah, too small to be among the clans of Judah, from you shall come forth for me one who is to be ruler in Israel; whose origin is from of old, **from ancient times**. | **New Revised Standard Version**<br>But you, O Bethlehem of Ephrathah, who are one of the little clans of Judah, from you shall come forth for me one who is to rule in Israel, whose origin is from of old, **from ancient days**. |
| **The Jerusalem Bible**<br>But you (Bethlehem) Ephrathah, the least of the clans of Judah, out of you will be born form me the one who is to rule over Israel; his origin goes back to the distant past, to the **days of old**. | **The New Jerusalem Bible**<br>But you (Bethlehem) Ephrathah, the least of the clans of Judah, from you will come form me a future ruler of Israel whose origins go back to the distant past, to the **days of old**. |
| **The International Critical Commentary**<br>And thou, Beth Ephrathah, the least among the clans of Judah, from thee one will come forth for me, who will be ruler over Israel, whose origins are from of old, **from ancient days**. | **Young's Literal Translation of the Holy Bible**<br>And thou, Bethlehem Ephratah, little to be among the chiefs of Judah! From thee to Me he cometh forth — to be ruler in Israel, from the **days of antiquity**. |

# Part XI

# Who is the Messiah?

## Genesis 49:10

The scepter shall not depart from Judah, nor a lawgiver from between his feet, until Shiloh comes; And to Him *shall be* the obedience of the people.

## Hosea 3:4-5

For the children of Israel shall abide many days without king or prince, without sacrifice or sacred pillar, without *ephod* or *teraphim*. [5]Afterward the children of Israel shall return and seek the Lord their God and David their king. They shall fear the Lord and His goodness in the latter days.

## Hosea 6:6

For I desire mercy and not sacrifice, And the knowledge of God more than burnt offerings.

## Hosea 14:2-3

Return O Israel to the Lord your God, for you have stumbled in your iniquity. [3]Take with you words and return to the Lord. Say: You shall forgive all iniquity and teach us the good way, and **let us render for bulls the offering of our lips** (וּנְשַׁלְּמָה פָרִים שְׂפָתֵינוּ).

## Psalm 68:35

Awesome is God in His sanctuary, the God of Israel; He gives power and strength to His people. Blessed be God! *(see also Isaiah 45:5-6)*

## Isaiah 43:10-11

"You are My witnesses," declares the Lord, "And My servant whom I have chosen, In order that you may know and believe Me, And understand that I am He. Before Me there was no God formed, And there will be none after Me. [11]I, I am the Lord, and besides me there is no savior!"

**Missionaries interpret Genesis 49:10 to mean that a king from the tribe of Judah would rule continuously over the Jewish people without pause. Based on their rendering of the verse, they argue that Judaism is essentially a defective religion, having no king, blood sacrifice, or high priest as outlined in the Bible. Accordingly, they insist, Christianity is the only true faith because it alone recognizes and embraces the reign of Jesus as king, sacrifice, and high priest (Mat. 27:11, 37; Acts 17:7; Eph. 5:2; Heb. 2:17, 3:1, 4:14, 9:26). Is this claim of the Church that it alone is the only true heir to the biblical faith, which the Jews have long abandoned, because it recognizes the uninterrupted reign of Jesus as king, high priest and sacrifice? Nothing can be further from the truth.**

**This Christian interpretation of Genesis 49:10 is completely erroneous. Genesis 49:10 does not suggest that the Davidic dynasty would rule without interruption. For example, all Christians concede that no king from the tribe of Judah reigned during the second temple period, which lasted for more than 400 years! This verse foretells that the legitimate royal ruler over the children of Israel would emerge exclusively from the tribe of Judah. It does not mean that there would be no period in Jewish history where no king would reign.**

**In fact, the Bible specifically predicts that there would be a protracted period of time in which the Jewish people would have no king. Contradicting all these missionary claims, Hosea 3:4-5 clearly states that the nation of Israel would endure "many days" without a king, sacrifice, or high priest (*ephod*) until the culmination of the messianic age. This prophecy shatters this missionary argument. The Jewish people are today without a king, sacrificial system, or high priest just as Hosea had foretold. Moreover, the church's claim to have a king, sacrifice, and high priest places an enormous strain on Christian theology.**

**There is not a single instance in the Hebrew scriptures where the Jewish people are instructed to worship or place their faith in a crucified messiah or demigod (Ex. 20:2-3; Deut. 4:35; 6:14; 32:39; Hos. 13:4). Nowhere in Tanach is there even a suggestion that an innocent person can die as an atonement for the wicked. These ideas are regarded as hostile and widely condemned in the Jewish scriptures (Ez. 18:1-23; Ex. 32:33).**

**The prophets of Israel called upon the penitent in exile to confess their sins and prayerfully repent directly to God for a complete atonement (I Kings 8:46-50). We await the coming of the messiah as our king who will be a descendant from the tribe of Judah, not a virgin.**

**Moreover, Hosea did not leave his people without spiritual guidance as they would endure turbulent life outside the land of Israel. He explicitly explained the method how the Jewish people would replace the sacrificial system during our long exile. What about all the animal sacrifices prescribed in the book of Leviticus? Can the Jewish people spiritually survive without the shedding of blood for an atonement? Missionaries claim they cannot. The Bible disagrees.**

**For this reason, Hosea's eye-opening declaration in 14:2-3 is crucial. In these two verses, Hosea discredits the foundation of Christian teachings, and instructs the Jewish people to replace the sacrificial system with prayer during their protracted exile. "Render for bulls the offering of our lips," Hosea declares.**

**The New International Version Bible, however, found the theological message contained in the final segment of Hosea 14:3 ("let us render for bulls the offering of our lips") so troubling that they altered the prophet's last words of the text to read, "that we may offer the *fruit* of our lips," thereby concealing Hosea's original message.**

**Ecclesiastes 12:13**

Let us hear the conclusion of the whole matter: Fear God, and keep His commandments: for this *is* the whole *duty* of man.

After King Solomon declares in his book of Ecclesiastes that all earthly pleasures are vanity, he finally sums up man's central purpose in life: fear God and keep the *mitzvot* (commandments). Although this teaching is the quintessential message of the Jewish faith, it stands in stark contrast to the teachings of the Church. If, as Paul and other New Testament authors insist, man is incapable of keeping the commandments of the Torah, why does Ecclesiastes insist that this is the whole duty of man? Furthermore, why doesn't King Solomon state that the central purpose of man is to believe that Jesus died for our sins? (John 3:16; 17:3)

**Jonah 3:10**

And God saw their works, that they turned from their evil way; and God repented of the evil, that he had said that he would do unto them; and he did *it* not.

**Isaiah I:16-18**

Wash, cleanse yourselves, remove the evil of your deeds from before My eyes, cease to do evil. 17Learn to do good, seek justice, strengthen the robbed, perform justice for the orphan, plead the case of the widow. 18Come now, let us reason together, says the Lord. If your sins prove to be like crimson, they will become white as snow....

**Deuteronomy 4:12**

"And the Lord spoke to you out of the midst of the fire. You heard the words, but saw no image; *you* only *heard* a voice."

According to Christian theology, the atonement that the people of Nineveh enjoyed could not have occurred. Church doctrine is clear on this matter: man cannot atone for his sins through own repentance and initiative. The Church maintains that a person is incapable of achieving salvation by his own deeds (Romans 3:10). Man's only hope for the cleansing of his iniquity is through the Cross. Nothing but believing in Jesus will save you (Mark 16:16, John 3:16, 14:6). Yet, while this teaching is the center piece of Christian theology, it is controverted by the teachings of the Jewish scriptures.

For example, the uplifting conclusion in the Book of Jonah clearly demonstrates that bloodless repentance expiates sin and is the desire of God (Jonah 3:10).

The opening verses of the Book of Isaiah also reveals this salvation plan. The book of Isaiah opens with a harsh censure of the nation of Israel. Few chapters in the Bible are as brutally critical of the Jewish people as Isaiah is in his opening sermon. In Isaiah 1:16-18, however, the prophet almost unexpectedly soothes his wayward nation by teaching them both the essence of atonement and the way to achieve it. He assures the nation of Israel that if they turn from their sinful ways and care for the downtrodden, their sins will be forgiven. Isaiah's message, like the other Jewish prophets, stands in stark contrast to the declaration in the Book of Hebrews that "without the shedding of blood there is no atonement." [1]

Moreover, if, as missionaries insist, belief in Jesus is the only conduit to atonement and salvation, Isaiah's first chapter would have been an ideal place for the prophet to inform us that in order to expiate our sins we must all believe in Jesus and thus be covered by the blood of the Cross. Why isn't this teaching stated clearly in even one verse anywhere in the Jewish scriptures? In stark contrast, the Jewish prophets, as if with one *clear* voice, testify that repentance *alone* atones for sin.[2]

---

1 Hebrews 9:22 2 Deuteronomy 4:26-31; I Kings 8:46-50; Isaiah 55:6-9; Jeremiah 7:3-23; Ezekiel 18:1-23; Hosea 6:6; 14:2-3; Psalm 40:7-9 (6-8); 51;51:16-19; Proverbs 10:2; 11:4; 16:6; Daniel 4:24; II Chronicles 6:36-39

# Why Doesn't Judaism Accept the Christian Messiah?

## Ezekiel 37:1-28

***Ezekiel's Vision of the Valley of Dry Bones***

The hand of the Lord was upon me, and He brought me out by the spirit of the Lord and set me down in the middle of the valley; and it was full of bones. 2 And He caused me to pass among them round about, and behold, *there were* very many on the surface of the valley; and lo, *they were* very dry. 3 And He said to me, "Son of man, can these bones live?" And I answered, "O Lord God, Thou knowest." 4 Again He said to me, "Prophesy over these bones, and say to them, 'O dry bones, hear the word of the Lord.' 5 Thus says the Lord God to these bones, 'Behold, I will cause breath to enter you that you may come to life. 6 And I will put sinews on you, make flesh grow back on you, cover you with skin, and put breath in you that you may come alive; and you will know that I am the Lord.'" 7 So I prophesied as I was commanded: and as I prophesied, there was a noise, and, behold, an earthquake; and the bones came together, bone to its bone. 8 And I looked, and behold, sinews were on them, and flesh grew, and skin covered them; but there was no breath in them. 9 Then said he unto me, "Prophesy unto the wind, prophesy, son of man, and say to the wind, 'Thus saith the Lord God: Come from the four winds, O breath, and breathe upon these slain, that they may live.'" 10 So I prophesied as He commanded me, and the breath came into them, and they came to life, and stood on their feet, an exceedingly great army.

***Ezekiel's Vision Is Explained: the Jewish People Will Be Restored***

11 Then He said to me, "Son of man, these bones are the whole house of Israel; behold, they say, 'Our bones are dried up, and our hope has perished. We are completely cut off.'"

***The Resurrection of the Dead: "Then You Will Know That I Am Lord"***

12 "Therefore prophesy, and say to them, 'Thus says the Lord God,' Behold, I will open your graves and cause you to come up out of your graves, My people; and I will bring you into the land of Israel. 13 Then you will know that I am the Lord, when I have opened your graves and caused you to come up out of your graves, My people. 14 And I will put My Spirit within you, and you will come to life, and I will place you on your own land. *Then you will know* that I, the Lord, have spoken and done it,'" declares the Lord.

***The Restoration of the Ten Lost Tribes (Judah and Israel Will be Reunited)***

15 The word of the Lord came again to me saying, 16 "And you, son of man, take for yourself one stick and write on it, 'For Judah and for the sons of Israel, his companions'; then take another stick and write on it, 'For Joseph, the stick of Ephraim and all the house of Israel, his companions.' 17 Then join them for yourself one to another into one stick, that they may become one in your hand. 18 And when the children of thy people shall speak unto thee, saying, 'Wilt thou not show us what thou meanest by these?' 19 say to them, 'Thus says the Lord God, 'Behold, I will take the stick of Joseph, which is in the hand of Ephraim, and the tribes of Israel, his companions; and I will put them with it, with the stick of Judah, and make them one stick, and they will be one in My hand.' 20 And the sticks on which you write will be in your hand before their eyes. And say to them, 21 'Thus says the Lord God, Behold, I will take the sons of Israel from among the nations where they have gone, and I will gather them from every side and bring them into their own land; 22 and I will make them one nation in the land, on the mountains of Israel; and one king will be king for all of them; and they will no longer be two nations, and they will no longer be divided into two kingdoms. 23 And they will no longer defile themselves with their idols, or with their detestable things, or with any of their transgressions; but I will deliver them from all their dwelling places in which they have sinned, and will cleanse them. And they will be My people, and I will be their God.'"

***The Davidic Kingdom Will be Restored and the Commandments Observed***

24 "And My servant David will be king over them, and they will all have one shepherd; and they will walk in My ordinances, and keep My statutes, and observe them. 25 And they shall live on the land that I gave to Jacob My servant, in which your fathers lived; and they will live on it, they, and their sons, and their sons' sons, forever; and David My servant shall be their prince forever. 26 And I will make a covenant of peace with them; it will be an everlasting covenant with them.

***The Third Temple will Stand Forever: "Then the Nations Will Know that I am Lord"***

And I will place them and multiply them, and will set My sanctuary in their midst forever. 27 My dwelling place also will be with them; and I will be their God, and they will be My people. 28 And the nations will know that I am the Lord who sanctifies Israel, when My sanctuary is in their midst forever."

**The 37th chapter of the book of Ezekiel stands out as one of the most detailed Biblical utterances describing the messianic age, where the prophet vividly describes the final redemption.**

**Why isn't there even a hint that the messiah will die or come twice in these monumental messianic verses? Bear in mind that the prophet mentions the messiah often in this chapter. Why doesn't Ezekiel mention the Cross even once? Yet these are the things you *will* find here: the ingathering of the Jewish exiles, the resurrection of the dead, the messiah's reign on the throne of David, the Jewish people faithfully keeping the commandments of the Torah, and the building of the final Temple that will stand forever in Jerusalem.**

**So, if anyone should ever ask you why Judaism doesn't accept the Christian messiah, ask him to read Ezekiel 37.**

# The following related articles can be found in Part XV of this study guide:

## Part XII

# Judaism and Christianity On Satan: Why We Differ

**Genesis 4:7**

"If you do well, will you not be accepted? And if you do that which is not well, sin lieth at the door, unto you shall be his desire, and **you shall rule over him**."

**Immediately after the transgression in the Garden of Eden, the Almighty declares that although sin is lurking behind the door, you can master over him.**

## Isaiah 45:7

| King James Version | New International Version |
|---|---|
| "I form the light, and create darkness: I make peace, and **create evil** (רָע): I the Lord do all these things." | "I form the light and create darkness, I bring prosperity and **create disaster**; I, the Lord, do all these things. |

## Was it God or Satan?

| II Samuel 24:1 | I Chronicles 21:1 |
|---|---|
| And again the anger of the Lord was kindled against Israel, and He moved David against them to say, "Go, number Israel and Judah." | And Satan stood up against Israel, and provoked David to number Israel. |

**At first glance, the parallel verses above (II Samuel 24:1 and I Chronicles 21:1) seem contradictory. Although these two accounts appear in different books of the Bible, they both describe the same event: King David's ill-fated census of the Jewish people.**

**The Torah forbids the act of performing a headcount of the Jewish people. This prohibition is found in Exodus 30:11-15 where the Torah clearly warns that if this commandment is violated, a devastating affliction would come upon the people. As a result, David's census brought about a dreadful plague. The glaring difference between these two narratives is obvious. Whereas in II Samuel 24:1 it was *God* who moved David to number the Jewish people, in I Chronicles 21:1 *Satan* provoked David to perform the census. Which was it? Was it God or Satan? While at first glance this question may seem trivial, yet because the mention of Satan is scarce in the Jewish scriptures (although quite common in the New Testament), a careful study of this rare occurrence can prove invaluable.**

**For the church, this contradiction is unreconcilable. In Christian theology Satan is the chief enemy and arch opponent of God. Satan opposes the Father's goals. As a result, Christian theology insists that the chief adversary of God has no inclination to fulfil the will of God. In short, these two passages are in conflict, and place considerable strain on Christian doctrine concerning Satan.[1]**

**For the Jewish faith, this apparent contradiction poses no problem because Satan is only an angelic agent of God. As a servant of the Almighty, Satan was faithfully carrying out the divine will of his Creator as he does in all his tasks. I Chronicles' mention of Satan gives us insight into how the Almighty moved the heart of King David; Satan was used to provoke King David perform a census.**

**Satan is one of the many angels mentioned in the Bible. It is worth noting that the Hebrew word for angel is *malach*, meaning messenger. The same is true for the English word angel, derived from the Greek word *angelos*, which also means messenger. Throughout the Bible, an angel is a messenger of God who carries out the divine will of the Almighty. Throughout the Jewish scriptures there is not one example where any angel, Satan included, who opposes God's will.**

---

[1]Christian Bible commentators struggle considerably in their attempt to reconcile this problem. Although their explanations vary, the common theme in their responses is almost always a regurgitation of the problem itself. They maintain that both the Satan of the Jewish scriptures and the Satan in Christian theology are true; Satan is both the servant of God and at the very same time the enemy of God. To quote the *NIV Study Bible* commentary on I Chronicles 21:1 (Zondervan: 1985) , *"Although scripture is clear that God does not cause anyone to sin, it is also clear that man's and Satan's evil acts are under God's sovereign control."* Although this is a remarkable and necessary concession, it doesn't begin to resolve the original problem which is irreconcilable in Christian theology.

# In Whose Merit Will Israel Be Saved?

| Isaiah 59:20 | Romans 11:26 |
| --- | --- |
| And the Redeemer shall come to Zion, and **unto them that turn from transgression in Jacob**, saith the Lord. | And so all Israel shall be saved: even as it is written, "There shall come out of Zion the Deliverer; **He shall turn away ungodliness from Jacob**." |

| Isaiah 59:21 | Romans 11:27 |
| --- | --- |
| As for me, this is my covenant with them, saith the Lord; My spirit that is upon thee, and my words which I have put in thy mouth, shall not depart out of thy mouth, nor out of the mouth of thy seed, nor out of the mouth of thy seed's seed, saith the Lord, from henceforth and for ever. | For this is my covenant unto them, **when I shall take away their sins**.<br>**Pauline interpolation** — **Original Isaiah text** |

**In Isaiah 59:20, the prophet brings into view an inspiring and uplifting picture of the messianic age. In a repeating literary pattern unique to the Book of Isaiah, this chapter opens with a harsh criticism of the obstinate sinner, forgiveness to the penitent faithful, and dramatically ends with the comforting promise of the messianic age.**

**In 59:20, Isaiah describes this final redemption when the messiah will come to his people who have turned away from transgression. These stirring words set the stage for the extraordinary prophecies in the next chapter where Isaiah holds up the picture of Israel, a righteous people, whose light will serve as a guide for all the surrounding gentile nations (60:1-22).**

**For Christians, however, Isaiah 59:20 presents a serious theological problem because in the third chapter of the Book of Romans, Paul insists that no one can merit his own salvation. One of the most fundamental underpinnings of Christian doctrine on salvation is the Pauline teaching that the cross alone, not our own good deeds and heart-felt repentance, can save.[1] Who then is the Redeemer coming to in Jacob if no one can turn from transgression?**

**Paul therefore rearranges the words of Isaiah 59:20 in the Book of Romans (11:26) so that Isaiah appears to predict that it will be the Redeemer [Jesus] who will turn away sin from Jacob. This, of course, is not what the prophet predicts. As mentioned above, the original verse declares that the messiah will come to those who have repented of transgression. It is not difficult, therefore, to understand why Paul found it necessary to manipulate Isaiah's message.**

**In the following verse Paul continues to tamper with the text in order to make it congruous with his alterations of the previous verse. Romans 11:27 was designed to appear as a continuation of Isaiah's message when he writes, "And this is my covenant unto them, when I shall take away their sins." Although the first half of this verse, "And this is my covenant unto them," is correctly quoted from the first part of Isaiah 59:21, the second half has disappeared. Paul expunged the latter half of Isaiah's verse and instead inserts a contrived text, "When I shall take away their sins." Paul interpolated this segment in order to support his modifications of Isaiah's previous verse (11:26).**

---

[1] Paul bases this assertion primarily on the verse from Genesis 15:6, *"And he [Abram] believed in the Lord; and he counted it to him for righteousness."* In both Romans 4:3 and Galatians 3:6, Paul sets out to prove from this verse that faith alone is what saves man — not his observance of the Law. Paul insists that this verse clearly demonstrates that Abraham was considered righteous through faith alone and not by his deeds.

This quote, however, is taken out of context. A little further on in the Book of Genesis, the Torah describes the very fabric of Abraham's faith. In Genesis 26:5, the Bible declares that *"Because Abraham obeyed Me and kept My charge, My commandments, My statutes and My laws."* It was Abraham's unwavering obedience to the commandments of the Almighty in spite of the challenging tests placed before him that revealed his unyielding faith in God.

# Who is the 'Morning Star,' Jesus or Satan?

| Isaiah 14:12 | Revelations 22:16 |
|---|---|
| "How you have fallen from heaven, O **morning star**, son of the dawn! You have been cut down to the earth, You who have weakened the nations!" | "I Jesus have sent mine angel to testify unto you these things in the churches. I am the root and the offspring of David, and the bright and **morning star**." *(See II Peter 1:19)* |

**Isaiah 27:9**

Therefore through this Jacob's iniquity will be forgiven; And this will be the full price of the pardoniing of his sin: When he makes all the altar stones like pulverized chalk stones; *When* Asherim and incense altars will not stand.

**Isaiah proclaims that the "full price" of Jacob's iniquity will be fully atoned when the Jewish nation finally destroys the alters and idols of heathens. This prophecy completely contradicts Christianity's most cherished doctrine: it is the blood of Jesus alone that atones for man's manifold sins. According to Christian theology, destroying idolatry and heathen altars is irrelevant to salvation.**

# The Devil and the Jews

**John 8:44**

"**Ye [Jews] are of your father the devil**, and the lusts of your father ye will do. He was a murderer from the beginning, and abode not in the truth, because there is no truth in him. When he speaketh a lie, he speaketh of his own: for he is a liar, and the father of it."

**Revelations 2:9**

"I know your works, tribulation, and poverty (but you are rich); and I know the blasphemy of those who say they are Jews and are not, but are a **synagogue of Satan."** *(See also Rev. 3:9)*

**Matthew 28:11-15**

Now while they were going, behold, some of the guard came into the city and reported to the chief priests all the things that had happened. When they had assembled with the elders and consulted together, they gave a large sum of money to the soldiers, saying, **"Tell them, 'His disciples came at night and stole Him away while we slept.'** And if this comes to the governor's ears, we will appease him and make you secure." So they took the money and did as they were instructed; **and this saying is commonly reported among the Jews until this day.**

**The following related article can be found in Part XV of this study guide:**

## Part XIII

# Bearers of the Torch

# "Jews Go Home"

*- By William Eiken -*

The Gazette Telegraph of Colorado

*(reprinted in more than 250 newspapers throughout North America)*

"Jews Go Home!" - Well, now this is nothing new. Never in the past have you taken this gentle suggestion to move on. But Heaven forbid, suppose just this once you thought that this expression of a few sick people actually expressed the conviction of all the people in this wonderful land of ours, and all of you started to pack your bags and leave for parts unknown.

"Jews Go Home, we don't want Jews, we want oil!" But before you leave, could you do me a favor? Would you leave behind your formula for the Salk Vaccine with me before you leave? You wouldn't be so heartless as to let my children contract polio?

And would you please leave your knack for government and politics, and persuasion and literature and your good food. And would you please leave me with the secret of your desire to succeed?

And please have pity on us. Please show us the secret of how to develop such geniuses as Einstein and Steinmetz and so many others who have helped us all. After all, we owe you a lot for the atomic bomb, most of our rocket research, and perhaps the fact that we are alive today. Instead, we could have been looking up from our chains and from our graves at Hitler, old but glad, driving slowly by in one of our Cadillacs had he succeeded in reaching the atom bomb and not us.

On your way out, Jews, will you do me another favor? Will you please drop by my house and pick me up too? I'm not sure I could live too well in a land where you were not to be found. For if ever you were to leave, love goes with you, democracy and morality goes with you, everything I and my buddies fought for in World War II goes with you. God goes with you.

Just pull up in front of my house, slow down and honk because so help me, I'm going with you too.

Yours sincerely,

William Eikin.

# "You Are My Witnesses!"

## 1. *"You Have Been Shown So That You Will Know"*

Only take heed to yourself, and diligently keep yourself, so that you do not forget the things your eyes have seen. Do not let [this memory] leave your hearts all the days of your lives. Teach them to your children and your children's children, [10]about the day you stood before the Lord your God in Horeb.... [11]Then you came near and stood at the foot of the mountain, and the mountain burned with fire to the midst of heaven, with darkness, cloud, and thick darkness. [12]And the Lord spoke to you out of the midst of the fire. You heard the sound of the words, but saw no form; you only heard a voice.

***Deuteronomy 4:9-12***

כִּי שְׁאַל-נָא
לְיָמִים רִאשֹׁנִים....

**You might inquire about times long past**, going back to the time that God created man on earth, [exploring] one end of the heavens to the other, see if anything as great as this has ever happened, or if the like has ever been heard. [33] Has any nation ever heard God speaking out of fire, as you have, and still survived? [34]Has God ever done miracles, bringing one nation out of another nation, with tremendous miracles, signs, wonders, war, a mighty hand and outstretched arm, and terrifying phenomena, as God did for you in Egypt before you very eyes? [35] You are the ones who have been shown, so that you will know that God is the Supreme Being, and there is none besides him. [36]From the heavens, He let you hear His voice admonishing you, and on earth He showed you His great fire, so that you heard His words from the fire. [37] It was because He loved your fathers, and chose their children after them, that [God] Himself brought you out of Egypt with His great power. [38]He will drive away before you nations that are greater and stronger than you, so as to bring you to their lands, and give them to you as a heritage, as [He is doing] today. [39]Realize it today and ponder it in you heart: God is the Supreme Being in heaven above and on earth beneath — there is no other.

***Deuteronomy 4:32-39***

If your brother, the son of your mother, your son or your daughter, the wife of your bosom, or your friend who is as your own soul, secretly entices you, saying, 'Let us go and serve other gods,' which you have not known, neither you nor your fathers, [7]of the gods of the people which are all around you, near to you or far off from you, from one end of the earth to the other end of the earth, [8]you shall not consent to him or listen to him, nor shall your eye pity him, nor shall you spare him or conceal him;

***Deuteronomy 13:6-8***

## 2. *A Nation Beares Testimony*

Everyone who is called by My name, whom I have created for My glory; I have formed him, yes, I have made him. Bring out the blind people who have eyes, and the deaf who have ears. Let all the nations be gathered together, and let the people be assembled. [9]Who among them can declare this, and show us former things? Let them bring out their witnesses, that they may be justified; Or let them hear and say, 'It is truth.' [10]"You are My witnesses!" says the Lord, "And My servant whom I have chosen, That you may know and believe Me, And understand that I am He. Before Me there was no God formed, nor shall there be after Me. [11]I, even I, am the Lord, And besides Me there is no Savior. [12]I have declared and saved, I have proclaimed, And there was no foreign god among you; therefore you are My witnesses," says the Lord, "that I am God."

***Isaiah 43:8-12***

# "Remember — Do Not Forget"

## 3. *Remember the Slavery in Egypt*

And you shall remember that you were a slave in the land of Egypt, and the Lord your God redeemed you; therefore I command you this today.

***Deuteronomy 15:15 (see also 16:12)***

You shall not pervert the justice due an alien or an orphan, nor take a widow's garment in pledge. [18]But you shall remember that you were a slave in Egypt, and that the Lord your God redeemed you from there; therefore I am commanding you to do this thing.

***Deuteronomy 24:17-18***

**The nation of Israel is commanded to remember the events that they were witness to and personally experienced. Only when it becomes evident that the Torah was not written at a later date or dates, but at the time the events themselves occurred, is it conceivable that the entire nation would shoulder the responsibility to remember.**

## 4. *Remember the Events in Egypt*

You shall not be afraid of them; you shall well remember what the Lord your God did to Pharaoh and to all Egypt: [19]the great trials which your eyes saw and the signs and the wonders and the mighty hand and the outstretched arm by which the Lord your God brought you out.

***Deuteronomy 7:18-19***

## 5. *Remember the Exodus*

And Moses said to the people, "Remember this day in which you went out from Egypt, from the house of slavery; for by a mighty hand the Lord brought you out from this place. Nothing leavened shall be eaten."

***Exodus 13:3***

You shall not eat leavened bread with it; seven days you shall eat with it unleavened bread, the bread of affliction (for you came out of the land of Egypt in haste), in order that you may remember all the days of your life the day when you came out of the land of Egypt.

***Deuteronomy 16:12***

## 6. *Remember Receiving the Torah at Sinai*

But take care and watch yourselves closely, so as neither to forget the things that your eyes have seen nor to let them slip from your mind all the days of your life; make them known to your children and your children's children.

***Deuteronomy 4:9***

**The Torah turns to the Nation of Israel in the first person and emphatically commands: "You shall remember, You shall remember!" No nation would have accepted such a detailed command to remember that which was seen and experienced had these events not actually occurred. The emphasis which is placed on remembering clearly evidences that the memory of these events carved itself deeply in the consciousness of the nation.**

## 7. *Remember the Journey in the Wilderness*

And you shall remember all the way which the Lord your God has led you in the wilderness these forty years, that He might humble you, testing you, to know what was in your heart, whether you would keep His commandments or not.

***Deuteronomy 8:2***

# Holocaust Revisionism

**Austin J. App**

Former associate professor of English at LaSalle College, Philadelphia, is the author of numerous neo-Nazi pamphlets, one, for example, called *"Did Six Million Really Die? The Truth at Last."*

**Arthur Butz**

Professor of engineering at Northwestern University and author of *"The Hoax of the Twentieth Century,"* denying the death camps and the extermination of millions of Jews. Claims of fabrication of the Holocaust by Jews seeking to enlist support for Israel by appealing to popular guilt feelings.

**Willis Carto**

Founder of the Institute for Historical Review (1978) in Torrance, CA. The I.H.R. Publishes journals and sponsors conventions designed to whitewash Nazi war crimes by denying the Holocaust. Carto is also the treasurer of the "Liberty Lobby" in Washington D.C. Which publishes the "*Spotlight*," a weekly publication long known for its diatribes against Israel and the American Jewish community.

**Thies Christopherson**

64 year-old journalist and leader of the Christians and Farmers Initiative, continues to write and lecture in the Federal Republic of Germany in defense of the Nazi regime and in propagation of the canard that there was no Holocaust. In addition to leading his group, he publishes tracts and pamphlets under the auspices of Critical Review Publications. A close associate of the American Hitlerite George Dietz, he has been a frequent visitor and lecturer in the USA and Canada.

**Leon Derelle**

Author of articles in praise of the S.S. of which he was a member...currently hiding in Spain to escape a death sentence for war crimes committed in his native Belgium...contributor to the I.H.R. journal.

**Robert Faurisson**

Holds a Ph.D. from the Sorbonne in Paris...was dismissed from his position as professor of French at Lyons University for revisionist views and convicted by a French court for defaming the victims of the Holocaust. He claims that the Nazi gas chambers never existed and that facts about the Holocaust and the number of victims have been grossly exaggerated.

**Edgar Geiss**

As recently as January 1979, 54 year-old Geiss formed a citizens' actions group to combat what he described as the "lies" about German war guilt, the concentration camp gassings and the murder of Jews.

**David McCalden**

Also known as Lewis Brandon, co-founder of the Institute for Historical Review....sponsor of "Truth Missions," a front for the defamation of Simon Wiesenthal and the propagation of Holocaust revisionism in Manhattan Beach, Ca.

**George Pape**

President of the German-American Committee of Greater New York (a cultural organization with over 50 branches in the metropolitan area) objected to the introduction of teaching the Holocaust in the school system with the words: "there is no real proof that the Holocaust actually happened."

**Paul Rassinier**

French author and a pioneer of this revisionist approach, speaks of "The Lie of Auschwitz."

**Manfred Roeder**

A 57 year-old disbarred lawyer is the leader of the 100 member German Citizens Initiative. Without a steady income and facing imprisonment because of his neo-Nazi activities, Roeder became a fugitive from justice who found refuge with friends and associates in North and South America. While a fugitive, he established a working relationship with the "Aryan Nations," a small vitriolic, violence-prone American anti-Semitic group located in Idaho. Currently he is serving his sentence in a German prison, having been taken into custody by German authorities in September 1980, as he sought surreptitiously to return to the Federal Republic.

**Erwin Schonborn**

68 year-old journalist and publisher from Frankfurt is the founder and fuehrer of the Combat League of German Soldiers. Seeking a political base, he at one time contemplated offering one Hildegart Lachert, a 62 year-old accused former Maidanek concentration camp guard, as a candidate for the European Parliament. Sentenced in 1979 to 18 months imprisonment for slandering former concentration camp victims, he nevertheless continues to be active.

**Charles Weber**

Professor of German at the university of Tulsa...author of "The Holocaust: 120 Questions and Answers," a conglomeration of distortions and half-truths trivializing Nazi guilt during World War II. Contributor to the I.H.R. journal. Article authored by Weber recently appeared in an "Aryan Nations" pamphlet.

**Ernst Zundel**

German-Canadian revisionist and major international publisher of anti-Semitic material and distributor of pro-Nazi literature convicted for knowingly spreading false information about the Holocaust.

## Trials of War Criminals Before the Nuernberg Military Tribunals

Opening statement of the Prosecution
by Brigadier General Telford Taylor, December 9, 1946

We need look no further than the law which the Nazis themselves passed on the 24th of November 1933 for the protection of animals. This law states explicitly that it is designed to prevent cruelty and indifference of man towards animals and to awaken and develop sympathy and understanding for animals as one of the highest moral values of a people. The soul of the German people should abhor the principle of mere utility without consideration of the moral aspects. The law states further that all operations or treatments which are associated with pain or injury, especially experiments involving the use of cold, heat, or infection, are prohibited, and can be permitted only under special exceptional circumstances. Special written authorization by the head of the department is necessary in every case, and experimenters are prohibited from performing experiments according to their own free judgment. Experiments for the purpose of teaching must be reduced to a minimum. Medico-legal tests, vaccinations, withdrawal of blood for diagnostic purposes, and trial of vaccines prepared according to well-established scientific principles are permitted, but the animals have to be killed immediately and painlessly after such experiments. Individual physicians are not permitted to use dogs to increase their surgical skill by such practices. National Socialism regards it as a sacred duty of German science to keep down the number of painful animal experiments to a minimum.

If the principles announced in this law had been followed for human beings as well, this indictment would never have been filed. It is perhaps the deepest shame of the defendants that it probably never even occurred to them that human beings should be treated with at least equal humanity.

***"The Medical Case", Volume I, page 71***

"The receptivity of the great masses is very limited, their intelligence is small, but their power of forgetting is enormous. In consequence of these facts, all effective propaganda must be limited to a very few points and must harp on these in slogans until the last member of the public understands what you want him to understand by your slogan. As soon as you sacrifice this slogan and try to be many-sided, the effect will piddle away, for the crowd can neither digest nor retain the material offered. In this way the result is weakened and the end entirely canceled out...

The magnitude of a lie always contains a certain factor of credibility, since the great masses of the people in the very bottom of their hearts tend to be corrupted rather than consciously and purposely evil, and that, therefore, in view of the primitive simplicity of their minds, they more easily fall a victim to a big lie than to a little one, since they themselves lie in little things, but would be ashamed of lies that were too big."

***Adolf Hitler, Mein Kampf***

---

"The Jews inflicted two scars on mankind. Circumcision on his body and a conscience on his soul."

***Adolf Hitler, Mein Kompf***

# Historical Parallels — "Our eyes have seen!"

## In Jerusalem, June 14th to 18th, 1981, the World Gathering of Jewish Holocaust Survivors:

*Ernest Michel, Chairman of the World Gathering:*

My name is Ernest Michel. Auschwitz number one zero four nine nine five. Like many of you I had a dream that one day — if we live — we could come and stand together.

This is a reunion of a special group of people for which there is no parallel anywhere. We want to stand together once more before time runs out, united in freedom as we were in slavery. We want to see in each others eyes and in the eyes of our children the proof of our survival and the joy that comes from being alive and free. But there is more than that. We survivors want to tell those who try to rewrite the history and deny that the Holocaust ever happened: Our eyes have seen. Our ears have heard. Our nostrils were filled with the acrid fumes from the gas chambers drifting over our camp. Day after day. Week after week. Year after year. These hands [Michel holds his hands up in the air] have carried more corpses than I care to remember. So don't tell us it never happened. We were there.

This gathering could not have taken place 10 or 20 years ago. It took time for wounds to heal enough for us to meet. This is why this event took almost 40 years to come into being, and that is why we shall never meet as one group again. It has become fashionable to invoke the memory of the Holocaust - so much has been written, so much has been dramatized. It is *we* who have lived it, *we* who have survived it, *we* of whom they write, *we* of whom they speak. So, today, it is our turn. Today, *we* speak. Despite the memories of the past, we have built new lives. Many of us have second families — so many of the first were exterminated. We have children, grandchildren. We have sanctified the names of those we lost — we have contributed to Jewish tomorrows. A number of people have asked: Why are you doing this? Why do you want to meet? Why recall a past such as you've had. Why not leave it alone? Our response, straight and simple: we survived for a purpose. Already something constructive has emerged from this gathering.

Represented here are almost 1,000 members of the Second Generation. I am pleased to announce that they have formed here in Jerusalem a Second Generation International Network whose major purpose will be to carry on the memory of the Holocaust. Like you, I will never forget this week, the seeking, the finding, then that first look of recognition. Aren't you? Aren't you? Weren't you? Block 14? Commando 35? From the ghetto? The embrace — the touch — God, how good it felt to see each other, to be together — the tears, the smiles, the memories, the stories: It will take a while to climb down from the mountain of this emotional high of this unforgettable and unrepeatable week. As long as I live the faces of this four days will be indelibly etched in my memory, when our tears turned to laughter and our sadness to joy.

### Lucy Dawidowicz

Can all these lies change the truth? Can a honest and intelligent person believe in a criminal and absurd falsehood which claims that Nazi Germany never murdered 6 million Jews? Who can give credence to the monstrous lie that Auschwitz never housed a gas chamber? To our chagrin, these are not merely rhetorical questions. While writing this article, a young man who works on a radio program in North America approached me and asked if I would be willing to debate Robert Faurisson on the air. When I replied angrily that it would be a travesty of justice and decency to give such a man a public platform, the young man answered: "Why are you opposed to dealing with a problem which is up for debate?!" I asked him if, in his opinion, the murder of European Jewry was included in the category of "up for debate." Has it not been proven as a historical fact? "I wouldn't know," he answered, "I wasn't born yet; I am only 30."

***(From an article by Lucy Dawidowicz in Ma'ariv, April 30, 1981 - Hebrew)***

"Some of the Israelis claim that God gave them this country. First, I do not believe that God loves Jews fore than He loves Christians and Moslems. Secondly, who were the witnesses?"

***(Dr. Mahmoud, Arab Journalist, East Jerusalem)***

### Elie Wiesel, speaking at a press conference:

"The Second Generation is the most meaningful aspect of our work. Their role in a way is even more difficult than ours. They are responsible for a world they didn't create. They who did not go through the experience must transmit it."

***Hillel Goldberg, "A Holocaust Theology: The Survivors' Statement - Part I" Tradition 20(2) 1982***

# Remember

זָכוֹר אֵת
אֲשֶׁר־עָשָׂה
לְךָ...

*Deuteronomy 25:17*

This day, 16 Sivan 5741 Anno Mundi (18.6.81), in the 36th year of our liberation from the hands of the Nazis, we are all standing before the remnant of our Sanctuary in Jerusalem, to transmit the legacy of this generation to future generations to come.

We are members of the generation which lived through the Holocaust. "One of a city, two of a family" survived. Some are scattered amongst the nations, from Holocaust to Dispersion; others came to Zion, from Holocaust to Redemption.

Ours is the generation of our children; they are standing here with us today, children without grandparents. And the generation of our children's children is also with us.

The memory of the six million, burnt in the fires of the Holocaust, is with us here as we transmit our everlasting legacy: Remember, and let nothing be forgotten! Remember what evil men did to us! Remember, we are a people scattered and dispersed amongst the nations in all countries - forget not!

Let memory be turned into deed! Let our broken fragments be brought together and become one people! Let our dispersed ones be brought together to one country, to become one amongst the nations, our State one amongst other states.

Let the desolation be rebuilt until our people can dwell securely in its land, in Israel, and there shall be no one to make us afraid; until it can "eat the fruits of its own labors and be content."

Let every Jew view himself as through he had been scorched in the fires of the Holocaust, for the obligation lies on him to remember and not to forget, to turn memory into action — to restore the life and culture of our people.

**Thousands of Holocaust Survivors at the Western Wall for the final ceremony of the World Gathering of Jewish Holocaust Survivors and the reading of "The Legacy"**

*Thursday evening. The closing ceremony at the Western Wall. 6,000 memorial candles. 1,000 people per candle. Six million....This was the evening of the future: the transmission of the "legacy." In six languages (Hebrew, Yiddish, English, French, Ladino and Russian), a survivor read the legacy and the son or grandson of a survivor received it. For 45 minutes, 10,000 people sat in perfect silence as an Israeli, an Australian, a New Yorker, a Parisian, and another Israeli survivor read in each of the six languages:*

# The Legacy

"We **take this oath!** We take it in the shadow of flames whose tongues scar the soul of our people. We vow in the name of dead parents and children; we vow with our sadness hidden, our faith renewed; we vow we shall never let the sacred memory of our perished Six Million be scorned or erased.

We **saw them hungry**, in fear; we saw them rush to battle; we saw them in the loneliness of night - true to their faith. At the threshold of death; we saw them. We received their silence in silence; merged their tears with ours.

Deportations, executions, mass graves, death camps, mute prayers, cries of revolt, desperation, torn scrolls, cities and towns, villages and hamlets, the young the old, the rich, the poor, ghetto fighters and partisans, scholars and messianic dreamers, ravaged faces, fists raised like clouds of fire, all have vanished.

We **take this oath!** Vision becomes word to be handed down from father to son, from mother to daughter, from generation to generation.

Remember **what the German killers and their accomplices did to our people**. Remember them with rage and contempt. Remember what an indifferent world did to us and to itself. Remember the victims with pride and with sorrow. Remember also the deeds of the Righteous Gentiles.

We **shall also remember the miracle of the Jewish rebirth** of the land of our ancestors, in the independent State of Israel. Here pioneers and fighters restored to our people the dignity and majesty of nationhood. From the ruin of their lives, orphans and widows built homes and old-new fortresses on our redeemed land. To the end of our days we shall remember all those who realized and raised their dream, our dream, of redemption to the loftiest heights.

We **take this oath** here in Jerusalem, our eternal spiritual sanctuary. Let our legacy endure as a stone of the Temple Wall. For her prayers and memories burn. They burn and burn and burn and will not be consumed."

Abraham Zelezniakov

Reading the Legacy of Survivors and Response of the Second Generation

Menachem Rosensaft

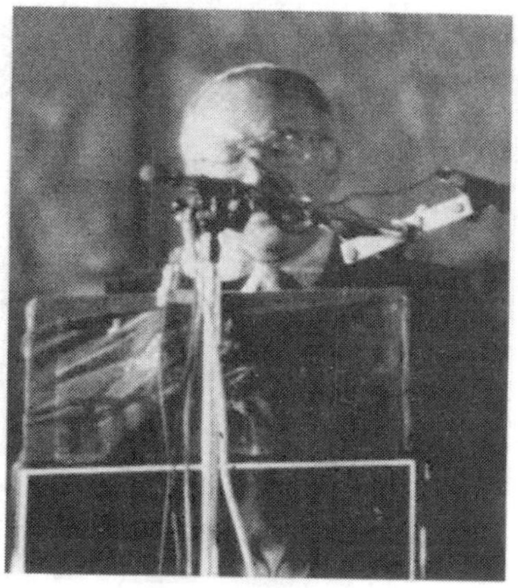

Norbert Wollheim

Chaim Zlotogorski

Yaakov Lerner

Marcel Stourze

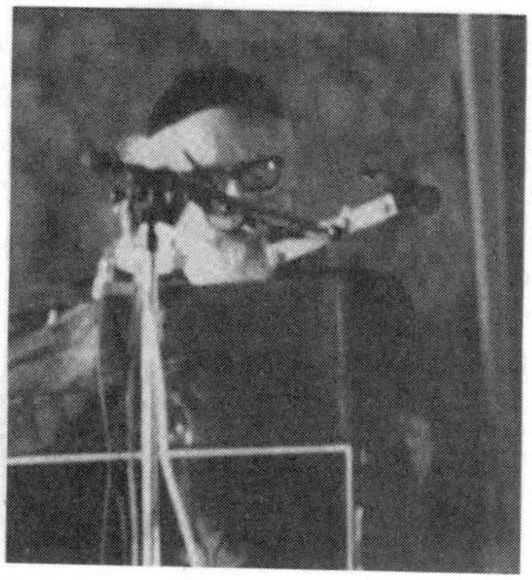

Mordecai Karasso

# The Second Generation Accepts the Legacy

"We accept the obligation of this legacy.

We are the first generation born after the darkness. Through our parent' memories, words and silence, we are linked to that annihilated Jewish existence whose echoes permeate our consciousness.

We dedicate this pledge to you, our parents, who suffered and survived; to our grandparents, who perished in the flames; to our vanished brothers and sisters, more than one million Jewish children, so brutally murdered; to all Six Million whose unyielding spiritual and physical resistance, even in the camps and ghettos, exemplifies our people's commitment to life.

We pledge to remember!

We shall teach our children to preserve forever that uprooted Jewish spirit which could not be destroyed.

We shall fight anti-Semitism and all forms of racial hatred by our dedication to freedom throughout the world.

We affirm our commitment to the State of Israel and to the furtherance of Jewish life in our homeland.

We pledge ourselves to the oneness of the Jewish people.

We are your children!"

# Transmission to Future Generations: The Testimony

## 8. *Gathering of the Survivors*

And in the fortieth year, on the first day of the eleventh month, Moses spoke to the people of Israel according to all that the Lord had given him in commandment to them.

***Deuteronomy 1:3***

Today, you are all standing before the Lord your God; the heads of your tribes, your elders, and your officers, all the men of Israel, [10]your little ones, your wives, and the sojourner who is in your camp, both he who hews your wood and he who draws your water, [11]that you may enter into the covenant with the Lord your God, and into His oath which the Lord your God is making with you today.

***Deuteronomy 29:9-11***

## 9. *The Testimony*

You might inquire about times long past, going back to the time that God created man on earth, [exploring] one end of the heavens to the other, see if anything as great as this has ever happened, or if the like has ever been heard. [33]Has any nation ever heard God speaking out of fire, as you have, and still survived? [34]Has God ever done miracles, bringing one nation out of another nation, with tremendous miracles, signs, wonders, war, a mighty hand and outstretched arm, and terrifying phenomena, as God did for you in Egypt before your very eyes? [35]You are the ones who have been shown, so that you will know that God is the Supreme Being, and there is none besides Him.

***Deuteronomy 4:32-35***

And Moses summoned all Israel and said to them: "You have seen all that the Lord did before your eyes in the land of Egypt, to Pharaoh and to all his servants and to all his land, [2]the great trials which your eyes saw, the signs, and those great wonders; [3]but to this day the Lord has not given you a mind to understand, or eyes to see, or ears to hear. [4]I have led you forty years in the wilderness; your clothes have not worn out upon you, and your sandals have not worn off your feet; [5]you have not eaten bread, and you have not drunk wine or strong drink; that you may know that I am the Lord your God."

***Deuteronomy 29:1-5***

## 10. *The Eye Witness Accounts*

And Moses summoned all Israel, and said to them, "Hear, O Israel, the statutes and the ordinances which I speak in your hearing this day, and you shall learn them and be careful to do them. [2]The Lord our God made a covenant with us in *Horeb*. [3]Not with our fathers did the Lord make this covenant, but with us, who are all of us here alive this day. The Lord spoke with you face to face at the mountain, out of the midst of the fire."

***Deuteronomy 5:1-3***

You must now realize that I am not speaking with your children, who did not know and who did not see the lesson the Lord your God [taught] through His greatness and His mighty hand and His outstretched arm -- [3]His signs and His acts which He did in the midst of Egypt, to Pharaoh king of Egypt, and to all his land; [4]what He did to the army of Egypt, to their horses and their chariots: how He made the waters of the Red Sea overflow them as they pursued you, and how the Lord has destroyed them to this day; [5]what He did for you in the wilderness until you came to this place.... [7] your eyes have seen every great act of the Lord which He did.

***Deuteronomy 11:2-7***

## 11. *Transmission to Future Generations*

But it is not with you alone that I am making this covenant and oath. [14] I am making it both with those who are standing there with us today before God our Lord, and with those who are not yet here with us today. [15] You know full that we lived in Egypt, and that we also passed through the territories of the nations you encountered. [16] You saw the disgusting, putrid idols that they have, made of wood and stone, gold and silver.

***Deuteronomy 29:13-16***

Only take heed and watch yourself very carefully, so that you do not forget the things that your eyes saw. Do not let [this memory] leave your hearts, all the days of your lives. Teach you children and children's children about the day you stood before the Lord your God and Horeb.

[10] It was then that God said to me, "Congregate the people for Me, and I will let them hear My words. This will teach them to be in awe of Me as long as they live on the earth, and they will also teach their children."

***Deuteronomy 4:9-10***

I will open my mouth in a parable; I will utter dark sayings of old, [3] which we have heard and known, and our fathers have told us. [4] We will not conceal them from their children, but tell to the generation to come the praises of the Lord, and His strength and His wondrous works that He has done. [5] For He established a testimony in Jacob, And appointed a law in Israel, which He commanded our fathers, That they should teach them to their children, [6] That the generation to come might know, even the children yet to be born, That they may arise and tell them to their children, [7] That they should put their confidence in God, And not forget the works of God, but keep His commandments.

***Psalm 78:2-7***

## 12. *Writing the Legacy*

Moses finished writing the words of this Torah in a scroll to the very end.

***Deuteronomy 31:24***

## 13. *Prohibition of Change*

Do not add to the word that I am commanding you, and do not subtract from it. You must keep all the commandments of the Lord your God, which I am instructing you.

***Deuteronomy 4:2***

## 14. *Formal Distribution of the Legacy*

Moses then wrote down this Torah. He gave it to Levi's descendants, the priests in charge of the ark of God's covenant, and the elders of Israel.

***Deuteronomy 31:9***

Now write for yourselves this song and teach it to the Israelites. Make them memorize it, so that this song will be a witness for the Israelites.

***Deuteronomy 31:19***

## 15. *Archive for Preservation of Testimony*

Moses then gave orders to the Levites who carried the Ark of God's covenant, saying, "Take this Torah scroll and place it inside the ark of the Lord your God, leaving it there as a witness."

***Deuteronomy 31:25***

# Kri and Kesiv - קרי וכתיב

What is to be read

What is to be written

Genesis 36:5 **(Original Hebrew)**

וְאָהֳלִיבָמָה יָלְדָה אֶת־(יעיש) [יְעוּשׁ] וְאֶת־יַעְלָם וְאֶת־קֹרַח אֵלֶּה בְּנֵי עֵשָׂו אֲשֶׁר יֻלְּדוּ־לוֹ בְּאֶרֶץ כְּנָעַן׃

Genesis 36:5 **(King James Version)**

And Aholibamah bare ***Jeush***, and Jaalam, and Korah: these are the sons of Esau, which were born unto him in the land of Canaan.

## Josh McDowell

*Evidence That Demands a Verdict*

*Geisler and Nix* make the following comment about how textual variations are counted: "There is an ambiguity in saying there are some 200,000 variants in the existing manuscripts of the New Testament, since these represent only 10,000 places in the New Testament. If one single word is misspelled in 3,000 different manuscripts, this is counted as 3,000 variants or readings."

Although he was dealing with fewer manuscripts than we have today, *Philip Shaff* in *Comparison to the Greek Testament and the English Version* concluded that only 400 of the 150,000 variant readings caused doubt about the textual meaning, and only 50 of these were of great significance.

*Here's Life Publishers, Inc.: San Bernardino, CA, 1979, page 44 .*

# Transmission to Future Generations

## 16. *Parents to Children*

Teach your children to speak of them, when you are at home, when traveling on the road, when you lie down and when you get up.

***Deuteronomy 11:19***

These words which I command you today must remain on your heart. [7] Teach them to your children and speak of them when you are at home, when traveling on the road, when you lie down and when you get up.

***Deuteronomy 6:6-7***

## 17. *The Foundations of Morality*

You must show love toward the foreigner, since you were foreigners in the land of Egypt.

***Deuteronomy 10:19***

Do not pervert justice for the proselyte or orphan. Do not take a widow's garment as security for a loan. [18] You must remember that you were a slave in Egypt, and the Lord your God then liberated you. It is for that reason that I am commanding you to do this. [19] When you reap your grain harvest and forget a sheaf in the field, you must not go back to get it. It must be left for the foreigner, orphan and widow, so that the Lord your God will bless you, no matter what you do.... [22] I am commanding you to do this because you must remember that you were a slave in Egypt.

***Deuteronomy 24:17-22***

## 18. *Weekly Day of Spiritual Rejuvenation*

Observe the Sabbath to keep it holy, as God your Lord commanded you. [13] You can work during the six weekdays, and do all your work, [14] but Saturday is the Sabbath to God your Lord, so do not do anything that constitutes work.... [15] You must remember that you were slaves in Egypt, when the Lord your God brought you out with a strong hand and an outstretched arm. It is for this reason that the Lord your God has commanded you to keep the Sabbath.

***Deuteronomy 5:12-15***

## 19. *Number Sign (Tattoo) on Body*

This is My covenant between Me, and between you and your offspring that you must keep: You must circumcise every male. [11] You shall be circumcised through the flesh of your foreskin. This shall be the mark of the covenant between Me and you. [12] Throughout all generation, every male shall be circumcised when he is eight days old....

***Genesis 17:10-12***

## 20. *Special Garments — Yellow Badge With the Star of David*

God spoke to Moses, telling him to speak to the Israelites and have them make tassels on the corners of their garments for all generations. They shall include a twist of sky-blue wool in the corner tassels. These shall be your tassels, and when you see them, you shall remember all of God's commandments so as to keep them....I am the Lord your God who brought you out of Egypt to be your God. I am the Lord your God.

***Numbers 15:37-41***

## 21. *Excerpt From the Scroll on Head and Heart*

[These words] shall be to you as a sign on your hand and as a memorial between your eyes, that the law of the Lord may be in your mouth; for with a strong hand the Lord has brought you out of Egypt.

***Exodus 13:9***

## 22. *Excerpt From the Scroll on Doorpost*

Write them on [parchments affixed to] the door posts of your houses and gates.

***Deuteronomy 6:9***

## 23. *Membership Sanctions*

Do not intermarry with them. Do not give your daughters to their sons, and do not take their daughters for your sons.

***Deuteronomy 7:3***

I see [this nation] from mountain tops, and gaze on it from the heights. It is a nation dwelling alone at peace, not counting itself among the nations.

***Numbers 23:9***

## 24. *Yearly Family Gathering: Transmission to the Next Generation*

When your son asks you in time to come, "What is the meaning of the testimonies and the statutes and the ordinances which the Lord our God has commanded you?" [21]then you shall say to your son, "We were Pharaoh's slaves in Egypt; and the Lord brought us out of Egypt with a mighty hand; [22]and the Lord showed signs and wonders, great and grievous, against Egypt and against Pharaoh and all his household, before our eyes; [23]and he brought us out from there, that he might bring us in and give us the land which he swore to give to our fathers.

***Deuteronomy 6:20-23***

## 25. *Commemoration of Deliverance: Potato Peels and Stale Bread*

You shall eat no leavened bread with it; seven days you shall eat it with unleavened bread, the bread of affliction — for you came out of the land of Egypt in hurried flight — that all the days of your life you may remember the day when you came out of the land of Egypt.

***Deuteronomy 16:3***

## 26. *Commemoration of Traveling to the Promised Land by Ship*

You shall dwell in booths for seven days; all that are native in Israel shall dwell in booths, [43]that your generations may know that I made the people of Israel dwell in booths when I brought them out of the land of Egypt: I am the Lord your God.

***Leviticus 23:42-43***

## 27. *Commemoration of Founding International Networks*

And you shall count from the morrow after the Sabbath, from the day that you brought the sheaf of the wave offering; seven full weeks shall they be.... [21]This very day shall be celebrated as a sacred holiday when no service work may be done. This is an eternal law for all generations, no matter where you may live.

***Leviticus 23:15-21***

# By David Ben Gurion

About 300 years ago a ship set sail for the new world and its name was the Mayflower. Its passengers were Englishmen who had become disgusted with their government and their society. They set out in search of some deserted shore to establish a new life for themselves. They landed in America and they were the first founders of that land and that people. This was an important event in the history of both England and America. And for this reason, to this day, every American child knows of the Mayflower, the pilgrims, Plymouth Rock and November 25, Thanksgiving Day.

I am, however, very interested in knowing if any Englishman, or American for that matter, is aware of the hour and the day that the Mayflower set sail? Does any child or even adult know how many pilgrims there were on this historical voyage? What were the names of their families? What did they wear? What did they eat? Where did they get water to drink? What path did they navigate and what happened en route?

Behold, it was more than 3,300 years ago that the Jews set out from Egypt. Every Jewish child all over the world - in America, Soviet Russia, Yemen, and Germany - knows exactly how his ancestors left at dawn on the 15th of Nissan. What did they wear? "Their loins were girded, their sandals were on their feet and their staffs were in their hands? (Exodus 12:11). They ate matzot and they arrived at the Red Sea after a seven-day journey. These children also know the route that their ancestors traveled and what events transpired during their 40-year trek in the wilderness. They ate Manna and Quail, they drank water from the Well of Miriam. They arrived at the borders of the Promised Land on the banks of the Jordan River facing Jericho. They know the names of their ancestors and they can quote them to you from the Five Books of Moses.

Till this day, Jews the world over eat the same matzot for seven days starting from the 15th of Nissan each year. And they relate the story of the Exodus and the tribulation that the Jews have suffered from the day they left their land and wandered into exile. And they end by shouting two phrases that children and parents and grandparents have been saying for thousands of years: 'Now we are slaves. Next year we will be free men. Now we are here in exile. Next year we will be in Jerusalem....' in the land of Israel. This is the nature of the Jews."

From Ben Gurion's speech in front of the Anglo-American Investigation Committee of the United Nations, 1948

**Credits**:
The text used in *Bearers of the Torch* has been adapted from the Arachim source book, *Pathways to the Torah*.
Photographs on pages 143 and 145 were copied with permission from the book, *From Holocaust to Redemption: Bearing Witness*. Published by The World Gathering of Jewish Holocaust Survivors; 1984.

## Part XIV

# Paul and the Christian Corruption of the Jewish Scriptures

## Why did the author of the book of Luke interpolate the phrase "Recovery of Sight to the Blind" into the mouth of the Prophet Isaiah?

| Luke 4:18-19 | Isaiah 61:1-2 *(KJV)* |
|---|---|
| The Spirit of the Lord is upon me, because he has anointed me to preach the gospel to the poor; he has sent me to heal the brokenhearted, to proclaim liberty to the captives and **recovery of sight to the blind**, to set at liberty those who are oppressed; [19]to proclaim the acceptable year of the Lord. | The Spirit of the Lord God is upon me; because the Lord hath anointed me to preach good tidings unto the meek; he hath sent me to bind up the brokenhearted, to proclaim liberty to the captives, and the opening of the prison to them that are bound; [2]to proclaim the acceptable year of the Lord, |

### Romans 9:24-26

Even us, whom he also called, not only from the Jews but also from the Gentiles? As he says in Hosea: "I will call them 'my people' who are not my people; and I will call her 'my loved one' who is not my loved one, and, it will happen that in the very place where it was said to them, 'You are not my people,' they will be called 'sons of the living God.'"

**In Romans 9:25, Paul erroneously claims that a prophecy from the Book of Hosea (2:25) proves that the gentiles, who, he asserts, were originally not God's people, would be called "My people."**

**Paul, however, ripped Hosea 2:25 completely out of context. The first two chapters of the book of Hosea are clearly referring to the future restoration of the ten exiled tribes of the Northern Kingdom of Israel who will finally be called "My people" in the messianic age. This prophecy is not speaking about the gentiles, as Paul argues.**

### Hosea 1:3-9

So he went and took Gomer the daughter of Diblaim; which conceived, and bare him a son. And the Lord said unto him, "Call his name **Jezreel**; for yet a little while, and I will avenge the blood of Jezreel upon the house of Jehu, and will cause to cease the kingdom of the house of Israel. And it shall come to pass at that day, that I will break the bow of Israel in the valley of Jezreel." And she conceived again, and bare a daughter. And God said unto him, "Call her name **Lo'rachamah**: for I will no more have mercy upon the house of Israel; but I will utterly take them away. But I will have mercy upon the house of Judah, and will save them by the Lord their God, and will not save them by bow, nor by sword, nor by battle, by horses, nor by horsemen." Now when she had weaned Loruhamah, she conceived, and bare a son. Then said God, "Call his name **Lo'ammi**: for ye are not my people, and I will not be your God."

### Hosea 2:25 *(Christian Bible 2:23)*

And I will sow her for Myself in the land. I will also have compassion on her who had not obtained compassion, And I will say to those who were not My people, 'You are My people!' And they will say, "*Thou art* my God!"

### Isaiah 7:14-16

Therefore the Lord himself will give you a sign. Look, the young woman is with child and shall bear a son, and shall name him Immanuel. He shall eat curds and honey by the time he knows how to refuse the evil and choose the good.

For before the child knows how to refuse the evil and choose the good, the land before whose two kings you are in dread will be deserted.

**Isaiah 7:3-4**

Then the Lord said to Isaiah, "Go out to meet Ahaz, you and your son ***Shear-yashuv***, at the end of the conduit of the upper pool on the highway to the Washer's Field, [4]and say to him, 'Take heed, be quiet, do not fear, and do not let your heart be faint because of these two smoldering stumps of firebrands, because of the fierce anger of Rezin and Aram and the son of Remaliah."

**Isaiah 8:18**

"See, I and the children whom the Lord has given me are signs and portents in Israel from the Lord of hosts, who dwells on Mount Zion."

**The names given to the children of a prophet symbolized the destiny of the people to whom they were preaching. Therefore, whereas Hosea's children were given names which pointed to the demise of the Northern Kingdom of Israel, i.e. *"Lo-Amee"* ("You are not my people"), the names of Isaiah's children, on the other hand, indicated the divine preservation and protection the Almighty would bestow upon the Southern Kingdom of Judah. i.e. *"Shear-Yashuv"* (The remnant will remain). See Isaiah 8:18.**

**Galatians 3:6-9**

Just as Abraham "believed God, and it was accounted to him for righteousness." Know ye therefore that they which are of faith, the same are the children of Abraham. [8]And the scripture, foreseeing that God would justify the heathen through faith, preached before the gospel unto Abraham, *saying*, In thee shall all nations be blessed. [9]So then they which be of faith are blessed with faithful Abraham.

**Genesis 15:5-6**

And he brought him forth outside, and said, "Look now toward heaven, and tell the stars, if thou be able to number them: and he said unto him, So shall thy seed be." [6]And he [Abraham] believed in the Lord, and He counted it to him for righteousness.

**Genesis 26:4-5**

And I will make thy seed to multiply as the stars of heaven, and will give unto thy seed all these countries; and in thy seed shall all the nations of the earth be blessed; [5]**Because that Abraham obeyed My voice, and kept My charge, My commandments, My statutes, and My laws**.

**Genesis 12:2-3**

"I will make you into a great nation and I will bless you; I will make your name great, and you will be a blessing. [3]I will bless those who bless you, and whoever curses you I will curse; and all peoples on earth will be blessed through you."

**Genesis 15:2-5**

Abram said, "O Lord God, what will You give me, since I am childless, and the heir of my house is Eliezer of Damascus?" [3]And Abram said, "Since You have given no offspring to me, the one born in my house is my heir." [4]Then behold, the word of the Lord came to him, saying, "**This man will not be your heir; but one who will come forth from your own body, he shall be your heir**." [5]And he brought him forth outside, and said, "Look now toward heaven, and tell the stars, if thou be able to number them: and he said unto him, So shall thy seed be."

## Galatians 3:15-16

Brethren, I speak in terms of human relations, even though it is only a man's covenant, yet when it has been ratified, no one sets it aside or adds conditions to it. [16]Now the promises were spoken to Abraham and to his seed. He does not say, "And to seeds," as referring to many, but rather to one, "And to your seed," that is, Christ.

## Genesis 17:19

And God said, Sarah thy wife shall bear thee a son indeed; and thou shalt call his name Isaac: and I will establish my covenant with him for an everlasting covenant, and with his **seed** (לְזַרְעוֹ) after him.

**Paul insists that the promise given to Abraham where God would make a covenant with his "seed," rather than his "seeds," clearly demonstrates that this covenant was being made to only one *singular* individual. This can only be Jesus, concludes the "Apostle to the Gentiles."**

**This shocking theological claim which Paul argues in Galatians 3:15-16 is, however, completely flawed. The Torah only uses the word "seed" rather than the word "seeds" when referring to the entire Nation of Israel. Numerous examples are listed below.**

## Genesis 13:16

And I will make thy **seed** (זַרְעֲךָ) as the dust of the earth: so that if a man can number the dust of the earth, then shall thy **seed** (זַרְעֲךָ) also be numbered.

## Genesis 15:5

And he brought him forth abroad, and said, Look now toward heaven, and tell the stars, if thou be able to number them: and he said unto him, So shall thy **seed** (זַרְעֶךָ) be.

## Genesis 16:10

And the angel of the Lord said unto her, I will multiply thy **seed** (זַרְעֵךְ) exceedingly, that it shall not be numbered for multitude.

## Genesis 22:17

That in blessing I will bless thee, and in multiplying I will multiply thy **seed** (זַרְעֲךָ) as the stars of the heaven, and as the sand which is upon the sea shore; and thy **seed** (זַרְעֲךָ) shall possess the gate of his enemies;

## Genesis 26:4

And I will make thy **seed** (לְזַרְעֲךָ) to multiply as the stars of heaven, and will give unto thy **seed** all these countries; and in thy **seed** (בְזַרְעֲךָ) shall all the nations of the earth be blessed;

## Genesis 46:6

And they took their cattle, and their goods, which they had gotten in the land of Canaan, and came into Egypt, Jacob, and all his **seed** (זַרְעוֹ) with him.

## II Kings 11:1

And when Athaliah the mother of Ahaziah saw that her son was dead, she arose and destroyed all the **seed** (זֶרַע) royal.

## 2 Chronicles 20:7

Art not thou our God, who didst drive out the inhabitants of this land before thy people Israel, and gavest it to the **seed** (לְזֶרַע) of Abraham thy friend forever? *(see also Mal. 2:15)*

**Genesis 3:15**
And I will put enmity between thee and the woman, and between thy **seed** (זַרְעֲךָ) and her seed; he shall bruise thy head, and thou shalt bruise his heel.

**I John 3:8**
He that commiteth sin is of the devil; for the devil sinneth from the beginning. For this purpose **the son of God was manifested, that he might destroy the works of the devil.**

**Hebrews 2:14**
Forasmuch then as the children are partakers of flesh and blood, he also himself likewise took part of the same; that **through death he might destroy him that had the power of death, that is, the devil**;

**I Samuel 2:20**
And Eli blessed Elkanah and his wife, and said, The Lord **give thee seed (זֶרַע) of this woman** for the loan which is lent to the Lord. And they went unto their own home.

**Genesis 4:7**
If you do that which is well, would that not be accepted? And if you do that which is not well, sin lies by the door, you shall be his desire, and you shall rule over him.

**Genesis 3:20**
And Adam called his wife's name Eve; because she was the mother of all living.

**I Thessalonians 2:18**
Wherefore we would have come unto you, even I Paul, once and again; **but Satan hindered us**.

## Part XV

# Rabbi Singer Answers Questions

# A Lutheran Doesn't Understand Why Rabbi Singer Doesn't Believe in Jesus: A Closer Look at the "Crucifixion Psalm"

## Question:

Dear Rabbi Singer,

I am a Lutheran living in Switzerland and have been reading your web page with interest. I admire your commitment to your faith, yet I am perplexed as to why you so assuredly reject Jesus Christ as your messiah. He came not only for the gentiles, but for the Jews as well. He was born to a Jewish mother and came to the Jewish people.

Because you are a rabbi, I am particularly perplexed as to why you have not willingly accepted Christ. You surely have read the 22nd Psalm which most clearly speaks of our Lord's crucifixion. Read verse 16. It states, "Dogs have compassed me; the assembly of the wicked has enclosed me; they pierced my hands and my feet." Of whom does the prophet speak other than our Lord? This Old Testament prophecy could only be foretelling Jesus' unique death on the cross. What greater proof is needed that Jesus died for the sins of mankind than this chapter which was written a thousand years before Jesus walked this earth?

I know that the Jews have been maligned and persecuted by so-called Christians. This has certainly left a bad taste in the mouths of the Jewish people against Christ; but certainly you must know, rabbi, that these were not real Christians, for a believer in Christ must love the Jew, for his Savior is a Jew.

Many Jewish people accuse Christians of anti-Semitism, and one can understand from where this bias is coming; for the Jews have been persecuted by those who claim to be Christian, but they are not. The true Christian loves the Jewish people.

Yours,

## Answer:

This is certainly one of the more surprising letters that I have received in recent memory. There is nothing about your question that is unusual or uncommon; I receive questions about this most-debated Psalm regularly. It is rather the denomination with which you proudly identify that caught me by surprise.

How odd that a Lutheran would proclaim that the tormentors of the Jews "were not real Christians," yet you apparently are not embarrassed to identify yourself with a denomination that is called after, and founded on, the teachings of Martin Luther. Among all the Church Fathers and Reformers, there was no mouth more vile, no tongue that uttered more vulgar curses against the Children of Israel than this founder of the Reformation whom you apparently revere. Even the anti-Semitism of the New Testament and the church fathers pales in comparison to the invectives launched by Luther's impious tongue during his lifetime.

In your letter you declared with certainty that those "so-called Christians" who "maligned and persecuted" the Jewish people "were not real Christians." Do you believe that the founder of your church, Martin Luther, should be counted among those who are not real Christians? Have you not read his odious volume entitled, *Of the Jews and Their Lies*? If you are familiar with this and other indecent works of Luther, do you also believe that this German Reformer lost his salvation because his maniacal

**For Luther's complete work**
***"Of the Jews and Their Lies,"*** **go to:**
**www.outreachjudaism.org/luther1543new.html**

hatred for the Jew prevented him from being an upstanding member of Christendom? If this is in fact what you believe, why would you belong to a church that boasts his unblessed name?

These burning questions do not apply to you and other members of your denomination alone. Every member of the Protestant church and every Christian who looks to the Reformers as vessels of God must wonder aloud whether God would use anti-Semites to carry out a sacred task? For virtually all the other leaders of the Reformation held the Jewish people in utter contempt as well. Martin Bucer's sneering disdain for the Jews is legendary; and, although Calvin's epithets against the Jews are less plentiful than Luther's abundant invectives, this disparity is not due to Calvin's piety. Rather, it is unlikely that Calvin, the father of the Presbyterian and Reformed Church, encountered any Jews at all during lifetime. Although the Swiss Reformer lived in countries where Jews were forbidden to reside, his words were no less disturbing than those of Martin Luther (see page 4-5).

Although evangelicals proudly declare that true believing Christians love the Jewish people, this assertion is not consistent with the annals of history. With few exceptions, the tormentors of the Jewish people emerged out of the fundamentalist Church. Remarkably, denominations that evangelical Christians regard as heretical, such as The Church of the Latter Day Saints and Jehovah's Witnesses, do not have a strong history of anti-Semitism. Liberal-leaning Christian denominations such as the Unitarian and Methodist churches also have for the most part resisted this teaching of contempt that is so ensconced in Christendom's shameful history.

The consistent and unyielding pattern of Jew-hatred that has for so long gripped the imagination of the true believer cannot be attributed to coincidence or to a remarkable quirk of history. The accounts in the New Testament — the most cherished book of the devout Christian — already display the animus of the early church toward the Jews, portraying them as the people of the devil: cunning, traitorous, corrupt, deceitful, and conspiring. In essence, whatever it is that humanity abhors, that is precisely how the Jews are depicted in the Christian Bible. Without rest, post-canonical Christian literature continued to perpetuate this dark image of the Jew. There can be little doubt as to why Christians believe of the Jews what common sense would forbid them to believe of anyone else. To some extent, Luther and his countless followers who eagerly embraced his shameful message were together willing followers of a body of literature that scandalized, smeared, and ultimately condemned the children of Israel to an unimaginable history.

Moreover, in an effort to distance Christians from a compelling Jewish message, the founders and defenders of Christianity methodically altered selected texts from the Jewish scriptures. This rewriting of *Tanach* was not done arbitrarily or subtly. The Church quite deliberately tampered with the words of the Jewish scriptures in order to bolster their most startling claim: The Old Testament clearly foretold that Jesus of Nazareth is the Messiah. With this goal in mind, missionaries manipulated, misquoted, mistranslated, and even fabricated verses in *Tanach* in order to make Jesus' life fit traditional Jewish messianic parameters and to make traditional Jewish messianic parameters fit the life of Jesus.

Bear in mind, the Jewish scriptures were written in Hebrew, not in seventeenth century King James English. What has made Christian believers so vulnerable to Bible tampering is that almost none of them can read or understand the Hebrew Bible in its original language. Virtually no Christian child in the world is taught the Hebrew language as part of a formal Christian education. As you and countless other Christians earnestly study the Authorized Version of the Bible, there is a blinding yet prevailing assumption that what you are reading is Heaven-breathed. Tragically, virtually every Christian in the world reads the translation of men rather than the Word of God. On the other hand, every Jewish child in the world who is enrolled in a Jewish school is taught to read and write Hebrew long before he or she even heard the name of Luther.

Unbeknownst to you and parishioners worldwide, the King James Version and numerous other Christian Bible translations were meticulously shaped in order to produce a message that would sustain and advance church theology and exegesis. This aggressive rewriting of biblical texts has had a devastating impact on Christians throughout the world who unhesitatingly embrace these twisted translations. As a result, Christians earnestly wonder, just as you have, why the Jews, who are the bearers and protectors of the divine oracles of God, have not willingly accepted Jesus as their messiah.

What evangelicals fail to understand, however, is that the passionate resistance of the Jew to the teachings of Christianity has little to do with the Church's bad manners and the direct result of the Church's contrived and therefore implausible message. This stunning conclusion, however, is impossible for Christians to accept without bringing injury to their own faith and world view.

Remember, in Christian theology the Jews are not just another worldly tribe whose beliefs conflict with the teachings of the church. Quite the contrary, the religion of Christianity readily concedes that the Jews were God's "firstborn" — the people who were chosen to receive and protect the divine oracles of God. The spiritual principles of such a priestly nation cannot be dismissed lightly. As a result, Christendom systematically engaged in a thorough ad hominem assault against the Jewish people, slandering them as a nefarious, demonic nation. It isn't difficult to understand how polemical literature against the Jews became a common feature in church writings. By declaring that the Jew rejects the claims of the Church as a result of Christian anti-Semitism, as you insist, or the Jew's spiritual blindness, evangelicals spare themselves the festering anguish that self-searching and self-doubt invariably create.

To understand the brazen manner in which the church tampered with the Jewish scriptures, let's examine the verse that you insist "*proves*" that Jesus is the messiah. Psalm 22:16 in the King James Version (KJV) reads,

> Dogs have compassed me; the assembly of the wicked have enclosed me; they ***pierced*** my hands and my feet.

It isn't difficult to understand why Christians are so confident that this verse contains a clear reference to Jesus' crucifixion. "This Old Testament prophecy could only be foretelling Jesus' unique death on the cross." "Of whom other than Jesus could the Psalmist be speaking?," missionaries ask. They insist that the Bible could not be referring to any other person in history but the man that bore the marks of the Cross.

Apparently, you were so impressed by this argument that you wondered how a rabbi like myself could miss this reference to Jesus' crucifixion. Paradoxically, well-educated Jews are utterly repelled by the manner in which the church rendered the words of Psalm 22:17.[1]

> Whereas in a Jewish Bible this verse appears as Psalm 22:17, in a Christian Bible it appears as 22:16. To avoid confusion, this verse will be referred to as Psalm 22:17 throughout this article.

To understand how Christian translators rewrote the words of King David, let's examine the original Hebrew words of this verse with a proper translation.

| Psalm 22:17 (16) | | |
|---|---|---|
| Correct Translation | Hebrew | King James Version (16) |
| For dogs have encompassed me; a company of evildoers have inclosed me; like a **lion**, they are at my hands and my feet. | כִּי סְבָבוּנִי כְּלָבִים<br>עֲדַת מְרֵעִים הִקִּיפוּנִי<br>כָּאֲרִי יָדַי וְרַגְלָי׃ | For dogs have compassed me, the assembly of the wicked have inclosed me; they **pierced** my hands and my feet. |

Notice that the English translation from the original Hebrew does not contain the word "pierced." The King James version deliberately mistranslates the Hebrew word *kaari* (כָּאֲרִי) as "pierced," rather than "like a lion," whereby misleading the reader into a false allusion that this Psalm is describing the Crucifixion. The Hebrew word כָּאֲרִי does not mean pierced but plainly means "like a lion. The end of Psalm 22:17, therefore, properly reads "like a lion they are at my hands and my feet." Had King David wished to write the word "pierced," he would never have used the Hebrew word *kaari*. Instead, he would have written either *daqar* or *ratza*, which are common Hebrew words in the Jewish scriptures. These common words mean to "stab" or "pierce." Needless to say, the phrase "they pierced my hands and my feet" is a not-too-ingenious Christian contrivance that appears nowhere in Tanach.

Bear in mind, this stunning mistranslation in the 22nd Psalm was not born out of ignorance. Christian translators were well aware of the correct meaning of this simple Hebrew word. They fully understood the meaning of the word כָּאֲרִי and deliberately twisted their translations of this text. The word *kaari* can be found in many other places in the Jewish scriptures and they correctly translated כָּאֲרִי "like a lion" in all places in Christian Bibles where this word appears with the exception of Psalm 22 – the Church's cherished "Crucifixion Psalm."

For example, the identical word *kaari* is also found in Isaiah 38:13. In the immediate context of this verse King Hezekiah is singing a song for deliverance from his grave illness. In the midst of his supplication he exclaims in Hebrew "שִׁוִּיתִי עַד־בֹּקֶר כָּאֲרִי." Notice that the last word in this phrase (moving from right to left) is the same Hebrew word *kaari* that appears in Psalm 22:17. In this Isaiah text, the *King James Version* correctly translates these words "I reckoned till morning that, as a lion...." As I mentioned above, Psalm 22:17 is the only place in all of the Jewish scriptures that any Christian Bible translates *kaari* as " pierced."

It must be noted that the authors of the New Testament were not responsible for inserting the word " pierced" into the text of Psalm 22:17. This verse was undoubtedly tampered with years after the Christian canon was completed. Bear in mind, during the latter half of the first century, when the New Testament writers were compiling their Greek manuscripts, Psalm 22:17 was still in pristine condition; thus, when the authors of the New Testament read this verse, they found nothing in the phrase " like a lion they are at my hands and my feet" that would advance their teachings. As a result, Psalm 22:17 is never quoted in the New Testament. Missionaries, who insist that the Christian translation of this verse reflects the original words of King David, must wonder why there was not one New Testament author who deemed this supposed allusion to the crucifixion worthy of being mentioned in his writings.

The reckless Bible tampering that was done to this verse is becomes obvious with only a cursory reading of the entire 22nd Psalm. Throughout this chapter, King David routinely uses an animal motif to describe his enemies. The Psalmist poignant references to the "dog" and "lion" are, therefore, common metaphors employed by the Psalmist. In fact, David repeatedly makes reference to the "dog" and "lion" both before and after Psalm 22:17. For King David, these menacing beasts symbolize his bitter foes who continuously sought to destroy him. This metaphor, therefore, sets the stage for the moving theme of this chapter. Although David's predicament at times seems hopeless, this faithful king relied on God alone for his deliverance. As the Psalmist eagerly looks to God for deliverance from his adversaries, he conveys the timeless message that it is the Almighty alone Who can save the faithful in times of tribulation. Let's examine a number of verses in this chapter that immediately surround Psalm 22:17 as they appear in the King James Version.

**King David, the author of Psalm 22, identifies his enemies as "lions" in the verses that immediately precede and follow Psalm 22:17 (16)**

| Psalm 22:12-13 (KJV) | Psalm 22:20:21 (KJV) |
|---|---|
| Many bulls have compassed me: strong *bulls* of *Bashan* have beset me round. 13They gaped upon me *with* their mouths, *as* a ravening and a roaring **lion**. | Deliver my soul from the sword; my darling from the power of the **dog**. 21Save me from the **lion's** mouth: for thou hast heard me from the horns of the unicorns. |

As mentioned above, it is obvious when reading this larger section of the 22nd Psalm that King David is using an animal motif — most commonly lions — as an animated literary device, in order to describe his pursuers and tormentors. This striking style is pervasive in this section of the Bible. In fact, each and every time the word "lion" appears in the Book of Psalms, King David is referring to a metaphoric lion, rather than a literal animal.

For example, in the 17th Psalm King David appeals to the Almighty to rescue him from the hands of his enemies, the "lion." Bear in mind, an examination of the 17th Psalm is of great relevance to our study because in many respects Psalm 17 and 22 are sister chapters, both with regard to their literary motif and driving theme. In the

17th Psalm, he is seeking deliverance from his adversaries as in Psalm 22. In Psalm 17:8-12, the he pleads with God for deliverance from the "lion," as he cries out,

> Hide me under the shadow of Your wings, from the wicked who oppress me, from my deadly enemies, who compass me about. They are enclosed in their own fat; with their mouths they speak proudly. They have now compassed us in our steps; they have set their eyes bowing down to the earth, **like a lion** that is greedy of his prey, and as it were a young **lion** lurking in secret places.

Fearing that he has been abandoned by God, David implores the Almighty to answer his supplications for help, mitigating any question as to the identity of the psalmist. It is explicitly clear from the very first verse of this chapter that the person speaking is King David.

> "Lord, how long wilt thou look on? Rescue my soul from their destruction, my darling from the **lions**."

Moreover, missionaries are confronted with another stunning problem in their effort to interpellate the words of this Psalm into a first century crucifixion story. In the simplest terms, this text that Christians eagerly quote is not a prophecy, nor does it speak of any future event. This entire Psalm, as well as Psalm 23:1-3 that follows, contains a famous personal prayer in which King David cried out to God from the depths of his pain and anguish – a fugitive from his family and former friends who betrayed him. Accordingly, the stirring monologue in this chapter is all in the first person. Fearing that he has been abandoned by God, David implores Him to answer his supplications for help, mitigating any question as to the identity of the psalmist. It is explicitly clear from the very first verse of this chapter that the person speaking is King David..

Understandably, Trinitarian Christians are confronted with another staggering problem; attributing this to anyone other than David, i.e. Jesus is nonsensical, considering that most Christians deem Jesus and God to be one entity. In the beginning of this chapter the Psalmist cries aloud,

> "My God, my God, why have You forsaken me? Why are You so far from helping me, and from the words of my groaning? O my God, I cry in the daytime, but You do not hear; and in the night season, and am not silent." (Psalm 22:1-3)

Why would Jesus, whom Trinitarians insist is God, complain that "God is so far from helping me?" To whom was he complaining? How could God, the first Person of the Trinity, not hear the cries of God – the second Person of the Trinity? To whom is this supposed god/man complaining? Finally, why would God be complaining to God? Confused, the bewildered speaker beseeches an answer from a silent God, whom he believes is ignoring his supplications. In the verses that follow, David questions his feelings of abandonment when enumerating the times when God did listen and intervene on behalf of his ancestors. If God and Jesus were truly one entity, then how or why would God not understand His predicament? How can God wonder why God doesn't hear His own prayers? Furthermore, who are God's ancestors? Applying the words of Psalm 22 to Jesus challenges even the most fertile imagination and places an enormous strain on Church teachings.

The nagging question that comes to mind is: Why did the King James Version translate the Hebrew word כָּאֲרִי *(kaari)* in Isaiah 38:13 correctly, "like a lion," yet deliberately mistranslate this same word as "pierced" in Psalm 22:17? These Christian translators were clearly aware of the correct meaning of the word *kaari*, as evidenced by their translation of Isaiah 38:13. Why then did they specifically tamper with Psalm 22?

To fully understand the Church felt compelled to revise the 22nd Psalm, it is essential to grasp the central role this chapter plays in traditional Christian teachings. Church fathers have always cherished Psalm 22 as a chapter that explicitly describes in vivid detail the agony of the Passion Narratives and provides the Gospel's script for Jesus' crucifixion. Segments of this Psalm are quoted extensively in the New Testament as a fulfillment of an Old Testament prophecy of the crucifixion. The most notable quote from Psalm 22 appears in the first two Gospels and is found in the chapter's opening verses, "My God, my God, why have You forsaken me?" Matthew and Mark place this desperate monologue in the mouth of the crucified Jesus as his last dying words.[2] These two Gospels resourcefully use Psalm 22 as one of many palettes from which to paint the brutal picture of a tormented crucified savior. All of the Gospels[3] similarly use Psalm 22:19 (22:18 in a Christian Bible) in their crucifixion narratives, and Hebrews 2:12 quotes Psalm 22:23 to explain why the messiah had to suffer for humanity.

Psalm 22 has, therefore, always been a vital text to the Church and was used repeatedly in order to retroject the life of Jesus back into the "Old Testament." In so doing, missionaries sought to lend credibility to their claim that Jesus is the messiah as was foreordained by the ancient Jewish prophets. For Christendom, the Psalmist's original intent was superseded by their interest in applying this entire chapter to Jesus' passion, no matter how extensive the revisions would be. The Church, therefore, did not hesitate to tamper with the words of the 22nd Psalm so that its verses would reflect and sustain its Christian message. Isaiah 38:13, on the other hand, possesses no Christological value to the church and was neither quoted nor used by the church fathers to propagate their teachings. The Church, therefore, had no need to mistranslate it; and thus it was left intact.

Interestingly, the stunning mistranslation in this chapter did not escape the notice of the missionary world. In fact, this controversy has attracted quite a bit of attention from Christians dedicated to Jewish evangelism. For example, Moshe Rosen, the founder of Jews for Jesus, advances a rather inventive response to this controversy over the appearance of the word "pierced" in Christian translations of Psalm 22. In his widely distributed book, *Y'shua*, Rosen readily concedes that the Hebrew word *kaari* does mean "like a lion," and not "pierced"; yet it is on this very point where he makes his argument.

He suggests that although the word "pierced" does not exist in the Hebrew Masoretic text, it is possible that a scribe may have inadvertently changed the word "pierced" into "like a lion" by modifying one small Hebrew letter. In his own words he writes,

> We can probably best understand what happened when we realize that, in Hebrew, the phrase "they have pierced" is *kaaru* while "like a lion" is *kaari*. The words are identical except that "pierced" ends with the Hebrew letter *vav* and "lion" with a *yod*. *Vav* and *yod* are similar in form, and a scribe might easily have changed the text by inscribing a *yod* and failing to attach a vertical descending line so that it would become a *vav*.[4]

While Rosen's proposition is quoted frequently by missionaries, it contains numerous remarkable flaws. Transforming *kaari* (כָּאֲרִי) into *kaaru* (כָּאֲרוּ) by changing the letters *kaf* (כ), *alef* (א), *raish* (ר), *yod* (י), which means "like a lion," into *kaf* (כ), *alef* (א) , *raish* (ר), *vav* (ו),does not create the Hebrew word for "pierced," as Rosen suggests. In fact, *kaaru* doesn't mean anything. In other words, this word *kaaru* does not exist in the Hebrew language; it's little more than Semitic gibberish. Rosen's claim that some anonymous scribe may have inadvertently changed *kaaru* into *kaari* is wholly unfounded and completely untenable.

In order to concoct a word that resembles *kaaru*, one would not only have to change the letter *yod* into a *vav*, but the letter *alef* would have to be removed altogether. This alteration would create the three-letter word *karu* (כָּרוּ), spelled *kaf, raish, vav*. *Karu*, however, doesn't mean "pierced" either. It means to "excavate" or "dig." As mentioned above, the words used in *Tanach* for "pierce" or "stab" are *daqar* or *ratza*, never *karu*, which does not have the connotation of "piercing" – as in puncturing through something.

For example, the King James Version renders אָזְנַיִם כָּרִיתָ לִּי in Psalm 40:7 (verse 6 in a Christian Bible) metaphorically as "mine ears hast thou opened." The Hebrew word כָּרִיתָ contains the same root as the word כארו (without the א *aleph*) that Christians claim is in Psalm 22:17, and it literally means "ears you have dug for me."

Within the context of Psalm 40:7, the meaning is clear, by digging or excavating his ear, the Psalmist is able to hear and perceive what God did and didn't desire. If *karah* could be translated as " pierce," this would mean that the Psalmist is piercing or stabbing his ears to hear God more clearly! The word כרו means to "open" or "excavate," not rip through flesh.

In recent years, a conservative, evangelical Christian professor of Religious Studies at Trinity Western University, Canada, made the assertion that an ancient, second century manuscript supports the reading of "pierced" in Psalm 22. In his book, *The Dead Sea Scrolls Bible* (2002), Dr. Peter Flint claims that scraps of scroll found the Nahal Hever Cave support the Christological reading rather than the Messoretic Text which clearly reads, "like a lion." The Nahal Hever Cave is located about 30 km south of Qumran. The document Flint is making reference to is designated as 5/6HevPs.

Bear in mind that the Nahal Hever manuscripts are considerably younger than the Dead Sea Scrolls. While the Qumran Dead Sea Scrolls manuscripts predates the first Jewish War (66 CE), the manuscripts from Nahal Hever came from a later period; between the two Jewish Wars (between 70 CE and 135 CE). Despite the claims made by Professor Flint in the *Dead Sea Scrolls Bible*, the passage in 5/6HevPs does not "unambiguously read pierce."

| Hebrew | Translit | Meaning | Comment |
|---|---|---|---|
| כארי | *Kaari* | "Like a lion" | This is the word which appears in all the Mesoretic texts in the world. |
| כארו | *Kaaru* | Does not exists in the Hebrew language | Christians claim that this non-existent word means "pierced," and appears in the Nahal Hever Cave. |
| כרו | *Karu* | "Dig" or "excavate" | The root of this word appears many times in Tanach. It does not mean to "pierce" through flesh. |

**The scrap from Psalm 22 found at Nachal Hever (5/6Hev - Col. XI, frag. 9) with the text under investigation from Psalm 22:17 enhanced.**

The above image was digitally enhanced, and it is difficult to discern by studying the faint, ancient text whether the word in question ends in a elongated י *(yud)* or a shortened ו *(vav)*. Unlike other ancient texts, the writing on this script found at Nahal Hever is not sharp or uniform. If, for arguments sake, we conclude that the debated word written in the Nahal Hever script is כארו (*ka'aru*), as Rosen and Flint argue, it is obvious that this anomaly is the result of the scribe's poor handwriting or spelling mistake. There is clear evidence, in fact, from an obvious spelling mistake in the script itself that the second century scribe was not meticulous. The very next word after the debated word is "my hands." The Hebrew word in Psalm 22:17 is ידי *(yadai)*. The Nahal Hever scribe, however, misspelled this word [as well] by placing a the extra letter ה (*hey*) at the end of the word, thus the Nahal Hever 5/6HevPs reads ידיה instead of the correct ידי. The Hebrew word ידיה (*yadehah*) means "her hands," not "my hands."

Moreover, as explained, there is no verb in the Hebrew language as כארו (*ka'aru*). In order to create the word "dig" or "excavate" in the Hebrew language, the א (*aleph*) would have to be removed from the word כארו as well. Again, כארו *(ka'aru)* is Hebrew gibberish.

Rosen is not the only church apologist to use scribes and rabbis of antiquity to defend the Christian translation of Psalm 22. In fact, missionaries more frequently refer to the *Septuagint* to justify the manner in which Christian Bible translators render Psalm 22:17. They argue that the *Septuagint*, a Greek translation of the entire Old Testament, which was completed by 72 rabbis more than 200 years before the Christian century, renders the last phrase of Psalm 22:17 as "they pierced my hands and my feet." From this they conclude that even the rabbis who lived before the first century believed that the last clause of this verse reads "pierced" rather than "like a lion."

Evangelists are typically quite fond of this response because it enables them to circumvent the often-troubling original Masoretic Hebrew Bible. This notion may seem strange at first glance; yet, Christians typically begin their assault on Judaism by swearing allegiance to the Hebrew scriptures, more often than not, they will renounce this vow in order to rescue their dubious proof-texts.

While somewhat secondary, the Church as well as Enlightenment philosophers such as Immanuel Kant have consistently held a more favorable view of Jews, i.e. the ancient Hebrews of the Old Testament who lived prior to the first century than those who lived during and after the death of Jesus. The Jewish translators of the *Septuagint* are of course pre-Christian, and are, therefore, held in higher regard in the eyes of the Christendom than those Jews who rejected the claims attributed to Jesus.

Despite the overwhelming popularity of the contention that the Greek translation of 72 rabbis supports the use of the word "pierced" in Psalm 22:17, this explanation is completely without merit. It is universally conceded and beyond doubt that the rabbis who created the original Septuagint only translated the Five Books of Moses and nothing more. This undisputed point is well attested to by the Letter of Aristeas,[5] the Talmud,[6] Josephus,[7] the church fathers,[8] and numerous other critical sources. In other words, these ancient 72 rabbis did not translate the Book of Psalms. The Book of Psalms belongs to the third section of the Jewish scriptures called the *Ketuvim*, the Writings. This is an entirely different segment of Tanach from the Torah, which was the only section translated by the 72 rabbis. In essence, this missionary argument is predicated on a fabrication.

Moreover, even the current Septuagint of the Five Books of Moses, is an almost complete corruption of the original Greek translation that was compiled by the 72 rabbis more than 2,200 years ago at the request of King Ptolemy II of Egypt.[9] This fact is well known to us because the Talmud[10] records how these 72 translators distinctly rendered 15 phrases of the Torah in their translation. Of these 15 unique translations, only two of them are currently extant.[11] Extrapolating from this, we must conclude that the vast bulk of the current Septuagint, even of the Torah, is now the translation that was forged by the 72 Jewish scribes.

The Septuagint that is currently in our hands — especially the sections that are of the Prophets and Writings — is a Christian work, doctored and edited exclusively by Christian hands. That said, there is little wonder why the Septuagint is so esteemed by Christendom, particularly by the Greek Orthodox Church, which regards it as Sacred Scripture. (I address the subject of the unreliability of the Septuagint more thoroughly in an article entitled, *A Christian Defends Matthew by Insisting That the Author of the First Gospel Used the Septuagint in His Quote of Isaiah to Support the Virgin Birth* (see page 227).

Although Christendom is predisposed to a reverence for the Scriptures written in Greek, the children of Israel regard only the Hebrew Bible given to us by our prophets as holy and authoritative. It is these sacred texts that we diligently pore over day and night. No translation of the Bible, no matter how widely used by churches and academicians, holds any influence over learned and pious among our people.

Do not think in your heart that the Jewish people have missed the stirring messianic message contained in *Tanach* or we somehow do not understand our own Bible. It is our nation of Israel which is ordained to protect the integrity of these Holy Scriptures, our people who brought these sacred oracles to the world's nations, and it is our people to whom these promises were addressed.

With best wishes for a happy and healthy New Year, I remain very sincerely yours,

Rabbi Tovia Singer

**Footnotes:**

1. Although in a Jewish Bible this verse appears as Psalm 22:17, in a Christian Bible it appears as 22:16. So as not to create confusion, I refer to this controversial verse as Psalm 22:17 throughout this article.

2. In the book of Luke, Jesus' last dying words are, "Father, forgive them for they know not what they do." In John's Gospel, Jesus' last words are "It is finished."

3. Matthew 27:35; Mark 15:24; Luke 23:34; John 19:24.

4. Rosen, Moishe. *Y'shua*. Chicago: Moody, 1982, p. 45-46.

5. This Letter of Aristeas ($2^{nd}$-$3^{rd}$ century B.C.E.), written by a Hellenistic Jew, describes the events leading up to and surrounding the writing of the original *Septuagint*. There is considerable disagreement as to the date when this was written.

6. Tractate *Megillah*, 9a.

7. Josephus, preface to *Antiquities of the Jews*, Sec 3. For Josephus' detailed description of events surrounding the original authorship of the *Septuagint*, see Josephus' *Antiquities of the Jews*, XII, ii, 1-4.

8. For example, St. Jerome, in his preface to the *Book of Hebrew Questions*, addresses this issue and concedes that, "Add to this that Josephus, who gives the story of the seventy translators, reports them as translating only the Five Books of Moses; and we also acknowledge that these are more in harmony with the Hebrew than the rest." *Nicene and Post-Nicene Fathers*. Peabody: Hendrickson, Volume 6. P. 87.

9. Ptolemy II, also known as "Philadelphus," reigned from 283 to 245 B.C.E.

10. Tractate *Megillah*, 9a-9b.

11. Of these 15 phrases which appeared in the original *Septuagint* (Genesis 1:1; 1:26; 2:2; 5:2; 11:7; 18:12; 49:6; Exodus 4:20; 12:40; 24:5; 24:11; Leviticus 11:6; Numbers 16:15; Deuteronomy 4:19; 17:3), only Genesis 2:2 and Exodus 12:40 are found in the current Septuagint.

# Does the Hebrew Word *Alma* Really Mean "Virgin"?

## Question:

Dear Rabbi Singer,

I have listened to your tapes and I have also read a number of your articles on your web site regarding Christ's virgin birth and you make some very good points. I have discussed this issue with my pastor and although he did remark that he finds your arguments "interesting" he brought up a good argument (I think). He asked that if the Hebrew word alma only meant "young woman" and not "virgin," why is it that in every place the word alma appears in the Bible it is always referring to a virgin? I think he has made a good point and will relate your answer to him. I thank you in advance.

## Answer:

Your pastor's contention that "every place the word *alma* appears in the Bible it is always referring to a virgin" is incorrect. This is not the first time that I have come across a Christian who has made this erroneous assertion; and each and every time I hear it I am puzzled as to why these apologists do not do their research before making this claim. This is especially the case in our modern age where computer technology has made simple word studies so quick and easy to research. I will briefly explain your question for the readers of our website who are unfamiliar with this subject.

For nearly two millennia the church has insisted that the Hebrew word *alma* (עַלְמָה) can only mean "virgin." The church must hold this position because Matthew 1:22-23 translates alma in Isaiah 7:14 as "virgin." The first Gospel quotes this well-known verse to provide the only "Old Testament" proof text for the supposed virgin birth of Jesus. The stakes are high for Christendom, because if the Hebrew word *alma* does not mean virgin, Matthew is misquoting the prophet Isaiah, and both a key tenet of Christianity and the credibility of the first Gospel collapses.

How accurate is this Christian claim? The only place to explore this issue is in the Jewish scriptures. If the Hebrew word *alma* means virgin, then each usage in the Bible must be either a clear reference to a virgin or at the very least appear ambiguous. The word *alma* appears in the Jewish scriptures seven times. If even one reference clearly refers to a woman who is not a virgin, then Matthew's rendition of Isaiah 7:14 becomes untenable.

One of the places where the uncommon Hebrew word *alma* appears in the Bible is in Proverbs 30:18-20 which reads,

> There are three things which are too wonderful for me, for which I do not understand: [19]the way of an eagle in the sky, the way of a serpent on a rock, the way of a ship in the middle of the sea, and the way of a man with a young woman [*b'alma*]. [20]This is the way of an adulterous woman: she eats and wipes her mouth, and says, "I have done no wrong."

In the above three verses, King Solomon compares a man with an *alma* to three other things: an eagle in the sky, a serpent on a rock, and a ship in the sea. What do these three things all have in common? They leave no trace. After the eagle has flown across the sky, it is impossible to determine whether an eagle had ever flown through that particular airspace. Once a snake has slithered over a rock, there is no way to discern that the snake had ever crossed there (as opposed to a snake slithering over sand or grass, where it leaves a trail). After a ship has passed across the sea, its wake comes together and settles behind it and thus there is no way to discern whether a ship had ever moved through this body of water. Similarly, King Solomon declares that once a man has been sexually intimate with an alma, i.e. a young woman, no trace of sexual intercourse is visible, unlike a virgin who will leave behind a discharge of blood after her hymen is broken.

Therefore, in the following verse (verse 20) King Solomon explains that once this adulterous woman eats" (a metaphor for her fornication), she removes the trace of her sexual activity, "wipes her mouth, and says, I have done no wrong." The word *alma* clearly does not mean virgin.

In the same way that in the English language the words "young woman" have no bearing on whether virginity is present or not, in the Hebrew language there is no relationship between the words *alma* and virgin. On the contrary, it is usually a young woman who bears children. Had Isaiah wished to speak about a virgin, he would have used the word *betulah*[1] (בְּתוּלָה) not *alma*. *Betulah* is a common word in the Jewish scriptures, and can only mean "virgin."

Sincerely yours,

Rabbi Tovia Singer

# Footnote:

[1]In fact, although Isaiah used the Hebrew word *alma* only one time in his entire corpus (7:14), the prophet uses this word virgin (*betulah*) five times throughout the book of Isaiah (23:4; 23:12; 37:22; 47:1; 62:5).

# 'Dual Prophecy' and the Virgin Birth

## Question:

*One of the methods you used in your tape series to refute missionary claims is to point out the context of the prophecy. For example, you point out that the seventh chapter of Isaiah cannot be a prophecy about Jesus' virgin birth because it suggests that the prophecy was to have been fulfilled in Ahaz's lifetime, some 700 years before Jesus.*

*Still, maybe this is a "double prophecy," a prophecy about a boy to be born in the days of Ahaz and also a prophecy to the birth of Jesus. The context is only for the first application of this double prophecy. Rabbi, do you have any comments?*

## Answer:

When missionaries are confronted with the glaring problem that the context of Isaiah 7:14 is unrelated to the messiah or a virgin birth, they often argue that Isaiah 7:14 is a "dual prophecy." In order to fully grasp the massive theological problem missionaries are seeking to escape with using this response, I will first describe the traumatic events that are unfolding in the seventh chapter of Isaiah which are completely inconsistent with Matthew's application of these passages to his virgin-birth story.

To begin with, the word "virgin" does not appear in the seventh chapter of Isaiah.

The author of the first Gospel deliberately mistranslated the Hebrew word הָעַלְמָה *(ha'almah)* as "a virgin." This Hebrew word, however, does not mean "a virgin." It simple means "the young woman," with no implication of virginity. Most modern Christian Bibles[1] have corrected this erroneous translation, and their Bibles now correctly translate this Hebrew word as "the young woman." (see page 33)

Matthew, however, not only changed the meaning of the word הָעַלְמָה to apply this verse from the Jewish scriptures to the virgin birth, he also completely ripped Isaiah 7:14 out of context in order to apply it to his birth narrative of Jesus.

The seventh chapter of the Book of Isaiah begins by describing the military crisis that was confronting Ahaz, King of the Southern Kingdom of Judah. In about the year 732 B.C.E. the House of David was facing imminent destruction at the hands of two warring kingdoms: the northern Kingdom of Israel and the Kingdom of Syria. These two armies had laid siege to Jerusalem. The Bible relates that the House of David and King Ahaz were gripped with fear. Chapter seven relates how God sent the prophet Isaiah to reassure King Ahaz that divine protection was at hand – the Almighty would protect him, their deliverance was assured, and these two hostile armies would fail in their attempt to subjugate Jerusalem. In Isaiah 7:1-16 we read,

> And it came to pass in the days of Ahaz son of Jotham, son of Uzziah, king of Judah, that Rezin, king of Aram, and Pekah son of Remaliah, king of Israel, marched on Jerusalem to wage war against it, and **he could not wage war against it**. It was told to the **House of David**, saying, "Aram has allied itself with Ephraim," and **his heart and the heart of his people trembled** as the trees of the forest tremble because of the wind. The Lord said to Isaiah, "Now go out toward Ahaz, you and Shear-Yashuv your son to the edge of the conduit of the upper pool, to the road of the washer's field, and you shall say to him, 'Feel secure and calm yourself, do not fear, and let your heart not be faint because of these two smoking stubs of firebrands, because of the raging anger of Rezin and Aram and the son of Remaliah. Since Aram planned harm to you, Ephraim and the son of Remaliah, saying: "Let us go up against Judah and provoke it, and annex it to us; and let us crown a king in its midst, one who is good for us." So said the Lord God, "Neither shall it succeed, nor shall it come to pass . . . ."' The Lord continued to speak to Ahaz, saying, "Ask for yourself a sign from the Lord, your God; ask it either in the depths, or in the heights above." Ahaz said, "I will not ask, and I will not test the Lord." Then he said, "Listen now, O House of David, is

> it little for you to weary men, that you weary my God as well? Therefore the Lord, of His own, shall give you a sign: Behold the young woman is with child, and she shall bear a son, and she shall call his name Immanuel. Cream and honey he shall eat when he knows to reject bad and choose good; for, when the lad does not yet know to reject bad and choose good, the land whose two kings you dread, shall be abandoned."

It is clear from this chapter that Isaiah's declaration was a prophecy of the unsuccessful siege of Jerusalem by the two armies of the Kingdoms of Israel and Syria, not a virgin birth more than 700 years later. If we interpret this chapter as referring to Jesus' birth, what possible comfort and assurance would Ahaz, who was surrounded by to overwhelming military enemies, have found in the birth of a child seven centuries later? Both he and his people would have been long dead and buried. Such a sign would make no sense.

Verses 15-16 state that by the time this child reaches the age of maturity ("he knows to reject bad and choose good"), the two warring kings, Pekah and Rezin, will have been removed. We see, in II Kings 15-16, that this prophecy was fulfilled when both kings were assassinated. With an understanding of the context of Isaiah 7:14 alone, it is evident that the child born in Isaiah 7:14 is not referring to Jesus or to any future virgin birth. Rather, it is referring to the divine protection that Ahaz and his people would enjoy from their impending destruction at the hands of these two enemies, the northern Kingdom of Israel and Syria.

This is where the Christian response of a dual prophecy comes in. Missionaries attempt to explain away this stunning problem of Matthew's complete indifference to the biblical context of Isaiah 7:14 by claiming that Isaiah's words to Ahaz had two different applications. They concede that the first application of Isaiah's prophecy must have been addressed to Ahaz and his immediate crisis. That child that was born contemporaneously and the first leg of this dual prophesy was fulfilled at the time of Ahaz, 2,700 years ago.

Missionaries insist, however, that the second leg of this dual prophecy applied to Jesus' virgin birth 2,000 years ago.

Using this elaborate explanation, missionaries maintain that Matthew's use of Isaiah 7:14 is entirely appropriate. In short, these Christians claim that Isaiah's prophecy was fulfilled twice: once in 732 B.C.E., and a second time in the year 1 C.E. Problem solved. Or is it?

The self-inflicted problems spawned by this far-reaching explanation are manifold. To begin with, the notion of a dual prophecy was fashioned without any biblical foundation. Nowhere in the seventh chapter of Isaiah does the text suggest a second fulfillment.[2] This alien notion of a dual prophecy was contrived in order to conceal a stunning theological problem – the seventh chapter of Isaiah is describing a contemporaneous, traumatic civil war which occurred 2,700 years ago, not the birth of a messiah centuries later. Simply put, the Book of Matthew ripped Isaiah 7:14 completely out of context.

Moreover, if, as missionaries argue, the Hebrew word *almah* can only mean a "virgin," and, as they insist, Isaiah 7:14 was fulfilled twice, who was the first virgin to conceive during Ahaz's lifetime? Were there two virgin births? Meaning, if Christians claim that the virgin birth of Isaiah 7:14 was fulfilled twice, who then was the first virgin to deliver a baby boy in 732 B.C.E.? Bear in mind that these missionaries assert that the word *almah* can only mean "virgin." Are they suggesting that Mary was not the only virgin in history to conceive and give birth to a son?

Furthermore, if missionaries contend that the seventh chapter of Isaiah contains a dual prophecy, how do the verses that follow, Isaiah 7:15-16, apply to Jesus where the prophet continues to discuss this lad? Isaiah 7:15-16 states,

> Cream and honey he shall eat when he knows to reject bad and choose good; 16 for, when the lad does not yet know to reject bad and choose good, the land whose two kings you dread, shall be abandoned.

If the seventh chapter of Isaiah contains a dual prophecy, at what age did the baby Jesus mature? Which were the two kingdoms identified by the prophet Isaiah that were abandoned during Jesus' lifetime? Who, during the first century C.E., "dreaded" the Kingdom of Israel when there had not been a Northern Kingdom of Israel in existence for 700 years? When did Jesus eat cream and honey? Does this biblical somersault make any sense? It is devoid of reason because this wild assertion of a dual prophecy was born out of a hopeless attempt to explain away Matthew's transparent mistranslation of the Jewish Scriptures.

Best wishes for a happy Chanukah.

Very truly yours,

Rabbi Tovia Singer

## Footnotes:

1. Many modern Christian translators have corrected Matthew's mistranslation of Isaiah 7:14 and correctly translate the Hebrew word *"almah"* as a "young woman." (see page 33).

2. I once heard a missionary try to explain away the problem of the unbiblical nature of a dual prophecy by claiming that in the seventh chapter of Isaiah, the prophet addressed himself to King Ahaz in both the singular "you" and the plural "you." (Although in the English language no such distinction exists, in the Hebrew language "you" can be expressed in both the singular and the plural.) He went on to explain that at times the prophet addressed Ahaz alone, and in other places in this chapter, the prophet addressed the House of David. He concluded, therefore, that whenever the prophet addressed the House of David or spoke in the plural "you," he was addressing the future virgin birth of Jesus seven centuries later. On the other hand, whenever the prophet addressed Ahaz or spoke in the singular "you," he was addressing the immediate crisis regarding Ahaz and the two kingdoms who were poised to defeat him. In Isaiah 7:14, he argued, the Hebrew word *"la'chem"* is a plural "you" and it therefore was addressing the future virgin birth of Jesus which was associated with the House of David, not Ahaz and his immediate military crisis.

   I replied to him that this chapter quite clearly declares that it was both the House of David and Ahaz who were threatened by the immediate crisis, not just Ahaz alone. Every reference to the House of David and plural "you" which was addressed to the entire Davidic House referred only to the military crisis described in this chapter. In fact, in the second verse in this chapter, Isaiah relates that both Ahaz and the House of David were informed of the immediate crisis of the two warring kingdoms. This verse, therefore, goes on to say, that both his heart (Ahaz — singular) and the heart of the people (the House of David — plural) trembled with fear. It was not Ahaz alone who was terrified of these two hostile armies, but the entire House of David as well.

   The reason that the prophet saw fit to repeatedly address Ahaz as the House of David and in the plural "you" throughout this chapter was because Ahaz was a wicked king and as such was personally undeserving of God's merciful intervention. Nevertheless, the Almighty did save Ahaz through the merit of the House of David.

The reason these two kingdoms laid siege to Jerusalem was to undermine the throne of David (Isaiah 7:6). In II Samuel 7:12-16, the Almighty promised King David that the House of David — his dynasty — would be preserved regardless of the worthiness of the king. God rescued King Ahaz in the merit of the House of David – the Davidic Covenant – not as a result of Ahaz's own piety. Accordingly, the prophet delivers this profound message by addressing King Ahaz both as the House of David and in the plural "you."

# How do Missionaries Paint the Virgin Birth Into the Mouth of Rashi?

## Question:

I had spent six years in the messianic movement until my family asked me to study your tape series with an open mind. I did and as a result, I have returned to Judaism. I have been a religious Jew for more than a year. Ever since I left, however, a Christian friend of mine who knew me when I was a believer has been trying to prove to me that I was wrong for leaving. I keep telling him that I have no doubts about my faith as a Jew, yet he still hasn't given up.

Recently, he told me and then showed me in this book of his, that Rashi, the most important Jewish commentator on the Bible, says in Isaiah 7:14 that the word "alma" means "virgin." Is this true? How do I respond to him? Thank you rabbi for all you have done for me.

## Answer:

It is wonderful to hear about your return to the Jewish faith, and it does my heart good to know that our tape series, *Let's Get Biblical*, helped you on your journey back to our God and your people. Over the years, this tape series has helped so many individuals return to their Jewish faith. There is nothing that gives me more joy than to welcome a Jew back from the Church. Welcome home.

As to your question regarding Rashi's commentary on Isaiah 7:14, it is a common practice for missionaries to selectively use rabbinic literature when it suits their purposes, yet to reject the words of the rabbis when it does not sustain their cause. The misuse of rabbinic literature becomes particularly disturbing when missionaries quote rabbinic statements that simply do not exist.

One of the most stunning examples of this sort of missionary corruption of rabbinic literature is of Rashi's commentary on Isaiah 7:14. In an effort to rescue their indefensible position that the Hebrew word הָעַלְמָה (*ha'almah)*[1] means a virgin, missionaries brazenly insist that Rashi, the most famous medieval Jewish commentator on the Bible, says that the mother of the child was a virgin. This is a stunning assertion considering that no such statement like this exists in Rashi's commentary on this verse. In fact, the word virgin never appears anywhere in Rashi's commentary on Isaiah 7:14. What missionaries have done here is misquote the words of this medieval commentator in order to buttress Matthew's untenable translation of Isaiah 7:14.

One of the most well known missionary books to flagrantly misquote Rashi in this manner is David Stern's *Jewish New Testament Commentary.* On pages 6-7 of his book, Stern writes,

> The most famous medieval Jewish Bible commentator, Rabbi Shlomo Yitzchaki ("Rashi," 1040-1105), who determinedly opposed christological interpretation of the *Tanakh,* nevertheless wrote on Isaiah 7:14, "Behold, the *`almah* shall conceive and bear a son and shall call his name *Immanu'el.*' This means that our Creator will be with us. This is the sign: The one who will conceive is a girl (*na'arah*) who never in her life has had intercourse with any man. Upon this one shall the Holy Spirit have power." (*Mikra'ot G'dolot, ad loc.*)

The fact is that Stern's quote of Rashi simply does not exist. What Stern has done is deliberately change the words of Rashi in order to provide his readers with a completely distorted, christological version of Rashi's commentary. In essence, Stern has tampered with the words of the commentator Rashi just as Matthew had altered the words of the prophet Isaiah.

Here is what Rashi actually says on this verse:

> Immanuel: Meaning, that our Rock will be with us, and this is the sign: She is a young girl and has never **prophesied** (*nitneviet*: נתנבאית)

Missionaries have mistranslated the Hebrew word *nitneviet* in Rashi's commentary to mean "sex" or "intercourse." This translation is preposterous. The Hebrew word *nitneviet* means "prophesied," not "intercourse." The root of the Hebrew word *nitneviet* is common in the Hebrew language. It is related to the Hebrew word *navie* which means "a prophet," a word with which most students of the Bible are familiar.

It is unfortunate , yet predictable, that missionaries do to the words of Rashi what Matthew did to the words of Isaiah.

Once again, welcome home to the Jewish faith, and may the Merciful One continue to guide you. With best wishes for a happy Chanukah.

Rabbi Singer

## Footnote:

1. The Hebrew word *ha'almah* means "the young woman," with no implications of virginity.

# A Christian Defends Matthew by Insisting That the Author of the First Gospel Used the Septuagint in His Quote of Isaiah to Support the Virgin Birth

## Question:

Rav Singer,

Why did you say Christians mistranslate the scripture by saying "almah" doesn't mean "virgin," when their translation of virgin comes from the Septuagint's "parthenos," not the Hebrew "almah"? "Parthenos" does mean "virgin."

They didn't mistranslate but used a different text. This is pretty well known, did you not know? I don't think this is a very good thing to have on your page.

## Answer:

Your inquiry will undoubtedly make an enormous contribution to our website because contained within your question are some of the most commonly held misconceptions regarding Matthew's rendering the Hebrew word *alma* as virgin in Matthew 1:23. Placing your question on our website will therefore benefit countless others who are confused by the same mistaken presuppositions imbedded in your question.

Your assertion that Matthew quoted from the Septuagint is the most repeated argument missionaries use in their attempt to explain away Matthew's stunning mistranslation of the Hebrew word *alma*. This well-worn response, however, raises far more problems than it answers.

To begin with, your contention that "*parthenos* does mean virgin" is incorrect. The Greek word *parthenos* can mean either a young woman or a virgin; for this reason the Greek word *parthenos* can be found in the *Septuagint* referring to someone who is not a virgin. For example, in Genesis 34:2-4, Shechem raped Dinah, the daughter of the patriarch Jacob, yet the Septuagint refers to her as a *parthenos* after she had been defiled. The Bible reports that after Shechem had violated her, "his heart desired Dinah, and he loved the damsel (LXX: *parthenos*) and he spoke tenderly to the damsel (LXX: *parthenos*)." Clearly, Dinah was not a virgin after having been raped, and yet she was referred to as a *parthenos*, the very same word the Septuagint used to translate the Hebrew word *alma* in Isaiah 7:14.

Moreover, the Septuagint in our hands is not a Jewish document, but rather a Christian one. The original Septuagint, created some 2,200 years ago by 72 Jewish translators, was a Greek translation of the Five Books of Moses alone. It therefore did not contain the Books of the Prophets or Writings of the Hebrew Bible such as Isaiah, which you asserted that Matthew quoted from. The Septuagint as we have it today, which includes the Prophets and Writings as well, is a product of the Church, not the Jewish people. In fact, the Septuagint remains the official Old Testament of the Greek Orthodox Church, and the manuscripts that consist of our Septuagint today date to the third century C.E. The fact that additional books known as the Apocrypha, which are uniquely sacred to the Roman Catholic and Orthodox Church, are found in the Septuagint should raise a red flag to those inquiring into the Jewishness of the Septuagint.

Christians such as Origin and Lucian (third and fourth century C.E.) had an enormous impact on creating and shaping the Septuagint that missionaries use to advance their untenable arguments against Judaism. In essence, the present Septuagint is largely a post-second century Christian translation of the Bible, used zealously by the Church throughout the centuries as an indispensable apologetic instrument to defend and sustain Christological alterations of the Jewish scriptures.

The ancient *Letter of Aristeas*, which is the earliest attestation to the existence of the Septuagint confirms that the original Septuagint translated by rabbis more than 22 centuries ago was of the Pentateuch alone and not the Books of the Prophets such as Isaiah. The Talmud also states this explicitly in Tractate Megillah (9a), and Josephus as well affirms that the Septuagint was a translation only of the Law of Moses in his preface to *Antiquities of the Jews*.[1] Moreover, St. Jerome, a church father and Bible translator who could hardly be construed as friendly to Judaism, affirms Josephus' statement regarding the authorship of the *Septuagint* in his preface to *The Book of Hebrew Questions*.[2] Likewise, the Anchor Bible Dictionary reports precisely this point in the opening sentence of its article on the Septuagint which states, "The word '*Septuagint*,' (from Lat. *septuaginta* = 70; hence the abbreviation LXX) derives from a story that 72 elders translated the Pentateuch into Greek; the term therefore applied originally only to those five books."[3]

In fact, Dr. F.F. Bruce, a preeminent professor of Biblical exegesis, keenly points out that, strictly speaking, the *Septuagint* deals only with the Pentateuch and not the whole Old Testament. Bruce writes,

> The Jews might have gone on at a later time to authorize a standard text of the rest of the Septuagint, but . . . lost interest in the Septuagint altogether. With but few exceptions, every manuscript of the *Septuagint* which has come down to our day was copied and preserved in Christian, not Jewish, circles.[4]

Regarding your assertion that Matthew was quoting from the Septuagint, nowhere in the Book of Matthew does the word Septuagint appear, or, for that matter, is there any reference to a Greek translation of the Bible ever mentioned in all of the New Testament; and there is good reason for this silence. The first century church was well aware that a Jewish audience would be thoroughly unimpressed by a claim that Jesus' virgin birth could only be supported by a Greek translation of the Bible. They understood that if Jews were to find their Christian message convincing, they would need to assert that it was the actual words of the prophet Isaiah that clearly foretold Mary's virgin conception, not from the words of a Greek translation. Therefore, in Matthew 1:22-23, the author of the first Gospel insists that it was "spoken of the Lord by the prophet, saying, 'Behold, a virgin shall be with child . . . .' " Matthew loudly makes the point that it was specifically the prophet's own words that proclaimed the virgin birth, not the words of any translator.

Isaiah, of course, did not preach or write in Greek, and therefore the word *parthenos* never left the lips of the prophet throughout his life. All 66 chapters of the Book of Isaiah were spoken and then recorded in the Hebrew language alone. Matthew, however, was attempting to place in the mind of his intended Jewish readers that it was the words of prophet Isaiah himself who declared that the messiah would be born of a virgin. Nothing of course could be further from the truth.

Furthermore, this contention becomes even more preposterous when we consider that the same missionaries who attempt to explain away Matthew's mistranslation of the Hebrew word *alma* by claiming that Matthew used a *Septuagint* when he quoted Isaiah 7:14 also steadfastly maintain that the entire first Gospel was divinely inspired. That is to say, these same Christian missionaries insist that every word of the New Testament, Matthew included, was authored through the Holy Spirit and is therefore the living word of God. Are these evangelical apologists therefore claiming that God needed a Greek translation of the Bible and therefore quoted from the Septuagint? Did the passing of 500 years since His last book cause God to forget how to read Hebrew that He would need to rely on a translation? Why would God need to quote from the Septuagint?

Matthew's mistranslation of the Hebrew word *alma* was deliberate, not the result of his unwitting decision to quote from a defective Greek translation of the Bible. This is evidenced by the fact that the context of Isaiah 7:14 is not speaking of the birth of a messiah at all.[5] This fact remains obvious even to the most casual reader of the seventh chapter of Isaiah.

For Matthew, the prophet's original intent regarding the young woman in Isaiah 7:14 was entirely superseded by his fervid desire to somehow prove to the Jewish people that the virgin birth was prophesied in the Hebrew scriptures. Bear in mind that the author of the first Gospel — more than any other writer in the New Testament — shaped and contoured his treatise with the deliberate purpose of promoting Christianity among the Jews. In essence, Matthew was writing with a Jewish audience in mind. He understood that in order to convince the Jewish people to embrace Jesus as the messiah, it was essential to demonstrate his claim of the virgin birth from the Jewish scriptures. Luke, in contrast, was writing for a non-Jewish, Greek audience and therefore makes no attempt to support his version of the virgin birth from the Hebrew Bible.

In his attempt to promote numerous Christian creeds amongst the Jews, Matthew was faced with a serious quandary. How would he prove that Jesus was the messiah from the Jewish scriptures when there is no relationship between the Jesus of Nazareth of the New Testament and the messianic prophecies of the Jewish scriptures? How was he going to merge newly inculcated pagan myths, such as the virgin birth, into Christianity with a Hebrew Bible in which a belief in a virgin birth was unknown?

In order to accomplish this daunting task, verses in the Hebrew scriptures were altered, misquoted, taken out of context, and mistranslated by the author of the Book of Matthew in order to make Jesus' life fit traditional Jewish messianic parameters, and to make traditional Jewish messianic parameters fit the life of Jesus. In essence, he had to claim that it was the Hebrew prophets themselves who foretold that Jesus was the messiah. It is therefore no coincidence that no other writer of the New Testament misuses the Jewish scriptures with abandon to the extent that Matthew does throughout his Gospel.

The irony of all this Bible manipulation is that the first Gospel was written for the sole purpose of convincing a Jewish audience that Jesus was the promised messiah. Yet, if the Book of Matthew had never been written, the Church would almost have certainly been more effective in its effort at evangelizing the Jews. In essence, had promoters of Christianity avoided the kind of scripture tampering that can be found in virtually every chapter in the Book of Matthew, the church might have enjoyed far more success among the Jews as did previous religions that targeted the Jewish people for conversion.

For example, the priests of Baal did not attempt to bolster the validity of their idol worship by misquoting the texts of the Hebrew Bible, as Matthew did. Yet, the Bible reports that Baal gained enormous popularity among the Jewish people. In contrast, once the nation of Israel was confronted with a corruption of their sacred scriptures by authors and apologists of the New Testament, their apostasy to Christianity for the most part became untenable and the Jewish people throughout history remained the most difficult nation for the Church to convert. Consequently, whereas the Gospels of Mark, Luke, and John enjoyed overwhelming success among their targeted gentile audiences, the Gospel of Matthew played an enormous role in the ultimate failure of the Church to effectively convert the Jews to Christianity, at least the knowledgeable ones.

Best wishes for a happy Purim.

Sincerely yours,

Rabbi Tovia Singer

# Footnotes:

1. Josephus, preface to *Antiquities of the Jews*, section 3. For Josephus'

detailed description of events surrounding the original authorship of the *Septuagint*, see Josephus, *Antiquities of the Jews*, XII, ii, 1-4.

2. St. Jerome, preface to *The Book of Hebrew Questions*, Nicene and Post-Nicene Fathers, Volume 6. Pg. 487. Hendrickson. (see page 34)

3. *The Anchor Bible Dictionary*. Excerpt from "*Septuagint*," New York: Vol. 5, pg. 1093. (see page 34)

4. F.F. Bruce, *The Books and the Parchments*, p.150.

5. The seventh chapter of the Book of Isaiah begins by describing the military crisis that was confronting King Ahaz of the Kingdom Judah. In about the year 732 B.C.E. the House of David was facing immanent destruction at the hands of two warring kingdoms: the northern Kingdom of Israel and the Syrian kingdom. These two armies had laid siege to Jerusalem. The Bible relates that the House of David and King Ahaz were gripped with fear. In response these two warring armies, God sent the prophet Isaiah to reassure King Ahaz that divine protection was at hand — the Almighty would protect him, their deliverance was assured, and these two hostile armies would fail in their attempt to subjugate Jerusalem.

   It is clear from this chapter that Isaiah's declaration was a prophecy of the unsuccessful siege of Jerusalem by the two armies of the Kingdoms of Israel and Syria, not a virgin birth more than 700 years later. If we interpret this chapter as referring to Jesus' birth, what possible comfort and assurance would Ahaz, who was surrounded by two overwhelming military forces, have found in the birth of a child seven centuries later? Both he and his people would be long dead and buried. Such a sign would make little sense.

# Sin and Atonement

## Question:

Not being a Jew or a "Jew for Jesus," I am confused by this "blood sacrifice" argument between the two groups. I am tryingto understand. I believe in Christ and am a Christian. I agree with your assessment that the offering the Lord truly wants is a broken heart and contrite spirit full of repentance. I also believe that "blood sacrifice" is not necessary for forgiveness as you have, with excellent scriptural support, stated very well.

My question is related to your beliefs in the atoning nature of the Messiah. Regardless of whether Jesus is THE Messiah or not, I am surprised that the arguments you present diminish the significance of the Messiah's role. My Jewish friends have always impressed me with their strong reverence for the Messiah and his role in their future. If I have read you correctly, you do not accept the concept of expiation. Please help me understand.

I am also confused with the use of Ezekiel 18:1-4, 19-23 as proof against the ability of one to atone for another's sins.

This text was not intended to be extrapolated to this point. It was simply as intended: A correction of those in that day who were propagating the idea that the sin of a father will rest upon his children. Ezekiel was dealing with those who teach that the sins of the father rest upon the children because the fall of Adam and Eve caused suffering on their children. It is clearly this false doctrine Ezekiel was trying to destroy.

Any clarification on these issues would be greatly appreciated and hopefully allow me to dispel confusion. I believe in asking the believer what he believes, not going to someone else and getting their "interpretation." I hope you can appreciate this sincerity.

## Answer:

I have been asked both of your questions by many Christians in the past, although not often with the earnestness and openness that comes across in your letter. You have essentially asked two questions, and I will address each separately.

Regarding your first question, the Bible is clear on the subject of the role of the messiah.[1] It should be noted that although there are many sections throughout the Jewish Scriptures that vividly describe how the world will be forever transformed with the arrival of the Messianic Age, very few discuss the messiah personally. The vast bulk of messianic scripture in Tanach[2] depicts the state of perfection that the world will achieve at the End of Days.

In contrast, parishioners pray to and venerate Jesus without pause. Jesus' name emerges repeatedly during Church services. This stunning contrast should be a "Red Flag" for and seeker of the truth

The Hebrew scriptures are quite clear that the significance of the messiah himself pales in comparison to the utopian age that his arrival will usher in.

The reason Judaism does not accept the Christian messiah is because Jesus filled none of the messianic prophecies clearly foretold in the Jewish scriptures. The following is an overview of the central messianic prophecies outlined in the Jewish scriptures that both Judaism and Christianity agree are messianic:

## *World Peace*

And he shall judge among the nations, and shall rebuke many people; and they shall beat their swords into plowshares, and their spears into pruning hooks. Nation shall not lift up sword against nation, neither shall they learn of war any more. (Isaiah 2:4)

The wolf also shall dwell with the lamb, and the leopard shall lie down with the kid; and the calf and the young lion and the fatling together . . . and the sucking child shall play on the hole of the cobra . . . . (Isaiah 11:6-8)

## *Universal Knowledge of God*

. . . for the earth shall be full of the knowledge of the Lord, as the waters cover the sea. (Isaiah 11:9)

No longer shall one teach his neighbor or shall one teach his brother, saying, "Know the Lord," for they shall all know Me, from their smallest to their greatest," says the Lord . . . . (Jeremiah 31:33)

And the Lord shall be king over all the earth. In that day shall there be one Lord, and His name one. (Zechariah 14:9)

## *Resurrection of the Dead*

Thy dead men shall live, together with my dead body shall they arise. Awake and sing, ye that dwell in dust, for thy dew is as the dew of herbs, and the earth shall cast out the dead. (Isaiah 26:19)

And many of them that sleep in the dust of the earth shall awake, some to everlasting life, and some to shame and everlasting contempt. (Daniel 12:2)

Therefore, prophesy and say to them, "So says the Lord God, 'Lo! I open your graves and cause you to come up out of your graves as My people, and bring you home to the land of Israel. Then you shall know that I am the Lord, when I open your graves and lead you up out of your graves as My people.'" (Ezekiel 37:12-13)

## *Ingathering of Israel*

. . . I will bring thy seed from the east, and gather you from the west. I will say to the north, "Give up," and to the south, "Keep not back, bring My sons from far, and My daughter from the ends of the earth." (see also Jeremiah 16:15, 23:3; Isaiah 11:12; Zechariah 10:6; Ezekiel 37:21-22)

## *Building of The Third Temple*

. . . and I will set My Sanctuary in the midst of them forevermore. My temple also shall be with them. Yes, I will be their God and they shall be My people. And the heathen shall know that I the Lord do sanctify Israel, when My sanctuary shall be in the midst of them forevermore. (See also Ezekiel 37:26-28, 40-48; Isaiah 33:20)

When we consider that messianic claims have been made by countless individuals and enthusiastic followers, not one of them have fulfilled any one of the prophecies clearly outlined in the Jewish scriptures.

When the Christian claim of Jesus' messiahship is considered, it is quite clear that the very opposite had occurred during the century that marks the birth of Christianity. In fact, during this catastrophic first century, there was no resurrection of the dead as prophesied by Daniel and Isaiah. Instead, the Romans slaughtered many hundreds of thousands of Jews during this period. Neither was there an ingathering of the exiles. Instead, the Jewish people were exiled from their land and dispersed throughout the Roman Empire. Nor did the universal knowledge of God occur. Rather, as a result of this exile, the knowledge of Torah and its observance decreased. There was no Temple built at any time during the first century; instead, the temple in Jerusalem was destroyed in the year 70 C.E. Clearly, there is no relationship between what the Bible says about the messiah and what the Messianic movement espouses about Jesus.

With regard to your second question, it is essential for you to understand that the Jewish people do not read their Bible as if it were a history book. Those teachings that are inscribed throughout the Jewish Bible were not only appropriate for the time they were recorded, rather their prophecies are indispensable for all generations that would follow. *A righteous person cannot die vicariously for the sins of the wicked.* Every edification and instruction of the Torah and the Prophets are as meaningful and timely today as they were the day they were first preached.

Scripture, therefore, provides very few dates for reckoning Biblical chronology. These dates do appear, but you have to carefully peice the information to stretch out a contiguous time line. Moreover, the Bible is entirely silent on what had transpired over the course of many decades during the lives of men like Abraham and Moses. This does not suggest that Abraham did nothing spiritually valuable during those silent years. Rather, only those crucial events that provide eternal teachings and are relevant for all future generations were inscribed in the Bible.

Even the first Christians were well aware of this principle. In II Timothy 3:16 Paul says, "All Scripture is given by inspiration of God, and is profitable for doctrine, for reproof, for correction, for instruction in righteousness." Bear in mind, at the time that II Timothy was written, the Christian Bible did not yet exist. Chronologically, the letters of Paul were among the earliest books in the New Testament. The author of this Pastoral Epistle was only referring to the Jewish scriptures.

In the 18th chapter of Ezekiel, the prophet was teaching his people a fundamental biblical principle: A righteous person cannot die vicariously for the sins of the wicked. This notion was identified as thoroughly pagan and was to be avoided by the Jewish people at all costs, and is taught emphatically throughout the 18th chapter of Ezekiel. In verses 20-23, the prophet declares that repentance alone provides full forgiveness of sin. Never are blood-sacrifices or the veneration of a crucified messiah mentioned throughout Ezekiel's thorough and inspiring discourse on sin and atonement.

Ezekiel's teaching was not new. The Jewish people were warned throughout the Torah never to offer human sacrifices. When Moses offered to have his name removed from the Torah in exchange for the sin that the Jewish people had committed with the golden calf, the Almighty abruptly refused Moses' offer.[3] Moses, who was righteous with regard to the golden calf, could not suffer vicariously for the sin of the nation. Rather, only the soul that sinned would endure judgment.

Regarding your comment on the sin in the Garden of Eden, the consequences of the fall of Adam and Eve are not to be appended to Ezekiel's 18th chapter. Nowhere in this chapter is the sin in the Garden of Eden ever mentioned. In fact, Ezekiel outlines many of the sins that the wicked may have committed, and yet not one of them is eating from the forbidden fruit of the tree of knowledge of good and evil. On the contrary, all of the sins outlined are those that were never committed in the Garden of Eden. As mentioned above, this chapter is a prophetic teaching on sin and atonement in general, and a vigorous condemnation of the thoroughly pagan belief in vicarious atonement.

Finally, I am puzzled by the fact that you have identified yourself as a Christian and yet at the end of your letter you refer to the teaching that the fall of Adam and Eve has affected and caused suffering to their future children as a doctrine that "Ezekiel was trying to destroy." This comment surprises me because this is a foundational Christian doctrine.

The Church teaches that all of mankind is utterly infected with the stain of the Original Sin. As a result, Christendom argues that man is incapable of achieving "salvation" through his own initiative. Man's "totally depravity" is complete. His only hope of salvation is through the Cross. This is the cornerstone of Paul's theology throughout his Epistles, especially in the Book of Romans.

I agree with your assessment that the doctrine of Original Sin is contrary to the teachings of the prophets. In fact, the Church's doctrine of Original Sin and total depravity has no greater foe than the prophet Ezekiel.

Thank you for your sincere questions. Happy Chanukah!

Yours,

Rabbi Tovia Singer

## Footnotes:

1. This subject is addressed at length in the letter entitled, *The Christian Messiah?* (Page 353)

2. The Hebrew word תנך *(Tanach)* refers to the entire corpus of the Jewish Scriptures, and is an acronym that stands for the Torah, Prophets, and the Writings.

3. Exodus 32:31-33.

# Did the Passover Lamb Foreshadow the Crucifixion of Jesus?

## Question:

I want to first commend you on your web site which is laid out quite well and has helped me understand more about traditional Jewish thinking on Christ. Although I am a born again Christian, I do not support groups such as the Messianics who sit on the fence regarding Judaism and Christianity. You either follow Judaism or Christianity; you can't pretend to follow both at the same time. This has led to Jews for Jesus following rabbinic customs that are not a part of the teachings of Christ.

With that said, my question to you is: Why have the Jewish people rejected Jesus as their sacrificial lamb who is the sin bearer for mankind when the atoning blood of Jesus is so ever-present in the Paschal lamb in the Book of Exodus. I ask this question because you are a rabbi and profess to believe in the teachings of the Old Testament; so how is it that you do not see the atonement of the blood of the lamb which was placed on the doorposts that first Passover Seder night in Egypt? I look forward to your answer.

## Answer:

Evangelical Christians often draw a comparison between the Paschal Lamb and Jesus, insisting that the former foreshadows the latter. This idea is advanced in the New Testament, particularly in the fourth Gospel, where John portrayed Jesus as the fulfillment of the Passover lamb. Yet how valid a point is this? What is the meaning of this holiday sacrifice? Is there a relationship between this offering and atonement for sin?

The Bible relates in Exodus 12:3-13 that when the Jewish people were preparing themselves for the momentous Exodus from Egypt, God commanded them to slaughter a year-old sheep or goat on the 14th day of the first month (Nissan) and to place its blood publicly on the outside doorposts of their homes. Because Christians insist that the blood of the Paschal lamb foreshadowed the atonement of the blood of Jesus at Calvary, it behooves us to question the soundness of this claim.

The Passover lamb did not atone for sin and accordingly, this idea is nowhere to be found in the Jewish scriptures. It goes without saying that the notion that the Paschal Lamb is a representation of a crucified savior or an atonement is alien to the teachings of the Torah and is not even mentioned by the first three Gospels.

A mindful study of the Jewish scriptures reveals that the Paschal Lamb was alluded to long before the Exodus from Egypt. Centuries earlier, Abraham's faith was tested by God when he commanded him to sacrifice his beloved son Isaac. Genesis 22:7-8 relates that as the two ascended Mount Moriah together, Isaac turned to his father and asked,

> "Here is the fire and the wood, but where is the lamb for the offering?" Abraham then replied, "God will see to a lamb for an offering, my son."

The question that comes to mind is, what happened to that lamb that Abraham promised? A few verses later we find that ram was sacrificed rather than a lamb! Where was the lamb to which Abraham was prophetically referring?

The answer of course is that our father Abraham was prophetically alluding to the Paschal lamb. Just as God tested Abraham's faith to demonstrate his worthiness to be the father of the chosen people, the young Jewish nation also had to have their faith tested to show their worthiness to participate in the exodus from Egypt, to receive the Torah at Mount Sinai, and to become the progenitors of the covenant people who would forever be known as "a light to the nations."

In ancient Egypt during the time of the Exodus, the lamb was deified and worshiped. It was forbidden to molest a lamb in any way; such an act was considered a crime punishable by death.

For this reason Moses refused Pharaoh's initial offer that the Jews bring their sacrifice to God while remaining in Egypt, following the third plague of lice. Moses explained to Pharaoh that it would be impossible for his people to sacrifice these animals in this land because the Egyptians would execute us for carrying out this ceremony (Exodus 8:25-26).

The Almighty, therefore, tested the faithfulness of the Jewish people by commanding them to kill Egypt's sacred god and publicly place the lamb's blood on their doorposts for all to see. Only those Israelites who, like Abraham, demonstrated that they feared nothing but the God of Israel were deemed worthy to have their homes "passed over" during the tenth and final plague.

It is worth noting that the synoptic gospels, i.e. the gospels of Matthew, Mark, and Luke, do not associate Jesus with the Paschal Lamb, whereas the Book of John does. The synoptic gospels specify that Jesus was crucified on the first day of Passover - the 15th day of Nissan. Written several decades after the synoptic gospels, John's gospel has Jesus crucified on the eve of Passover, the 14th day of Nissan, when the lambs were slaughtered. As a result, the Passover Seder is noticeably absent in the Book of John's Passion Narrative. (See pages 365-370)

Yours,

Rabbi Tovia Singer

# Could Jesus' Death Atone for Any Kind of Sin?

## Question:

Dear Rabbi Singer,

A mutual friend of ours introduced me to your site. I work with Michael Flanigan of Palestine, TX. I am a gentile Christian who has many questions. I have found a lot of fascinating reading on your site. Michael and I have been discussing atonement and sacrifice as of late. Now bear in mind that I am by no means a biblical scholar, so, I apologize if my questions seem silly. Would it not be possible for the death of Y'shua to apply as an unintentional sin sacrifice with His death applying when an individual asks Him into his/her life initially? Thereafter, sins would be forgiven as intentional sins through repentance. I hope you are able to make sense of my question. I am learning much through my conversations with Michael and listening to your tapes. I will continue to visit your website in the future.

Thank you for your time.

## Answer:

Your question is not silly at all. I will first explain your question more clearly so that visitors to our website who are unfamiliar with this subject will have a better understanding of what you are asking.

Missionaries claim that the blood sacrificial system is man's only hope for atonement; they insist that there can be no forgiveness of sin without the shedding of blood. They maintain that the Bible sets forth only blood atonement to expiate sin. Evangelical Christians assert that for the past nineteen centuries, since the destruction of the second Temple in 70 C.E., Jews have lacked the essential and indispensable animal sacrificial system for atonement. Consequently, they maintain, God must have provided a blood atonement in place of the animal sacrifices of the past. This sacrifice, they insist, is the death of Jesus on the cross.

In support of their claim that atonement can only be achieved through the shedding of blood, missionaries cite Leviticus 17:11, which reads,

> This is because the life of the flesh is in the blood, and I have given it to you upon the altar to make atonement for your souls; for it is the blood that makes atonement for the soul.

They conclude from this verse that only by being covered in the blood of the cross can man have any hope of being forgiven by God for his sins.

In response to this argument, I have explained that contrary to the missionary claim that blood sacrifice is the only method of atonement in the Bible, there are three methods of atonement, which are clearly defined in the Jewish scriptures; the sin sacrifice, repentance, and charity. Moreover, the sin sacrifice (called in the Jewish scriptures as *korban chatat*) did not atone for all types of sin, but rather, only for man's most insignificant iniquity: unintentional sins. The sin sacrifice was inadequate to atone for a transgression committed intentionally. The brazen sinner was barred from the sanctuary, and had to bear his own iniquity because of his rebellious intent to sin against God. The *Torah* teaches this fundamental principle in Numbers 15:27-31.

> **If a person sins unintentionally**, then he shall offer a one-year-old female goat for a sin offering. The priest shall make atonement before

> the Lord for the person who goes astray when he sins **unintentionally**, making atonement for him that he may be forgiven . . . . **The person who does anything defiantly**, whether he is native or an alien, that one is blaspheming the Lord; and that person shall be cut off from among his people, because he has despised the word of the Lord and has broken His commandment, that person shall be completely cut off; his guilt shall be on him.

Your question is excellent: "If the sin sacrifice was necessary in order to atone for unintentional sin, didn't Jesus then have to die for those sins committed unwittingly?"

The answer to your question is simple. Jesus could not die for anyone's sins, whether they were committed intentionally or accidentally. To begin with, the Jewish people were strictly prohibited from offering human sacrifices under any circumstances. There is not one place throughout the entire corpus of the Jewish scriptures where human sacrifices are condoned. In fact, over and over again, the Bible warns the Jewish people that it is a grave sin to bring a human being as a sacrifice. In the Book of Leviticus, only distinct species of animals are permitted for use in blood sacrifices.

The ancient pagan religions promoted the same idea about atonement as Christendom continues to preach today (e.g. *Molech*). They would joyfully offer a child into the fires of their sacrificial offering in order to expiate their sins and appease the gods. Why would a child sacrifice be used in this pagan ritual rather than an adult? The reason is because a child is thoroughly innocent of sin. A child, they reasoned, could not have committed iniquity and thus mirrored the animal sacrifice which also had to be unblemished. The *Torah* therefore admonishes the children of Israel never to offer human sacrifices, and forewarned Jewish people of terrible consequences if this commandment were violated.

This message was carefully communicated at Mt. Moriah where Abraham was prepared to offer up his beloved son Isaac as a sacrifice. At that crucial juncture in history when Abraham was ready to sacrifice Isaac, the Almighty admonished him that He did not want the human sacrifice, and directed Abraham to sacrifice the ram caught in the thicket instead. The Almighty's directive – that he only wanted animal sacrifices rather than human sacrifices – was immediately understood. This teaching has never departed from the mind and soul of the faithful children of Israel.

Moreover, if missionaries want to use Leviticus 17:11 to bolster their claim that blood sacrifices are indispensable for procuring an atonement, they must use all of the verse, not just a part of it. Leviticus 17:11 specifically says that the blood of the sacrifice must be placed "upon the altar to make atonement for your souls." That is to say, Leviticus 17:11 explicitly declares that blood can only effect atonement if it is placed on the altar. Jesus' blood, however, was never placed on the altar. If the church is going to take the "blood" part of the verse literally, they must also take the "altar" part literally as well. Jesus' blood was never sprinkled on the altar, and therefore his death could not provide atonement for anyone.

Finally, the prophets loudly declared to the Jewish people that the contrite prayer of the penitent sinner replaces the sacrificial system. Therefore, atonement for unintentional sins today is expiated through devotional supplication to God, the Merciful One.

In fact, in Hosea 3:4-5, the prophet foretold with divine exactness that the nation of Israel would not have a sacrificial system during the last segment of Jewish history until the messianic age. Hosea 3:4-5 reads,

> . . . for the children of Israel shall abide many days without king or prince, **without sacrifice** or sacred pillar, without *ephod* or *teraphim*. Afterward the children of Israel shall return and seek the LORD their God and David their king. They shall fear the LORD and His goodness in the latter days.

In the words of the Bible, this period of time would last for many days. Yet, despite the repeated proclamations of the church that the crucifixion of Jesus serves as a sin sacrifice today, the words of Hosea were meticulously fulfilled, and we are without an animal sacrificial system today.

Given the spiritual magnitude of this remarkable prophecy, Hosea was compelled to reveal how the ecclesiastical Temple functions were it to be replaced. In essence, if the prophet is testifying that the nation of Israel will indeed be without a sacrificial system during their long exile until the messianic age, what are we to use instead? How are the Jewish people to atone for unintentional sin without a blood sacrifice during their bitter exile? What about all the animal sacrifices prescribed in the Book of Leviticus? Can the Jewish people get along without animal offerings? Missionaries claim they cannot. The Bible disagrees.

For this reason, the statement in Hosea 14:2-3 is crucial. In these two verses, Hosea reveals to his beloved nation how they are to replace the sacrificial system during their protracted exile. The prophet declares that the Almighty wants us to "render for bulls the offering of our lips." Prayer is to replace the sacrificial system. Hosea 14:2-3 states,

> Take words with you, and return to the LORD. Say to Him, "Take away all iniquity; receive us graciously, for we will **render for bulls the offering of our lips**."

The prophets never instruct the Jews to worship any crucified messiah or demigod; nor does scripture ever tell us that an innocent man should die as an atonement for the sins of the wicked. Such a message is utterly antithetical to the teachings of the Jewish scriptures. Rather, it is the prayers of the sinner that would become as bulls of the sin offerings.

King Solomon echoes this sentiment as well. In I Kings 8:46-50, King Solomon delivers a startling prophetic message as he inaugurates the first Temple that had just been completed. In his inauguration sermon, King Solomon forewarns that one day the Jewish people would be driven out of the land of Israel, and be banished to the land of their enemies, near and far. During their exile they would fervently desire to repent of their sins. King Solomon then declares that they are to face Jerusalem from their exile, confess their sins, "and God will hear their prayers in heaven, and forgive them for all their transgressions."

There was no mention of a cross or a dead messiah in King Solomon's prophetic message. Only the contrite and repentant prayer of the remorseful sinner can bring about a complete atonement. Although King Solomon's timeless message stands out as a theological impossibility in Christian terms, it remains the centerpiece of the Jew's system of atonement throughout his long and bitter exile.

Best wishes for a happy Passover.

Sincerely yours,

Rabbi Tovia Singer

# Does Judaism Believe in Original Sin?

## Question:

Dear Rabbi Singer,

Does the Jewish faith have a teaching comparable to that of "original sin" in the Christian tradition? By this I mean the teaching that all human beings are born with an innate tendency to disobey God. In my particular Christian tradition, water baptism is required for the removal of this sin. Would you please comment.

Thanks for your assistance.

## Answer:

The term "original sin" is unknown to the Jewish scriptures, and the Church's teachings on this doctrine are antithetical to the core principles of the Torah and its prophets. Moreover, your comment that your Christian denomination teaches that water baptism is essential for the removal of sin may rattle the sensitivities of more Christians than anything I am going to say. Nevertheless, you have raised a number of important issues that must be addressed. Before answering your question, however, it is important that our website visitors understand the Christian doctrine on original sin.

According to church teachings, the mortal sin committed by our first parents in the Garden of Eden had catastrophic consequences for the human race. Most importantly, Christendom holds that these devastating effects extend far beyond the curses of painful childbirth and laborious farming conditions outlined in the third chapter of Genesis.

This well-known church doctrine posits that when Adam and Eve rebelled against God and ate from the forbidden Tree of Knowledge, all of their descendants became infected with the stain of their transgression. Moreover, as a consequence of this first iniquity, man is hopelessly lost in a state of sin in which he has been held captive since this fall. As a result, he is powerless to follow the path of obedience and righteousness by his own free will. Rather, missionaries contend, because all are born with an innate and uncontrollable lust for sin, humanity can do nothing to merit its own salvation. In essence, man is totally depraved and true free will is far beyond his grasp. "Totally depraved" may seem to be a harsh way for a Christian doctrine to depict mankind's dire condition, yet this is precisely the term used by the church to describe man's desperate, sinful predicament. It is only through faith in Jesus, Christendom concludes, that hopeless man can be saved.

You stated in your question that the doctrine of original sin teaches that "all human beings are born with an innate tendency to disobey God." While this statement is superficially correct, it fails to convey the far-reaching scope of this church doctrine. Although Christianity does teach that the entire human race is born with an evil inclination, this tenet encompasses a far more extreme position than the one that you briefly outlined. In fact, missionaries insist that as a result of the fall in the Garden of Eden, man's unquenchable desire for sin is virtually ungovernable. In Christian terms, man is not inclined toward sin but more accurately is a **slave** to sin. As a result, the church concludes, short of converting to Christianity, humanity can do nothing to save itself from hell.

Bear in mind, there is good reason for the Church's uncompromising stand on this cherished doctrine. The founders of Christianity understood that if man can save himself from eternal damnation through his own initiative and obedience to God, the Church would have very little to offer the human race. Moreover, if righteousness can be achieved through submission to the commandments outlined in the Torah, what possible benefit could Jesus' death provide for mankind? Such self-probing thoughts, however, were unimaginable to those who shaped primitive Christianity.

Despite the zealous position missionaries take as they defend this creed, the Christian doctrine of original sin is profoundly hostile to the central teachings of the Jewish scriptures. Over and over again the Torah loudly dismisses the notion that man has lost his divinely endowed capacity to freely choose good over evil, life over death. This is not a hidden or ambiguous message in the Jewish scriptures. On the contrary, it is proclaimed in virtually every teaching that Moses directs to the children of Israel.

In fact, in an extraordinary sermon delivered by Moses in the last days of his life, the prophet stands before the entire nation and condemns the notion that man's condition is utterly hopeless. Throughout this uplifting exhortation, Moses declares that it is man alone who can and must merit his own salvation. Moreover, as he unhesitatingly speaks in the name of God, the lawgiver thoroughly rejects the notion that obedience to the Almighty is "too difficult or far off" and declares to the children of Israel that righteousness has been placed within their reach.

The thirtieth chapter of Deuteronomy isn't quiet on this matter and its verses read as though the Torah is bracing the Jewish people for the Christian doctrines that would confront them many centuries later. As the last Book of the *Pentateuch* draws to a close, Moses admonishes his young nation not to question their capacity to remain faithful to the *mitzvoth* of the Torah. Deuteronomy 30:10-14 states:

> . . . if you will hearken to the voice of the Lord your God, to keep His commandments and His statutes which are written in this Book of the Law; if you turn unto the Lord thy God with all your heart and with all your soul; for this commandment which I command you this day is not too hard for you neither is it too far off. It is not in heaven, that you should say, "Who shall go up for us to heaven, and bring it to us, and make us hear it, that we may do it?" Neither is it beyond the sea that you should say: "Who shall go over the sea for us, and bring it unto us, and make us to hear it that we may do it?" The word is very near to you, in your mouth and in your heart, **that you may do it**.

The Jewish people have drawn great comfort and encouragement from this uplifting promise. For the Church, however, Moses' strong message created a theological disaster. How could the authors of the New Testament reasonably insist that man's dire condition was hopeless if the Torah unambiguously declared that man possessed an extraordinary ability to remain faithful to God? How could the church fathers possibly contend that the *mitzvoth* in the Torah couldn't save the Jewish people when the Creator proclaimed otherwise? How could missionaries conceivably maintain that the commandments of the Torah are too difficult when the Torah declares that they are "not far off," "not too hard," and "you may do it"?

This staggering problem did not escape Paul's attention. Bear in mind, the author of Romans and Galatians constructed his most consequential doctrines on the premise that man is utterly depraved and incapable of saving himself through his own obedience to God. In chapter after chapter, he directs his largely gentile audiences toward the cross and away from Sinai, as he repeatedly insists that man is lost without Jesus.

Yet, how could Paul harmonize this wayward theology with the Jewish scriptures in which his teachings were not only unknown, but thoroughly condemned? Even with the nimble skills that Paul possessed, welding together the Church's young doctrine of original sin with diametrically opposed teachings of the Jewish scriptures would not be a simple task.

Employing unparalleled literary manipulation, however, Paul manages to conceal this vexing theological problem with a swipe of his well-worn eraser. In fact, Paul's innovative approach to biblical tampering was so remarkable that it would set the standard of scriptural revisionism for future New Testament authors.

A classic example of this biblical revisionism can be found in Romans 10:8 where Paul announces to his readers that he is quoting directly from scripture as he records the words of Deuteronomy 30:14. Yet as he approaches the last portion of this verse, he carefully stops short of the Torah's vital conclusion and expunges the remaining segment of this crucial verse. In Romans 10:8 Paul writes,

> But what does it say? "The word is near you, in your mouth and in your heart" (that is, the word of faith which we preach).

Predictably, the last words of Deuteronomy 30:14, "that you may do it," were meticulously deleted by Paul. Bear in mind that he had good reason for removing this clause – the powerful message contained in these closing words rendered all that Paul was preaching as heresy.

This stunning misquote in Romans stands out as a remarkable illustration of Paul's ability to shape scriptures in order to create the illusion that his theological message conformed to the principles of the Torah. By removing the final segment of this verse, Paul succeeded in convincing his largely gentile readers that his Christian teachings were supported by the principles of the Hebrew Bible.

| Compare | |
|---|---|
| **Deuteronomy 30:14** | **Romans 10:8** |
| But the word is very near to you, in your mouth and in your heart, **that you may do it**. | But what does it say? "The word is near you, in your mouth and in your heart" (that is, the word of faith which we preach). |

The question that immediately comes to mind is: How can Paul deliberately remove a vital clause from Moses' message and still expect to gain a following among the Jewish people? While considering this question, we can begin to understand why Paul attained great success among his gentile audiences and utterly failed among the Jews who were unimpressed with his contrived message.

It is for this reason that although both Paul and Matthew quoted extensively from the Jewish scriptures, they achieved a very different result. Paul was largely a minister to gentile audiences who were ignorant of the Jewish Bible (the only Bible in existence at the time). As a result, they did not possess the skills necessary to discern between genuine Judaism and Bible tampering. These illiterate masses were, as a result, vulnerable, and eagerly consumed everything that Paul taught them. In fact, throughout the New Testament it was exclusively the Jewish apostates to Christianity who challenged Paul's authority, never the gentile community.

Matthew, on the other hand, directed all of his evangelism and Bible quotes to Jewish audiences. Jewish people, however, were keenly aware of Matthew's manipulation of their Bible. As a result, the first Gospel failed to effectively reach its intended Jewish readers. It required little more than a perfunctory reading of the first few chapters in the Book of Matthew for Jewish people to determine that there was no prophecy in Isaiah that foretold that a virgin would give birth to a messiah. Likewise, the Jewish people were doubly unimpressed with Matthew's claim that the messiah was to be a resident of Nazareth, when no such prophecy existed. The people of Israel concluded that Matthew had engaged in a willful and unrestrained corruption of their sacred scriptures. Consequently, the author of the first Gospel failed in his effort to convert his targeted Jewish audiences to Christianity.

Ironically, there was no individual in history who was more responsible for the strong resistance of the Jewish people to the Christian message than Matthew. In contrast, the person most responsible for the church's unparalleled success among the gentiles was unquestionably the apostle Paul. Not surprisingly, throughout the biblical narrative, gentiles had always had a terrible time discerning chaff from wheat, truth from heresy; and the Jews were repeatedly warned never to emulate them. Tragically, some of our people missed this crucial message.

Paul, however, should have been tipped off that his teachings on original sin were misguided and that his broad-brushed characterization of humanity was erroneous. In fact, the Jewish scriptures repeatedly praised numerous men of God for their unwavering righteousness. For example, the Bible declared that men like Calev1 and King Josiah2 were faithful throughout their extraordinary lives. Moreover, because of their devotion to their Creator, Abraham and Daniel were the objects of the Almighty's warm affection as He tenderly referred to Abraham as "My friend,"[3] and Daniel, "beloved."[4] These extraordinary people did not merit these remarkable superlatives because they believed in Jesus or depended on a blood atonement; but rather, it was their devotion to God and unyielding obedience to His Torah that shaped their lives.

Job's unique loyalty to God stands as a permanent enigma to Christian theology as well. Here was a man who was severely tested by Satan and endured unimaginable personal tragedies, yet despite these afflictions, Job remains the model of the righteous servant of God. While in Christian theology Job's personal spiritual triumph is a theological impossibility, in Jewish terms it stands out as the embodiment of God's salvation program for mankind. Job didn't rely on Jesus to save him and he certainly did not turn to the cross for his redemption; rather, it was his unswerving obedience to God that made his life a lesson for all of humanity.

Paul's unfounded doctrine of original sin sullies the exemplary legacies of these and many other great men of God. Moreover, Christians must ponder whether it is an insult to the Creator to label all of God's human creation depraved.

Quite unwittingly, Luke committed a striking theological blunder that severely undermined Paul's teachings on original sin. In the first chapter of Luke, the evangelist seeks to portray Elizabeth, who is the cousin of Mary, and her husband Zechariah as the virtuous parents of John the Baptist. Yet in his zeal to characterize the baptizer's mother and father as saints, Luke unwittingly writes,

> "Both of them were upright in the sight of God, observing all the Lord's commandments and regulations blamelessly." (Luke 1:6)

The question that comes to mind is how can missionaries possibly harmonize Paul's insistence that all humanity is depraved when Luke insists that Elizabeth and

Zechariah were to be regarded as "blameless"? This is a stunning gaffe for Luke to make when it was he who eagerly promoted Paul in his Book of Acts. Doesn't Luke's assertion that this couple observed "all the Lord's commandments" fly in the face of Paul's central teaching that no one is capable of keeping the *mitzvoth* of the Torah? Is it not a fact that Christianity teaches that this task is impossible?

Paul never lived to read the Book of Luke, yet throughout his epistles Paul sidesteps any statement in the Jewish scriptures that could undermine his teaching on original sin. For example, immediately after the sin of Adam and Eve is narrated, the Torah declares that man can master his passionate lust for sin. In Genesis 4:6-7, God turns to Cain and warns him,

> If you do what is right, will you not be accepted? If, though, you do not do what is right, sin is crouching at your door; it desires to have you, **but you shall master over it**.

For Christian architects like Paul, Augustine, and Calvin, this declaration of man's ability to restrain and govern his lust for sin is nothing short of heresy. Moreover, the fact that the Torah places these assuring words immediately following the sin in the Garden of Eden[5] is profoundly troubling for the Church. How can depraved humanity control its iniquity when the Book of Romans repeatedly insists that man can do nothing to release himself from sin's powerful grip? Yet notice that there is nothing in the Eden narrative that could be construed as support for Paul's teaching on humanity's dire condition. On the contrary, in just these two inspiring verses, the Torah dispels forever the church's teachings on original sin.

There is one final point to be addressed in a passing statement you raised in your question. I was somewhat puzzled by your comment that your brand of Christianity teaches that "water baptism is required for the removal of this sin." It is not uncommon for Christians to relate some personal tidbit about their religious beliefs somewhere in the course of their question. What was so surprising about your comment, however, is that your church has simply replaced one commandment with another. On the one hand, your church teaches that the commandments explicitly ordained by the Torah are to be abandoned by believing Christians. Yet in the very same breath, your church then introduces this brand new commandment declaring that its parishioners must undergo a water baptism to be saved. It would seem more logical that if you were going to contemplate observing commandments, you might as well devote your loyalty to those *mitzvoth* ordained by God rather than those introduced by your pastor and deacons.

The notion that man is saved by being washed in water or forgiven through human blood is unknown to the Jewish scriptures. The Almighty does, however, clearly lay out His sovereign plan for His covenant people when he declares, "See, I have set before you today life and good, death and evil." (Deuteronomy 30:15) What is this "life" and "good" of which the Torah speaks? Missionaries insist that the Jewish nation must convert to Christianity and believe in a crucified messiah in order to be saved. The Torah, however, disagrees. Throughout the Hebrew Bible the Almighty unambiguously declares that the children of Israel are to draw near to Him with intense love and faithfully keep His commandments. This is the desire of the Creator. Moses beseeches the children of Israel,

> I command you today to **love the Lord your God, to walk in his ways, and to keep his commands**, decrees, and laws; then you will live and increase, and the Lord your God will bless you in the land you are entering to possess. (Deuteronomy 30:16)

Abraham, the father of the Jewish nation, remained intensely loyal to God's commandments and, as a result, the Torah regards our first patriarch as the paradigm of faithfulness.

> I will make your descendants multiply as the stars of heaven; I will give to your descendants all these lands, and in your seed all the nations of the earth shall be blessed **because Abraham obeyed My voice and kept My charge, My commandments, My statutes, and My laws**. (Genesis 26:4-5)

The Almighty did not give us desires that we cannot govern or commandments that we could not keep. The Torah was not delivered to angels, it was given to the children of Israel long after our first ancestors transgressed in the Garden of Eden.

In Jewish terms, sin is not a person, it's an event, and that event happened yesterday. In chapter after chapter, the prophets of Israel beseech those who lost their way to turn back to the Merciful One because today is a new day.

Best wishes for a happy Purim.

Very sincerely yours,

Rabbi Tovia Singer

## Footnotes:

1. Numbers 14:24.

2. II Kings 22:2.

3. Isaiah 41:8.

4. Daniel 9:23; 10:11; 10:19.

5. The sin in the Garden of Eden is found in the third chapter of Genesis.

# Why Didn't the Red Ribbon on the Head of the Scapegoat Turn White in 30 C.E.?

## Question:

I was wondering about a story that a "Hebrew-Christian" told me recently. He said that there was a scarlet cloth which would turn white every year when the high priest atoned for the sins of the people. When Jesus died, around 30 A.D., the cloth would no longer turn white when the priest atoned for sins because Jesus was the final atonement. I've read this story in other sources, and I wondered what you have to say about it.

## Answer:

This assertion with which you were confronted has, in the last decade, attracted wide interest in the evangelical world. In fact, I am somewhat surprised that it has taken this long for one of our website visitors to write in with this question.

In spite of the popularity this issue has gained in the Christian world in recent years, this contention stands out as one of the most bizarre arguments used by those who seek to convert the Jewish people to Christianity. What makes this line of reasoning so odd is that it seeks to use the Talmud to prove that Jesus is the messiah. While many readers of our website would simply be surprised to learn that missionaries would point to the Talmud to prove the validity of the Christian religion, in reality, this misuse of rabbinic literature is widespread.

Those who have navigated through the plethora of Hebrew-Christian websites are well aware of how widespread this abuse of Jewish literature has become in recent years. Moreover, by probing this surprising missionary approach, we can gain enormous insight into the schizophrenic technique that Christendom so often takes in its cherished work of Jewish evangelism.

Bear in mind, missionaries rarely shy away from an opportunity to condemn the Oral Law as the nimble work of men rather than the oral transmission handed down to us by Moses, our teacher. In fact, there are few issues that seem to produce the visceral passions of the Hebrew-Christian world as does the mere mention of the *Talmud*. These evangelicals fervently insist that the written Bible alone is reliable and divinely inspired and often scornfully mock traditional Jews as practicing a "rabbinic Judaism." Needless to say, Christians rarely use this acrid label in a manner that is meant to be flattering.

Paradoxically, whenever missionaries feel the urge to advance their position by quoting from the Talmud, they undergo a spontaneous conversion as they happily and unhesitatingly point to the works of the Talmud with a newfound regard for its truthfulness and inspiration. Yet the very same Talmud, which evangelicals gleefully use to advance their tenuous positions, also unambiguously states that Jesus of Nazareth was neither virtuous nor the messiah. This pick-and-choose approach that missionaries unflinchingly embrace doesn't appear to bother those dedicated to Jewish evangelism.

Nevertheless, it is essential that we examine this well-worn argument with which you were confronted. In Tractate Yoma 39b, the Talmud quotes a *Baraisa*[1] that discusses numerous remarkable phenomena that occurred in the Temple during the Yom Kippur service. More specifically, the Talmud states that there was a strip of scarlet-dyed wool tied to the head of the scapegoat[2] which would turn white in the presence of the large crowd gathered at the Temple on the Day of Atonement. The Jewish people perceived this miraculous transformation as a heavenly sign that their sins were forgiven. The Talmud relates, however, that 40 years before the destruction of the Second Temple the scarlet colored strip of wool did not turn white. The text of the Talmud which missionaries quote states,

> The Rabbis taught that forty years prior to the destruction of the Temple the lot did not come up in the [high priest's] right hand nor

did the tongue of scarlet wool become white . . .

Citing the above statement, missionaries contend that the year the scarlet ribbon ceased to turn white coincides with the time that Jesus was crucified. They go on to insist that 40 years prior to the destruction of the second Temple corresponds to the year 30 C.E.,[3] which is approximately the time of Jesus' crucifixion. They conclude, therefore, that the cessation of the whitening of the scarlet ribbon clearly indicates that God was no longer accepting animal sacrifices, and the Jewish people, therefore, needed to turn to Jesus as their only avenue for atonement. Ultimately, this argument asserts that the reason why the scarlet strip of wool did not turn white in the year 30 C.E. was due to the fact that the sins of the Jews were not forgiven because they did not accept Jesus as their messiah.

As unimaginable as it would seem, particularly for those readers who are familiar with this well-known section of the Talmud, this argument has gained widespread attention over the last few years. In fact, the first time I heard this polemic used I watched in disbelief as a spellbound church audience turned pale when their pastor excitedly expounded on this quote from the Talmud in his sermon. It was a particularly disheartening spectacle to observe. Had any one of the parishioners in the audience gone to the local library and examined this entire section of the *Talmud*, they would have quickly realized that this quote had been misapplied and misused.

Before we examine this statement in the Talmud, there are two issues which need to be raised here. The first point is that it is my hope that our website readers have noticed what those who advance this argument have done; they have attached an exegesis to the text of the Talmud that reflects a self-serving theology. In essence, missionaries are claiming that the reason why the strip of scarlet wool did not turn white must be attributed to the fact that the Jews rejected Jesus. This is a preposterous notion. In fact, if evangelicals wish to engage in this sophomoric approach, a far more congruous argument could be made here using their same line of reasoning. We can, utilizing the same course of logic, conclude that the reason the scarlet strip of wool did not turn white was due to the fact that masses of wayward Jews had followed the false messiah, Jesus of Nazareth. In other words, rather than attributing the reason for the scarlet strip of wool not turning white to the rejection of Jesus, it can be more steadily asserted that the reason this transformation didn't occur was due to the fact that many Jewish people had shamefully embraced Christianity. In fact, such an interpretation would be far more consistent with the whole of the Talmud.

Bear in mind, I am not suggesting that this is the correct understanding of this text.

It is not. We shall soon see that this section of the Talmud is unrelated to either of these explanations. I have made this point, however, to illustrate the self-serving nature of this circular missionary argument.

The second point, however, presents a far more serious problem for Christian apologists. If in fact, as the "Hebrew-Christian" insisted, the reason that the scarlet wool strip did not turn white was "because Jesus was the final atonement," and there was thus no longer any need for animal sacrifices, why then are the same animal sacrifices coming back? Christians have very little room to maneuver on this matter because the Bible is quite clear that the animal sacrificial system will be restored in the messianic age. In fact, in the last nine chapters of the Book of Ezekiel, the prophet describes in vivid detail the elaborate rituals and lofty ceremonies which will occur in the third and final messianic Temple. In chapters 43-44, Ezekiel clearly states that the animal sacrifices will be reinstated in their full glory. This simple fact should at least give Hebrew-Christians pause before they boldly proclaim that the transformation of the scarlet strip of wool had ceased due to the fact that God had done away with animal sacrifices. Clearly, God has not done away with them as evidenced by the fact that these elaborate Temple rituals will be restored with the advent of the messiah.

Let us now examine the Talmudic discussion from which this quote is derived. As you will discover, this text was carefully quoted out of its original context. Once this crucial background is restored and understood, it will become clear that this quote does nothing to advance any Christian theology.

Tractate Yoma[4] is wholly given over to laws pertaining to Yom Kippur. Although missionaries cite the above statement which appears on page 39b, the discussion leading up to this quote begins on the previous page, 39a. Quoting from a *Baraisa*, the Talmud begins with a discussion of the deteriorating spiritual condition of the Jewish people during the second Temple period. Throughout this fascinating discourse, the miraculous events that transpired during the Temple ceremonies are the barometer by which the *Baraisa* measures the religious decline of the nation of Israel during this difficult epoch in Jewish history. The period of time examined in this assessment begins with the era during which Shimon HaTzaddik[5] officiated as the high priest until the time that the Romans destroyed the second Temple in the year 70 C.E. More specifically, the Talmud breaks this period down into three successive stages, with the first stage being the most meritorious, the second marking a gradual spiritual decline, and the third the most deleterious.

The *Baraisa* begins by recounting the miraculous events that repeatedly occurred during the forty years when Shimon HaTzaddik officiated as high priest. The *Baraisa* then continues to relate how the appearance of these miracles progressively diminished in the years that followed his death. These events are as follows:

1) The lot inscribed *"LaHashem,"* would always appear in the right hand of the high priest[6] during the *Yom Kippur* service.

2) The strip of scarlet-dyed wool which was tied to the head of the scapegoat always turned white during the *Yom Kippur* service.

3) The western-most lamp of the Temple menorah remained lit until the priest would use its fire to kindle the next day's lamps.

4) The pyre on the altar did not require any additional wood to sustain a strong fire.

5) There was a blessing upon the first fruits of the *Omer*, the two loaves offered on *Shevuoth*, and on the twelve loaves of the showbread so that each priest was satisfied with a portion no larger than the size of an olive.

The faithfulness and goodwill that Shimon HaTzaddik engendered during his public tenure as high priest profoundly inspired the nation. His most famous maxim was, "The world exists on three things: the Torah, divine worship, and acts of kindness" (*Pirkay Avot* 1:2). He is described as a person who took great thought and consideration regarding his fellow man.[7] His extraordinary character effected the people deeply, and this manifested itself with a host of miraculous phenomena in the Temple, the House of Shimon's dedication.

Following his death, however, the Jewish people were unable to sustain the spiritual heights which they had achieved during Shimon HaTzaddik's lifetime. As a result, they digressed into a downward spiritual spiral from which they never recovered. This decline continued and worsened as the second Temple era continued to unfold. The *Baraisa* therefore relates that after the death of Shimon HaTzaddik the occurrence of these miracles became sporadic; there were some years when these miraculous signs occurred, and there were other years when they did not. This spiritual decay plunged to its lowest point during the last 40 years of the second Temple period. The *Baraisa* records that none of the above miracles occurred during these last four decades of the second Temple.

The question that immediately comes to mind is: In what dreadful sins did the children of Israel indulge during these last ill-famed 40 years of the second Temple that proved so devastating to their spiritual subsistence? What brought about the end of the miraculous events that were commonplace in the years that Shimon HaTzaddik served as high priest and periodically in the years that followed his death?

With virtually no knowledge of the works of the Talmud, missionaries boldly insist that the scarlet ribbon not whitening relates to the crucifixion of Jesus. As you probably suspect by now, this contention is wholly without merit. Moreover, this Christian assertion entails a misuse of Jewish literature in order to advance a theology that is unknown to the Talmud. The Talmud, in fact, clearly and painfully records the sins that brought about the deplorable spiritual condition of the Jewish people during this last turbulent four decades of the second commonwealth. When quoting this Talmudic text, however, missionaries are careful to sidestep the crucial backdrop of this quote in the Talmud. By so doing, they deprive the uninitiated listener of indispensable knowledge and the vital tools to effectively respond to this argument.

What makes the Christian use of this Talmudic quote so preposterous is the fact that the miracles in the Temple did not suddenly end in the year 30 C.E. as missionaries would have you think. On the contrary, the disappearance of miraculous phenomena began immediately following the death of Shimon HaTzaddik, which occurred many centuries before the destruction of the second Temple. In essence, there was not a sudden watershed event that caused supernatural events to end. The cessation of miraculous phenomena in the Temple was brought about by a slow spiritual decay among the Jewish people that lasted for many hundreds of years.

Although there were a number of sins that were rampant among the nation of Israel throughout this spiritual decline, there was no iniquity that was as self-destructive as the interpersonal baseless hatred that was pervasive among the Jewish people during this difficult time. This dreadful self-inflicted wound had infected the Jewish people and ultimately brought about the destruction of the second Temple.[8] The *Talmud* bears record to this spiritual decay, and declares that this national tragedy reached its height exactly 40 years prior to the destruction of the second Temple. It was during this turbulent time that murders became so widespread that the *Sanhedrin*[9] ceased to judge capital crimes such as homicide.[10]

Under ordinary conditions, the *Sanhedrin* rarely carried out capital punishment. In fact, the Talmud proclaims that a *Sanhedrin* which put more than one person to death in 70 years was unflatteringly regarded as a "Killer *Bais Din*."[11] The Jewish judicial system was not set up for a lawless society where murder among the nation of Israel was widespread. It is for this reason, and under these deplorable conditions, that the glory of the Temple was dimmed, the miracles in the sanctuary ceased, and the *Sanhedrin* withdrew itself from adjudicating capital punishment.

Although the termination of miraculous events in the Temple was unrelated to Christian theology, it bore testimony to a time in history when Jewish people in great numbers turned against each other.

I will add one final note in order to bring all of the above parts together. To illustrate this final point, however, I will raise a number of basic questions. Bear in mind, missionaries insist that God had discontinued the animal sacrificial system and replaced it with Jesus' sacrificial death on the cross. How can we know that the ending of the miraculous transformation of the scarlet ribbon was not connected to the ending of the animal sacrificial system, as missionaries contend? How can we be certain that the cessation of the whitening of the scarlet ribbon was entirely unrelated to the blood sacrificial system? Moreover, how can we be sure that the reason this miracle ended 40 years before the destruction of the second Temple was due to the deplorable lack of social justice and brotherly kindness among the Jewish people?

Finally, what is the meaning behind this mysterious ritual of tying a scarlet ribbon to the head of the scapegoat with the anticipation that it would miraculously turn white? To begin with, why was the wool of the ribbon dyed scarlet? Why didn't they use a blue or green ribbon? Why would it have to turn white to indicate that their iniquities were cleansed? Moreover, how could the nation know that the marvelous transformation from scarlet to white was a clear indication that their sins had been forgiven? In essence, how do the colors scarlet and white relate to social justice and brotherly love? What is the connection between the color of the ribbon and the spiritual state of the children of Israel?

The answer to all these perplexing questions is addressed clearly in the Hebrew Bible. In the first chapter of the Book of Isaiah, the prophet severely castigates the Jewish people for their woeful sins. No where in this epic chapter does the prophet condemn his people for violating the Sabbath or eating unkosher food. This was not the spiritual crisis which confronted the nation; rather, the prophet cries aloud that their lack of social justice and unconscionable abandonment of the weak that robbed the masses of their spiritual sustenance and connection to God. They abandoned these cornerstone tenants, mindlessly turning against each other. The nation was especially indifferent to needs of the most vulnerable members of society – the widow, the fatherless and the destitute. With a visceral condemnation of his people, Isaiah berates the nation with the biting words virtually unparalleled in the Jewish scriptures. He compares his people to Sodom and Gomorrah and warns that if this is the manner with which you treat your fellow man, then God rejects your Sabbaths and New Moons. "When you beseech Me with your many prayers, I will not hear them for your hands are stained with blood."[12] "There was a time," Isaiah laments, "that the city was filled with righteousness, but now it has become a harlot, filled with murderers!"[13]

It is painfully difficult to read the opening verses of this chapter. As we listen to the pounding words of the prophet, there is a mortifying and numbing sense that all hope is lost. Reconciliation is impossible; God will never take us back. It is, though, precisely at this most desperate juncture that Isaiah proclaims the unimaginable: Hope is not lost and God's tender mercy is within your grasp. What, though, should we do to possess this undeserved mercy? How can these seemingly unforgivable sins be forgiven? Does the prophet then announce that we must believe in a crucified messiah to gain our atonement? Is a blood sacrifice recommended as the solution to our desperate sinful predicament? Missionaries would have us think so, but Isaiah disagrees. The prophet, therefore, instructs,

> "Wash yourselves; make yourselves clean; remove the evil of your doings from before my eyes; cease to do evil, learn to do good; seek justice, correct oppression; defend the fatherless, plead for the widow. Come now, let us reason together," says the Lord, **"though your sins are like scarlet, they shall be as white as snow; though they are red like crimson, they shall become like wool.** If you are willing and obedient, you shall eat the good of the land."[14]

With the prophet's reassuring words before us, we can now understand why the miracle surrounding the transformation of the scarlet ribbon was uniquely connected to the atonement achieved through social justice and brotherly kindness rather than blood atonement. If your sins that are as the scarlet-colored ribbon are to be forgiven and become white, indulge in acts of kindness and put an end to murder and baseless hatred. These precious words fell on deaf ears during the last 40 years of the second Temple.

The prophet Isaiah begins his first chapter with a warning to his wayward nation that blood sacrifices were counterproductive in the eyes of God as a means of atonement, and pleads with the people not to depend on them. Thus, the moving portrait of the scarlet thread transforming to white stands as a living monument to the prophet's inspiring message on bloodless atonement. Needless to say, this profound teaching deals a fatal blow to the core teachings of the Church.

Missionaries attempt to counter this point by claiming that Isaiah was simply condemning insincere sacrifices; but this assertion is without merit and opposed by the prophets of Israel. Isaiah loudly declares that charity and acts of kindness alone atone for man's most grievous sins, as he repeatedly and resoundingly trivializes blood sacrificial system, casting it as an inefficacious ceremony that cannot atone man's deliberate sins. Isaiah revisits this stern message, warning that blood sacrifices for sin are an abomination to in his closing chapter:

> Whoever sacrifices a bull is like one who kills a man, and whoever offers a lamb, like one who breaks a dog's neck; whoever makes a grain offering is like one who presents pig's blood, and whoever burns frankincense, like one who worships an idol... (Isaiah 66:3)

While Shimon HaTzaddik officiated for 40 years as high priest, the nation was inspired by his good will and they emulated him. As a result, the atonement outlined in Isaiah was efficacious and the scarlet ribbon always turned white. The people knew that God had forgiven them.

In the years that followed the death of Shimon HaTzaddik, the people's dedication to his golden rule slacked off, and consequently, there were some years when the ribbon turned white and others when it did not.

Sadly, we can now also understand why 40 years prior to the destruction of the second Temple this auspicious miracle ended. It was during these calamitous four decades when Isaiah's words of condemnation were personified.

Even as I write this letter, in the shadow of Yitzhak Rabin's assassination, it is still difficult to imagine a time when baseless hatred could have become so widespread that murders had became commonplace among my people. I vividly recall the traumatic days that followed the death of Rabin. It seemed as though humanity was almost overcome by a sense of stunned bewilderment. Men and women wondered aloud how something like this could have happened. I recall how deeply people were stunned, not just by the fact that the leader of the Jewish State was assassinated, but even more appalling, it was a Jew who had committed this crime. How could this mindless hatred have emerged among Jews, people wondered. Yet it did.

As we contemplate the despotic period that brought about the destruction of the

Second Temple, let us free ourselves of this spiritual affliction and turn toward each other with Godly affection. May this repentance bring about the coming of the true messiah, quickly in our time.

Sincerely yours,

Rabbi Tovia Singer

# Footnotes:

1. A *Baraisa* is a statement made by a *Tanna* which was not included by Rabbi Yehudah Ha'nasi (approximately 200 C.E.) in the Mishnah.
2. See Leviticus 16:7-10.
3. The Second Temple was destroyed by the Romans in the year 70 C.E.
4. The Aramaic word *Yoma* means "The Day," and it refers to *Yom Kippur*, the Day of Atonement.
5. Shimon HaTzaddik (Simon the Just) succeeded Ezra during the early part of the second Temple period and officiated as high priest for forty years. Shimon was called *"HaTzaddik"* because of his faithfulness and his kindness to his countrymen (*Josephus Antiquities* 12:157).
6. The high priest would randomly pick two lots from a box. One was inscribed *"LaHashem,"* and the other was inscribed, *"LaAzazel,"* (see Leviticus 16:8-10). It was considered an auspicious sign if the lot inscribed *"LaHashem"* appeared in the right hand of the high priest.
7. Ecclus. [*Sirach*] 1, 4.
8. Talmud, Yoma 9b.
9. The *Sanhedrin* is the name for the Jewish court system.
10. Talmud, Sanhedrin 41a; Avodah Zara 8b.
11. Talmud, Makkos 7a. *"Bais Din,"* literally, a "House of Law," refers to a Jewish court.
12. Isaiah 1:15.
13. Isaiah 1:21.
14. Isaiah 1:16-19.

# When a Pastor Demands Charity

## Question:

Dear Rabbi,

I was watching a television evangelist one Sunday, and something he said really struck me. According to him, unless people pay tithes they will suffer. Actually his words were that they would "get their butts kicked by life." I was horrified, Rabbi. Would you tell me what Judaism teaches about tithing and its purpose.

Thank you.

## Answer:

It is a mitzvah (commandment) from the Torah for every Jew -- whether impoverished or wealthy -- to give ten percent of his income to charity. This act of giving alms to the poor is held in high esteem by the Jewish people. Moreover, the Bible teaches us that this mitzvah acts as an atonement for sin. This message is declared to Nebuchadnezzar in the Book of Daniel (4:24)[1] and is the central theme of the opening message of the Book of Isaiah.

In the beginning of the Book of Isaiah, the prophet declares how alms to the poor and downtrodden expiates man's iniquities. The first chapter of Isaiah begins with a harsh condemnation of the nation of Israel. Few chapters in the Bible are as brutally critical of the Jewish people as Isaiah is in the beginning of his first chapter. In the 16th verse, however, the prophet almost unexpectedly soothes his wayward nation by teaching them both the essence of atonement and the way to achieve it. He assures the nation of Israel that if they turn from their sinful ways and care for the downtrodden, their sins will be forgiven. Isaiah's message, like that of the other Jewish prophets, stands in stark contrast to the declaration in the Book of Hebrews that "without the shedding of blood there is no atonement."[2]

As an aside, I find this Christian pastor's message that those who fail to tithe will "suffer" to be rather puzzling. According to mainline Protestant theology, salvation cannot be achieved through any form of "works" or deeds. Tithing would certainly fall into this category of works. There is little doubt that this church leader is attempting to instill fear within the congregation in order to secure some rather plump offerings.

Sincerely yours,

Rabbi Tovia Singer

**Footnotes:**

1. "Therefore, O king, may my counsel be acceptable to you. Atone for your sins with righteousness, and your iniquities with mercy to the oppressed, so that your prosperity may be prolonged." This verse appears as 4:27 in a Christian Bible.

2. Hebrews 9:22.

# The Haftorah and Isaiah 53: Are the Jews Hiding Something?

## Question:

Dear Rabbi,

Missionaries claim that we are so "scared" of Isaiah 53 that we have omitted it from the Haftorah reading when it comes up. I know this can't be true, but what should be my response when this is brought up? Thank you.

## Answer:

This well-worn claim that the Jews have deliberately removed Isaiah 53 from the *Haftorah* because they are "so scared" that upon hearing this chapter read aloud from the pulpit, worshipers might bolt from their synagogues for the local baptism pool, is one of the most popular arguments used by missionaries to sustain their christological interpretation of Isaiah 53. This argument, however, is so devoid of merit that I often find it difficult to know where to begin in my response. Let's start with a little background on the Jewish custom to read a portion of the *Haftorah* on the Sabbath day.

Those unfamiliar with the source of the custom to read the *Haftorah* might conclude from this missionary argument that the Jews read all of the Prophets during the yearly cycle (as we do the entire Pentateuch) and we somehow only leave out Isaiah 53 from the annual reading of the *Haftorah*. Actually, less than five percent of the prophets are read during the Sabbath service throughout the year.

The Jewish people adopted the custom to read the *Haftorah* long before the advent of Christianity. During the traumatic events that led to the festival of Chanukah, Antiochus Epiphanes IV (ruled from 175-164 B.C.E.) decreed that it was forbidden for the Jews to read the Torah in his effort to eradicate the Jewish faith. To circumvent this spiritual crisis, the Jewish people began to read from a selected portion of the Prophets on each Sabbath to substitute the designated reading from the Torah. This custom was retained after the decree was rescinded.

The particular Sabbath portion of the Prophets was carefully selected for one of two reasons. Either because the theme of a segment of the Prophets closely correlated to the portion of the Torah read that week, or because that section of the Prophets thematically corresponded to a festival or a historical circumstance during that Sabbath. It is therefore easy to understand why Isaiah 53 is never read in the synagogue. Isaiah 53 bears no relationship to any of the chapters of the Pentateuch and is unrelated to any holiday or historical circumstance on the Jewish calendar and therefore it was never included in any *Haftorah* portion.

It probably would come as a surprise to many missionaries that not only is Isaiah 53 never read in the synagogue on the Sabbath, but neither are Isaiah chapters 3, 13, 23 or 33 for that matter. It should be obvious that Christian polemics played no role in the *Haftorah* selection as evidenced by the fact that Isaiah 9:5-6 is read in the *Haftorah*, which is a text widely used by missionaries to support their claims.

Needless to say, this missionary argument is particularly preposterous when we consider that the custom to read the *Haftorah* in the synagogue was implemented more than 2,150 years ago, long before the Christian era. It is puzzling why missionaries are unaware of this fact when the custom to read the *Haftorah* is mentioned quite clearly in the New Testament (Acts 13:14-15), long before the Jewish people could have an inkling that a heretical sect would emerge that would misinterpret this extraordinary chapter.

This remarkable claim that the Jews expunged Isaiah 53 from the *Haftorah* is probably the most anti-Semitic argument used by missionaries. It thrives on and perpetuates the medieval Christian portrait of the Jews – a cunning, scheming, diabolical bunch – who are capable of rejecting Jesus, although deep down – in their heart of hearts, believe in him and have conspired to make sure that every other Jew rejects him. Only the Devil is capable of this dastardly deed. In other words, although the Devil knows the truth and believes in God, he rejects Him and seduces others to do the same. This personification of the Jew as the Devil (John 8:44) is as old as Christianity itself and things haven't changed much.

Yours,

Rabbi Tovia Singer

# Isaiah 53: Did Jesus Have Long Life?

## Question:

My question pertains to an objection you raised in your tape series regarding the christological reading of Isaiah 53, specifically verse 10. This verse says that the Servant's days will be prolonged. Jesus, however, died young. However, if we were to believe in the resurrection, that Jesus rose in the flesh, why can we not say that his life has been prolonged? The human side of him would now be about 2,000 years old. One would think that this could be called having a prolonged life. Is there a fault in this reasoning?

Expanded study of Isaiah 53 on pages 68-80

## Answer:

Before answering your question, we should begin with a brief overview of the 53rd chapter of Isaiah[1] for our readers who are unfamiliar with this most-debated section of the Bible.

The 53rd chapter of Isaiah is the last of the four famed "Servant Songs"[2] at the end of the Book of Isaiah. These four "Servant Songs," which are found in Isaiah 41-53, are chapters pregnant with stunning End Time prophecy and comfort for the children of Israel. The prophet soothes his traumatized Servant by unveiling the glorious redemption of the righteous remnant of Israel, who is repeatedly identified as God's servant. Isaiah 53 is the culmination of Isaiah's narrative which describes the Almighty's servant-nation who, after a brutal and seemingly endless exile, is elevated and redeemed in the eyes of her former oppressors – the gentile nations.

The 53rd chapter of Isaiah begins with an extraordinary soliloquy expressed by the surprised gentile kings of nations at the End of Days as they finally behold the righteous remnant of the Jewish people raised up and glorified. The redemption of Israel is not at all what her non-Jewish neighbors expected.

The astonished reaction of the gentiles to the Messianic Age is a common theme in the Hebrew prophets, and the baffled reaction of the gentiles is recorded in Isaiah 53 with greater clarity than any other chapter in the Bible. What startling news will astound the world's leaders? What will they finally grasp that will amaze them beyond measure? Everything that they have ever heard or considered is in stark contrast to what they will finally witness in the Messianic Age. They will place their hands over their mouths in numbed bewilderment as they behold the glory of the remnant of the Jewish people, finally vindicated and redeemed by the "arm of the Lord." Let's examine Isaiah 52:15-53:1, which are the introductory verses to Isaiah 53:

> So shall he startle many nations; kings shall shut their mouths because of him; for that which has not been told them they shall see, and that which they have not heard they shall understand. Who has believed what we have heard? And to whom has the arm of the Lord been revealed?

In verses two through eight, the kings of nations continue to speak as they sorrowfully express their heartfelt confession. They finally understand that as a result of the sins of their peoples, the nation of Israel had suffered brutally throughout their long and bitter exile. In the past, these world leaders surmised that because the Jewish people stubbornly refused to embrace the ways of their nations the Jews were stricken and smitten by God. But now, as they bear witness to the glorious messianic redemption, they will be astounded, for they will finally understand that Israel suffered as a result of the destructive arrogance and devastating reckless behavior of their own peoples.

By Isaiah 53:9, however, the speakers are no longer the gentile kings, but rather the Almighty Himself. In 53:10, the verse about which you were asking, God is enumerating the blessings that are bestowed on those who have chosen the path of devotion and "have made their souls a restitution." These manifold blessings mirror the promised blessings to the faithful at the end of the Book of Deuteronomy. In these last chapters of the Pentateuch, the Almighty promises prolonged life and children to those who are devoted to the life-giving teachings of the Torah.

And now we come to your question. In an effort to support their christological position, missionaries often try to argue that Isaiah 53 is speaking about Jesus. In fact, Isaiah 53 stands out as the biblical text most used by missionaries. There are, however, countless ways to prove from this chapter and the chapters that surround it that Isaiah 53 is referring to the faithful remnant of Israel and not to the Christian messiah.

In Isaiah 53:10, the verse about which you were asking, the servant is promised long life and seed. Let's read Isaiah 53:10.

> And the Lord wished to crush him, He made him ill; if his soul makes itself restitution, he shall see seed, He shall prolong his days, and God's purpose shall prosper in his hand.

For the church, this verse presents numerous staggering problems. To begin with, Jesus did not have any biological children. The Hebrew word זרע *(zerah)*, which means "seed" used in Isaiah 53:10 can only refer to biological offspring when used in connection with a person's children, never metaphoric children, such as disciples. The Hebrew word that can refer to metaphoric children is ben. Moreover, according to church teachings, Jesus died when he was approximately 30-40 years old, only about half the life span of a man as declared by King David in Psalm 90:10. Obviously, neither the blessing of seed, nor the blessing of long life has been fulfilled in Jesus' case.

Missionaries attempt to ameliorate this serious problem by explaining that Jesus had long life in the resurrection where he lives forever. Therefore, they would argue, as you have pointed out, that Jesus indeed lived a very long life.

This response, however, does little to relieve their problem. To begin with, the Hebrew words יאריך ימים *(ya'arich yamim),* meaning "long life" in this verse do not mean or refer to an eternal life which has no end, but rather a lengthening of days which eventually come to an end. These Hebrew words are therefore never applied in Tanach to anyone who is to live forever. In fact, the words *ya'arich yamim* appear in a number of places throughout Jewish scriptures, including Deuteronomy 17:20, Deuteronomy 25:15, Proverbs 28:16, and Ecclesiastes 8:13. In each and every verse where this phrase appears, these words refer to an extended mortal life, not an eternal one. When the Jewish scriptures speak of an eternal resurrected life, as in Daniel 12:2, the Hebrew words לחיי עולם *(l'chayai olam)* are used.

Missionaries are confronted with staggering problems in this verse. Bear in mind that virtually all missionaries zealously espouse the doctrine of the Trinity. This tenet declares that Jesus was not just a man, but God Himself, manifested in the flesh and the second Person in the triune godhead. This is no small matter in Christian theology. I have encountered many Hebrew-Christians who were expelled from Messianic conference or denied membership in a Messianic congregation because they questioned this cherished and well-guarded doctrine.

In order to have a better understanding of this doctrine, we need to go back to the Council of Nicea where it all began. Assembled by the Emperor Constantine in 325 C.E., was the most important council in church history in both its scope and focus. Luther called it "the most sacred of all councils."[3] At the Council of Nicea it was declared that Jesus was of the same substance (Greek: *homousios*) as the Father. In essence, according to this Christian belief, Jesus shared one being with the Father and in full deity. This doctrine does not hold that Jesus was half God and half man. Rather, in the original language of this foundational Christian creed, he is "God of God, Light of Light, very God of very God . . ."[4]

Bearing all this in mind, how can God be promised long life? Even if missionaries argue that this blessing in Isaiah 53:10 is referring to that time after Jesus' supposed resurrection, how can God promise Himself, or give Himself anything for that matter? Moreover, how can God be promised longevity when He is eternal? How can God bestow the blessing of long life upon a messiah, who the Church insists, exists for eternity? Such a blessing would be absurd. Furthermore, why is God talking to Himself?

Finally, it is essential to carefully study the surrounding chapters of Isaiah 53 in order to grasp a clear understanding of the "Suffering Servant." The context of Isaiah 53 immediately reveals that the prophet is speaking of the nation of Israel in the singular. It is a tragedy that few missionaries are as familiar with the 52nd and 54th chapters of Isaiah as they are with the 53rd. The consequence of this unbalanced knowledge is obvious.

Isaiah 52 and 54 both serve as an indictment against the Christianization of Isaiah 53. To this day I have yet to encounter a Christian who can recite these chapters from memory. This cannot be said of Isaiah 53, which evangelicals can spout off by heart without hesitating.

The contiguous relationship between Isaiah 52 through 54 is evident because the theme, poetic structure, and motif of Isaiah 53 closely mimics the illustrative language of Isaiah 52 and 54. As in Isaiah 53, Isaiah 52 and 54 clearly identify Israel in the singular, suffering innocently as a result of the vile wickedness of the gentile nations. In addition, all three of these exhilarating chapters vividly describe the glorious redemption of Israel in full view of the gentiles, her former persecutors.

For example, in Isaiah 52:4 the prophet recounts that "Assyria oppressed him [Israel] without cause." This concept, in Isaiah 52, that the nation of Israel innocently suffered as a single individual at the hands of the gentiles, is precisely the same underlying theme of Isaiah 53. In Isaiah 54, the prophet recounts how Israel, in the singular, is "despised," "forsaken," and "afflicted." These are the identical descriptions of the nation of Israel found in the previous chapter, Isaiah 53. In fact, it is so manifestly evident from these chapters that Isaiah 53 is speaking of the righteous remnant of Israel, that a great many Christian commentators unhesitatingly agree that this chapter speaks of no one else but the Almighty's Chosen People. If Hebrew-Christians would pore over the entire Book of Isaiah with the same zeal as they do Isaiah 53, few of them would have abandoned the faith of their ancestors.

Over the years, so many Hebrew-Christians have turned to me and pondered aloud as they finally decided to leave the church, "Why weren't you there with the answers 11 years ago when I first got involved?" My response is always the same, "The answers to your questions were always there. I just teach the Bible."

Sincerely yours,

Rabbi Tovia Singer

**Footnotes:**

1. Although this text is most commonly referred to as Isaiah 53, in actuality it refers to the 15 verses beginning with Isaiah 52:13 and

ending with 53:12.The chapter break at the end of 52:15 is artificial.

2. These verses in the Servant Songs include:

**Isaiah 41:8-9**

But thou, Israel, art My servant, Jacob whom I have chosen, the seed of Abraham My friend. Whom I grasped from the ends of the earth, and from it nobles I called you, and I said to you, "You are My servant"; I chose you and I did not despise you.

**Isaiah 44:1-2**

Yet hear now, O Jacob My servant and Israel, whom I have chosen. So said the Lord your Maker, and He who formed you from the womb shall aid you. Fear not, My servant Jacob, and *Jeshurun* whom I have chosen.

**Isaiah 44:21**

Remember these, O Jacob and Israel, for thou art My servant; I have formed thee; thou art My servant, O Israel, thou shalt not be forgotten of Me.

**Isaiah 45:4**

For the sake of My servant Jacob, and Israel My chosen one, and I called to you by your name . . . .

**Isaiah 48:20**

Leave Babylon, flee from the *Chaldeans*; with a voice of singing declare, tell this, publicize it to the end of the earth; say, "The Lord has redeemed His servant Jacob."

**Isaiah 49:3**

And said to me, thou art My servant, O Israel in whom I will be glorified!

3. Gordon Rupp, *Luther's Progress to the Diet of Worms* (New York: Harper and Row Publishers, 1964), pp. 66.

4. *The Third Ecumenical Council. The Council of Ephesus*, p. 202).

# Monotheism and Idiolatry

## Question:

I'm confused. I know that Christianity is pure paganism. I still believe that Yeshua ben Josef from Nazaret is not only the Messiah, but he is God. Not the second part of a three-part-God, but God himself. I am looked down upon because of my belief. I have been buried by my family, and the other Jews through out the world that I communicate with via internet do not consider me a Jew any more, even though I am more orthodox in my observance of Judaism then most of them are. The Christians do not accept me either because of the way I feel about their faith. I believe that God gave his life to forgive me and gave me the ability to obey his law without breaking the smallest of his commandments. Why is Judaism so unforgiving?

## Answer:

I am surprised that you, who I presume firmly embraces the core tenets advanced in the New Testament, are wondering "Why is Judaism so unforgiving?" I think that the ideas attributed to Jesus, or "Yeshua," as you call him, should haunt your soul. The Christian Bible triumphantly declares that those who don't believe in Jesus are condemned to an "eternal lake of fire" and everlasting damnation (Mark 16:16, II, Thes.1:8). If you consider forgiveness a sacred virtue, how do you find comfort in a religion that regards Anne Frank, a girl murdered by the Nazis during the spring of 1945, as a permanent citizen of hell for not believing in Jesus? Why is the God of the New Testament so unforgiving? I would think that a forgiving God would consider the hell on earth that Anne endured at Auschwitz and Bergen Belsen sufficient to atone for unwillingness to accept "Yeshua."

The Jewish Scriptures, the Fountain of the Living Waters, is the only cornerstone of the Jewish faith. Although you apparently adopted some the traditions of the Jewish people, perhaps your family and friends recognize that your core beliefs are indistinguishable from the Christianity that you outwardly condemn.

Why does Judaism regard your professed beliefs as hostile to the God of Israel? There is no greater sin than idolatry. Your worship of a man as God violates the very first of the Ten Commandments:

> And God spoke all these words, saying, "I am the Lord thy God, which have brought thee out of the land of Egypt, out of the house of bondage. Thou shalt have no other gods before me." (Exodus 20:1-2)

Moreover, the Bible warns us...

> God is not a man that He should lie, nor a mortal that He should change His mind. (Numbers 23:19)
>
> And also the Eternal One of Israel will not lie nor change His mind; for he is not a man, that He should change His mind. (I Samuel 15:29)
>
> Do not put your trust in princes, nor in the son of man, in whom there is no salvation! (Psalm 146:3)

The Merciful One repeatedly warns the Jewish people to turn away from other gods. As a result of this sin, ten tribes were exiled by Assyria 2,700 years ago. The prophet Hosea warned the Northern Kingdom of Israel that idol worship would lead to their demise. There is, however, wonderful news here. Listen to the words of Isaiah:

> Seek the Lord while he may be found, call upon him while he is near; let the wicked forsake his way, and the unrighteous man his thoughts. Let him return to the Lord, that he may have mercy on him, and to our God, for he will abundantly pardon, for my thoughts are not your thoughts, neither are your ways my ways, says the Lord; for as the heavens are higher than the earth, so are my ways higher than your ways and my thoughts than your thoughts. (Isaiah 55:6-9)

In his startling and uplifting sermon, the prophet promises that repentance alone atones for sin. This is Judaism.

I find it difficult to understand why you have chosen this belief that Jesus was God when John's Jesus says:

> . . . because I go to the Father; **for the Father is greater than I**. (John 14:28)

Clearly, the author of the fourth Gospel did not regard Jesus as equal with God, as you profess to believe. Below, I enclosed some Bible references for you to study.

If you are not sure Who the God of Israel is, the Bible gives us a hint in this matter. Scripture warns us that one day you will worship other gods that your fathers did not know (Deuteronomy 28) and this iniquity will bring about national disaster. So ask yourself this question. "Did my great grandfather worship "*Yeshua ben Josef*" as God?" If the answer to that question is "no" then it is time to come home to your God and your people.

I look forward to welcoming you.

Rabbi Tovia Singer

**List of Bible References:**

**Deuteronomy 4:11-12**

You came near and stood at the foot of the mountain while it blazed with fire to the very heavens, with black clouds and deep darkness. Then the Lord spoke to you out of the fire. You heard the sound of words but saw no image; there was only a voice.

**Deuteronomy 4:35**

You are the ones who have been shown, so that you will know that God is the Supreme Being, and there is none other besides Him!

**Deuteronomy 4:39**

Know therefore today, and take it to your heart, that the Lord, He is God in heaven above and on the earth below; there is no other!

**Deuteronomy 6:14**

You shall not follow other gods, any of the gods of the peoples who surround you!

**Deuteronomy 32:39**

See, now, that I, I am He -- and no god is with Me . . . .

**I Samuel 2:2**

There is none holy as the Lord. There is none beside Thee; neither is there any Rock like our God.

**I Kings 8:27**

For will God indeed dwell on the earth? Behold the heaven and heaven of heavens cannot contain Thee; how much less this house that I have built?

**I Kings 8:60**

So that all the nations of the earth may know that the Lord is God and that there is no other!

**II Kings 19:19**

Now, O Lord our God, deliver us from his hand, so that all kingdoms on earth may know that You alone, O Lord, are God. (see also Psalm 113:5)

**Isaiah 40:18**

"To whom then will you liken God? To what likeness will you compare Him?"

**Isaiah 40:25**

"To whom then will you liken Me, that I should be his equal?" says the Holy One.

**Isaiah 42:8**

I am the Lord, that is My name, and My glory will I not give to another, neither My praise to graven images!

**Isaiah 43:10-11**

"You are My witnesses," declares the Lord, "and My servant whom I have chosen, so that you may know and believe Me and understand that I am He. Before Me no god was formed, nor will there be one after Me. I, even I, am the Lord, and besides Me there is no Savior."

**Isaiah 44:6-8**

This is what the Lord says, Israel's King and Redeemer, the Lord Almighty, "I am the first and I am the last; apart from Me there is no God! Who then is like Me? Let him proclaim it. Let him declare it and lay it out before Me . . . . Do not tremble, do not be afraid. Did I not proclaim this and foretell it long ago? You are My witnesses. Is there any God besides Me? No, there is no other Rock; I know not one."

**Isaiah 44:24**

Thus said the Lord, your Redeemer, the One who formed you from the womb, "I am the Lord Who makes everything, Who stretched forth the heavens alone, Who spread out the earth by Myself."

**Isaiah 45:5-6**

I am the Lord, and there is no other; besides Me there is no God . . . . I will strengthen you . . . in order that they know from the shining of the sun and from the west that there is no one besides Me; I am the Lord and there is no other!

**Isaiah 45:21-22**

. . . Who announced this from before, who declared it from the distant past? Is it not I, the Lord, and there is no God apart from Me, a righteous God and a Savior; there is none but Me. Turn to Me and be saved, all you ends of the earth; for I am God, and there is no other!

**Isaiah 46:5**

To whom shall you liken Me and make Me equal and compare Me that we may be alike?

**Isaiah 46:9**

Remember the first things of old, that I am God and there is no other; I am God and there is none like Me.

**Hosea 13:4**

I am the Lord your God, Who brought you out of Egypt. You shall acknowledge no God but Me, no Savior except Me!

**Joel 2:27**

You shall know that I am in the midst of Israel, and I am the Lord your God, there is no other; and My people shall never be ashamed.

**Malachi 2:10**

Have we not all one Father? Has not one God created us? Why should we betray, each one his brother, to profane the covenant of our forefathers?

**Psalm 73:25**

Whom have I in heaven but You? The earth has nothing I desire besides You.

**Psalm 81:8-9**

Hear, O My people, and I will admonish you; O Israel, if you would listen to Me! Let there be no strange god among you; nor shall you worship any foreign god.

**Nehemiah 9:6**

You alone are the Lord; You made the heavens, the heavens of the heavens and all their host, the earth and all that is upon it, the seas and all that is in them, and You give life to all, and the heavenly host bow down before You.

**I Chronicles 17:20**

O Lord, there is none like You, neither is there any God beside You, according to all that we have heard with our ears!

# Have Christians Discovered the Doctrine of the Trinity in the *Shema* prayer?

## Question:

I am about to begin a conversion process. My boyfriend is Jewish and I wish to convert before we marry. I have believed for many years that this is the way for me and will be the way in which I bring up my children.

I have a born-again Christian friend coming to visit me next weekend. She has been very involved in Messianic Judaism (even though she is a gentile) and I know she is going to have a big talk with me. I want to be able to answer her intelligently. I know exactly the one she is going to throw at me and I would like some help with the answer. She is going to talk about the time in the bible (can't remember where it is) when they bought back a sample of the fruits of the promised land. Apparently it says that they bought "echad" grapes. The word "echad," although it refers to ONE, is talking about a BUNCH of grapes. Therefore, when we talk about Adonai Echad," we can be talking about three gods in one.

None of this rings true for me, but I want to be well thought out on all of this. Would you please help ASAP. (She is arriving next weekend!)

## Answer:

I am very pleased that you have asked this question because I am certain that some of our Jewish readers will be surprised by your dilemma. How can I be so sure that they will be stunned by simply reading your question? Imagine the astonished reaction of a Jew (who has his monotheism intact) as he discovers from your question that missionaries employ his cherished national creed, **"Hear O Israel, the Lord is our God, the Lord is *one*"** (אֶחָד – Hebrew: *echad*), to prove the doctrine of the Trinity. To the surprise of many, Trinitarians will often use this most-sacred text which declares the Oneness of God to support their belief in a triune nature of God. The doctrine of the Trinity has no greater foe than the declaration in Deuteronomy 6:4. Let's examine this strange missionary argument more closely.

To support their claim that there are multiple persons within the godhead, missionaries insist that the Hebrew word אֶחָד *(echad),* meaning "one" at the end of Deuteronomy 6:4 does not mean an absolute one. Rather, they argue, this verse can only signify a "compound unity," or many things in one. They will often cite two verses to support this assertion. The first is the one you have mentioned, Numbers 13:23 reads,

> Then they came to the Valley of Eshcol, and there cut down a branch with *one* אֶחָד *(echad)* cluster of grapes; they carried it between two of them on a pole. They also brought some of the pomegranates and figs.

The second is Genesis 1:5, which reads,

> . . . and there was evening and there was morning, *one* (אֶחָד *echad*) day.

From these verses, they insist, it is clear that the Hebrew word אֶחָד *(echad)* can only mean a fusion of a number of things into one.

Although this assertion is as flawed as the doctrine it seeks to support, for those who lack an elementary knowledge of the Hebrew language, this argument can be rather puzzling.

The word *echad* in the Hebrew language functions in precisely the same manner as the word "one" does in the English language. In the English language it can be said, "these four chairs and the table constitute **one** dinette set," or alternatively, "There is **one** penny in my hand." Using these two examples, it is easy to see how the English word "one" can mean either many things in one, as in the case of the dinette set, or one alone, as in the case of the penny.

Although the Hebrew word *echad* functions in the exact same manner, evangelical Christians will never offer biblical examples where the word *echad* means "one alone." Thus, by only presenting scriptural verses such as Genesis 1:5 and Numbers 23:13, it creates the illusion to the novice that the word *echad* is somehow synonymous with a compound unity. Nothing, of course, could be further from the truth. For example, Deuteronomy 17:6 reads,

> At the mouth of two witnesses, or three witnesses, shall he that is worthy of death be put to death; but at the mouth of one (אֶחָד – *echad*) witness he shall not be put to death.

or Ecclesiastes 4:8 reads,

> There is one (אֶחָד – *echad*) alone, without a companion; yes he has neither son . . .

In the above two verses the exact same Hebrew word is used, and clearly the word *echad* is referring to one alone, not a "compound unity."

There is a question that immediately comes to mind: If the Hebrew word אֶחָד *echad* can signify either a compound unity or one alone, how can one tell which definition is operative when studying a verse? The answer is: The context is always determinative. In the exact same way the word "one" is understood in the English language, that is, from the context. "Four chairs and a table make up ***one*** dinette set" is a compound unity, and "Hear O Israel, the Lord is our God, the Lord is ***one*** is unsullied monotheism.

I thank you for your question, and may the Merciful One guide you in your conversion process.

Sincerely yours,

Rabbi Singer

# Did Jesus Claim to be God?

## Question:

I have heard Christian missionaries claim that Jesus deliberately screened or veiled his divine nature on earth, so when he is asked a question by one of his disciples about the time of the end he can honestly answer, that no man, not even the Son knows the time of the end, only the Father. Then, when he says elsewhere that he and the Father are One, he is speaking about his ontological identity with the Father. Please comment on this and post it on your web site.

Thank you.

## Answer:

If the one God of the universe, Creator of the heavens and the earth, wanted to convey to His people that He alone was God and there was no other who shared this unique distinction with Him, what words would He use so that there would be no possibility for error? What phrase could He have selected so that there would be no chance of misunderstanding? If you or I wanted to describe the unique oneness of God in a way that could not be misinterpreted, how would we express this? Would we not have used the words that Moses reported God to have said in Deuteronomy 32:39,

> "See now that I myself am He! There is no god besides Me . . ."

As a result of this and many other inspiring affirmations throughout the Jewish scriptures,[1] faithful Jews to this day will only worship the One life-giving God of Israel -- alone.

No prophet in Tanach ever remained silent on this foundational teaching. As if with one voice, they pleaded with their often-wayward nation never to compromise their faith for anything other than the unwavering monotheism that they tirelessly preached. Over and over again, the Hebrew Bible declared with deliberate clarity in its most celebrated creeds that the Almighty alone is God, and there is no other. Nothing was ever "screened," nothing was ever "veiled." It could not be, because the very survival of the Jewish people depended on it. The Torah intimately connects the faith in one indivisible God with the national experience of the Jewish people throughout their long history. Dreadful suffering was the consequence for any defection from the uncompromising monotheism that the Almighty demanded of His people.

Throughout the Jewish scriptures, God never "screened or veiled his divine nature." In fact, Isaiah unequivocally proclaimed that the Almighty did not reveal Himself in darkness or in a hidden or veiled fashion. In Isaiah 45:19 the prophet, speaking in the Almighty's name, declares that,

I have not spoken in secret, from somewhere in a land of darkness; I have not said to Jacob's descendants, "Seek Me in vain." I, the Lord, speak the truth; I declare what is right.

Although the belief in the unity of God is taught and declared on virtually every page of the Jewish scriptures, the doctrine of the Trinity is never mentioned anywhere throughout the entire corpus of the Hebrew Bible. This is understandable when we consider that primitive Christianity, in its earliest stages, was still monotheistic. The authors of the New Testament were completely unaware that the Church they had fashioned would eventually embrace a pagan deification of a triune deity. Although the worship of a three-part godhead was well known and fervently venerated throughout the Roman Empire and beyond in religious systems such as Hinduism and Mithraism, it was quite distant from the heretical Judaism out of which Christianity emerged. However, when the Greek and Roman rather than the Hebrew began to dominate the church, it created a theological disaster from which Christendom has never recovered. By the end of the fourth century, the doctrine of the Trinity was firmly in place as a central tenet of the church, and strict monotheism was formally rejected by Vatican councils in Nicea and Constantinople.[2]

This absorption of a triune godhead into Christianity created serious problems for post-Nicene Christian apologists. How would they harmonize this new veneration of Jesus as a being who is of the same substance as the Father with a New Testament that portrays Jesus as a separate entity, subordinate to the Father, and created by God? How would they now integrate the teaching of the Trinity with a New Testament that recognized the Father alone as God? In essence, how would Christian apologists merge a first and second century Christian Bible which was monotheistic with a much later church which was not?

This task was particularly difficult because throughout the Gospels and Paul's letters Jesus never claims to be God. On the contrary, the Jesus of the New Testament makes it crystal clear that he is not God, but rather an agent of God. For example, in John 14:28, the author of the fourth Gospel has Jesus declare,

> "I go unto the Father, for my Father is greater than I."

The example you mentioned illustrates this particularly well. In the thirteenth chapter of the Book of Mark, Jesus is asked by four of his disciples when the Tribulation period will occur. In 13:32 Jesus responds,

> But of that day and that hour knows no man, no, not the angels which are in heaven, neither the son, but the Father.

The problems this verse creates for Trinitarians are staggering. If Jesus were coequal with the Father, how could the Father have information that Jesus lacked? That is to say, if Jesus were God manifested in the flesh, as missionaries contend, how can God not know something? If somehow the second Person of the godhead didn't know, how did the first Person find out? Moreover, if, as some Trinitarians persist, the son was limited by his human nature, why didn't the Holy Spirit know?

Christians cannot simply explain away this verse by insisting that it was Jesus' human or humble nature that did not know. This is because the doctrine of the Trinity does not hold that Jesus was half God and half man. Rather, Jesus was one hundred percent God and one hundred percent man. His substance as God was not diminished because of his human nature. As the ecclesiastical Athanasian Creed explicitly states:

> The divinity of the Father, Son, and Holy Spirit is one, their glory equal, their majesty coeternal. What quality the Father has, the Son has, and the Holy Spirit has.

Few statements defining the nature of the triune godhead have so plainly spelled out the nature of the doctrine of the Trinity as does this durable fourth century creed.

Some missionaries will argue, as you point out, that Jesus' statement in John 10:30, "I and my Father are one," demonstrates that Jesus considered himself God. The Greek word hen (one), however, does not imply being a part of the same substance. We see this clearly in John 17:11 and 17:21-22 where Jesus prays to God that the disciples may be one (hen) as are Jesus and God. Clearly, Jesus is requesting that the disciples be of one unified purpose, not of the same substance or part of the Trinity.

Moreover, John 10:30-34 is particularly revealing. The fourth Gospel describes how when the Jews heard Jesus proclaim, "I and my Father are one," they immediately wanted to stone him. When Jesus asks them why they wanted to kill him, the Jews responded because "you claim to be God." Upon hearing this, Jesus asked, "Is it not written in your law, 'I have said you are gods'?" This response is one of the most important statements in the Book of John, and should at least give Trinitarians pause.

The verse is found in Psalm 82:6 where the Bible refers to judges who teach God's divine law as gods. This title was bestowed on them because they were teachers of the Almighty's divine law, not because they were actually God in any way. This usage is quite common in the Jewish scriptures. For example, in Exodus 7:1 Moses is called a god because he was God's representative to Pharaoh. In essence, Jesus' reply supports the very opposite of what missionaries are trying to put forth. Jesus, as depicted by John, is explaining that his identification with God is comparable to the Jewish judges' identification with God.

The fact remains that no author in the New Testament ever advanced the doctrine of the Trinity. It took many years from the time the last Gospel was completed for the defenders of the church to promote this alien creed.

Sincerely yours,

Rabbi Tovia Singer

**Footnotes:**

1. See page 84-85

2. The Council of Nicea and Constantinople were convened in 325 and 381 C.E., respectively. At the Council of Nicea the nature of Jesus was determined to be of the same substance (*homousios*) as the Father, and at the Council of Constantinople this doctrine was ratified and the doctrine of the Trinity was expressly declared to be a foundational Church teaching. (See Question and Answer entitled, *Isaiah 53: Did Jesus have long life?* on page 283)

# Did Someone Find the Doctrine of the Trinity In the First Chapter of the Bible? To Whom Was God Speaking When He Said, "Let Us Make Man in Our Image?

## Question:

Dear Rabbi Singer,

A Messianic Jew is working overtime to try to convince me that I need JC. She recently showed me Genesis 1:26, "Let US make man in OUR image," stating that JC was part of creation with God, plural Us and Our being the proof. Can you explain the plural in this verse to me? I want to have an intelligent answer. I am trying very hard to learn more of my Jewish religion, as I was raised in a non-religious home. The only Bible I own is the one she gave me and it is a King James.

## Answer:

The doctrine of the Trinity has no greater foe than the prophets of the Hebrew Scriptures. It is on the strength of these sacred texts that the Jew has preserved the concept of one, single, unique Creator God Who alone is worthy of worship. Missionaries undertake an impossible task when they seek to prove the doctrine of the Trinity from the Jewish scriptures.

No prophet remained silent on the uncompromising radical monotheism demanded by the God of Israel. The Jewish people, therefore, to whom these sublime declarations about the nature of the Almighty were given, knew nothing about a trinity of persons in the godhead.

Because the prophets relayed their divine message on the nature of God with such timeless, transparent, clarity, very few verses in Tanach could be summoned by the Church to support for their alien teachings on the doctrine of the Trinity. Understandably, though, the defenders of Christendom parade the few verses that they insist support the notion that there is a plurality in the godhead.

One of the most popular verses used by missionaries as a proof text in support of the doctrine of the Trinity is Genesis 1:26. This verse appears frequently in missionary literature despite of the fact that this argument has been answered countless times throughout the centuries and numerous Christian scholars have long abandoned it. Let's examine Genesis 1:26:

> And God said, "Let **us** make man in **our** image, after **our** likeness; and they shall rule over the fish of the sea, and over the fowl of the sky, and over the cattle, and over all the earth, and over every creeping thing that creeps upon the earth."

With limited knowledge of the Jewish scriptures, missionaries advance the above verse in as evidence that there was a plurality in the godhead which forged the Creation. What other explanation could adequately account for the Torah's use of the plural pronouns such as "us" and "our" in this verse?

This argument, however, is grievously flawed. In fact, a great number of Trinitarian Christian writers have long discarded the notion that Genesis 1:26 implies a plurality of persons in the godhead. Rather, Christian scholars overwhelmingly agree that the plural pronoun in this verse is a reference to God's ministering angels who were created previously, and the Almighty spoke majestically in the plural, consulting His heavenly court. Let's read the comments of a number of preeminent Trinitarian Bible scholars on this subject.

For example, the evangelical Christian author Gordon J. Wenham, who is no foe of the Trinity and authored a widely respected two-volume commentary on the Book of Genesis, writes on this verse,

> Christians have traditionally seen [Genesis 1:26] as adumbrating [foreshadowing] the Trinity. It is now universally admitted that this was not what the plural meant to the original author.[1]

If you had attended any one of my lectures you would know that the *New International Version* is hardly a Bible that can be construed as being friendly to Judaism. Yet, the *NIV Study Bible* also writes in its commentary on Genesis 1:26,

> **Us . . . Our . . . Our.** God speaks as the Creator-king, announcing His crowning work to the members of His heavenly court. (see 3:22; 11:7; Isaiah 6:8; I Kings 22:19-23; Job 15:8; Jeremiah 23:18)[2]

Charles Caldwell Ryrie, a highly regarded Dispensationalist professor of Biblical Studies at the Philadelphia College of Bible and author of the widely read Bible commentary, *The Ryrie Study Bible*, writes in his short and to-the-point annotation on Genesis 1:26,

> Us . . . Our. Plurals of majesty.[3]

The Liberty Annotated Study Bible, a Bible commentary published by the fundamentalist Reverend Jerry Falwell's Liberty University, similarly remarks on this verse,

> The plural pronoun "Us" is most likely a majestic plural from the standpoint of Hebrew grammar and syntax.[4]

The 10-volume commentary by Keil and Delitzsch is considered by many to be the most influential exposition on the "Old Testament" in evangelical circles. Yet in Keil and Delitzsch's commentary on Genesis 1:26, we find,

> The plural "We" was regarded by the fathers and earlier theologians almost unanimously as indicative of the Trinity; modern commentators, on the contrary, regard it either as *pluralis majestatis* . . . No other explanation is left, therefore, than to regard it as *pluralis majestatis* . . .[5]

The question that immediately comes to mind is: What would compel these evangelical scholars – all of whom are devout Trinitarians – to determinedly reject the notion that Genesis 1:26 supports the doctrine of Trinity? Why do they conclude that God is speaking in this famed verse in His majestic address to the angelic hosts of Heaven? Why are the commentaries of the above conservative Christian writers completely consistent with the age-old Jewish teaching on this verse?

The answer to this question is simple. If you search the Bible you will find that when the Almighty speaks of "us" or "our," He is addressing His ministering angels. In fact, only two chapters later, God continues to use the pronoun "us" as He speaks with His angels. At the end of the third chapter of Genesis the Almighty relates to His angels that Adam and his wife have eaten from the Tree of Knowledge and must therefore be prevented from eating from the Tree of Life as well; for if man would gain access to the Tree of Life he will "become like one of us." The Creator then instructs his angels known as *Cherubim* to stand at the gate of the Garden of Eden waving a flaming sword so that mankind is prevented from entering the Garden and eating from the Tree of Life. Let's examine Genesis 3:22-24:

> Then the Lord God said, "Behold, the man has become like one of ***Us***, to know good and evil. And now, lest he put out his hand and take also of the tree of life, and eat, and live forever" – therefore the Lord God sent him out of the Garden of Eden to till the ground from which he was taken. So He drove out the man; and He placed *cherubim* at the east of the Garden of Eden, and a flaming sword which turned every way, to guard the way to the tree of life.

This use of the majestic plural in Genesis 3:22-24 is what is intended by the *NIV Study Bible's* annotation on Genesis 1:26 (above). At the end of its comment on this verse, the *NIV Study Bible* provides a number of biblical sources from the Jewish scriptures to support its position that:

> "God speaks as the Creator-king, announcing His crowning work to the members of His heavenly court." The verses cited are: Genesis 3:22, 11:7, Isaiah 6:8, I Kings 22:19-23, Job 15:8, and Jeremiah 23:18. These verses convey to the attentive Bible reader that the heavenly abode of the Creator is filled with the ministering angels who attend the Almighty and to whom He repeatedly refers when using the plural pronoun "Us."[6]

I will close this letter with one final note.

Outsiders often wonder what powerful force binds the Jewish people united in faith. This is not so odd a question when we consider the internal conflicts that has followed our people throughout our troubled history. Bear in mind, regardless of the turbulent quarrels that fester among us, the oneness of God remains the binding thread which unites the Jewish people in history and witness. The teachings of the Torah were designed to set forever in the national conscience of the Jewish people the idea that God is one alone and therefore the only Savior worthy of our devotion and worship.

Sincerely yours,

Rabbi Tovia Singer

## Footnotes:

1. Gordon J. Wenham, *Word Biblical Commentary on Genesis*, Word Books, 1987, p. 27.
2. *NIV Study Bible*, Grand Rapids: Zondervan, 1985, p. 7.
3. Charles Caldwell Ryrie, *The Ryrie Study Bible* (Dallas Theological Seminary), Chicago: Moody Press, 1978, p. 9.
4. Jerry Falwell (Executive Editor), *Liberty Annotated Study Bible*, Lynchburg: Liberty University, 1988, p. 8.
5. Keil & Delitzsch, *Commentary on the Old Testament*, Peabody: Hendric., 1989, Vol. I, p. 62.
6. A similar verse describing God as He converses with His ministering angels is found in the beginning of the sixth chapter of Isaiah, which reads:

> In the year that King Uzziah died, I saw the Lord sitting on a throne, high and lifted up, and the train of His robe filled the Temple. Above it stood *seraphim*; each one had six wings: with two he covered his face, with two he covered his feet, and with two he flew. . . Also, I heard the voice of the Lord, saying, "Whom shall I send, and who will go for Us?" Then I said, "Here am I! Send me." (Isaiah 6:1, 8)

# Did Someone Find the Doctrine of the Trinity In the Name of God? Why is God's Name "*Elohim*" in the Plural?

## Question:

Dear Rabbi Singer,

First, let me say that what you are doing is a great service to Jews and the religious community at large. You are setting the record straight - one that has needed correction for almost 2,000 years! Thank you.

Yesterday, a Christian business associate made a point that in the very first verse of Genesis G-d is referred to as "Elohim" which is plural. She also said that it is a plural form of three (something I have never heard before). That, she concludes, is proof of the Trinity! Why is G-d's name plural in this verse?

## Answer:

The claim advanced by your business associate is one of the more well-known arguments used by missionaries to defend the doctrine of the Trinity, their most guarded and untenable creed. It would be difficult to imagine a doctrine more hostile to the unflinching monotheism preached in the Jewish scriptures than the Christian claim that there is a plurality within the divine nature of God. Yet, armed with little knowledge of the Hebrew language, many Trinitarians brazenly argue that the name of God, as it appears in the first verse in the Bible, "proves" there are three distinct Persons in the godhead.

More specifically, missionaries point to the plural form of the Hebrew name of God אלהים (*Elohim*) which appears frequently in the Torah. They insist that the use of the Hebrew letters "ים" (*yod* and *mem*, pronounced "*im*") at the end of the word *Elohim* is a plural suffix, and provides ample evidence from *Tanach* that there is a plurality within the nature of God. Your business associate went out on an even more bizarre limb when she declared that this Hebrew syntax is somehow indicative of the "plural form of three."

I will begin by saying that you can rest assured that the Hebrew tongue is a foreign language to your business associate, and both of her contentions are erroneous. While her first assertion can be easily explained away by her lack of familiarity with the biblical language, her second point cannot. Her latter comment that the plural suffix in *Elohim* is indicative of "a plural form of three" is particularly preposterous, and illustrates the desperation and frustration some Trinitarians display in their rash effort to defend this alien Church creed.

While I too have never heard any missionary make the astounding claim that plurals somehow mean "a plural form of three," I could sense from where this irresponsible contrivance is coming. If you examine the few verses evangelicals use from the Jewish scriptures as they seek to buttress the doctrine of the Trinity, you will notice that none of them, even in Christian terms, speaks of three persons. In essence, her flawed declaration was born out of a desperate desire to weave the Trinity out of whole Jewish cloth. This is an impossible task.

Bear in mind, there is no mystery as to the origins of the Trinity, nor is there any secret how this aberrant doctrine emerged. The doctrine of the Trinity was forged out of the crucible of the Catholic Church long after the Christian century. It is, therefore, no wonder that this pagan doctrine was unknown to authors of the New Testament (see pages 88-90). Church history reveals that it was not until three hundred years after the birth of Christianity that the doctrine of the Bianity (325 C.E.) and Trinity (381 C.E.) received formal approval in the Christian community. These well-documented events occurred under circumstances confused with political agitation and radical dissension. In essence, the Jewish people never believed in a Trinity, and the church adopted it under enormous political pressure from the most pagan segments of the Catholic Church. Understandably, missionaries undertake a formidable task when they seek to prove this fourth century doctrine from a radically monotheistic *Torah* which is timeless. Let's examine your business associate's claim.

There is an enormous difficulty with the interpretation that the name *Elohim* signifies a sort of plurality in the godhead; for if *Elohim* implies a plurality of persons, how can missionaries explain that the identical word *Elohim* in *Tanach* refers to Moses as well? Regarding Moses, in Exodus 7:1, the *Torah* says,

> The Lord said to Moses, "See, I have made thee a **god** אלהים (*Elohim*) to Pharaoh, and Aaron thy brother shall be thy prophet." (KJV)

Are missionaries going to claim that there was a plurality of persons in Moses? Is your associate going to insist that Moses was part of a Trinity? The notion that Moses, who is called *Elohim* in the *Torah*, possessed more than one person is preposterous. Moreover, if the name of God is to signify a plurality in the godhead, why wasn't the name *Je-hovah*, which is by far the most frequently used name for God in the Jewish scriptures, also written in the plural? Clearly, this sort of Trinitarian argument is baseless.

The word *Elohim* possesses a plural intensive syntax and is singular in meaning. This is self-evident from the fact that the verb "created" ברה (*bara*) in Genesis 1:1 is in the singular. This linguistic pattern is well known and widely used throughout the Jewish scriptures. For example, I am certain that many of our website readers are familiar with the Hebrew word חיים *chayim*, meaning "life." Notice that this word contains the identical plural suffix "im," as in *Elohim*, yet it repeatedly means "life", in the singular, throughout the Bible. Examples are:

> And Rebekah said to Isaac, "I am weary of my life because of the daughters of Heth; if Jacob takes a wife of the daughters of Heth, like these who are the daughters of the land, what good will my **life** חיים (*chayim*) be to me?" (Genesis 27:46)
>
> You have granted me **life** חיים (*chayim*) and favor, and Your care has preserved my spirit. (Job 10:12)

The fact that the name of God, *Elohim*, does not in any way imply a plurality in the godhead is well known and widely recognized even among Trinitarian Christians. For example, in the *New International Version Study Bible* (NIV), which is hardly a Christian commentary that could be regarded as friendly to the Jewish faith, the Christian author writes in his commentary on Genesis 1:1:

> God created. The Hebrew noun *Elohim* is plural but the verb is singular, a normal usage in the OT when reference is to the one true God. This use of the plural expresses intensification rather than number and has been called the plural of majesty, or of potentiality. (*New International Version Study Bible*, Grand Rapids: Zondervan, 1985, p. 6.)

Finally, it is important that I clarify the crucial message which the name *Elohim* conveys to the Children of Israel. To be sure, two questions must be answered. 1) Why does the Torah employ this intensive plural name for the Almighty throughout the Torah? 2) Why is this name predominant throughout the creation narrative in the beginning of Genesis?

There is a fundamental principal regarding the many names of the Almighty as they appear in the *Torah* – they are exalted descriptions of the God of Israel. The name *Elohim*, which is not an exception to this rule, comes from the Hebrew root *el*, which means "might" or "power." This common root appears in a variety of words throughout the Jewish scriptures. For example, we find this word used in the famous opening words to Psalm 29, הבו לה' בני אלים *(havu la'donai b'nai **eylim**)*. This chapter is well known to the Jewish people because this Psalm is sung joyously in every synagogue as the Torah scroll is returned into the ark following a congregational reading. What do these noble words mean? "Ascribe to the Lord, O sons of the **mighty.**" *(New American Standard Bible)*

We also have a deeper understanding of the message behind the sacred name *Elohim*. The pagan world ascribed a separate god for each of the powers in the world, which they observed and on whom they depended. They gazed upon the life-giving and perplexing energy emanating from the sun, and they worshiped it as a god. They craved an abundant harvest and boundless fertility, and they appointed gods for them as well. The ancients were awestruck by the forces which sustained them, and venerated each of them with mysterious and sometimes gruesome rites.

The Torah of Israel had a very different and uplifting message for mankind. All the forces and energies in the universe, all the might and power that man could behold, emanated from the One Creator of the universe. This grand message was contained in the name of God, *Elohim*. All the forces of the world emerged from the God of Abraham, Isaac, and Jacob. This God, Creator of all matter, is alone worthy of worship. It is for this reason that *Elohim* appears almost exclusively as the name of God throughout the first two chapters of Genesis. In these two chapters, the Almighty is creating all the powers and forces which stir the universe.

You can now begin to understand why the nation of Israel, to whom God revealed Himself at the foot of Mount Sinai, knew nothing about a plurality of persons in the godhead. No fact could be more firmly established once all of our literature – both canonical and rabbinical – is used as our eternal guide. This matter is indisputable.

Best wishes for a happy and healthy New Year.

Sincerely yours,

Rabbi Tovia Singer

# Did God Divorce Israel? What does Jeremiah Mean by the Promise of a "New Covenant"?

## Question:

Rabbi,

How do you explain the divorce in Jeremiah? How do you explain that the Jewish people are divorced from God by His own word? How do we as Jews get back to God under the Law which prohibits us from coming back? I am not saying that we are no longer God's Chosen - I am saying that for us to be reconciled to God, it cannot happen under the Law. Would God have to bring a "new covenant" in to bring us back to Him? You may post this question.

Thank you.

**Answer:**

When you ask about the "divorce in Jeremiah," I am sure that you are referring to the parable in the opening verse of the third chapter of Jeremiah, where the prophet uses a harsh allegory to illustrate God's displeasure with His wayward nation. For the readers of our website who are unfamiliar with this subject, I will briefly explain your series of questions.

Using a jarring metaphor, Jeremiah compares Israel's spiritual disloyalty to an adulterous woman who has been put away by her husband whom she betrayed. The prophet then asks a biting question, "After she leaves him and marries another man, may he return to her again?" (Jeremiah 3:1) The unspoken answer is that he cannot. Deuteronomy 24:1-4 states that the original husband may never come back to his twice-divorced wife.

Your question therefore is how can Israel ever return to its rightful place as God's priestly nation? The prophet seems to indicate that she (Israel) has married another, namely, the gods of the heathen nations, and she is therefore unable to return as God's "firstborn son" (Exodus 4:22). How can Israel ever hope to restore herself with the Almighty when the Law of Moses seems to indicate that she cannot? How can the nation of Israel look to the commandments of the *Torah* for her salvation when, according to Jeremiah's metaphor, it is those very commandments that prevent her from returning?

The reason you have had difficulty understanding Jeremiah 3:1 is that you made two mistakes while reading the parable of Israel as the divorced wife. Your first error is you attempted to interpret a parable in a hyper-literal fashion. I find it puzzling that Christians, who should be quite familiar with the use of parables, have such difficulty understanding how Jeremiah is using the parable of the "divorced wife." Your second mistake is you read only half the parable. In fact, the answer to your question is embedded in the final clause of the very same verse. Let's first examine this parable more closely.

Jeremiah's purpose in using this parable is two-fold. First, the prophet wishes to vividly illustrate Israel's spiritual disloyalty to its Creator. Second, and most important, unlike the twice-estranged wife whose original husband cannot return to her, the prophet appeals to the Jewish people to repent and proclaims that it is their sacred mandate to be restored as God's chosen people. What is impossible with the forsaken woman is the destiny for the children of Israel. Let's look at the entire verse in context:

> They say, "If a man divorces his wife, and she goes from him and becomes another man's, may he return to her again?" Would not that land be greatly polluted? But you have played the harlot with many lovers; **"Yet return to Me," says the Lord**. (Jeremiah 3:1)

The central feature of the prophet's exhortation that you overlooked appears at the very end of the verse, " 'Yet return to Me', says the Lord." Jeremiah makes this plea five times throughout the chapter. The message of the prophet is clear: The mercy and compassion of the Almighty is far beyond the scope of man's comprehension. Whereas normally the betrayed husband would never take back his adulterous wife, our merciful God will forgive His wayward nation. While the transgressed husband would never part with his burning wrath against his estranged wife, Jeremiah points the way to forgiveness, reconciliation, and salvation with the Almighty. In contrast to the enraged husband who would never take back his unfaithful wife, God will, upon repentance, compassionately receive his disobedient people. What must Israel do to win the affection of its Maker?

> Just cry out to Me, "My Father, you are the Master of my youth!" (Jeremiah 3:4)

Yet how can this be? Will God's wrath not be kindled forever against His nation? Jeremiah responds with a rhetorical question.

> Will He remain angry forever? Will He keep it to eternity? (Jeremiah 3:5)

The Almighty's answer follows with a comforting oath promising Israel an eternal destiny and permanent union with the Almighty.

> "Return, O backsliding children," says the Lord, "for I am married to you. I will take you, one from a city and two from a family, and I will bring you to Zion." (Jeremiah 3:14)

The central message of the third chapter remains: The fate of disloyal Israel stands in stark contrast to an unfaithful wife. Whereas the adulterous woman may never return to her former husband, Jeremiah beckons the Jewish people back to the Almighty, and assures them of their eternal destiny to be forever married to their Maker.

Yet, by what means can the Jewish people return to God? A few chapters later, Jeremiah answers this question as he outlines for his disobedient nation how they are to end their persistent backsliding. In his seventh chapter, the prophet warns his people not to place their hopes on blood sacrifices or look to The Temple of the Lord to save them. Jeremiah proclaims that these institutions cannot deliver them from their brazen sins. Rather, they must turn away from idolatry and return to God by keeping the commandments. Please take a moment and study Jeremiah's remarkable message on atonement.

> So said the Lord of Hosts, the God of Israel, "Improve your ways and your deeds, I then will allow you to dwell in this place. **Do not rely on false words, saying, 'The Temple of the Lord, The Temple of the Lord, The Temple of the Lord are they.'** If you improve your ways and your deeds, if you perform judgment between one man and his fellow man, you do not oppress the stranger, an orphan, or a widow, and you do not shed innocent blood in this place, and you do not follow other gods for your detriment. I will then allow you to dwell in this place, in the land that I gave your forefathers from days of yore to eternity. . . So says the Lord of Hosts, the God of Israel, **"Add your burnt offerings upon your sacrifices and eat flesh; for neither did I speak with your forefathers nor did I command them on the day I brought them out of the land of Egypt concerning a burnt offering or a sacrifice. This thing did I command them saying, 'Listen to Me so that I am your God and you are My people, you walk in all the ways that I command you . . .'"** (Jeremiah 7:3-7, 21-23)

The seventh chapter of Jeremiah stands as a glaring indictment against the Church's most cherished creeds. For example, according to Christian doctrine, there is nothing man can do to merit salvation through his own "works" or repentance. Atonement, Christendom argues, can only be achieved through the shedding of innocent blood. Throughout the seventh chapter of Jeremiah, however, the prophet proclaims the very opposite message on atonement. Repeatedly, Jeremiah loudly declares that God does not desire blood sacrifices but rather repentance alone for man's grievous sins.

Finally, as we study the words of Jeremiah, pay careful attention to what is noticeably absent from the prophet's message. The cornerstone teachings of the Church are nowhere to be found in the Book of Jeremiah. As a result, this chapter presents a monumental theological problem for Christians. Why isn't there one word throughout the prophet's admonishment about believing in Jesus for salvation? Bear in mind that this prophecy contains the essential guide into a pure relationship with God for those who have lost their spiritual path. Why didn't Jeremiah, as he points his wayward nation in the direction of Godliness, direct the Jewish people to Jesus' atoning death at Calvary? Why did Jeremiah instead prophesy that the day will come when the Jewish people will be restored to their land as a result of their own heartfelt repentance (Jeremiah 3:14-18)? According to Christian doctrine, repentance alone can do nothing to save man from damnation. He can weep and wax forth with humble words of remorse from dawn until dusk, but without the blood of the Cross, missionaries argue, there can be no forgiveness of sin. Why didn't the prophet ever mention this foundational creed in his sermon on forgiveness or declare that the Jewish people would eventually be restored if they believed in Jesus as their Lord and Savior?

Moreover, why would Jeremiah prophesy that in this act of penitence, you will one day "call Me 'My Father,' and not turn away from Me" (3:4)? Why is there no mention in Jeremiah's prophecy of the Jewish people calling out to the Son or the Holy Spirit in repentance? In short, why is there not a word mentioned throughout Jeremiah's prophetic sermon on atonement regarding the foundational claims of Christendom? It is not only what the prophet does say, but also what he doesn't say that draws our attention.

Your next question argues that Jews can only find salvation through a "new covenant" or New Testament (the Greek word διαθήκης *(diatheke)* means both a "covenant" and a "testament"). This "new covenant," missionaries argue, is the covenant of the cross that was fulfilled nearly 2,000 years ago when the blood of Jesus was shed for the sins of mankind. Moreover, Christians insist, this new covenant was prophesied in Jeremiah 31:31-34, which states:

> "Behold, days are coming," declares the Lord, "when I will make a new covenant (בְּרִית *bris*) with the House of Israel and with the House of Judah. Not like the covenant (*bris*) which I made with their fathers in the day I took them by the hand to bring them out of the land of Egypt, My covenant which they broke, although I was a husband to them," declares the Lord. "But this is the covenant which I will make with the house of Israel after those days," declares the Lord, "I will put My law within them, and on their hearts I will write it; and I will be their God, and they shall be My people. No more shall every man teach his neighbor, and every man his brother, saying, 'Know the Lord,' for they all shall know Me, from the least of them to the greatest of them," says the Lord, "for I will forgive their iniquity, and their sin I will remember no more."

Missionaries maintain that Jeremiah's "new covenant" is an unveiled reference to the New Testament, which speaks of salvation by believing in the atoning death of Jesus:

> . . . for this is my blood of the new testament, which is shed for many for the remission of sins. (Matthew 26:28)

What of the Sinaitic covenant founded on the keeping of the *Torah's* commandments? Commenting on Jeremiah 31:31, the author of the Book of Hebrews declares that the Torah's life-giving commandments are obsolete and concludes:

> In that He says, "A new covenant," He has made the first obsolete. Now what is becoming obsolete and growing old is ready to vanish away. (Hebrews 8:13)

In short, the New Testament writer pronounces that the covenant God made with the Jewish people has expired. The Jewish people no longer have to keep the commandments of the Torah. Salvation comes by believing in Jesus as high priest, sacrifice, and messiah. It is therefore not difficult to understand how the Calvinist author Arthur W. Pink, in his *An Exposition of Hebrews*, argues,

> It is exceedingly difficult, if not quite impossible, for us to form any adequate conception of the serious obstacles presented to the mind of a pious Jew, when any one sought to persuade him that Judaism had been set aside by God and that he must turn his own back upon it.[1]

While some people find Pink's conclusion reprehensible, this Reformed author is a committed Christian. He is simply drawing the conclusion clearly conveyed in the Book of Hebrews. Essentially, the Book of Hebrews is a multifaceted polemic against the Church's elder rival: Judaism.

In order to answer your question regarding Jeremiah's prophecy of a "new covenant," you must first understand how the New Testament has misapplied and altered Jeremiah 31:31-34, and then secondly, try to grasp the prophet's message in these four well-known verses.

As mentioned above, missionaries argue that Jeremiah 31:31-34 is a prophecy of an event that occurred nearly 2,000 years ago with Jesus' death on the cross. They insist that this is the new covenant that replaced the old, decaying Mosaic covenant forged with Israel.

This Christian rendering of Jeremiah's prophecy of a "new covenant," however, is an extraordinary reconstruction of the prophet's own words. Jeremiah 31:31-34 is not a prophecy that occurred 2,000 years ago, or any time in the past. Rather, it is a prophecy that will be fulfilled in the future messianic age.

The fact that Jeremiah 31:31-34 begins with the prophet addressing both the "House of Israel and the House of Judah" clearly indicates that Jeremiah is speaking to a fully restored Jewish people. This, however, was not at all the case at the time when Christians claim the new covenant was fulfilled in Jesus' death – quite the contrary. During the Christian century there was no House of Israel in existence because Assyria had exiled the Kingdom of Israel more than 700 years earlier (approx. 732 B.C.E.). Moreover, in the first century of the common era, the Jewish people were spread throughout the Roman Empire and beyond. Thus, even the "House of Judah" was not all in the Promised Land during Jesus' lifetime.

In short, the era of the new covenant has not yet arrived. Rather, Jeremiah's prophecy addresses a future messianic age when the entire Jewish people – both Judah and Israel – will be restored together in their rightful place – the land of Israel (Ezekiel 37:15-22). To the contrary, there had been no time in history when the Jewish people were more fractured and dispersed than during the first century C.E. when, according to the author of Hebrews, Jeremiah's prophecy of a new covenant was supposedly fulfilled.

Moreover, a cursory reading of verse 31:34, further confirms that Jeremiah's prophecy is not speaking of a Christian cross 2,000 years ago but rather a restored Jewish people in the future messianic era. Missionaries often overlook verse 34 and emphasize only 31:31-33 when quoting Jeremiah's declaration of a new covenant. This oversight has proved to be devastating to their understanding of this prophecy, because verse 31:34 sheds so much light on the future new covenant era. Jeremiah 31:34 states:

> No more shall every man teach his neighbor, and every man his brother, saying, "Know the Lord," **for they all shall know Me, from the least of them to the greatest of them, says the Lord;** for I will forgive their iniquity, and their sin I will remember no more.

The above verse declares that the age of the new covenant will be realized during an epoch of the universal knowledge of God. It will occur when no one will have to teach his neighbor about God, "for they all shall know Me, from the least of them to the greatest of them . . ." Did this occur durin any part of the first century C.E., or at any time since? Does every human being "know the Lord"? This is hardly the case. The Church is spending many hundreds of millions of dollars annually in order to convert masses worldwide to Christianity. There are roughly one billion Moslems and Hindus in the world today who, according to Christian teachings, do not know the Lord; and there are an untold number of atheists throughout the globe who certainly do not know the Lord. Has Jeremiah's prophecy of a "new covenant" as yet been fulfilled by anyone's standards? Are we living in a time when each and every person "knows the Lord"? Hardly.

The Hebrew word בְּרִית (*bris*) in Jeremiah 31:31 does not mean a Bible or refer to a new salvation program or *Torah.* The word *bris* always refers to a covenant, promise, or a contract. This covenant was made with the Jewish people while they were still in the wilderness – long before they entered the Promised Land.

In the 28th and 29th chapters of Deuteronomy, Moses told the children of Israel that if they remained faithful to God in the land they were about to enter, then the Almighty would bestow upon them manifold blessings and flourish in the Holy Land. On the other hand, if they turned away from the Lord, they would be driven out of Israel into a bitter exile in the land of their enemies. We are all familiar with the events that followed when the Jewish people broke their side of the covenant and they were sent into diaspora.

These four verses in Jeremiah 31:31-34 are part of an ongoing theme throughout the Book of Jeremiah. Jeremiah's unique literary motif is to contrast the redemption of the children of Israel from Egypt with their final redemption in the messianic age – vividly illustrating how the latter will far outshine the former. In Jeremiah 23:7-8, the prophet makes this clear when he proclaims,

Therefore, behold, the days are coming, says the Lord, when men shall no longer say, "As the Lord lives who brought up the people of Israel out of the land of Egypt," but, "as the Lord lives who brought up and led the descendants of the house of Israel out of the north country and out of all the countries where He had driven them." Then they shall dwell in their own land.

In the 31st chapter of the Book of Jeremiah, the prophet continues to contrast the exodus from Egypt with the messianic age. He foretells that unlike the exodus from Egypt when the Jewish people were brought into the land of Israel and exiled centuries later because they broke their original covenant as a result of their iniquities, in the messianic age, the Jewish people will enter into a "new covenant" when they will be permanently restored to their land, never to be exiled again.

As declared by every Jewish prophet, the covenant that God has with the Jewish people is eternal. No words in the Christian Bible or interpolation of the Jewish scriptures can ever change this eternal oath. The prophet Isaiah proclaimed this vow more than 2,700 years ago,

"With a little wrath I hid My face from you for a moment; but with everlasting kindness I will have mercy on you," says the Lord, your Redeemer. "This is like the waters of Noah to Me; for as I have sworn that the waters of Noah would no longer cover the earth, so have I sworn that I would not be angry with you, nor rebuke you. The mountains shall depart and the hills be removed, but My kindness shall not depart from you, nor shall My covenant of peace be removed," says the Lord, Who has mercy on you (Isaiah 54:8-10).

Remarkably, the contorted manner in which Hebrews rendered Jeremiah's prophecy promulgates the precise opposite message of the prophet's original intent. Hebrews misconstrues Jeremiah's prophecy to be understood that God had somehow disregarded His covenant with Israel when, in fact, the prophet's message is that God's unique relationship with the Jewish people is bound in Heaven and can never be destroyed.

Moreover, in Jeremiah 31:35-36, the prophet exclaims the Lord's reaffirmation of His eternal covenant with the children of Israel:

> Thus says the Lord, Who gives the sun for light by day and the fixed order of the moon and the stars for light by night, Who stirs up the sea so that its waves roar – the Lord of hosts is His name: **If this fixed order were ever to cease from My presence, says the Lord, then also the offspring of Israel would cease to be a nation before Me forever**. Thus says the Lord: If the heavens above can be measured, and the foundations of the earth below can be explored, then I will reject all the offspring of Israel because of all they have done.

Jeremiah's prophecy of an eternal Jewish people presents the Church with a serious theological problem because the New Testament went to great lengths to undermine the Jewish sacred texts. In fact, the author of Hebrews deliberately changed the words of Jeremiah in order to reverse the prophet's original message.

In Hebrews 8:9, while quoting Jeremiah 31:32, the Christian author changed a most crucial word in the last clause of Jeremiah 31:32:

> . . . My covenant which they broke, although I was a ***husband*** to them.

The book of Hebrews does not merely misquote Jeremiah, but entirely changes the verse to fit their anti-Judaic agenda. Changing the text to:

> . . . because they did not continue in My covenant, and I ***disregarded*** them, says the Lord."

The Hebrew word בָּעַלְתִּי (*ba'altee*) means a "husband," not "to disregard." This is a stunning alteration of the words of Jeremiah; to be a "husband" conveys the precise opposite message "disregard." How dare the author of Hebrews change the word of God in order to persuade readers of the authenticity and superiority of Christianity, and the obsolescence of Judaism? When New Testament authors wantonly tamper with the Jewish scriptures, do they not convey the very opposite message?

| Hebrews 8:9 | Jeremiah 31:32 |
|---|---|
| ...because they did not continue in My Covenant, and I disregarded them (ἠμέλησα), says the Lord. | ...My covenant which they broke, although I was a **husband** (*ba'altee* בָּעַלְתִּי) to them. |

Furthermore, in contrast to the message of Hebrews 8:13, the life-giving commandments of the *Torah* have no expiration date. Moses declared that these commandments are eternal.

> The secret things belong unto the Lord our God; but the things that are revealed belong unto us and **to our children forever, that we may do all the words of this law** (Deuteronomy 29:28 [29:29]).

> The works of his hands are verity and judgment; all his **commandments are sure. They stand fast forever and ever**, and are done in truth and uprightness (Psalm 111:7-8).

Moreover, the prophets foretold that the Jewish people will observe the commandments of the Torah after the messiah arrives. In fact, the Jewish scriptures prominently testify that the faithful observance of the *Torah* will be the emblematic feature of the messianic era.

> And I shall give them one heart, and shall put a new spirit within them. And I shall take the heart of stone out of their flesh and give them a heart of flesh, that **they may walk in My statutes and keep My ordinances, and do them**. Then they will be My people, and I shall be their God. (Ezekiel 11:19-20)

> My servant David will be king over them, and they will all have one shepherd. **They will follow my laws and be careful to keep my decrees**. (Ezekiel 37:24)

> And many peoples shall come, and say: "Come, let us go up to the mountain of the Lord, to the house of the God of Jacob; that he may teach us his ways and that we may walk in his paths," **for out of Zion shall go forth the law**, and the word of the Lord from Jerusalem. (Isaiah 2:3)

So let's ask ourselves the following question: Do Hebrew-Christians, who insist that the messiah has already come, keep the commandments of God? Do members of Messianic congregations actually observe the *mitzvoth* of *Shabbat* and *Kashruth* as clearly outlined in the Jewish scriptures? For example, do those Jews who have converted to Christianity refrain from kindling a fire or carrying any object on the Sabbath day as the Bible explicitly decrees (Exodus 35:3; Jeremiah 17:19-20)? The answer is that they do not. Yet, why are they not obedient to these commandants if they insist the messiah has already come? Who, in reality, diligently and joyfully adheres to these life-giving precepts? The faithful remnant of the Jewish people who utterly reject the teachings of Christianity.

Paradoxically, Hebrew-Christians misguidedly point to Jeremiah's new covenant to explain their continued indifference to the commandments mandated in the Torah, when in fact the central messianic prophecy in the Bible declares that the Children of Israel will diligently keep the commandments as a result of the coming of the messiah.

Finally, let's consider which grievous sin the Jewish people committed that brought down the wrath of God upon them in the first place. In which iniquity did Israel indulge that brought about Jeremiah's bitter reproach? The appalling sin of idolatry; they had violated the first of the Ten Commandments. The Jewish people worshiped gods that their fathers had not known. They indulged in idol worship and heathen practices of the surrounding gentile nations. Let us consider whether a pious Jew ever read the third chapter of Jeremiah, and as a result was somehow moved to convert to Christianity.

More than 3,300 years ago the Torah warned the Jewish people that they would one day serve gods that their fathers didn't know (Deuteronomy 28:36). When a Jew becomes a Hebrew-Christian, whether he then calls himself Messianic or Baptist, did this occur as a result of the teachings of his grandfather or great grandfather? Did he come to this theological conclusion by fervently studying the Torah in a *yeshiva*?

Did he find the doctrine of the Trinity in the Book of Jeremiah, or by any other prophet in Tanach? This is certainly never the case. Hebrew-Christians learn and adopt their spiritual craft from the gentiles who evangelized them – just as prophesied in the Jewish Scriptures.

Sincerely yours,

Rabbi Tovia Singer

**As a postscript, our readers should be excited to know that the author of this letter, who has spent many years of his life as a Hebrew-Christian, has returned to the truth and beauty of the Jewish faith. "Give thanks to the Lord, for He is good! His mercy endures forever."** (Psalm 136:1)

**Footnote:**

1. Pink, Arthur W., *An Exposition of Hebrews,* Baker Book House, Grand Rapids, MI; 1984: pp. 1065.

# Will God Only Save the Jews?

## Question:

Dear Rabbi,

I would agree with most of what you said in the above noted commentary ["Has God Divorced Israel? What Is the Meaning of the 'New Covenant' Promised in Jeremiah?"], except your broad sense of rejection of when the Lord did or did not establish the new covenant. My overriding concern and question for you to consider is this. Will God only save the Jews? You never ever show any salvation path for gentiles. It is here where your arguments hit the deepest rooted question. Were the Jews chosen by God as the only people to be saved? Surely this cannot be so. I would further add, your concern only for the Jews is understandable from a human perspective, but shows a rather hard hearted and unspiritual approach to God who has done so much for all of us.

Finally, your reference to the Christian commentary was rather limited as the author is only saying that the Jew does not have to abandon Judaism to believe in Jesus. It is in fact that Jesus, as you have heard and rejected, was the fulfillment of the Law so that God would bring us to a new covenant of Grace through His Son and place His Spirit in the hearts of all mankind who believe in Jesus... The Law has NOT been set aside but has been fulfilled by the only one who could keep the Law. For surely neither you nor I nor any man is righteous enough to keep God's law in full...and one cannot stand in the judgement if he has violated any of the Law. So these issues need to be addressed in your heart and between you and God. I have come to my own deep and personal resolution with our Creator. I wish you all the rich blessings of God, especially His salvation which I feel is intended for all mankind.

## Answer:

After reading your question carefully, it became abundantly clear that you have a skewed understanding of the Jewish people and our faith. You charge Judaism with holding out salvation to the Jew alone, when in fact nothing could be further from the truth. Quite the contrary, it is the Church which has no room in heaven for those who do not believe in Jesus, and instead of spending eternity in a lush paradise, non-Christians are relegated by the New Testament and its Church to an eternal lake of hell-fire (2 Thessalonians 1:8). Such narrow teachings, however, are alien and utterly abhorrent to the Jewish people.

The faith of Israel proclaims that the merciful Redeemer holds out a distinct salvation program for both the Jews and the gentiles. The faith of the children of Israel does not condemn the masses of non-Jewish humanity to everlasting separation from God, as your question suggests. Rather, Scriptures offer a path of salvation to all righteous people – both Jew and gentile. I have written an article which addresses this subject in much greater detail entitled, *What is a Former Christian Minister to Do, Convert?* (See page 413.)

Are the Jewish people proud? Yes, but we want all of humanity to be proud. Were we chosen? Yes, but for what purpose? For power, happiness, rest and security in our possessions? No. Rather to be a light to the nations - to show all nations an example of a people who are not afraid to stand upright on the earth. To regard no man as God, and to be the protectors and teachers of the divine oracles of the Torah. This is why we are the chosen people of God.

With respect to my comment regarding the anti-Dispensationalist author Arthur W. Pink, you are being overly charitable when you defend his supersessionist position. I am going to assume that your defense of this Calvinist writer is born out of a lack of familiarity with his Christology. Bear in mind that Pink's quote1 from his *An Exposition of Hebrews* appears in chapter 102 entitled, *The Passing of Judaism*. This jarring title is quite revealing. Other section names in his book are equally telling, such as *The Inferiority of Judaism* and *The Superiority of Christianity*. To further illustrate this point, in his chapter, "*The Passing of Judaism*," Pink applauds the Bible commentator and advocate of replacement theology Matthew Henry (17-18th century) when he writes,

> "We believe that Matthew Henry was on the right track when he said, 'It is by the Gospel from heaven that God shook to pieces the civil and ecclesiastical state of the Jewish nation, and introduced a new state of the church, that cannot be removed, shall never be changed for any other on earth, but shall remain till it be made perfect in heaven. 'The apostle [Paul] is still supplying proof that the Hebrew believers were no longer connected with Judaism, but were to come to the antitypical Zion."[2]

Finally, your letter defiantly proclaims that man is unable and unfit to keep the Torah. The readers of this letter can rest assured that you did not derive this cynical teaching from the Jewish scriptures, for such an idea is unknown to the timeless message of Tanach. The Hebrew scriptures are filled with testimonials proudly describing the towering character of godly men like Abraham, whom God tenderly called "My friend."[3] Calev and Josiah, to name a few, knew righteousness throughout their faithful lives.[4] Your statement, "neither you nor I nor any man is righteous enough to keep God's law in full" could only have been derived from the Greek letters of Paul, not the Hebrew letters of the Jewish prophets.

The fundamentalist church blindly labels the human condition as depraved, utterly incapable of meriting salvation by their own action. But, shall we call ourselves wretchedly sinful? Were we not created in the image of God? Is it not an insult to God to call ourselves spiritually defective and utterly sinful? Self-criticism is good, but what is the purpose of humility and self-criticism? Is it not to learn from one's errors and do better in the future? However, if we carry humility to such a point that one says "I am utterly lost and no action of mine can ever be good," then the incentive to improvement has been abolished, and excessive humility becomes an excuse for lack of effort. This is the ultimate consequence of grim Christian doctrines such as Total Depravity.

You proclaim that "Jesus was the fulfillment of the Law," but what does that really mean? Are we to understand that it as a declaration that a Jew need not observe the life-giving commandments of the Torah? What do you mean when you assert that the Jew does not have to abandon Judaism to believe in Jesus? When you refer to "Judaism," you most certainly do not mean Jewish culture or customs such as eating bagels and lox and donning a *yarmulke*? We all know that Christianity has no doctrine or opinion on such matters. In fact, there have been a number of popes who have been known to put on a yarmulke every now and then, and if my sources are correct, bagels and lox are becoming a pretty big hit amongst Protestants. Clearly, when you refer to the Jew and his Judaism, you must therefore be saying that the Jew is to continue to observe the *mitzvot* of the Torah just as he was commanded. What does Jesus' alleged fulfillment of the Torah have to do with the nation who were charged to keep the Torah forever and ever? When you reassure the Jew that he need not abandon his Jewishness, does this mean that the converted Jew is to keep the *mitzvot* with devotion, or can he abandon his Jewishness because "Jesus fulfilled the Law?" You can't have it both ways. This is a crucial question, because a meaningful message must be attached to the statement that the Jew doesn't have to "abandon Judaism to believe in Jesus." Well, which is it? Are we to continue to observe the Torah or has Jesus somehow fulfilled the commandments so we no longer have to keep them?

I ask these questions in order to give you some insight into the spiritual schizophrenia that Christianity displays as it grapples with Jews and Judaism. And this sort of playing both sides of the fence repeatedly manifests itself when Jews are converted to Christianity. I have seen many pastors squirm in discomfort as they are confronted with this unsettling question.

I am unsure whether this letter has opened your eyes, or perhaps given you some insight into the Jew and his faith. If you ever wondered why or how the faithful remnant of Israel so stubbornly refuses to worship any man as God or abandon the precious commandments of the Torah, remember what we saw and heard more than

3,300 years ago. Prior to his death, our teacher Moses stood at the border of the Promised Land and looked at Joshua before the entire nation of Israel and said, "Be strong and of good courage."

Very sincerely yours,

Rabbi Tovia Singer

## Footnotes:

1. Pink writes in his book, *An Exposition of Hebrews* the following:

   > "It is exceedingly difficult, if not quite impossible, for us to form any adequate conception of the serious obstacles presented to the mind of a pious Jew, when any one sought to persuade him that Judaism had been set aside by God and that he must turn his own back upon it." (Pink, Arthur W., *An Exposition of Hebrews*, Baker Book House, Grand Rapids, MI; 1984: pp. 1065.)

2. Ibid., p. 1069-1070.
3. Isaiah 41:8
4. Numbers 14:24; II Kings 22:2

# "The Lord Said to My Lord..." To Whom Was the Lord Speaking in Psalm 110:1?

## Question:

Dear Rabbi Singer,
A co-worker and friend of mine, who I know is a fundamentalist Christian, recently asked me what Jews think about the Trinity. I told him that the concept is not part of our religion and that Jews believe in only one God. He went on to ask me to explain Psalm 110 to him, which starts in English, "The Lord said unto my Lord . . ." To him this is yet another proof of the trinity. I could not give him an answer to his question. Would you please explain the meaning of this.
Thank You.

## Answer:

Psalm 110 represents one of the New Testament's most stunning, yet clever, mistranslations of the Jewish scriptures. Moreover, the confusion created by the Christianization of this verse was further perpetuated and promulgated by numerous Christian translators of the Bible as well. As you will soon see, some Christian translators, to their credit, refrain from rewriting this text in Psalm 110.

The story of the Church's tampering with Psalm 110 is so old that it begins in the

Christian canon itself. In the Gospels we find the church's first use of Psalm 110, and it begins with a question. In Matthew 22:41-44 Matthew's Jesus turns to the Pharisees and asks them,

> What do you think about the Christ? Whose son is he?

The question in laymen's terms is, "Of whom is the messiah supposed to be a descendant?"

> They said to him, "The son of David." He said to them, "How then does David in the spirit call him 'Lord,' saying, 'The Lord said to my Lord, "Sit at My right hand, till I make your enemies your footstool?"' If David then called him Lord, how is he his son?" No one was able to answer him a word, neither did any man from that day forth ask him any more questions. (Matthew 22:41-44)

Although the above conversation as portrayed in the first Gospel could not have occurred, this narrative has been replayed over and over again in the imagination of countless Christians for nearly two millennia.

It's a great story to the Christian believer – Jesus really showed those Pharisees how little they knew! Yet, this is precisely why this story could never have transpired. No Jew, who had even a superficial knowledge of the Jewish scriptures, would have ever found Jesus' argument compelling, let alone a conversation-stopper. The depth of knowledge that the Pharisees possessed of Tanach was astounding.

In order to grasp the manner in which the original Hebrew text was manipulated to create the above storyline, let's take a closer look at the original verse from which Matthew's Jesus quoted. The New American Standard Bible (NASB), one of the most widely read Christian Bibles in use today, translates Psalm 110:1 in the following manner,

> The **Lord** said unto my **Lord**, "Sit thou on my right hand, till I put thine enemies underneath thy feet."

It appears from the NASB translation that the "Lord," which is God, "said unto to my Lord" – who missionaries would have you believe is Jesus (David's "Lord") – "Sit thou on my right hand, till I put thine enemies underneath thy feet."

Is the above verse speaking about Jesus? Not at all, yet look at the first word "Lord" in the verse. Now look at the second word "Lord" (they are only three words apart). Did you notice any difference between these two words in this fundamentalist Bible? They are identical because the Christian translator carefully masked what it actually says in the text of the original Hebrew.

Although the two English words in the NASB translation are carefully made to appear identical, in the original Hebrew text they are entirely different. Whereas the first word "Lord" in the Hebrew is a correct translation of יהוה, which is the Tetragrammaton (YHWH), the ineffable name of God, the second word "Lord" is a complete and deliberate mistranslation of the text. The second word "Lord" in the verse is an appalling translation of the Hebrew word לַאדֹנִי (pronounced *ladonee*).

The correct and only translation of *ladonee* is "to my master" or "to my lord." The Hebrew word *adonee* never refers to God anywhere in the Bible. It is only used for the profane, never the sacred. That is to say, God, the Creator of the universe, is never called *adonee* in the Bible. There are many words reserved for God in the Bible; *adonee*, however, is not one of them.

To illustrate this vital point, let's examine other places in the Bible where the exact same Hebrew word appears and find out how the same New American Standard Bible translates it there. Bear in mind, in none of the following examples do the Christian Bibles have any incentive for mistranslating the word *adonee*.

For example, we find the same Hebrew word, לַאדֹנִי (*ladonee*), used in the following two verses which have been translated by the same New American Standard Bible where the identical word is used as in Psalm 110:

> Then he and the men who were with him ate and drank and spent the night. When they arose in the morning, he said, "Send me away to my master (*ladonee*: לַאדֹנִי)." (Genesis 24:54, New American Standard Bible)

Jacob instructed the angels to bring the following message to his brother Esau:

> "Thus you shall say to my lord לַאדֹנִי (*ladonee*) Esau, 'Thus says your servant Jacob, "I have sojourned with Laban, and stayed until now."' (Genesis 32:4, New American Standard Bible).

The Hebrew word לַאדֹנִי (*ladonee*) used in the above two verses is referring to Abraham and Esau, respectively. Notice that the Hebrew word used in both verses is identical to the Hebrew word in Psalm 110:1. Why did the New American Standard Bible translate לַאדֹנִי correctly in Genesis 24:54 as "to my master," or in Genesis 32:4 as "to my lord," yet, for some reason, in Psalm 110:1 mistranslate it as "Lord"?

The answer is obvious. Both Genesis 24:54 and Genesis 32:4 are not texts used by the church to "prove" Jesus from the Jewish scriptures and therefore they had no reason to tamper with them. Psalm 110:1, on the other hand, is a verse that is flaunted by the New Testament and its missionaries as a verse that evangelicals insist "unquestionably points only to Jesus," and is deliberate mistranslation.

Some Christian translations are more transparent in their rendering of Psalm 110 than the New American Standard Bible. For example, the King James Version and a few other Bibles still render the second "Lord" as if it were sacred; however, they translate the first "LORD" in upper case. This is a helpful hint to the keen observer that there is a distinction between them. Of course, it's up to the curious Bible student to then look up the second "Lord" in a Hebrew Bible. Only such a deliberate and thorough investigation would uncover how the text was doctored.

It should be noted that while many Christian translators indulge in this manipulation of Psalm 110:1, some do not. Numerous modern Christian Bibles have corrected Matthew's mistranslation. For example, the Revised Standard Version and the New English Bible correctly render the Hebrew word ladonee as " to my lord," in Psalm 110:1, indicating that it is not speaking of God.

As mentioned above, this tampering with Psalm 110:1 began long ago in the Christian Bible itself. The Christian translators, who would later also mistranslate this verse, simply followed in the footsteps of the author of the first Gospel. If we look at the original Greek of Matthew 22:44 we find the same doctoring of the text in later Christian translations of the Book of Psalms. When Matthew has Jesus quote Psalm 110:1 to the Pharisees, the identical Greek word *kurios*[2] (pronounced koo-re-os) is used both times the word "Lord" appears in Matthew 22:44.

Finally, it is essential that I explain the meaning of Psalm 110:1. Of whom is this Psalm really speaking? To whom are the words "my master" or "my lord" referring?

The Psalm begins with the opening Hebrew words "Mizmor l'David." The word "*Mizmor*" means "a song," and thus the opening phrase of this Psalm is, "A Song of David." In fact, the word Psalms comes from the Greek word ψαλμοῖς (*psalmos*), which means "a song." This simple fact is unknown to many Bible readers.

Why would King David be writing these songs? For whom was he writing them? By whom were they to be sung? With these questions in mind, we can begin to understand the meaning of Psalm 110.

One of King David's greatest disappointments was God's refusal to allow him to build the first Temple in Jerusalem. Although David's son Solomon undertook that task, and eventually constructed the first Temple, David's umbilical connection to Solomon's Temple was significant.

For example, David founded the city of Jerusalem, the city where the Temple was built. In fact, both the city and the Temple were called after him, the City and Temple of David. Moreover, he made preparations for the building of the Temple, and even arranged for the Temple service (II Samuel 7; I Chronicles 14-17, 22-26). This is where the Book of Psalms played its central role. King David was a faithful servant of God who possessed extraordinary skills as a teacher, musician, and poet. In fact, King David authored most of the Book of Psalms. The original purpose for which King David composed the Book of Psalms was for the Levites to sing them in the Temple. The Levites would stand on a platform and joyfully chant these spiritually exhilarating Psalms to an inspired people; Psalm 110 was no exception.

> The Lord [God] said to my master [King David] "Sit thou at my right hand . . ."

For the church, however, the Psalmist's original intent was set aside because it was consumed with Christianizing this verse. Thus, the opening verse in Psalm 110 was altered in order to paint Jesus into the Jewish scriptures.

Here is some advice. The only way to recognize such rampant Christian tampering of the Bible is to be able to read it in the original, without the aid of the Christian translator. Therefore, give your children a good Jewish education. Remember, the success of groups like Jews for Jesus represents the unpaid bills of the Jewish people.

Sincerely yours,

Rabbi Tovia Singer

**Footnotes:**

1. This is the sacred name of God.

2. Although the two Greek words *kurios* in this verse are the same, they are written with a slightly different syntax. Whereas the Greek word for the first word "Lord" in Matthew 22:44 is *kurios*, the Greek word for the second word "Lord" is *kurio*, because the latter is in the dative case, indicating "to" or "for" which an action occurs. This Greek syntax functions similarly to the letter *l* (*lamed*) does as a prefix in the Hebrew language.

# Jewish Genealogy

## Question:

I am a Jew descended from and through the tribe of Levi. I live in an area of the country in the State of Montana where there are no rabbis. I have a gentile friend who seems to be somewhat of a biblical theologian. He questions how I know that I am a Levite, considering that all of the records of the twelve tribes of Israel were destroyed. Can you help me with some answers? Where is the proof? Is it still written somewhere, or has the information about my descendants been merely passed down through the generations orally? My parents are dead, so there is no one to ask. Can you help?

## Answer:

Your friend's assertion that all the genealogical records of the Jewish people were destroyed is untrue and unfounded. No such event ever occurred in Jewish history and there is no historian or ancient source that supports his claim. The genealogies of the twelve tribes of Israel were not stored in the Temple and they were never destroyed. Moreover, the majority of the Jewish people did not live in Israel during the first century and their genealogical records would have been unaffected by the destruction of Jerusalem and its Temple in 70 C.E.

With regard to your personal genealogical ancestry, bear in mind that there is no segment of the Jewish people who are more aware of their tribal affiliation and more mindful to properly transmit this distinctive ancestry than the tribe of Levi. It has always been critical for members of the tribe of Levi to be aware of their unique place and status among the nation of Israel. This is true for a number of reasons. For instance, there are numerous distinct laws that apply only to this tribe. For example, there are certain women who a priest (kohen), who is a descendant of the tribe of Levi, may not marry. In addition, a priest is prohibited from coming into contact with a dead body. Also, only descendants from the tribe of Levi are involved in the Aaronic Benediction ceremony celebrated every festival throughout the world. Simply put, every family from the tribe of Levi is known to the Jewish people.

Moreover, not only are the descendants of Levi keenly aware of their unique ancestry, but the Jewish community as a whole has always been well aware of their identity as well. For example, only members of the tribe of Levi are honored with the first two blessings during the Torah reading in the synagogue. Also, any descendant of the tribe of Levi is identified as such on all legal documents such as marriage contracts and divorces.

Bear in mind that there were hundreds of thousands of priests and Levites throughout the Roman empire during the first century. Did they all have sudden amnesia? Did they all forget who their fathers were? It was always well known and meticulously documented by the Jewish people who their ancestors were. This information was carefully passed down from father to son and was often recorded in a family's *Sefer Yuchsin* (a record book of family genealogy).

I found your question particularly interesting, because my family has a *Sefer Yuchsin* which dates my ancestry back to biblical times. In it, every male between Aaron the High Priest (Moses' brother) and myself is carefully recorded.

Yours,

Rabbi Tovia Singer, HaKohen

# The Christian Messiah?

## Question:

I used to be a Christian and I live in an area that is mainly Christian. I am now trying to live as a Buddhist. I would like information that proves that Jesus was NOT the Christ that the Christians claim. For instance, I do not see the end of war, the lion lying down with the lamb, or a changed world. Would you recommend a book or pamphlet that proves that Jesus is not the person who the Christians claim him to be.

## Answer:

The reason why Judaism does not accept the Christian messiah is simple and clear: There is no relationship between what the Jewish scriptures teach about the messiah and Jesus of Nazareth.

What does scripture say about the messiah and the age he will bring to the world? I would encourage you to read the 37th chapter of the Book of Ezekiel. In this famed text, the prophet clearly teaches that we can recognize the coming of the messiah when all of the following take place: the resurrection of the dead, the building of the final Temple that will stand forever in Jerusalem, the universal knowledge of God and obedience to His Torah is attained, the lost tribes (the Northern Kingdom of Israel whom Assyria carried off) return to Israel, as well as the complete restoration of the Jewish people to their land.

When we carefully consider that not a single one of these epic events ever occurred, we can be assured that although many thousands of individuals have claimed to be the messiah throughout the centuries, Jesus included, none of them ushered in any of the aforementioned prophetic requirements.

Moreover, when we ponder whether Jesus is the messiah, it is obvious that the very opposite events occurred immediately after the Christian movement began. During the first century C.E., the Romans slaughtered hundreds of thousands of Jews, Secondly, hundreds of thousands more were forced into exile or enslaved by the Romans, and thirdly, the Temple in Jerusalem was destroyed. Consequently, the knowledge of Torah and its observance decreased, and the nation of Israel was dispersed throughout the Roman Empire. Clearly, there is no correlation with what the Tanach prophesied about the Messianic Age with that which the Messianic movement teaches about the Christian messiah, Jesus.

Nonetheless, missionaries often insist that Jesus will somehow accomplish these things in a second coming. While this notion conveniently explains away any failed messiahship, it is completely and utterly antithetical to the Bible.

James, I also suggest that you read Ezekiel 37 for another reason. It would give you the opportunity to learn about the real messiah, for whose coming the Jewish people all yearn. As you consider the flaws of the Christian claim, remember that the nation of Israel stood at the foot of Mount Sinai and heard the voice of God and declared His testimonies to the world. It is the nation of Israel that bears the mark of the covenant and attests to the world that there is one God and no other. His name is not Buddha. It is the Lord, God of Israel, your Creator.

Yours,

Rabbi Tovia Singer

# Mary's Genealogy

## Question:

I am curious to know what happened during the 400 years or so between the Torah and the New Testament. Also, did the Jews have a king during Roman Era at all, and what was the function of the Sanhedrin? Why do they say he was the king of the Jews? To which Jews are they referring? Also, as far as the line of David goes, can we trace Mary and Joseph back to David? Were they even from any tribe at all?

## Answer:

I am going to assume that in your first question you are asking whether there was a legitimate Davidic king over the Jewish people during the Second Temple period. If this is in fact your question, the answer is no. Although there was a royal crown held by both the dynasty of the Hasmoneans and Herod, they were not legitimately anointed kings over the Jewish people, because they were not heirs to the Davidic throne.

The answer to your second question is the *Sanhedrin* was the Jewish court system, not the seat of a king.

With regard to your third question, when Christians refer to Jesus as king of the Jews, they are in essence asserting that Jesus was the messiah, and the final heir to the throne of David. This claim, however, is self-defeating because it undermines the Christian claim that Jesus was conceived from a virgin.

According to both Matthew and Luke, Jesus was born of a virgin. This claim makes it impossible, however, for Christians to insist that Jesus was king of the Jews. This is because tribal lineage is traced only through a person's father. This is clearly stated in Numbers 1:18. According to Christian teachings, Jesus had only a human Jewish mother, not a human Jewish father. This human Jewish father would be essential for anyone to be a legitimate heir to the throne of David, which the real messiah will be.

With regard to your final question, Mary's genealogy is completely irrelevant to Jesus' supposed lineage from King David. Nowhere in the New Testament is Mary's genealogy traced. In both the first chapter of Matthew and in the third chapter of Luke, these New Testament authors provide a genealogy of Joseph alone. Although these two genealogies violently contradict each other, there is no suggestion in either of them that Mary's genealogy is connected to the House of David. As mentioned above, Joseph's genealogy is irrelevant to Jesus because according to Christian doctrine, Joseph was not Jesus' father.

It should be pointed out that both Catholic and Protestant traditions hold that whereas Matthew's genealogy is that of Joseph, Luke's genealogy is of Mary. Although this tradition is nowhere to be found in the New Testament, it was a necessary doctrine for the Church to adopt.

Nowhere in the third Gospel, or in the entire New Testament, for that matter, does it state that Mary was a descendant of the House of David. On the contrary, Luke 1:27 plainly asserts that it is Joseph who was from the House of David, not Mary. In fact, Luke claims that Mary was the cousin of Elizabeth, who he says was a descendant of Aaron the high priest,[1] placing her in the tribe of Levi, not David's tribe of Judah. Moreover, in Luke 2:4, the author writes that the reason it was necessary for Joseph and Mary to return to Bethlehem was because Joseph was from the House of David.

There are a number of reasons why the Church sought to claim that Luke's genealogy of Jesus is traced through Mary's line. To begin with, Paul claims in Romans 1:3 that Jesus was from the seed of David after the flesh. This has always been understood to mean that Paul was claiming that King David was the biological ancestor of Jesus. At the time when Paul penned the Book of Romans, he was completely unaware that Christendom would eventually claim that Jesus was born of a virgin. Consequently, the Church desperately needed to have Paul's statement correlate with the virgin-birth story. This dilemma was solved by the assertion that whereas Matthew's genealogy of Jesus was traced through Joseph's line, Luke's genealogy of Jesus was through Mary's lineage. In this way, Jesus could now be from the seed of David after the flesh through Luke's genealogy. Likewise, establishing Mary's lineage to King David, Luke's genealogy ostensibly solves the problem of what to do with Romans 1:3 (Paul), and establishes a physical link between Jesus and King David.

Finally, it seeks to resolve an awkward discrepancy between the conflicting genealogies contained in the books of Matthew and Luke. Whereas in Matthew's genealogy, Joseph's father is Jacob,[2] in Luke's genealogy it is Heli.[3] By claiming that Luke's genealogy is of Mary, Heli becomes Mary's father and Joseph's father-in-law. Surprisingly, Christendom's not-too-ingenious resolution to the conflicting genealogies in the Gospels has satisfied the unlettered minds of billions of Christians worldwide.

Yours,

Rabbi Tovia Singer

## Footnotes:

1. Luke 1:5
2. Matthew 1:16
3. Luke 3:23

# Who Killed Jesus?

## Question:

Dear Rabbi,

What can you answer to a "Christian" who claims that the Jews killed Jesus? I was too angry to think clearly of a good answer for that.

Thank you.

P.S. . . It's hard to be a Jew in Hawaii sometimes!

## Answer:

You shouldn't get so angry at Christians who insist that the Jews killed Jesus. Your outrage is being directed in the wrong direction. Your accuser simply accepted the dark portrayal of the Jews by the authors of the New Testament too seriously. The odious charge of deicide is clearly leveled against the Jewish people in the Christian scriptures. From the narratives in the Gospels and letters of Paul, there can be no doubt that the Jews alone are responsible for Jesus' death. In I Thessalonians 2:14-16, Paul writes,

> ". . . even as they have of the Jews, who both killed the Lord Jesus, and their own prophets, and have persecuted us; and they please not God, and are contrary to all men, forbidding us to speak to the Gentiles that they might be saved, to fill up their sins always; for the wrath is come upon them to the uttermost!"

Moreover, not only are the Jews completely vilified in the New Testament for Jesus' execution, but shockingly – the Romans are completely exonerated! This selective condemnation is not only directed toward those Jews who allegedly plotted and collaborated in Jesus' crucifixion, but holds all future generations of Jews accountable for this crime. Virtually all the Church Fathers regurgitate this devastating charge.

The author of the first Gospel goes out of his way to portray Roman leaders at the time as patsies of the Jews, wanting no part in Jesus' death. Matthew portrays Pontius Pilate as someone who strongly opposed Jesus' execution, and he symbolically washes his hands of the gruesome affair.[1] In fact, the Gospels consistently cast Pilate as the one trying to reason with the vindictive Jews, arguing for Jesus' vindication. The Jews, on the other hand, are cast as bloodthirsty, maniacal, and debased rabblers, demanding that Jesus be put to death. The benign caricature of Pontius Pilate in the gospels, on the other hand, is one of a melancholy, weak leader who finally relents to the Jews and reluctantly hands Jesus over to be crucified.

Mark also depicts Jesus as innocent of committing any crime against Rome, and Pilate as extremely reluctant to execute Jesus, blaming the Jews for his death.[2] In Matthew, Pilate washes his hands of Jesus's execution and reluctantly sends him to his death.[3] In Luke, Pilate not only agrees that Jesus did not conspire against Rome, but Herod Antipas, the tetrarch, admired Jesus as a saintly miracle worker,[4] and finds nothing treasonous in Jesus' actions.[5] In the book of John, shockingly, the warm feelings between the two are almost mutual, where Pilate finds no fault in Jesus,[6] and Jesus finds little sin in Pilate.[7]

It could be said that Matthew, singlehandedly, is responsible for the first blood libel against the Jews, wherein after the Roman governor allegedly pleads with the crowd to spare Jesus' life, they answer him, "We take his blood upon ourselves and our children!" Please see Matthew 27:22-25 (below). These chilling verses provide deep insight as to how the mind and soul of your acquaintance was poisoned by the slanderous words of the New Testament. Pilate said to the Jews:

> "What then shall I do with Jesus who is called Christ?" They all [the Jews] said to him, "Let Him be crucified!" Then the governor said, "Why, what evil has He done?" But they cried out all the more, saying, "Let Him be crucified!" When Pilate saw that he could not prevail at all, but rather that a tumult was rising, he took water and washed his hands before the multitude, saying, "I am innocent of the blood of this just Person. You see to it." All the people answered and said, **"His blood be on us and on our children."**

Moreover, in the book of John, which is considered by many to be the most anti-Semitic of all the Gospels, Jesus completely exonerates the Romans for the crucifixion while holding the Jews completely accountable for his execution. In a conversation between Jesus and Pilate, Jesus assures the Roman procurator of Judea that he has no power of his own, and therefore, "the one who delivered me to you [the Jews] bear the greatest iniquity" (John 19:11). In fact, nowhere in the New Testament are the Romans ever condemned for the crucifixion of Jesus. Predictably, this cannot be said about the Jews. This is made clear in the book of Acts where the Jews alone are condemned for the death of Jesus. Notice how the Roman culpability is never mentioned anywhere in this text:

> Therefore let all Israel be assured of this: God has made this Jesus, whom you crucified, both Lord and Christ. (Acts 2:36)

It is not difficult to understand why the Ethiopian Orthodox Church venerates Pontius Pilate as a saint, and according to Eastern Orthodox traditions, Pilate committed suicide out of remorse for having sentenced Jesus to death.

In stark contrast, according to noted historians, including Philo and Josephus, Pilate was renowned for his "his violence, thefts, assaults, abusive behavior, endless executions, and savage ferocity"[8] and a "cruel despot who executed troublemakers without a trial and ordered his soldiers to randomly attack, beat, and kill scores of Jews."[9] Not surprisingly, this record of Pilate's brutality is nowhere to be found in the New Testament. A cruel tyrant such as Pilate would not have hesitated to execute any leader whose followers posed a potential threat to Roman rule. The notion that the Jews would or could demand of Pilate to crucify Jesus is preposterous.

If you stop and think about it, the whole accusation of the Jews killing Jesus is rather ludicrous. On the one hand, the New Testament insists that it was the most wonderful thing for mankind to have an atonement through Jesus' death. On the other hand, the Jews are vilified by the same New Testament for killing him. If you take New Testament theology to its full logical conclusion, the Jews should have been praised in the New Testament for making this atonement possible, not condemned. Does all this make any sense? You [Jews] just can't win.

With regard to your request for advice on how to answer the Christian who accuses the Jews of killing Jesus, remember that you are dealing with someone who is operating out of a venomous hate for the Chosen People, the "apple of His eye" (Zechariah 2:8). He is probably not interested in understanding why his charges are preposterous. Instead, remind him that his Bible says that the Almighty will bless those who bless Israel, and curse those curse Israel (Genesis 12:3). In short, Jew-hatred is a sin that damns the soul.

It is important to bear in mind that although, as a result of this despicable charge of deicide, countless Christians have committed unspeakable atrocities against the Jewish people, albeit many decent Christians condemn it. The reason for their condemnation, however, is often varied. There is no doubt that many Christians denounce anti-Semitism because of their genuine affection for the Jewish people. Unfortunately, many Christians who loudly declare their love for the Jewish people and condemn this charge of deicide have an ulterior motive: They do not want to be perceived by their potential Jewish converts to Christianity as being anti-Semitic or associated with Christendom and its long history of hatred and violence against them.

Sincerely yours,

Rabbi Tovia Singer

**Footnotes:**

1. Matthew 27:22-25
2. Mark 15:8-15
3. Matthew 27:13-25
4. Luke 23:8
5. Luke 23:3-23
6. John 18:38
7. John 19:11
8. Philo, *On The Embassy of Gauis.* Book XXXVIII 299-305.
9. Josephus, Jewish War 2.9.2-4

# Did Jesus Rise from the Dead? What is the Evidence for the Resurrection?

## Question:

Dear Rabbi Singer:

I'm doing a project on missionary and counter-missionary groups. There is a very large section in my project that deals with theology. I have read your site as well as the Jews for Jesus site, and I must say that the information is both deep and extensive. I must commend you. Your site offers many good counter arguments to the validity of Jesus being the messiah. I have, however hit a stumbling block.

I checked your Q&A section on the web pages, but found very little dealing with "Jewish" explanations of the resurrection. I found that quite odd, as any Christian will tell you that Jesus' resurrection is the foundation of the Christian religion. I assume that we as Jews do not believe in Christ's resurrection, so how do we explain the resurrection? Did a bunch of crazy people decide to create a story about a resurrection? This story was passed on to the time when the Gospels were written, so how inaccurate can they be? The memory of someone 40 years ago isn't considered faulty today, so accounts from 40 years may have been altered, but

**all adhere to a resurrection story. What is the Jewish take on the resurrection?**

## Answer:

You certainly did not overstate the importance of the claim of Jesus' resurrection to the Church. As Paul candidly concedes, "If Christ has not been raised, your faith is futile and you are still in your sins" (I Corinthians15:17). In essence, the validity of Christianity stands or falls on this astounding claim. Because of the importance of this topic, I have dedicated an entire segment on the audio recording, *Confused Texts and Testimonies*, to this subject.

Bear in mind that Christianity is not the only religion to have declared that its savior or demigod resurrected from the grave. The story of a deity who defeated the grip of death is one of the most common themes embedded in the plethora of religions that have emerged since time immemorial. Your question, therefore, may be expanded even more widely because the claim of a divine savior who is born of a virgin birth, suffers a brutal death, and ascends to heaven was so very common among pagan and Gnostic religions during the first century (this was especially true for the regions around Tarsus, Paul's hometown). Mythologies throughout the Roman Empire and beyond contained widespread beliefs that notable mortals and god-men were born of virgins and returned from the dead. See accounts of Romulus, Apollonius of Tyana, Drusilla, Claudius, Dionysus-Bacchus, Tammuz, Mithra, Osiris, Krishna, and Buddha.

The question for the Jewish people is simple. Should we accept the numerous claims made by widespread religions of a miraculous resurrections from the dead simply because their zealous defenders promoted them? Claims of biased followers need to be particularly scrutinized, especially if they are the only claims that exist.

Since the belief in Jesus' resurrection is the foundation of Christianity, we should certainly examine the credibility of this story. What is the evidence for the belief that Jesus rose from the grave? Aside from the accounts in the New Testament, there is no independent supportive documentation, nor is there any circumstantial evidence. There is not even one contemporaneous historian who mentions one word about the resurrection. The entire claim hangs exclusively on the New Testament texts. Moreover, it was the creators and defenders of Christianity who promoted the stories of the resurrection. Their biased testimony must therefore be examined more carefully. Is this testimony reliable? As a seeker of truth, you are the judge.

Obviously, a judge must be impartial, and objectively weigh all of the relevant evidence. Realize this is not a routine case; your relationship with God is at stake. As an individual examining the case for the resurrection, you should not be swayed by conjecture or hearsay, but demand clear proof.

If you were the judge presiding over a murder case, you would want to be absolutely certain before convicting the defendant. If the prosecutor called his key witnesses, but each told a different story, his case would be very shaky. The defense attorney would argue for the acquittal of his client by demonstrating the weakness of the prosecutor's case. He would impeach the state's witnesses by showing how their accounts are contradictory.

The resurrection narratives in the Gospels may be convincing testimony for people who have not read them very carefully. As a responsible judge, though, you can't be satisfied with just a casual examination of the evidence, especially if biased witnesses gave the testimony. The stories told in the New Testament, and the passion narratives in particular, are so inconsistent, that the resurrection story collapses under careful scrutiny. The conflicting testimonies of the evangelists are so unreliable, that they would not stand up to critical cross-examination in any court of law. In fact, there is virtually not one detail of the crucifixion and resurrection narratives upon which all four Gospel authors agree. Yet, it is upon this story that the entire Christian religion stands or falls.

I have prepared the following three-part study to help you critically evaluate the case of the alleged resurrection of Jesus. This analysis consists of the crucial date of the crucifixion and the events that allegedly followed the resurrection.

Study the *crucifixion/resurrection chart* on page 130-131, which maps out the vast number of inconsistencies in the Passion Narratives among the four Gospels and the letters of Paul. Let's begin this examination of the resurrection stories by studying the date of the crucifixion as told by the four Gospels.

# The Crucifixion Date: On Which Day Was Jesus Crucified?

When examining the four crucifixion accounts as they are presented in the New Testament, it is difficult to identify a single event upon which all four Gospel writers agree. Even the date of the crucifixion is an issue of contention among the four Gospels.

A perfunctory examination of New Testament texts reveals that the Books of Matthew[1] Mark[2] and Luke[3] all agree that the Last Supper was actually a Passover *Seder*. Bearing in mind that Jesus was crucified on the very next day following the Last Supper, that would mean that according to all three synoptic[4] Gospels, Jesus was crucified on the first day of Passover, or the 15th day of the of the first Jewish month of *Nissan* (for example, if tonight were a Passover *Seder*, then tomorrow would be the first day of Passover[5]).

The author of the Book of John, however, completely contradicts a crucial element of the crucifixion story as they are presented in the first three Gospels. John maintains that Jesus was crucified on the eve of Passover, or the 14th day of *Nissan*. The Book of John identifies the date of the crucifixion in the following manner:

> "Now it was the **day of preparation** for the Passover... Then he handed him over to them to be crucified." (John 19:14-16)

The implications of this stunning contradiction cannot be overstated because both claims cannot possibly be true. In essence, this is not the sort of inconsistency that can be explained away with the claim that attributes the varying Gospel accounts to different perspectives of the Gospel writers. Jesus was crucified either of the eve of Passover, which is the 14th day of *Nissan*, as John contends, or on the first day of Passover, which is the 15th day of *Nissan*, as the Gospels of Matthew, Mark, and Luke maintain. Jesus could not have been crucified on both days.

Was the first Good Friday the first day of Passover? According to Matthew, Mark, and Luke, it was; according to John it was not.

As a result of this peculiar conflict over the crucifixion date, numerous other aspects of John's Passion Narrative differ radically from that of the synoptic Gospels.

For example, John's description of what transpired during the Last Supper had to be entirely different from the accounts of Matthew, Mark, and Luke. John cannot include a Passover *Seder* in his version of the Last Supper because according to his reckoning of the date of the crucifixion, the night of the Last Supper fell on the night of the 13th day of Nissan which was not a holiday. Accordingly, no aspect of the *Seder* ceremony occurs in John's Last Supper. In fact, in John's Last Supper, there is neither eating of the matzo, nor drinking of the wine, because the evening before the crucifixion does not occur on the festival of Passover. In the book of John (chapter 13), there is no mention of anyone drinking wine, or eating matzo and herbs as we find in Matthew, Mark, and Luke. John's account of the Last Supper contains no ceremonial supper; he only describes Jesus' washing the feet of the disciples.

Moreover, John begins his 13th chapter by saying, "Now before the festival of the Passover . . ." This is a stunning opening statement because according to Matthew, Mark, and Luke that momentous night wasn't "before the festival of Passover, but rather it was the festival of Passover. Also, according to John, when Judas Iscariot mysteriously leaves the Last Supper with the moneybag, the disciples immediately presume that he is taking money to purchase food for the festive meal (13:29). Why would Judas be purchasing food for the feast if, according to the first three Gospels, they had just eaten the "festive meal?"

Furthermore, John's story describes how, when the Jews were handing Jesus over to Pontius Pilate to be crucified on the morning of the crucifixion, "They [the Jews] themselves did not enter the headquarters, so as to avoid ritual defilement and to be able to eat the Passover."[6] (John 18:28) Why were these Jews concerned about not being able to eat the Passover? According to Matthew, Mark, and Luke they had already consumed the lamb because the Passover *Seder* took place the previous evening. This is not a problem for John because John states that Jesus was crucified on the eve of Passover, so that this statement makes perfect sense in his story. In contrast, the synoptic Gospels never mention in their accounts the fear the Jews had of entering the home of Pilate. Such concern would be preposterous because in Matthew, Mark, and Luke's story, the Jews had already eaten the Passover lamb the previous night.

The first question that naturally comes to mind is, why would John change the crucifixion date from the 15th day of *Nissan* to the 14th day? Why was it so important to the author of the fourth Gospel that Jesus be crucified on the eve of Passover rather than the first day of Passover, as the other three Gospels claim?

The simple answer becomes quite clear when we have a good understanding of what message John's Gospel was trying to convey to its reader.

Remembering that the book of John was the last of the four Gospels to be written, the author was trying to appeal to a second century church that had already become predominantly gentile. Bearing this in mind, John had to appeal to pagans of the Greco-Roman world whom he was addressing. This was accomplished by carefully integrating heathen practices with elements of the Jewish faith. The notion that an animal was to be revered and sacrificed as a god was well known and widely practiced throughout the Roman Empire[7], in Mystery Religions such as Mithraism, which flourished during the time that the Book of John was being written. John was well aware of this and seamlessly fused together the Mithraic sacrifice of the redeeming bull with the Jewish sacrifice of the Paschal lamb.

It is for this reason that only in John's Gospel does John the Baptist proclaim of Jesus, "Behold, the Lamb of God . . . ." (1:29, 36). In fact, of the four Gospels, only John ever equates Jesus with the Passover lamb. If Matthew, Mark, and Luke agreed with the fourth Gospel that the lamb was the antitype of Jesus, as John insisted, why is it that when the synoptic Gospels described the communion at the last supper, Jesus raised the matzo saying, "This is my body"? Instead, according to Jewish tradition, he should have raised the Paschal lamb. At mass, priests should be giving their parishioners a shank bone rather than a wafer for communion!

In addition, the story of the Roman soldiers who pierced the side of Jesus rather than break his legs on the cross (John 19:31-37) appears nowhere else in the New Testament. This brief narrative only fits into the theological story line of the fourth Gospel. This is because only the author of the Book of John was eager not to have Jesus' bones broken so as not to violate the prohibition of breaking the bones of the Paschal lamb found in the Book of Exodus (12:46).

Therefore, we have come to the reason that John places the crucifixion on the 14th day rather than the 15th. Because the *Torah* commands Israel to slaughter the Paschal lamb on the eve of Passover or on the 14th day of *Nissan* (Exodus 12:6), John's Jesus is also "slaughtered" i.e. crucified on the eve of Passover or the 14th day of *Nissan*.

# Both of these Contradictory Resurrection Stories Could Not have Occurred

## Matthew 28:1-10

1 After the Sabbath, as the first day of the week was dawning, Mary Magdalene and the other Mary went to see the tomb. 2 And suddenly there was a great earthquake; for an angel of the Lord, descending from heaven, came and rolled back the stone and sat on it. 3 His appearance was like lightning, and his clothing white as snow. 4 For fear of him the guards shook and became like dead men. 5 But the angel said to the women, "Do not be afraid; I know that you are looking for Jesus who was crucified. 6 He is not here; for he has been raised, as he said. Come, see the place where he lay. 7 Then go quickly and tell his disciples, 'He has been raised from the dead, and indeed he is going ahead of you to Galilee; there you will see him.' This is my message for you." 8 So they left the tomb quickly with fear and great joy, and ran to tell his disciples. 9 Suddenly Jesus met them and said, "Greetings!" And they came to him, took hold of his feet, and worshiped him. 10 Then Jesus said to them, "Do not be afraid; go and tell my brothers to go to Galilee; there they will see me."

## John 20:1-18

1 Early on the first day of the week, while it was still dark, Mary Magdalene came to the tomb and saw that the stone had been removed from the tomb. 2 So she ran and went to Simon Peter and the other disciple, the one whom Jesus loved, and said to them, "They have taken the Lord out of the tomb, and we do not know where they have laid him." 3 Then Peter and the other disciple set out and went toward the tomb. 4 The two were running together, but the other disciple outran Peter and reached the tomb first. 5 He bent down to look in and saw the linen wrappings lying there, but he did not go in. 6 Then Simon Peter came, following him, and went into the tomb. He saw the linen wrappings lying there, 7 and the cloth that had been on Jesus' head, not lying with the linen wrappings but rolled up in a place by itself. 8 Then the other disciple, who reached the tomb first, also went in, and he saw and believed; 9 for as yet they did not understand the scripture, that he must rise from the dead. 10 Then the disciples returned to their homes. 11 But Mary stood weeping outside the tomb. As she wept, she bent over to look into the tomb; 12 and she saw two angels in white, sitting where the body of Jesus had been lying, one at the head and the other at the feet. 13 They said to her, "Woman, why are you weeping?" She said to them, "They have taken away my Lord, and I do not know where they have laid him." 14 When she had said this, she turned around and saw Jesus standing there, but she did not know that it was Jesus. 15 Jesus said to her, "Woman, why are you weeping? For whom are you looking?" Supposing him to be the gardener, she said to him, "Sir, if you have carried him away, tell me where you have laid him, and I will take him away." 16 Jesus said to her, "Mary!" She turned and said to him in Hebrew, "Rabbouni!" which means Teacher. 17 Jesus said to her, "Do not hold on to me, because I have not yet ascended to the Father. But go to my brothers and say to them, 'I am ascending to my Father and your Father, to my God and your God.'" 18 Mary Magdalene went and announced to the disciples, "I have seen the Lord"; and she told them that he had said these things to her.

What is wrong with these two stories from the first and last Gospel? If read independently, the resurrection accounts presented by either Matthew or John appear viable if all the other New Testament accounts are ignored. When read side by side, however, these narratives collapse because it would have been chronologically impossible for both accounts to have occurred. In fact, the crucial events presented in these two Gospel narratives are so manifestly contradictory that even liberal Christians, who often allow for occasional mistakes that appear in the New Testament, must take pause.

This brief study will examine several unreconcilable contradictions in the variant Gospel accounts of the resurrection chronology in the books of Matthew and John. The following discrepancies, which we will now examine, have been selected because they cannot be harmonized or explained by such well-worn arguments as "each Gospel writer is giving us his own personal perspective." Such a rationalization becomes impossible because the above Gospel narratives are so irreconcilable that no explanation can account for the stark differences between them.

Matthew presents us with a post-resurrection story where the two Marys are greeted at the tomb by an angel who had just rolled away the stone from its entrance. After revealing to both women the empty place where Jesus' body once laid, the angel proclaims to them that Jesus had already risen from the dead. The angel goes on to instruct both Marys that they are to tell the disciples that Jesus had gone before them to the Galilee to meet them (Matthew 28:1-7).

If that encounter wasn't convincing enough for the two women, Matthew continues to relate how, after leaving the tomb, both Marys unexpectedly meet the resurrected Jesus himself, whom they both worship. Jesus then essentially repeats the angel's instructions to them, and sends the women to inform the disciples that they are to meet the resurrected Jesus in the Galilee. (Matthew 28:8-10)

Like Matthew's account, John's resurrection narrative also contains an empty tomb. However, that is where the similarities between the first and fourth Gospel end. In John's version of the first Easter morning, when Mary Magdalene arrives at Jesus' tomb, there is no angel to greet her with information about Jesus' whereabouts, or instructions about a rendezvous in the Galilee as we find in Matthew's account (Matthew 28:5-7). On the contrary, in John's story, after Mary finds the empty tomb, she concludes that someone had removed the body from the grave. Mary certainly had no reason to believe otherwise. She therefore quickly runs back to the disciples and reports, "They have taken the Lord out of the tomb, and we do not know where they have laid him!" (John 20:1-2).

The above account in two verses in the book of John could not have occurred in Matthew's post-resurrection narrative. How could Mary have not known that Jesus' body was not laid anywhere? In Matthew's story, the angel had already revealed to her that Jesus rose from the dead and had gone to the Galilee. It is therefore ludicrous for her to think that someone had moved the body when the angels had already informed her that Jesus' resurrection had occurred. Moreover, if the angel's instructions to her were not convincing enough, Matthew maintains that Mary also met the resurrected Jesus himself right after leaving the tomb (Matthew 28:9); and all this transpires before Mary ever sees the disciples! Why then in John's Gospel is Mary clueless as to where Jesus' body was moved, when according to Matthew, Mary had already heard from two reliable sources (the angel at the tomb and Jesus himself) that Jesus rose from the dead?

Further contradicting Matthew's post-resurrection account, John's story lacks the Roman guards whom Matthew places at the tomb to prevent anyone from removing Jesus' body. How could John's Mary have thought that someone removed the body, when according to Matthew, Roman soldiers were placed at the tomb for the specific purpose of preventing just such an occurrence? Obviously, the author of the fourth Gospel has no need for Roman guards at the tomb, so in John's crucifixion account they simply are not there.

This Gospel problem of the missing Roman soldiers in the Book of John raises another important issue. Missionaries often contend that it would have been impossible for anyone to have surreptitiously removed Jesus' corpse from the tomb because there were guards posted at the tomb who would have prevented such an occurrence. Therefore, they argue, without any possibility for the body to have been quietly whisked away, the only other logical conclusion is that Jesus must have truly arisen from the dead.

John's account, however, completely nullifies this argument, because according to his story line, this is precisely what Mary thought had happened. Mary clearly didn't feel as though the scenario of Jesus' body being removed was unlikely. In fact, according to John, that was her only logical conclusion. Clearly, Matthew's guards didn't dissuade John's Mary from concluding that someone had taken Jesus' body, because, in John's story, Matthew's Roman guards do not exist.

To compound the problem of the conflicting resurrection accounts even further,

John's Gospel continues to unfold with Mary returning to the tomb a second time, only to find two angels sitting inside the tomb. Mary is still unaware of any resurrection as she complains to the angels that someone had removed Jesus' dead body. As far as John's Mary is concerned, the only explanation for the missing body was that someone must have removed it, and she was determined to locate it (John 20:11-13). Although in Matthew's account the angel emphatically tells Mary about the resurrection (Matthew 28:5-7), in John's Gospel the angels say nothing about the resurrection. The angels only ask Mary, "Woman, why are you weeping?" Mary then inquires as to whether the angels have removed Jesus' body. Then, Mary turns and sees Jesus standing before her, but mistakes him for the gardener. Mary is still completely unaware of any resurrection, and therefore asks the "gardener" if he was the one who carried away Jesus' body. It is only then that Mary realizes that she was speaking to the resurrected Jesus (John 20:14-16).

It is at this final juncture of the narrative that the accounts of Matthew and John become hopelessly irreconcilable. The question every missionary must answer is the following: When Mary met Jesus for the first time after the resurrection, had the angel(s) already informed her that Jesus had arisen from the dead? According to Matthew, the angles did inform Mary of the resurrection, but in John's account they certainly did not. As we survey the divergent New Testament accounts of the resurrection, we are not just looking at contradictory versions, we are simply staring at two entirely different stories.

Many Christian apologists have argued that the inconsistent resurrection accounts are similar to a traffic accident that is viewed by four different witnesses – each who sees it has a distinct perspective. This might be a tenable idea if the evangelists were actually on the scene and watched the story unfold as the women approached the tomb. Yet, this was not the case. Not only were the Gospel writers not eyewitnesses, they didn't even write their accounts of the story until at least 40-70 years after it allegedly took place. Moreover, most of the inconsistencies in the resurrection narratives, e.g. date, time, and place cannot be dismissed as differences in perspective.

Philo of Alexandria (20 B.C.E.-50 C.E.), a renowned philosopher and a contemporary of Jesus, wrote extensively about his time. Yet, his entire corpus of works fails to mention a word regarding Jesus or his alleged resurrection. Josephus' silence on this matter is also deafening. Consequently, the only information we have of this 2,000-year-old tale is the Greek document called the New Testament. However, the moment our finger begins to navigate through its verses, we are confronted and appalled by the plethora of glaring irreconcilable inconsistencies. Every element of the resurrection narrative is recklessly contradicted by another.

There is, however, a more significant issue here – the source. When a number of people in different places and at different times write a description of an event that occurred in the significant past – whether a year ago, a decade ago, or a half a century ago – we expect and anticipate many contradictions. Why, you ask? Because humans are fallible, and are therefore likely to make unintentional and intentional errors. Accordingly, when we read descriptions of what transpired during a historical event, such as the assassination of JFK, disparities will inevitably exist among the accounts. Therefore, when various individuals witness a traffic accident and then attempt to clearly transmit the information they saw, errors will be made. This is what we expect from humans! The New Testament, however, does not make this claim. Its authors and those who promoted the Christian religion wanted us to believe that its content was divinely inspired, i.e. every word is from God! With this claim, we must hold it to an entirely different standard of accuracy – that of perfection. The time span from the first letters of Paul to the last words of Revelation is over a half a century. Moreover, these books were penned from one end of the Roman Empire to the other. Thus, if we are to assume they were written by mere mortals, without Heavenly inspiration, mistakes and inconsistencies are expected. God, however, is inerrant.

There is another difference between conflicting accounts of a traffic accident and conflicting accounts of the resurrection. The testimonies of a traffic accident are believable because they are likely to have occurred and make sense in our world. The resurrection story, on the other hand, is a biological and scientific impossibility. Thus, the only reason for believing its miraculous occurrence – defying all natural laws – is the believer's total reliance on the credibility of the divine author. Since the stunning contradictions clearly establish the human origins of the resurrection stories, we can no more accept their testimony than we can that of the Book of Mormon. Moreover, the resurrection story is a self-serving rationalization to account for a messianic failure.

I know there have been many frantic attempts to respond to some of the countless inconsistencies that exist in the Gospels. These answers, however, are so plainly contrived that even a perfunctory examination of these rationalizations cast serious doubt on the claim that they were divinely inspired. God doesn't suffer from human fallibility and certainly wouldn't present such a garbled account of what Christians consider the most crucial event in world history.

Best regards for a happy Passover.

Very truly yours,

Rabbi Tovia Singer

## Crucifixion/Resurrection Chart on pages 130-131

**Footnotes:**

1. Matthew 26:20-30.

2. Mark 14:17-25.

3. Luke 22:14-23.

4. The synoptic Gospels are those of Matthew, Mark, and Luke. The word synoptic comes from two Greek words that mean "the same view." Matthew, Mark, and Luke are referred to as the synoptic Gospels because these three Gospels tell a similar story, and there is a strong literary relationship among them.

5. Suggesting that the Last Supper might have been the second Passover Seder would not hold true in the land of Israel, but only in the Diaspora where it is customary to hold two Seders. Secondly, a second Seder would create a 48-hour problem instead of a 24-hour problem.

6. *Kohanim*, priests, avoided entering the homes of gentiles because it was a common practice for non-Jews to bury their dead in their homes.

7. This is particularly true of the pagan god Mithras. Belief in this deity flourished throughout the Roman Empire during the second and third centuries C.E. Similar to Christianity, Mithra was called the "Mediator" (see I Timothy 2:5), and one Mithraic hymn begins, "Thou hast redeemed us too by shedding the eternal blood."

# Who Was Jesus?

## Question:

Dear Rabbi Singer,

Apparently, you guys have not read about the foolishness of the Sanhedrin 2,000 years ago. Or perhaps, God has hardened your hearts.

"Eloi Eloi lama sabachthani?"

I'm sure you understand this as clearly as the *Sanhedrin* 2000 years ago understood this. Do you really believe that a poor carpenter born in Bethlehem of the lineage of David would be able to set circumstances in motion such that the prophets could be made to be fools? I believe that God and His prophets are bigger than that.

In the end you are forced to believe one of three things: Jesus was crazy and empowered by Satan for his miracles, or Jesus intentionally led people away from God and wanted to do this so much that he died at the hands of the Romans and Sanhedrin to fulfill this purpose, or that Jesus is Messiah – and as Messiah, would save any – even those who had him

**slain. My question to you is: Which do you believe that Jesus was? I would not mind this question and answer posted if you so choose to do so.**

## Answer:

As I sit here preparing to write down the answers to your questions, it is beginning to sink into my mind that in the first three paragraphs of your letter, you are not asking anything at all.

Your first paragraph begins with the words "You guys..." I have spent enough time in Brooklyn to know that this is your euphemism for "You Jews." No need to get into a tizzy. We Hebrews have been called worse.

Your unsubtle sentiments in paragraphs one and three are not unfamiliar to the Jewish people. It is noticeably consistent with the long-held Christian notion that contemporary Jews bear the same loathsome characteristics as their first century forebears who were held accountable in the New Testament for Jesus' crucifixion. Do not think, however, that I have an unsympathetic ear either. I understand your position. The New Testament paints the Jews in the darkest colors imaginable. Essentially, whatever it is that one considers detestable in a people, that is precisely how the Jews are portrayed in the Christian scriptures. The nation of Israel has paid a heavy price for this vilification.

Jews of subsequent generations retain the sinister reputation of the people who were said to have committed deicide, regardless of how far they are removed in time and place from the first century. This notion was vigorously espoused by virtually all of the Church Fathers and reformers as well as their countless eager followers from the moment Christianity was spawned. The New Testament contains maliciously fabricated stories of the *Sanhedrin*, who they unjustly blame for condemning Jesus to death. These stories are replete with so many contradictions and inconsistencies - both within the Gospels and outside of the Christian canon that they betray themselves as self-serving, contemptuous accusations, specifically designed to heap all of the blame for the crucifixion of Jesus squarely on the *yarmulke* of the Jew. This portrayal of the Jews in the Gospels, particularly in the Passion Narratives, has been devastating for European Jewry and is ultimately responsible for the unspeakable misery of untold millions of my people. The world's oldest hatred is alive and well.

With regard to the verse, "*Eloi Eloi lama sabachthani*?" attributed by the New Testament as Jesus' last words on the cross, it is actually lifted from the lips of King David and placed in the mouth of Jesus by the first two Gospel writers.[1] This passage appears in Psalm 22:2[2] where King David, who is its author and the one speaking throughout this chapter, is describing his own anguish and longing as he remained a fugitive from his enemies. It was from the very depths of David's despair when he cries out his heartfelt supplication, *"Eli, Eli, lamah azovtani ..."* In short, passionate words of despair and faith contained in the twenty second Psalm are not a prophecy about Jesus or any future figure. These celebrated verses do not peer into the future. Rather, these prayers, which are all, without exception, written in the first person by King David, painfully describe his own turbulent life, not the life of Jesus.

Furthermore, the words of this verse do not fit into Jesus' mouth from a Trinitarian viewpoint. The opening verses of this Psalm read,

> "My God, my God, why have You forsaken Me? Why are You so far from helping me, and from the words of my groaning? O my God, I cry in the daytime, but You do not hear; and in the night season, and am not silent."

Why would Jesus, the man/god of Christianity, be complaining that "God is so far from helping me?" How could God, the first Person of the Trinity, not hear the cries of God, the second Person of the Trinity? To whom is this supposed "God" complaining? The speaker here is moaning that God is not listening to him day and night, and questions his feelings of abandonment when enumerating in the next few verses the times that God did listen and intervene for his ancestors. How can God not understand his own predicament? Applying the words of Psalm 22 to Jesus challenges even the most fertile imagination, and places an enormous strain on Church teachings.

Your fourth paragraph essentially begins your first question. You ask how "a poor carpenter born in Bethlehem of the lineage of David would be able to set circumstances in motion such that the prophets could be made to be fools?" The prophets are never made fools into by the willful errors of mankind. Do you really think that people like Isaiah and Jeremiah were humiliated by the followers of deviant spiritual teachings and idolatry? Was it not these same men of God who pleaded without end that man should not turn away from the radical monotheism they vigorously proclaimed?

Moreover, your question could be asked of all the successful religions of the world.

How is it that Joseph Smith was able to set into motion the fastest growing religion in North America? How is that Mohammed was able to set into motion the fastest growing religion in the world? What about Hinduism with nearly a billion adherents? I am sure the priests of Baal were very proud of what they had set into motion as well. The first Book of Kings chronicles their success among the Jewish people. I could just hear them saying, "Look at what we have set into motion! The entire nation of Israel, with the exception of 7,000 stubborn Jews, is following us. Let's pray for these last 7,000 Jews that their hearts might not be hardened, that the scales over their eyes might be lifted, and they may worship Baal as do the rest of their brethren!"

Furthermore, from the Torah's vantage point, membership in a large successful religion has little to do with truth. On the contrary, the Torah foretold that the Jewish people would remain few in number where they would live among the heathens (Deuteronomy 4:27). In Deuteronomy 7:7, the Bible makes it clear that the intense love that the Almighty has for His people is not because they are great in number, for they are the fewest among the nations. There were many great nations and religions set into motion that became very successful. Their success, however, has little to do with the purity and truth of their worship. In other words, if you belong to a religion that comprises more than a quarter of the world's population, check your theology.

I am further puzzled by your reference to Jesus as being from "the lineage of David" when according to both Matthew and Luke, Jesus was born of a virgin and would therefore be unable to claim the rights to the Davidic line because tribal lineage is traced exclusively through a person's father. This is clearly articulated in Numbers 1:18. If you believe in the virgin birth – and I'm going to assume that you do – how do you proclaim that Jesus was from the line of David when according to your own doctrine Jesus lacked the human father with which to trace his lineage back to King David? According to Christian teachings, Jesus had only a human Jewish mother, not a human Jewish father. This human Jewish father would be essential for anyone to be a legitimate heir to the throne of David, which the real messiah will be.

Your last question has been asked of me by many Christians. It is a well-worn argument popularized by C.S. Lewis, and it seeks to cage a non-Christian into only three possible options regarding who Jesus was. These three options are: Was Jesus A) a liar B) a lunatic C) Lord? This line of questioning, however, is preposterous because there is a far more likely option that you had not offered me from which to choose: D) Jesus never claimed to be the messiah, but rather this was a claim placed in his mouth by others. In fact, option D is consistent with Jewish tradition regarding Jesus, which holds that Jesus never professed to be the messiah, although others would make this claim for him. It may be for this reason that Jesus almost[3] never claims to be the messiah throughout the New Testament.

For the Jewish people, it is completely unimportant who Jesus nor for that matter who Hare Krishna really were. If they are not who Christianity or Hinduism says they are, then it matters little whether they were liars, lunatics, plumbers, or carpenters. Their veneration is to be avoided at all costs.

Yours truly,

Rabbi Tovia Singer

**Footnotes:**

1. Matthew 27:46 and Mark 15:34. In Luke 23:46, Jesus' last statement is "Father, into thy hands I commend my spirit," and in John 19:30, it's simply, "It is finished."

2. In a Christian Bible this verse appears as Psalm 22:1.

3. Exceptions are: Matthew 16:15-17, John 4:26, and 17:3.

# Why Doesn't Judaism Have a King? Where is our Messiah?

## Question:

Dear Rabbi Singer,

I have been a Jewish Christian (Messianic Jew, meshumed, whatever) for 20+ years. I have been attending a Conservative temple recently and my rabbi there lent me your tape series. I listened to about six of the tapes and enjoyed your style and research very much. Thank you for your fair and even-handed presentation of both sides. (By the way, I do use an interlinear bible as you suggested and recommend it to everyone.)

While I am not a staff member of Jews for Jesus, I work with them fairly often as well as folks from Chosen People Ministries. Certainly I refer people to Isaiah 53 and other passages you covered, but I usually start with a different tack that you did not mention (in the six tapes I have heard so far). I wanted to get your opinion on this, or you could simply tell me, "That is on tape 14," for example, and I'd listen to that one.

My approach goes something along the lines of, "If not Jesus, then who?" The main scriptures I use are the promises that David's throne shall never go empty. There are lots of passages that say that, the main ones are Jeremiah 33:17-26 and I Chronicles 17:12-14. So if God promised that, then that must mean that there is a Davidic king right now. So "If not Jesus, then who?" In all fairness, some of the other passages seem to make the promise conditional ("if your sons walk in my ways") except that makes me uncomfortable because of the certainty of the Jeremiah 33 promise. I trust your view on this because you have made a defense of a literal fulfillment of other promises about which you have spoken on your tapes.
Thank you for your time on this.

## Answer:

Thank you for your thoughtful question; it does my heart good to know that you are enjoying the Let's Get Biblical tape series. When I first published this audio program in 1993, it was the Hebrew-Christian, such as yourself, whom I had in mind as its most important audience. Over the years, this audio series has grown and, as a result, many Jews who had joined the Church have since returned to their rich heritage. Please continue to study the Let's Get Biblical series, and I look forward to the day when I can welcome you home.

Although the answer to your question is addressed on the audio program *Who Is the Messiah?*, I believe that the point you raise is also of great interest to our website visitors.

Curiously, the biblical "tack" that you use does not directly seek to prove that Jesus is the messiah. Rather, you present a series of verses from the Jewish scriptures in order to demonstrate that Judaism is a defective religion. As you can well imagine, you have undertaken a formidable task. Although the methodology you employ entails a more roundabout approach to Jewish evangelism, this technique is used widely by missionaries dedicated to converting Jews to Christianity.

In your argument, you maintain that the Bible teaches that there is supposed to be a Davidic ruler sitting on the royal throne at all times. You also point out that although traditional Judaism lacks any ruler from the House of David, Christianity claims Jesus as its king. As a result, you conclude that only the Church, which claims Jesus as its king, can rightly claim spiritual legitimacy because it alone boasts a Davidic ruler as ordained by the Jewish scriptures.

Although this question has been asked of me many times in the past, you are the first to use the words of Jeremiah and I Chronicles to support this argument. In general, this contention is based on a verse found in Genesis. Far be it from me to tell a missionary how to conduct his evangelism; however, the verses you quote do not in any way convey the message that the throne of David is to be occupied without interruption. In fact all of these biblical texts clearly affirm the Davidic covenant -- God has set aside the royal throne for the descendants of King David alone. None of the verses you mentioned, however, teach that there will not be an interruption of David's throne.

For example, you quoted Jeremiah 33:17-26 to support your contention, yet this text does not refer to a period when Jewry is in its diaspora as it is today. On the contrary, these verses are messianic in nature, and the prophecies they contain have yet to be fulfilled. In essence, this prophecy specifically foretells the events that will follow the advent of the messiah, which even in Christian terms has not yet occurred. Christian commentators therefore acknowledge that these verses contain a future prophecy of a millennial kingdom. For example, Charles Caldwell Ryrie writes in his annotation on Jeremiah 33:14-26,

> The King-Messiah will emerge from the Davidic dynasty to rule in the millennial kingdom (see 23:5).[1]

In your reading of Jeremiah's words you made two serious errors that caused you to misconstrue the words of the prophet. Your first mistake was to take these verses out of context. Had you begun your quote one verse earlier, you would have quickly discovered that Jeremiah's words refer to a time in the future, and you would have concluded that this prophecy has no bearing on our time. Jeremiah 33:16 states:

> In those days Judah will be saved, and Jerusalem will dwell safely. This is the name by which she will be called: *'The Lord Our Righteousness.'*

Ponder this: Has Judah been saved? Does Jerusalem dwell safely? We are well aware of the answers to these questions. The children of Israel, therefore, abide without a king because the messiah has not yet come. In fact, the predicament of the people of Judah and the condition of the city of Jerusalem became much worse around the beginning of the first century C.E. than it ever had been before. In fact, if Jesus were the messiah, why isn't "Judah saved, and Jerusalem dwell safely." In fact, I can think of no greater proof that Jesus is not the messiah from the very chapter you quoted.

The prophet Jeremiah is speaking of a future eschatological era when the Jewish people will dwell in their holy city in peace and tranquility. Such a utopian age has not occurred since the glorious days of King Solomon. Only under these utopian circumstances will our anointed king again occupy the throne of David. This will occur, without interruption, only in the messianic age – just as the prophet foretold.[2]

Your second error, however, is far more puzzling because the very verses from which you quoted demonstrate that Jeremiah is speaking of an end-of-days prophecy. Let's take a quick look at Jeremiah 33:17-26:

> "...for thus says the Lord, "David shall never lack a man to sit on the throne of the house of Israel, nor shall the priests, the Levites, lack a man to offer burnt offerings before Me, to kindle grain offerings, and to sacrifice continually." The word of the Lord came to Jeremiah, saying, "Thus says the Lord, 'If you can break My covenant with the day and My covenant with the night, so that there will not be day and night in their season, then My covenant may also be broken with David My servant, so that he shall not have a son to reign on his throne, and with the Levites, the priests, My ministers. As the host of heaven cannot be numbered, nor the sand of the sea measured, so will I multiply the descendants of David My servant and the Levites who minister to Me.'" Moreover the word of the Lord came to Jeremiah, saying, "Have you not considered what these people have spoken, saying, 'The two families which the Lord has chosen, He has also cast them off?' Thus they have despised My people, as if they should no more be a nation before them." Thus says the Lord, "If My covenant is not with day and night, and if I have not appointed the ordinances of heaven and earth, then I will cast away the descendants of Jacob and David My servant, so that I will not take any of his descendants to be rulers over the descendants of Abraham, Isaac, and Jacob; for I will cause their captives to return, and will have mercy on them."

These 10 verses contain some of the most comforting messianic passages in the

Jewish scriptures. None of them, however, speaks of our current era as you suggested; rather, each of these verses foretells of a future messianic age that has yet to come.

You constructed your entire thesis on verse 33:17, which states:

> . . . for thus says the Lord, "David shall never lack a man to sit on the throne of the house of Israel . . .

Yet surprisingly, you ignored the following verse that is a vital part of the same sentence and prophecy. This selective reading of Jeremiah's prophetic message led you to erroneously conclude that the prophet speaks of all of Jewish history. This is a misinterpretation of Jeremiah's prophecy. Verse 18 continues,

> "...nor shall the priests, the Levites, lack a man to offer burnt offerings before Me, to kindle grain offerings, and to sacrifice continually."

As you are well aware, neither a priest nor a Levite has brought a burnt, grain or sacrificial offering in Jerusalem for over 1,900 years. The prophets of Israel foretold that the sacrificial system would be restored in all of its glory at the end of days. At what juncture therefore, will the royal throne of David once again seat a ruler? At the same time that the sacrificial system will be restored to its rightful place in Jerusalem – during the advent of the messiah, and not before.

In fact, in Hosea 3:4-5, the prophet reveals this divine plan of history as he declares that the Jewish people would remain for many days without a king, sacrifice or high priest (ephod) until the messianic age. Hosea 3:4-5 states:

> "...for the children of Israel shall abide many days without king or prince, without sacrifice or sacred pillar, without ephod or teraphim. Afterward the children of Israel shall return and seek the Lord their God and David their king. They shall fear the Lord and His goodness in the latter days."

This prophecy completely undermines your contention that Judaism is deficient because it lacks a Davidic king. The Jewish people are today without a king precisely as Hosea had foretold. Moreover, the Church's claim to have such a king places an enormous strain on Christian theology. Notice how Hosea, just as Jeremiah, connects the future king with future sacrifices as he declares that both of these ecclesiastical functions will only be restored in the "latter days."

In your question you also referred to I Chronicles 17:12-14 to support your contention. I Chronicles 17:12-14 states:

> He is the one who will build a house for Me, and I will establish his throne forever. I will be his Father, and he will be My son. I will never take My love away from him, as I took it away from your predecessor. I will set him over My house and My kingdom forever; his throne will be established forever.

As I mentioned above, I am somewhat surprised by the selection of verses from which you quoted to support your contention. I have yet to come across a Christian who used passages from Jeremiah and I Chronicles to support the claim that there can never be a moment without a king reigning on the throne of David. Missionaries typically use Genesis 49:10 to support this well-known argument. Although this text may appear at first glance to be somewhat more ambiguous than the scriptures you used, Christians zealously employ this verse to argue that the Torah states that the reign of Davidic kings will continue without interruption. Genesis 49:10 reads:

> "The scepter shall not depart from Judah, Nor a lawgiver from between his feet, Until Shiloh comes..."

What is the meaning of the uncommon Hebrew word "*Shiloh*"? Although there is some disagreement over the definition of this obscure word, there is a wide consensus among Jews and Christians that *Shiloh* is an uncommon reference to the messiah. Bear in mind, this verse is part of the blessing that Jacob bestowed on his son Judah, the ancestor of King David. Using Genesis 49:10, Christians argue that Jacob is revealing that the "scepter," the symbol of kingship, will never depart from the tribe of Judah even until the End of Days. Pointing to the fact that the Jewish people maintain that there is no Davidic king today, missionaries argue that Judaism is a defective and blinding religion that has turned its back on Jesus, king of the Jews.

Although it appears as though the Church has made a serious charge against the Jewish faith, this contention is born out of Christendom's inability to grasp one of the most important covenants in the Bible. The notion that the reign of a Davidic king will continue uninterrupted is unknown to the Jewish scriptures. This Christian creed has come about as the result of a skewed understanding of Jacob's blessing and a misinterpretation of a vital promise made by God to King David. In all of the verses that you quoted, the Bible declares that the legitimate royal throne of the Jewish people will never be occupied by anyone other than a member of the tribe of Judah and the House of David. I Chronicles 17:12-142 is therefore, one of the most well-known passages in the Jewish scriptures, because it contains God's everlasting covenant with King David – the irrevocable promise that the throne would never depart from his dynasty until the end of time.

Yet how can we be confident that this is the correct interpretation of the scripture's message? How can we know with certainty that the Bible is not suggesting that there would never be an interruption of a Davidic king to sit on the throne at every moment throughout history, as missionaries insist?

The answer is simple. Even the Church concedes that there was no king on the throne of David for five centuries! In other words, missionaries acknowledge that from the time the Babylonians removed King Zedekiah from his throne and destroyed the first Temple, there has been no king since who reigned over the Jewish people who was a descendant of the House of David. If the Christian rendering of these prophecies is correct, why was there no king from the House of David who ruled during those 500 years? No further evidence is necessary to demonstrate that the Church's interpretation of Genesis 49:10 and I Chronicles 17:12-14 is erroneous.

There is, however, a far more serious problem with which missionaries must contend with regarding their claim that Jesus was a direct descendant from the House of David. According to Christian teachings, Jesus was born of a virgin. Although this assertion in the New Testament provides an important record of pagan influences on first century of Christianity, it also deals a devastating blow to the Church's claim that Jesus is the messiah from the lineage of King David.

By insisting that Jesus was born of a virgin, Christendom therefore concedes that Jesus lacked the human Jewish father necessary to trace his lineage back to King David and the tribe of Judah. This patrilineal connection to the Davidic dynasty is vital for any claimant to the throne of David, because the lineage of the mother is irrelevant in this regard. The Torah clearly states that tribal affiliation is traced exclusively through the father.

> They assembled the entire congregation together on the first day of the second month, and they declared their pedigrees after their families, by the house of their **fathers**..." (Numbers 1:18)

Moreover, the author of the Book of Hebrews' strange assertion that Jesus was also a high priest further weakens the Church's claim that Jesus is eligible to rule as a

Davidic king. For example, the New Testament author writes:

> Therefore, holy brothers, who share in the heavenly calling, fix your thoughts on Jesus, the apostle and high priest whom we confess (Hebrews 3:1).
>
> Seeing then that we have a great high priest who has passed through the heavens, Jesus the Son of God, let us hold fast our confession (Hebrews 4:14).

This stunning claim that Jesus was high priest further undermines the church's claim that Jesus was a Davidic king. Simply put, the same man can never be both high priest and king. The high priest must be a descendant of Aaron (the brother of Moses), who was from the tribe of Levi. A Davidic king, on the other hand, has to trace his lineage from the House of David, descended from the tribe of Judah. It is impossible for the same person to be a descendant from both the tribes of Levi and Judah.

It isn't difficult to understand why the Book of Hebrews would repeatedly maintain that Jesus served as high priest – the notion that Jesus provided the ultimate sin sacrifice for the human race was vital to the core theology of this Pauline author. This astonishing claim, however, completely sabotages the missionary contention that Jesus was eligible to sit on David's throne.

There is no mystery as to how Christianity could find itself in this self-inflicted theological wound. During the first century, the Church had endured a severe theological transition. In its earliest years, the founders of Christianity sought out Jews to join their young movement. As the first century began to draw to a close, however, Christendom recognized that the Jewish people were by and large unimpressed with their message. The Church understood that if Christianity was going to flourish, they needed to attract converts from heathen communities that dotted the Fertile Crescent. Although the Church's swift adaptation at this crucial juncture was highly successful, it would have devastating consequences for the theological complexion of this once-Jewish heresy.

Quite rapidly, Christendom inculcated pagan teachings that were widely familiar to the citizens of the Roman Empire. Virtually all of the god-men and divine saviors of Persia, the Far East, North Africa, and Rome were born to a virgin mother.[3] As a result, the notion that Jesus was also born of a virgin quickly became well ensconced in the teachings of the very young Christian church.

Christianity would eventually import many other notable pagan beliefs into its teachings. Yet many of these creeds, such as the doctrine of the Trinity, would take a few more centuries and numerous political struggles until they were firmly a part of church orthodoxy. The belief that Jesus was born of a virgin, on the other hand, was adopted by the church so early that the New Testament was still being fashioned when it was embraced by first century Christians.

Christendom paid no small price for becoming the repository of pagan lore. The consequences for adopting the doctrine of the virgin birth created a theological disaster from which the Church has never recovered and rendered every royal and priestly claim it has made for Jesus impossible.

Sincerely yours,

Rabbi Tovia Singer

**Footnotes:**

1. Charles Caldwell Ryrie, *The Ryrie Study Bible* (Dallas Theological Seminary), Chicago: Moody Press, 1978, p. 1175.

2. See also II Samuel 7:12-16.

3. See accounts of Romulus, Apollonius of Tyana, Drusilla, Claudius, Dionysus-Bacchus, Tammuz, Mithra, Osiris, Krishna, and Buddha.

# Who is Satan?

## Question:

Dear Rabbi Singer:

When you were in Buffalo, NY in November of '96, during the extended question and answer time, you were asked your view on angels and specifically about Satan. I was astounded at your answer and was more astounded that the other rabbis present did not step into the discussion.

In your explanation of Satan and other fallen angels you attributed the creation of evil to G-d thus making Him responsible for evil. There are at least 87 references to G-d's holiness in Leviticus alone! In 11:44 G-d says, "I AM HOLY." Is not holiness the absence of sin? There are many scriptures to prove that G-d hates sin (evil), that He cannot tolerate evil in His presence. How, then, can you attribute evil to G-d? I am interested in the Biblical support for your statement.

I have a fair understanding of Judaism and have found nothing in all of my reading to support your view as traditional.

Awaiting your reply.

A seeker after truth

## Answer:

The rabbis to whom you made reference have spent their entire lives immersed in the study of the Jewish scriptures as well as other sacred literature and were, therefore, not "astounded" by the Judaism that was taught in Buffalo that evening, as you were.

Why weren't the rabbis stunned by these Jewish teachings on Satan? The answer is because according to the Hebrew Scriptures, the Almighty, Himself, placed both good and the evil into the world, in order that mankind would have the opportunity to exercise free will. Deuteronomy 30:15 states:

> "See, I [God] have set before thee this day life and good, and death and evil."

In Isaiah 45:7, the prophet describes God's creation plan when he reports the following:

> "I form the light, and create darkness; I make peace, and create evil;
> I the Lord do all these things."

I did not invent these verses, nor did I tamper with them. In fact, the Bible I used in the above quotations is the King James Version, which is a translation that could hardly be construed as friendly to the Jewish faith.

These edifying verses underscore the fundamental Hebrew biblical teaching of the Almighty's divine sovereign plan, which provides that every searching soul must confront evil, as well as good, in order to remain vigilant in ones personal search for perfect spiritual balance. The Almighty's gift of free will to humanity is what separates us from His other creations. For those committed to attaining a higher spiritual existence, the struggle towards living a life of virtue is only possible with the existence evil, which serves as a sort of spiritual and behavioral barometer.

The two verses, Isaiah 45:7 and Deuteronomy 30:15, however, pose a serious theological problem for Christians who maintain that God did not create Satan, the angel of evil. According to Christian doctrine, as you suggest in your question, Satan was the highest-ranking angel who, through his own act of spiritual defiance and outright disobedience, became the chief adversary and slanderer of God and the embodiment of evil in this world. In Christian theology God never created evil; He is only the author of righteousness and perfection, as you maintained in your question. Therefore, God could never create something as sinister as the devil himself. Rather, Satan's unyielding wickedness is the result of his own spiritual rebellion.

Although this well-known Christian doctrine has much in common with the pagan Zoroastrian Persian dualism from which it spawned, it is completely alien to the teachings of the Jewish scriptures. In fact, this Christian notion that Satan, in an act of outright defiance, ceased to function as God had intended him to, suggests that God created something imperfect or defective.

For the Jewish faith, Satan's purpose in seducing man away from God poses no problem because Satan is only an agent of God. As a servant of the Almighty, Satan faithfully carries out the divine will of his Creator as he does in all his tasks.

Satan is one of the many angels mentioned in the Bible. It is worth noting that the Hebrew word for angel is *malach*, meaning "messenger." The same is true for the English word angel, derived from the Greek word *angelos*, which also means "messenger." Throughout the Bible, an angel is a messenger of God who carries out the divine will of the Almighty. There is not one example in the Jewish scriptures where any angel, Satan included, who ever opposes God's will.

In no part of the Bible is this more evident than in the Book of Job. In the first chapter of Job, Satan appears with other angels before God and suggests that Job's steadfast faithfulness would not withstand personal pain and utter destitution. Satan then requests from God the chance to test Job's virtue. The Almighty grants this request, but He meticulously outlines for Satan what he may and may not do when putting Job to the test. Satan obediently follows his Creator's instructions. Job is immediately put to the test and, by the third chapter, begins to struggle. He questions his Maker as to why he was created and, in a moment of despair, wishes aloud that he had perished in his mother's womb. Still, by the end of this unparalleled biblical narrative, Job's virtue prevails over Satan's unyielding torment.

While in Christian terms Job's personal spiritual triumph is a theological impossibility, in Jewish terms it stands out as the embodiment of God's salvation program for mankind. In Deuteronomy 30:15, the Torah attests to this principle and in Isaiah 45:7, the prophet echoes this message when he declares that the Almighty Himself creates evil.

This biblical principle, however, was apparently too problematic for the Christian translators of the fundamentalist New International Version Bible. They clearly grasped that a Bible, which asserts that God creates evil, calls into question one of Christendom's most cherished teachings on salvation. How can the church insist that man is totally depraved when his God placed him in a world where he is free to choose good over evil? How can the Church hold to a doctrine of election or predestination when free will is man's to express? How can Christians maintain that God did not create evil when the Jewish scriptures clearly state otherwise?

Understandably, the NIV translators saw fit to alter the prophet's words by rendering the offensive Hebrew word rah as "disaster" instead of correctly translating it as "bad" or "evil." The NIV Bible therefore mistranslates Isaiah 45:7 to read:

> "I form the light and create darkness, I bring prosperity and create disaster; I, the Lord, do all these things."

The word "disaster" inserted by the NIV is so ambiguous that the uninformed reader would easily come to the conclusion that it refers to such things as earthquakes and hurricanes. This skewed understanding created by the NIV mistranslation effectively conceals Isaiah's original message. As mentioned above, the King James Version correctly translates this verse and renders the Hebrew word רָע *(rah)* as "evil."

One final point is in order. Christians often point to Isaiah 14:12 as a biblical reference to support their teachings of the final and complete downfall of Satan, which brings to an end the long and otherwise successful career of this fallen angel. Isaiah 14:12 states:

> "How you are fallen from heaven, O morning star! You have been cut down to the ground, you who weakened the nations!"

Christians argue that Isaiah's mention of the fallen "morning star" refers to the ultimate demise of Satan at the end of time, when he will finally be cast into an eternal lake of fire, as articulated in the twentieth chapter of the Book of Revelations.

There are, however, two serious problems with this assertion. First, if Christians maintain that the "morning star" is a reference to Satan, how do they explain

Revelation 22:16 where Jesus is called the "morning star" as well? Secondly, a cursory reading of the fourteenth chapter of Isaiah reveals that the "morning star" spoken of in Isaiah 14:12 is referring to Nebuchadnessar, the wicked King of Babylon, and not to Satan. The prophet explicitly names the king of Babylon as the subject of the prophecy.

> "That thou shall take up this proverb against the king of Babylon, and say, 'How hath the oppressor ceased, the golden city ceased!'" (Isaiah 14:4)

Throughout this chapter and the preceding chapter of Isaiah, the prophet foretells the rise and fall of this arrogant king who would use his unbridled power to plunder Jerusalem and destroy its Temple but, ultimately, would suffer a cataclysmic downfall. In 14:12, Nebuchadnezzar is compared to the planet Venus whose light is still visible in the morning, yet vanishes with the rise of the sun. Like the light of Venus, Nebuchadnezzar's reign shone brilliantly for a short time, yet, as the prophets foretold, it was eventually overshadowed by the nation of Israel whose light endured and outlived this arrogant nation who tormented and exiled her.

Yours,

Rabbi Tovia Singer

# Is There an Accurate Translation of the Jewish Scriptures?

## Question:

I am a Reform Jew and I occasionally find myself in debates online with Evangelical Christians about the nature of the Bible, and what is actually being said. Your site has become a very valuable resource for me, and I am interested in studying the Bible more closely. Since there are so many badly, or intentionally mistranslated versions of the Bible out there, I was wondering if you could tell me what you feel the most accurate English translation of the original Hebrew is?

## Answer:

Because the Hebrew and English language belongs to two different language families, accurately rendering the Jewish scriptures into the English language is never an easy task, and a literal word-for-word English translation would produce a Bible that would be difficult to read. A good translation must be accurate and readable – that is, it must reliably replicate the meaning of the text without sacrificing its readability.

The best translation of the Jewish scriptures is the Judaica Press Tanach series.

Rabbi Avraham J. Rosenberg has provided in his lucid translation a remarkably accurate rendition of the Jewish scriptures. It comes in about 30 volumes and it not only contains a translation of the *Messoretic* text, but of the great Jewish commentators as well. It will cost you a few hundred *shekalim* for the whole set, but it is a life-long investment and well worth the price.

Chabad's website has made the entire Judaica Press Tanach available free online at: http://www.chabad.org/library/bible_cdo/aid/63255/jewish/The-Bible-with-Rashi.htm

Yours,

Rabbi Tovia Singer

# But Look at How Believing in Jesus Changed My Life!

## Question:

Dear Rabbi Singer,

I am certain that the question will surface somewhere in this general commentary I am making. I hope you will bear with me until the question does arise.

For one who has been a Christian all his life, I find your commentaries very compelling and thought provoking, but, at times, dismaying, while there have always been questions in my mind inherent to matters of truth concerning the Gospels, and the remainder of the New Testament. The question is, as Pilate said it, What is truth? Everyone has a different version, and all claim their particular version to be the final word. Regarding your commentaries, I do not find anything that I would consider to be misleading or mean-spirited in your answers to your reader's questions when you criticize Christianity, but it is obvious to me that you base practically your entire criticism on legalism.

Jesus Christ had much to say about the legalism of the scribes and Pharisees in the context of how it applied to their religious worship. The one thing you seem to miss is that much of the teachings of Jesus related to the depth of the love of the individual towards God. I can understand how you can use legalism to apparently refute many of the claims of Christianity, so I believe my question is: How do you refute the almost unbelievable change in the character and personality of people after they are converted to Christ?

I have seen this again and again, so I believe my observations are, at least, reasonable. I have seen this change continue throughout lifetimes. What you seem to observe as a zeal to convert others is actually a zeal to help others, and of course to witness to that person for Christ. I am not aware of any pressure to convert. The basic premise is to show other people the change in your life and how it came about. As much as I am swayed by your legal criticism, I cannot deny the knowledge of Christ in my being, even when I sin. Surely, the God of all mankind would preempt a false religion, proclaimed in His name, which would lead millions from the true path and towards damnation. If this is not the case, then the existence of man on this world appears quite pointless.

Thanks for your time.

## Answer:

Because your letter touches on an intangible condition rooted in the heart of the believer, I am certain that many visitors to our website will not fully grasp the importance of your main question. It would not be an overstatement to say that your thoughtful letter contains one of the most important questions that could be asked of me.

Ever since I began working to help Jews return to Judaism, I have received numerous letters and listened to many stories from people like you, which are filled with personal anecdotes recounting how their lives were miraculously changed as a result of their newfound faith. Many of the accounts of these new believers describe how their drug addiction and alcoholism inexplicably ceased. Recently, I received a letter from a middle-aged Jewish woman who maintained that as a result of her conversion to Mormonism, her festering illnesses were miraculously cured. Following a recent lecture, a young man vividly recalled how his plaguing depression had lifted soon after he converted to the Catholic Church. For him, the euphoria that had now replaced his nagging bouts of depression bore testimony to the validity of the teachings of Roman Catholicism.

While I was speaking in Southern California a number of years ago, I met four young men who were members of Hare Krishna. It wasn't a planned meeting, we just happened to strike up a conversation as we were crossing the same busy street in Los Angeles. To my utter shock, three of these lost souls were Jews. As I listened attentively to the testimonials of these oddly dressed fellows, each of them carefully described how their newfound religion had transformed their lives. They joyfully spoke of their joining this eastern sect, and I could sense the elation and inner peace they felt. They were certain that what they believed was true and it was quite apparent that they were more spiritual now than they had ever been in their former lives.

When considered individually, such moving accounts seem quite impressive. Once these remarkable testimonials are examined as part of a larger pattern, however, they present us with a serious theological problem. Although each of these extraordinary stories may appear to the novice as evidence of the validity of their newly acquired faith, the fact remains that these variant religions cannot all be valid. When it comes to spiritual experiences and miraculous occurrences, things get very messy. The realm of faith would be very tidy if only one religion produced life-altering transformations and miraculous occurrences. To the dismay of the fervid believer, however, this may be the most disorganized arena of organized religion. In fact, the life-changing experience that you describe in your letter is a universal phenomenon produced by virtually all faiths. People from just about every religion claim an "almost unbelievable change in the character and personality" of those whom they touch, regardless of the truth of the doctrines they preach. In essence, there is no relationship between spiritual transformation that occurs in the heart of the faithful believer and the spiritual truth which he espouses.

Bear in mind, our planet is brimming with world religions such as Hinduism, Buddhism, and Islam, each of which boast many hundreds of millions of adherents. The multitudes of these devout believers, in their diverse faiths, all remarkably speak of the very same "character and personality" transformation that you describe within the context of your religion – Christianity. Yet, as we pay careful attention to their personal testimonials, which movingly recount how their religious faith has transformed them, it seems as if they all somehow belong to the same religion – their testimonials all breathe with the experience of a connection with the divine.

According to your doctrinal barometer, however, billions of these devoted faithful are lost souls merely following a "false religion." Realize, therefore, that their startling religious experiences cannot possibly speak of the validity of their theology. For example, Hinduism and Islam have radically different teachings on the nature of God, yet, how is it that Hindus, Christians, Mormons, and Muslims all experience this profound religious conversion, which you describe? This question becomes particularly puzzling when we consider your implied assertion that spiritual transformation among the faithful will point us in the direction of spiritual truth. All of these religions cannot possibly be transmitting truth; nevertheless, each of them does ignite profound spiritual changes within the character and personality of their devoted masses.

The question that therefore comes to mind is, why would God allow all religions, regardless of the theological untruths they espouse, to ignite a spiritual passion within the heart of the believer? The Bible contains a record of many individuals and nations who possessed fervent devotion to their idolatry. Nonetheless, their spiritual adultery is condemned as an utter abomination, regardless of the spirituality and transformation they derived. Why would the Almighty permit religions whose fundamental teachings have no basis in truth to produce life-transforming experiences and miraculous occurrences in the lives of their devout followers?

The answer is found in the beginning of Deuteronomy, where the Torah addresses this dilemma in an even more startling scenario. In Deuteronomy 13:1-2, the Bible raises the question of what to do when a "prophet" offers to show a miracle in order to lend credibility to his message. How are we to respond if, in fact, the promised miracle comes to pass just as he predicted? Should we then follow this "prophet" even if he encourages us to worship other gods which are unknown to our people? "You must not listen to the words of that prophet or dreamer," the Torah emphatically declares. God did not send him.

Why would the Almighty permit religions and prophets who teach unsavory doctrines to produce spiritual transformations and miraculous events? The answer lies in the verses that follow.

> The Lord your God is testing you to find out whether you love Him with all your heart and with all your soul. It is the Lord your God you must follow, and Him you must revere. Keep His commands and obey Him; serve Him and hold fast to Him. (Deuteronomy 13:3-4)

God is truly testing you with the experiences and observations you have had and made. This is your choice in a world where free will hangs in perfect balance. Will you worship the God of Israel alone or turn to gods whom the nation of Israel has not known? If we lived in a world where only one religion could produce spirituality and miraculous life-altering experiences, the precious balance of free will could not exist.

In the 18th chapter of I Kings, the Bible relates that when Elijah had challenged 450 priests of Baal to bring a sacrifice to their gods and see if their offering would be miraculously accepted with fire, there was a peculiar spectacle which followed. It seemed as though there was no doubt in the minds of these pagan worshipers that Baal would hear their supplications and consume their bullock with a heavenly fire. The Bible vividly recounts how they enthusiastically entreated Baal and prayed fervidly for a miracle all day. They even climbed on top of the altar and began to prance beside their sacrifice, but when that failed to secure a response from their gods, with frantic zeal they used knives and lancets to slice away flesh from their bodies. These prophets of Baal were on fire for their gods. Regardless of their unyielding zeal for their idols, they were commanded to turn away from these abominations.

In fact, the prophet Jeremiah warns us that the spirituality gained from following false prophets and corrupt teachers may become so encompassing and overwhelming that one may begin to have dreams regarding these prophets. Jeremiah concludes,

> . . . for thus says the Lord of hosts, the God of Israel, "Do not let your prophets and your diviners who are in your midst deceive you, nor listen to your dreams which you cause to be dreamed; for they prophesy falsely to you in My name. I have not sent them, says the Lord" (Jeremiah 29:8-9).

Jeremiah's message is clear. If the prophet's message has so permeated your being to the point that you are having dreams of these false prophets and their false teachings, you alone are the one who is responsible for these improper apparitions. God has not sent them.

Furthermore, at the very end of your question, you insist that "the God of all mankind would preempt a false religion in His name, which would lead millions from the true path, and towards damnation." This assertion is incorrect; for if your conclusion were accurate, why do these masses of spiritually blind believers make such deplorable choices about their religious affiliations? Why hasn't God in fact "preempted" these false religions? Why is Islam the fastest growing religion in the world when your Christianity is supposedly the only life-transforming truth? In essence, how could so many be so wrong about something so crucial as religion when, according to your reckoning, the Almighty would never "lead millions" away from His true path?

A careful reading of the Bible reveals that, in fact, God does not lead mankind away from His true path. This alone is an individual decision, and it will forever remain Man's domain. Your Creator never removed that decision from your grasp. As the Torah declares in Deuteronomy 30:15-19:

> See, I have set before you today life and good, death and evil, in that I command you today to love the Lord your God, to walk in His ways, and to keep His commandments, His statutes, and His judgments, that you may live and multiply; and the Lord your God will bless you in the land which you go to possess. If, though, your heart turns away so that you do not hear, and are drawn away, and worship other gods and serve them, I announce to you today that you shall surely perish; you shall not prolong your days in the land which you cross over the Jordan to go in and possess. I call heaven and earth as witnesses against you today, that I have set before you life and death, the blessing and the curse; therefore choose life, that both you and your descendants may live.

God permits man to become enraptured with false religions for the same reason He permits a married man to be attracted to women other than his wife. Free will is within your grasp. If this ordained tender balance of free will were ever compromised, virtue would remain beyond the reach of mankind. Don't, though, look to spirituality and miraculous life-changing events as your guide to truth in faith. Look to the Bible alone for this eternal instruction. Once you have committed your life to truth in the God of Israel, joyously take part in the spiritual food it provides. Never permit spiritual expressions to become your barometer for truth. Your foundation must be the Jewish scriptures.

Best wishes for a happy and healthy New Year.

Very sincerely yours,

Rabbi Tovia Singer

# What is a Former Christian Minister To Do? Convert?

## Question:

Shalom my friend,

I am an ordained minister who has been studying the Hebrew roots of Christianity for around 10 years. Over time I have been forced to "unlearn" much of what I inherited and learned at higher levels of education. The bottom line is that much of Christianity is a false faith which detracts from the true faith given to all mankind at Sinai: Biblical Judaism.

I am questioning converting. It seems to me that as a god-fearer I have the best of both worlds. Let me explain. Understanding the Laws of Noah, and then going on to choose those things that please Hashem and taking hold of His covenant in Isaiah 56 by acquiring other mitzvoth and incorporating them into my life... is this not a better position for me to be in than full conversion where I would then be obligated to fulfill all the 613? You see where I live there is not a Jewish community close which could support me. Buying foods and meats killed in a kosher manner, observing regulations of travel on the Sabbath, etc... these seem to be so difficult living in a Gentile society today which is blind to Torah. Can you advise for I value your comments very much.

Blessing on you and your family I pray. Shalom.

## Answer:

You are raising an important question which is asked of me almost daily. What should a former Christian do when he discovers that the Almighty's salvation program has never changed, and the path to express His eternal truth is still uniquely realized within the Jewish faith? This is a dilemma which confronts so many seeking souls who have emerged from the Church and have embarked on the very same spiritual journey you have.

Remember that you were created in the image of God and should walk in the path of the righteous gentile. This journey is realized by your commitment to observe the seven laws of Noah. There are thousands of men and women with your religious background who have come to proudly identify as a *Noachide*, or *B'nai Noah* (children of Noah). They diligently remain on this sacred path of observance of the seven Noachide laws, which will ultimately bring each of them into the presence of God for all eternity.

Be mindful that as you observe these seven *mitzvoth*, do not say in your heart, "I am performing these commandments because they make sense to my intellect and understanding." Rather, proclaim that you are fulfilling them because the God of Israel commanded you to keep them.

The seven Noachide commandments are:

1) The prohibition of idolatry
2) The prohibition of blasphemy
3) The prohibition of murder
4) The prohibition of theft
5) The prohibition of immoral sexual relations
6) The prohibition of eating the limb of a living animal
7) The commandment to establish courts to enforce the commandments

It is a mistake to suppose that since the children of Israel have 613 commandments and the children of Noah have seven commandments, that the ratio of spiritual worth of a gentile to a Jew is proportionally 7 to 613.

In reality, the seven *Noachide* laws are general categories of commandments, each containing many components and details, whereas the 613 commandments of the Torah are precise, each relating to one basic detail of the law of the Torah. Therefore, the numerical disparity in no way reflects the relative spiritual worth of the two systems of commandments.

Because of their profound spiritual connection to the nation of Israel, many righteous gentiles symbolically commemorate some of the Jewish festivals. For example, it is not uncommon for *B'nai Noah* to in some way celebrate the holiday of Rosh Hashanah, the Jewish New Year and Day of Judgment. This festival is of particular interest to the righteous gentile because God judges all of mankind on that day – the Jew as well as the gentile. Rosh Hashanah is also the day Adam, the first man, was created by God. Just as all mankind is descended from Adam, we are all also descendants from Noah.

The holiday of *Shevuoth* (the Festival of Weeks) is also of unique interest to the *Noachide* because the descendants of Noah received their commandments at that time as well. When the evening of *Shevuoth* arrives, righteous gentiles often spend the entire night contemplating the momentous occasion of the giving of the Torah to the children of Israel at Mt. Sinai. In essence, the affinity that the truly righteous gentile feels for the Jewish people ignites within his soul a fervent desire to cling to the God of Israel and His people.

Bear in mind though, whichever observances *B'nai Noah* choose to keep, they must not keep the Shabbat according to Jewish Law, for the observance of the Shabbat was set aside for the Jewish people alone.

> 16 The children of Israel shall keep the Sabbath, to observe the Sabbath throughout their generations, for an eternal covenant. 17 It is a sign between Me and the children of Israel for ever; for in six days the Lord made heaven and earth, and on the seventh day He ceased from work and rested. (Exodus 31:16-17)

There are gentiles, however, whose experience with the children of Israel runs much deeper than a feeling of profound affection for the Jew and his Torah. These individuals, throughout their lives, have often felt a longing and desire to be a part of the Jewish people. In fact, one middle aged woman recently confided in me that she inexplicably knew she was Jewish for as long as she could remember. This is not an uncommon phenomenon. Because the vast majority of *B'nai Noah* were brought up within the Christian religion, their attachment to the nation of Israel has always been more than just a passing interest or fascination.

Since in its most primitive beginnings, Christianity began as a heresy of Judaism, "Jews" play more than an incidental role in the Church. Nor is the role a flattering one, yet the mere mention of the Jew is enough to ignite a fervid and inquisitive spark within the soul of the destined convert. The discussion about the nation of Israel may have occurred at home, or even taken place in church or Sunday school. Nevertheless, this simple discussion generates an almost unbridled enchantment with the Jewish people. These are the gentiles who experience an irresistible calling to convert to Judaism.

Ironically, there are some gentiles who have this undeniable yearning to somehow connect to the Jewish people and mistakenly get caught up in the Messianic movement. When at first they hear about Christians who worship using Jewish symbols and liturgy, they become very excited. They imagine that this is precisely what they were looking for. They believe that they can finally express their desire to associate with Judaism by attending Messianic congregations. Once they get involved, however, they quickly realize that a Messianic "synagogue" is nothing more than an evangelical church deceptively designed to appear as a synagogue in order to lure those Jews who might otherwise resist the Christian trappings of a Church. They eventually grasp that the Messianic movement exists in order to generate the very opposite effect to which they wish to be a part. They realize that this modern movement seeks to make Jews into Christians, using nefarious means. In essence, they conclude quite correctly that the Messianic movement is thoroughly Christian, and look elsewhere for authentic expressions of Judaism.

The decision to convert to the Jewish faith is quite different than the commitment to continue as a *B'nai Noah*. For whereas the *Noachide* has embraced the faith of the Jewish people alone, the righteous convert, on the other hand, has in every manner become part of the Jewish people – sharing in full their Torah, as well as their wondrous history and eternal destiny.

The distinction between the righteous convert to Judaism and the Noachide is often difficult for Christians to comprehend. For whereas Christianity and Islam are both religions of creed alone, Judaism comprises both a faith and a distinct peoplehood. For example, if a Christian declares that he does not believe in Jesus, is he still a Christian? Or if a Moslem confesses that he does not trust in the prophet Mohammed, is he still a Moslem? Certainly not. On the other hand, if a Jew declares that he doesn't believe in God, or he has embraced the alien deities of surrounding peoples such as Hare Krishna or Jesus, is he still a Jew? Yes, a sinner who is called by the prophets to repent. Paradoxically, the word religion appears nowhere throughout the Bible. The Jewish people are referred to as an *"Am,"* a nation.

There exists a Jewish tradition or belief, which suspects that many of those unique individuals who genuinely yearn to convert to Judaism are actually gentiles who somehow possess a Jewish soul, and therefore tirelessly cries out to God for clarity of his or her true identity.

The request of a gentile to convert to Judaism is never taken lightly by a rabbi. On the contrary, this petition is considered with the utmost concern and apprehension. The rabbi or scholar who is asked to perform a conversion will in almost all situations repeatedly attempt to dissuade the petitioner from going on with his conversion and send the potential convert away. This effort of dissuasion will continue throughout the conversion process. For once a gentile has converted to Judaism, there is no going back. There can be no undoing of this eternal decision. Once the conversion has occurred, the convert is forever a Jew.

Bear in mind that there is no sin for a gentile to eat pork or violate the Sabbath. Once the conversion ceremony is completed, however, the Jew by choice is required to observe all 613 commandments as any other Jew. If a convert backslides and returns to his former heathen ways, the conversion that he has endured has now become his spiritual affliction. In a sense, he would have been far better off had he not converted, for before his conversion these iniquitous acts were not considered sinful, but as a Jew they are. Rabbis are extremely sensitive to this and carefully screen a potential convert.

We see this principle in the Bible as well. When Ruth entreated her mother-in-law, Naomi to return with her to the land of Israel and join the Jewish people, Naomi made three attempts to dissuade her daughter-in-law. Only after Naomi realized that Ruth was unshakable in her commitment to return did Naomi relent and bring her to her home in Bethlehem (Ruth 1:8-18). Ruth went on to become one of the most extraordinary women in Jewish history, and was the grandmother of King David.

May the Merciful One guide you on your own sacred path.

Sincerely yours,

Rabbi Tovia Singer

# Why did the Chief Rabbi of Rome Convert to Catholicism?

## Question:

I understand that the chief Rabbi of Rome, Rabbi Israel Zolli was a devout and serious Orthodox Jew as well as a learned scholar of the almud and of Semitic literature. Rabbi Israel Zolli was the Chief Rabbi of Trieste for many years (35, I think) before coming to Rome. I believe that there were several rabbis in his family. Would it not be the case that he knew about the arguments you present here with reference to the evidence on whether or not J.C. was the Messiah? Do you disagree with those who say that he converted to Roman Catholicism because he believed that Roman Catholicism is the fulfillment of Judaism and that J.C. was the Messiah? Do you have an opinion on why he converted to Roman Catholicism, and if you have an opinion on it, are you willing to share it?

Thank you.

## Answer:

Although Pope Pius XII – Hitler's Pope –took great pride in baptizing the former chief rabbi of Rome, the Catholic Church could hardly boast of "Zolli" to be a pious convert. This is because Rabbi Israel Zoller's apostasy to Catholicism had little to do with any spiritual conviction or theological satisfaction he found in the Roman church. Rather, it was the result of his ostracism and banishment after the Holocaust by the survivors of the Italian Jewish community, whom he callously abandoned during the war when he hid in the Vatican while fleeing the Nazis.

The following article, which appears in the Encyclopedia Judaica, discusses the subject of Rabbi Zoller's baptism.

> **Zoller (Zolli), Israel** (1881-1956), rabbi and apostate. Born in Brody, Galicia, Zoller spent a great part of his life in Italy. He was chief rabbi of Trieste after World War I, professor of Hebrew at the University of Padua from 1927 to 1938, and, from 1939, chief rabbi of Rome. At the beginning of September 1943, when the Germans entered Rome, he abandoned the community and took refuge in the Vatican. At the end of the hostilities he reappeared to assume his position as rabbi, but was rejected by the community because of his villainous behavior at the time when his community faced their greatest danger. On February 14, 1945, he converted to Catholicism, taking the name of Eugenio Maria (in homage to Pope Pius XII) and returned to the Vatican. In 1949 he was professor of Semitic epigraphy and Hebrew at the University of Rome. He was the author of a large number of works, especially of biblical interpretation, Jewish history, liturgy, and *talmudic* literature. Among his works are *Israele* ("Israel," 1935), *L'ebraismo* ("Judaism," 1953), and autobiographical reflections entitled *Before the Dawn* (1954). His translation of the tractate *Berakhot* was published by a Catholic publishing house (1968). Bibliography: L.I. Newman, A "Chief Rabbi" of Rome Becomes a Catholic (1945). *Encyclopedia Judaica*, Vol. 16, Page 1217.

Christians should not waste their time searching for trophies in the annals of history for "Orthodox Jews" who abandoned their faith in search of a showpieces for the Church. It will not take very long for them to find many "Orthodox Jews" who became Moslems and pagans; and it was not uncommon for these defectors to become leaders in their newfound religions. The Bible is filled with such nefarious opportunists who abandoned their faith in the one God of Israel and sold out the Jewish people in the process. In fact, there was a wicked king who was raised in an Orthodox home who sat on the throne of David for more than a half-century who also abandoned his Jewish faith. His name was King Manasseh the son of King Hezekiah. One could never hope to grow up in a more Orthodox home than Manasseh, whose father was a devout and righteous man. Yet, in spite of his Orthodox Jewish upbringing, this young man grew up to become the most evil king that had ever ruled the Jewish nation.

The Bible testifies that Manasseh worshiped Baal with great zeal, and encouraged the Jewish people to do likewise. Moreover, Manasseh was a far more sincere apostate than Israel Zoller. Manasseh certainly did not worship profane idols in order to escape persecution. Does this mean that the Jewish people should follow suit? Should the apostasy of one Jew, no matter how prestigious a position he holds among the nation of Israel, be a signal to others to turn their backs on their Creator as well?

The question that comes to mind is how can an intelligent, well-informed Jew abandon his faith? Shouldn't we anticipate that clever and erudite Jews would consistently make the correct spiritual choices in life? How is it that we find bright and knowledgeable people making disastrous decisions that have eternal consequences?

The answer is that emotions have no IQ. The lusts of the heart have no intelligence. The prophet Jeremiah therefore declared that, "The heart is deceitful above all things, and desperately wicked; who can know it" (Jeremiah 17:9)? In Numbers 15:37-39, the Torah commands the nation of Israel to wear *tzitsis* (fringes) on the corners of our garments so that "you do not follow the lust of your own heart and your own eyes which lead you astray." The difference between the intelligent man and the simpleton is not the correctness of their decisions, but rather the cunning sinner can more skillfully defend and justify his iniquity. Heaven is not reserved only for the intellectual.

The heart can only be a wonderful thing if is bound up with the Creator and His *Torah*. King David therefore beseeched God for this in his uplifting prayer in Psalm 119:36, "Turn my heart to your commandments, and not to selfish gain."

Yours,

Rabbi Tovia Singer

# The Gentiles are Coming!

## Question:

Dear Rabbi Singer,

I have just received my order of your tape series today. I live in Canada and I am a Seventh-day Adventist minister. To say the least, your recorded lectures are eye-opening. Obviously, I will have to make some radical changes in my life and profession, and family life will be impacted drastically. I would value your input as I process these changes. Being in my mid forties with a large family this is a pivotal time to make this change for all of us.

My immediate question is this: I am interested in researching an accurate list of the 613 mitzvot. Is it possible to secure an e-mail list of the 613 commandments? Alternately, in what written publication will I find these listed?

Thanks for your loving efforts to speak the truth. Better the truth than the comfortable and the familiar. You have spoken the truth and I treasure it even though it upsets previously-held beliefs. I feel relieved since you have lifted severe cognitive dissonance in my thinking on the theological front. Many thanks.

## Answer:

Although Outreach Judaism is an organization dedicated to helping Jews understand why Judaism does not accept the Christian messiah, we are clearly reaching far beyond the nation of Israel with our crucial message. When I founded this organization it never entered my mind that so many gentiles would be so deeply affected by our work. Over the years, however, it became abundantly clear to me that in spite of my original goals, there were larger plans in store for Outreach Judaism. I could have never anticipated the vast number of both lay people and pastors coming forward out of the evangelical church and embracing the One God of Israel. I encountered an enormous amount of vile anti-Semitism in my youth so I just assumed that "*goyim*" were, for some strange, irrational reason, repulsed by Jews and Judaism. In later years I discovered that my childhood conclusions about non-Jews were wrong.

To answer to your question, I would recommend Maimonides' *Sefer Hamitzvos* which has been translated into English by Rabbi Charles B. Chavel, and is published by *Soncino Press* in a two-volume set.

Please stay in touch and may the Merciful One continue to guide you. With best wishes for a happy Chanukah.

Very truly yours,

Rabbi Tovia Singer

# Coping With Christmas

## Question:

Hello, Rabbi. I hope Hashem has been blessing your work and family. As you may recall, I am a former Christian who is now living as a Noahide and considering conversion to Judaism. I am confronted again with the Christian holiday season and am starting to encounter some uncomfortable situations at home since my extended family still celebrates Xmas. Their love and happiness are important to me, and I would appreciate any suggestions you may have for negotiating these difficulties.

## Answer:

The month of December often ushers in a season of strained family relations particularly when its members are made up of different religious faiths. This is especially true when those faiths are Judaism and Christianity.

Of all Christian holidays, one would least expect Christmas to generate this much family tumult, considering that the church has long abandoned its claim that Jesus was actually born on December 25th. Moreover, virtually all Christian scholars agree that the reason Christendom adopted this date to celebrate the second member of the

Trinity's birthday is because the pagan Roman holiday Solstice, the great festival of the sun god, was celebrated on December 25th as well. It therefore comes as little surprise that Christianity's Jesus also shares his birth date with so many other notable pagan deities of the mystery religions, such as the Persian god Mithra, and a host of other gods who were venerated throughout the Roman empire and beyond.

As a rabbi, I recommend that you follow the sage advice of the prophet Jeremiah who condemned Christmas Trees as a pagan ritual 500 years before the advent of Christianity!

> Thus saith the LORD: "Learn not the way of the nations, and be not dismayed at the signs of heaven; for the nations are dismayed at them.
> 3 For the customs of the peoples are vanity; for it is but a tree which one cutteth out of the forest, the work of the hands of the workman with the axe. 4 They deck it with silver and with gold, they fasten it with nails and with hammers, that it move not." (Jeremiah 10:2-4)

In order for me to render some more concrete advice on how to diplomatically avoid setting off family fireworks this holiday season, I encourage you to write back with some more details about your family's dynamics and volatility. Happy Chanukah!

Yours,

Rabbi Tovia Singer

# A Contrite Minister Apologizes for the Church's Long History of Hate

## Question:

Dear Rabbi Singer:

It was informative to browse your site. I am a pretty typical Presbyterian, Reformed, Calvinist, gentile pastor. Each time I read comments of Luther, Calvin, and others in my tradition as reflected in "Reformers' Advice," I'm filled with tremendous sadness and heaviness. Obviously we will differ on most things that matter most to us, and I really am not writing to argue the issues your site addresses. I only wish to apologize for my spiritual forbears without qualification or excuse. I feel real shame over their attitudes, and I'm warned to keep a careful watch over my own.

I'm an evangelical. I wish for everyone to believe in Jesus as Messiah, obviously. My prayer, though, is that Christians who may browse Outreach Judaism will hit that section and do some serious introspection. We can be very arrogant, especially in times and places where "cultural Christianity" is dominant; for this, I'm deeply, deeply sorry. We've wronged you and dishonored our faith through arrogance, aggression, and silence.

## Answer:

Your letter has touched me deeply. It does my heart good to know that you, a gentile Christian, are disturbed by these burning words of hate directed against the Children of Israel. If you have not set out to destroy the Jewish nation, with your lips or your hands, either spiritually or physically, you have nothing for which to apologize. I am, however, puzzled why you would ever identify yourself as a Calvinist after reading those comments.

Virtually all the reformers and church fathers held the Jewish people in contempt and encouraged their utter destruction. These founders and defenders of Christendom are therefore enduring the recompense of their iniquity under the wrath of God, as promised in the twelfth chapter of the book of Genesis.

Understandably, after nearly two millennia of unimaginable suffering at the hands of both the Catholic and Protestant faithful, it becomes clear to the Jewish people that the consistent pattern of unrelenting hatred emanating from the Christian is no coincidence. For example, my people have not endured this pattern of merciless hate from the followers of other religions such as Hinduism, Buddhism, or Mormonism. Likewise, the Jewish people have not experienced this genocidal enmity from members of the more liberal expressions of Christianity such as Unitarians and Methodists. Historically, Christian anti-Semitism has come, almost without exception, from the most devout segment of Christian society: the fundamentalist evangelical community. This history of relentless cruelty has not gone unnoticed by the Jewish people.

Understandably, the nation of Israel must ask this question: What connection exists between the beliefs of the devout Christian and his unyielding hate directed against the children of Israel? Why has the fundamentalist Christian, almost without exception, been our source of bitter anti-Semitism and savage oppression for the past two millennia?

Many Christians contend that those Christians who have persecuted the Jews were not real Christians. This response is both self-serving and preposterous. In fact, the most grievous expressions of hate against my faith and my people have come from the evangelical Christian world that has committed itself to converting the Jewish people to Christianity.

Your message of contrition is a valuable one. Preach it tirelessly among the evangelical Christian community. They desperately need to hear and understand it.

Best regards for a happy Passover.

Very sincerely yours,

Rabbi Tovia Singer

## Part XVI

# Outreach Judaism Responds to Jews for Jesus

# Outreach Judaism Responds To Jews for Jesus

The central goal of Outreach Judaism is to respond directly and effectively to unyielding Christian missionaries who specifically target Jews for conversion. As overzealous, fundamentalist denominations grow worldwide and Jewish evangelism continues at a feverish pitch, the overwhelming task of Outreach Judaism becomes more vital than ever.

**The *Let's Get Biblical* audio series and study guide refutes missionary claims**

Our renowned *Let's Get Biblical* audio series and accompanying in-depth study guide has become one of the most effective educational tools to empower Jewish communities worldwide and counter the well funded and highly aggressive missionary movement. Introduced in 1993, this program has helped countless Jews and gentiles understand why Judaism does not accept the Christian messiah. Moreover, this groundbreaking work has inspired and empowered so many to understand so much about the beauty and truth of the Jewish faith.

**Jews for Jesus responds to Outreach Judaism on its website**

Jews for Jesus, the most well known and highly aggressive organization committed to converting Jews to Christianity, posted on its web page its response to one of our hallmark audio programs entitled, "Sin and Atonement" from Outreach Judaism's *Let's Get Biblical* series. Strangely, Jews for Jesus calls this section of its web page which seeks to rebut our audio series, "*Let's Get **Really** Biblical.*" Their choice of this title is puzzling given that whereas our *Let's Get Biblical* audio series – as the title suggests – quotes exclusively from the scriptures, there is not a single instance where Jews for Jesus quotes the Bible throughout the entire corpus of their response. Instead, Jews for Jesus draws all of their arguments to support their rebuttal from rabbinic and secular sources.

Throughout the Let's Get Biblical audio series I only quote from the Bible for a simple reason. Christians reject the validity of the Judaism's rabbinic literature (although they quote it incessantly when it suites their agenda), thus it would be pointless to use any other source other than Tanach to disprove the arguments made by missionaries. It is only the words of the Jewish Scriptures alone that can empower a Christian to thoroughly grasp why Judaism does not accept the Christian messiah. It is only the eternal words of Tanach that can guide a lost Jewish soul in the Church back to the God of Israel.

**Christian doctrines refuted in the presentation, *"Sin and Atonement"***

Prior to responding to Jews for Jesus' numerous arguments, I will highlight the fundamental points that I address in my lecture entitled "Sin and Atonement." This presentation confronts and responds to one of Christendom's most central claims against its elder rival, Judaism: How can man expiate his sin without the shedding of blood? Missionaries argue that man's sin can only be cleansed through a blood sacrifice. They contend that there can be no forgiveness of sin *without* a blood sacrifice.[1] Without the blood of Jesus, man is utterly hopeless, lost in a state of eternal sin.[2] To prove this doctrine, the church teaches that the Bible sets forth blood atonement alone to expiate sin.[3] Moreover, evangelical Christians assert that for the past two millennia, since the destruction of the second temple in 70 C.E., Jews lacked this essential and indispensable animal-sacrificial system for atonement. Consequently, they conclude, God must have provided a blood atonement in place of the animal sacrifices of the past. This sacrifice, they declare, is Jesus' death on the Cross – man's only hope for salvation.

To support this claim that atonement can only be achieved through the shedding of blood, missionaries cite Leviticus 17:11 which reads:

**Christians quote Leviticus 17:11 to prove that blood-sacrifice alone atones for sin**

> "This is because the life of the flesh is in the blood, and I have given it to you upon the altar to make atonement for your souls; for it is the blood that makes atonement for the soul."

With this verse in hand, Christians conclude that only by being covered in the blood of the Cross can man have any hope of being forgiven by God for his sins.

The lecture "Sin and Atonement" and its corresponding chapter[4] in the study guide responds to the above missionary argument in a variety of ways. The following is a brief overview of six crucial points elucidated in the presentation "Sin and Atonement."

# Overview of the Presentation "Sin and Atonement"

**Refutation I**
There are three methods of atonement in the Bible – Blood Sacrifice is the weakest form of atonement

Contrary to the missionary claim that blood-sacrifice is the only method of atonement in the Bible, there are three methods of atonement clearly defined in the Jewish scriptures: The sin sacrifice,[5] repentance[6] and charity.[7] Moreover, the קָרְבַּן חַטָּאת (*Korban chatat*), the sin sacrifice, did not atone for all types of sin, but rather, only for man's most insignificant iniquity: unintentional sins.[8] The sin sacrifice was inadequate to atone for a transgression committed intentionally. The brazen sinner was barred from the Sanctuary, and had to bear his own iniquity because of his rebellious intent to sin against God. The Torah declares this fundamental principle in the following manner:

> "If a person sins **unintentionally**, then he shall offer a one year old female goat for a sin offering. And the priest shall make atonement before the Lord for the person who goes astray when he sins unintentionally, making atonement for him that he may be forgiven... But the person who does anything **defiantly**, whether he is native or an alien, that one is blaspheming the Lord; and that person shall be cut off from among his people. Because he has despised the word of the Lord and has broken His commandment, that person shall be completely cut off; his guilt shall be on him." (Numbers 15:27-31)

**Refutation II**
Leviticus 17:11 does not suggest that atonement can only be achieved through the shedding of blood; rather, it explains the prohibition against consuming blood

Contrary to the Christian claim that Leviticus 17:11 proves that man can only atone for his iniquity through the shedding of blood, this verse only explains the prohibition of eating blood.

Missionaries have conveniently severed this verse from its original context, effectively concealing and distorting its message.

In the immediate context of Leviticus 17:11, we find that the Torah is speaking of the prohibition of eating blood, not the subject of sin and atonement. The Torah discusses blood atonement in this verse only as a byproduct of its central theme. This crucial message is lost when missionaries quote Leviticus 17:11 alone, without the surrounding texts as its proper background. Leviticus 17:11 begins with the conjunctive Hebrew word כִּי (*kee*), meaning "This is because..." Whenever a verse begins with this conjunction, it is explaining what has just been related in the previous verse. The previous verse, Leviticus 17:10, reads,

> "And any man from the house of Israel, or from the aliens who sojourn among them, who eats any blood, I will set My face against that person who eats blood, and will cut him off from among his people."

Leviticus 17:11 then continues this message and explains,

> "This is because the life of the flesh is in the blood, and I have given it to you upon the altar to make atonement for your souls; for it is the blood that makes atonement for the soul."

Thus, Leviticus 17:11 explains Leviticus 17:10 by revealing that consuming blood is forbidden because it may only be used in the act of sprinkling of an animal's blood on the altar for an atonement. It is a grievous sin to use it for anything else.[9]

Leviticus 17:10-11 is therefore outlining two fundamental principles about blood: 1) you may not eat it 2) amongst all the various rituals associated with the sin sacrifice, such as the laying of the hands on the animal, slaughtering, collecting, carrying, sprinkling, placing of the animal on the altar, it is only the sprinkling the blood on the altar that brings about the atonement. You therefore may not eat of the blood. This verse does not state or imply that one cannot have atonement for sin without a blood sacrifice. Such a message would contradict all of the Jewish scriptures which clearly highlight two other methods of atonement more efficacious and pleasing to God than a blood sacrifice: heartfelt repentance and charity.[10]

Although the statement "without the shedding of blood there is no forgiveness of sins" is found nowhere in the Jewish scriptures, it does appear in the Christian scriptures. In Hebrews 9:22 the author misquotes Leviticus 17:11 when he states:

> "Indeed, under the law almost everything is purified with blood, and

without the shedding of blood there is no forgiveness of sins."

Although this quote in Hebrews 9:22 is always cross referenced in a Christian study Bible with Leviticus 17:11, it is a deliberate misquote of the original text in the Torah.

Furthermore, if missionaries seek to hold up Leviticus 17:11 to bolster their position that blood sacrifices are indispensable for procuring an atonement, they must use all of the verse, and not dispense with any part of it. Leviticus 17:11 specifically says that the blood of the sacrifice must be placed "upon the altar to make atonement for your souls." That is to say, Leviticus 17:11 explicitly declares that blood can only effect atonement if it is placed on the altar. Jesus' blood, however, was never placed on the altar. If the church is going to take the "blood" part of the verse literally, they must also take the "altar" part literally as well. Jesus' blood was never sprinkled on the altar, and therefore his death could not provide atonement for anyone.

Moreover, the Torah strictly prohibited the Jewish people from offering human sacrifices under any circumstances. There is not one place throughout the entire corpus of the Jewish scriptures where human sacrifices are condoned. Throughout the Book of Leviticus, only distinct species of animals are permitted for use in blood sacrifices.

**Refutation III**
The prophets openly pronounced that repentance and charity are more favorable to God than a blood sacrifice

Throughout the Jewish scriptures, the prophets declared that repentance and charity are more pleasing to God for atonement than a blood sacrifice.

They repeatedly forewarned the Jewish people from becoming obsessed with blood offerings. Other methods of atonement were more efficacious and would even replace animal sacrifices. For example, King David cries out to God:

> "Rescue me from blood-guilt, O God, God of my salvation. 17 My Lord, open my lips, that my mouth may declare Your praise. 18 For You desire no offering, else I would give it, a burnt offering You do not favor. 19 The offerings of God are a broken spirit, a heart broken and crushed O God, that You will not despise. (Psalm 51:16-19)

King David declares in Psalm 40:7:[11]

> "Sacrifice and burnt offering You have not desired; **<u>but my ears You have opened</u>**; burnt offering and sin offering You have not required."

These words of the Bible are not consistent with the Christian doctrine that sin can only be expiated through the shedding of blood. Because the Psalmist's words were deeply offensive to the early church, Hebrews 10:5-6 altered Psalm 40:7 to read instead:

> "Sacrifice and offering You did not desire, **<u>but a body You have prepared for Me</u>**. In burnt offerings and sacrifices for sin you had no pleasure."

Notice how King David's original words, "but my ears You have opened" have been removed entirely in the Hebrews quote. Instead, this New Testament author replaced this expunged clause with the words "But a body you have prepared for Me." This is a startling alteration of the Jewish scriptures.

The notion that the sacrificial system is central faith and atonement was condemned as heretical by the contemporary prophets Hosea and Micah.

> For I desire goodness, and not sacrifice; and the knowledge of God more than burnt-offerings." (Hosea 6:6)

> "With what shall I come before the Lord, *and* bow myself before the High God? Shall I come before Him with burnt offerings, With calves a year old? [7]Will the Lord be pleased with thousands of rams, Ten thousand rivers of oil? Shall I give my firstborn *for* my transgression, The fruit of my body *for* the sin of my soul? [8]He has shown you, O man, what *is* good; and what does the Lord require of you but to do justly, to love mercy, and to walk humbly with your God?" (Micah 6:6-8)

In his book of Proverbs, King Solomon explicitly states that giving charity is more effective method to atone for sin than a sacrifice:

> Riches will not avail on the day of wrath, but charity will save from death. (Proverbs 11:4)

> With loving-kindness and truth will iniquity be expiated, and through

fear of the Lord one turns away from evil. (Proverbs 16:6)

> Performing charity and justice is preferred by God to a sacrifice. (Proverbs 21:3)

During the Babylonian exile, following the destruction of Solomon's temple, Daniel declared that charity atones for sin:

> "Nevertheless, O king, let my advice be agreeable to you. Redeem your error with charity, and your sin through kindness to the poor, so that there will be an extension to your tranquility" (Daniel 4:24).

**Refutation IV**
Hosea foretold that the Jewish people would be without a sacrificial system, and instructed us to replace animal offerings with prayer

In Hosea 3:4-5, the prophet foretold with divine exactness that the Nation of Israel would not have a sacrificial system during the last segment of Jewish history until the messianic age.

> "For the children of Israel shall abide many days without king or prince, without sacrifice or sacred pillar, without *ephod* or *teraphim*. Afterward the children of Israel shall return and seek the Lord their God and David their king. They shall fear the Lord and His goodness in the latter days" (Hosea 3:4-5).

In the words of the Bible, this period of time would last for many days. Yet, despite the repeated proclamations of the church that the crucifixion of Jesus serves as a sin sacrifice today, the words of Hosea were meticulously fulfilled.

Given the spiritual magnitude of this remarkable prophecy, Hosea was compelled to reveal how the ecclesiastical temple functions were to be replaced. In essence, if the prophet is testifying that the nation of Israel will indeed be without a sacrificial system during their long exile until the messianic age, what are we to use instead? How are the Jewish people to worship without blood sacrifices during their bitter exile? What about all the animal sacrifices prescribed in the Book of Leviticus? Can the Jewish people get along without animal offerings? Missionaries claim they cannot. The Bible disagrees.

For this reason, the statement in Hosea 14:2-3 is crucial. In these two verses, Hosea reveals to his beloved nation how they are to replace the sacrificial system during their protracted exile. The prophet declares that the Almighty wants us to "render for bulls the offering of our lips." Prayer is to replace the sacrificial system.

> "Take words with you, and return to the Lord. Say to Him, "Take away all iniquity; receive us graciously, For we will render for bulls the offering of our lips." (Hosea 14:2-3)

The prophets never instruct the Jews to worship any crucified messiah or demigod.[12] Nor does scripture ever tell us that an innocent man can die as an atonement for the sins of the wicked.[13] Such a message is utterly antithetical to the teachings of the Jewish scriptures. Rather, it is the lips of the sinner that is transformed into bulls of the sin offerings.

**Refutation V**
Ezekiel condemns the doctrine of vicarious atonement

The prophet Ezekiel warned against Christendom's central doctrine that an innocent human being can die for the sins of the wicked.

Throughout the 18th chapter, Ezekiel warned his people that this erroneous teaching, i.e. that a righteous man could die for another man's sins was contrary to the will of God. The way for the sinful man to come right by God is to turn away from his rebellious ways and repent. Thereby, the penitent is assured complete forgiveness. Throughout Ezekiel's uplifting sermon on the forgiveness of sin, blood sacrifices are never mentioned.

> The word of the Lord came to me, saying: "What do you people mean by quoting this proverb about the land of Israel, saying: `The fathers eat sour grapes, and the sons' teeth are set on edge?' As I live, declares the Sovereign Lord, you will no longer quote this proverb in Israel. For every living soul belongs to Me, the father as well as the son – they are Mine. Which ever soul sins, it shall die... Yet you ask: Why did the son not bear the sin of the father? But the son, justice and righteousness did he do, all My decrees did he safeguard and perform them. He shall surely live. The soul that sins, it shall die! The son shall not bear for the sin of the father, nor the father bear for the sin of the son. The righteousness of the righteous person shall be upon him, and the wickedness of the wicked person shall be upon him. As for the wicked man, if he should turn away from all his sins which he did, and safeguard all My decrees, and do justice and righteousness; he shall surely live. He will not die. All his transgressions which he committed will not be remembered against

him. For the righteousness which he did, he shall live. Do I desire at all the death of the wicked man – the words of my Lord, God – is it not rather his return from his ways, that he might live." (Ezekiel 18:1-4, 19-23)

**Refutation VI**
If Jesus was the final sacrifice, why will the sacrificial system be restored in the messianic age?

Finally, the New Testament is clear that the animal sacrificial system never could atone for sin in any permanent way,[14] and indeed the entire purpose of the animal sacrificial system was, in the language of the Book of Hebrews, foreshadowing Jesus' death on the cross.[15]

The New Testament therefore repeatedly declares that Jesus was the final sacrifice for all time, and there would no longer be any future need for the return of the animal sacrificial system.

> By that will we have been sanctified through the offering of the body of Jesus Christ once *for all.* (Hebrews 10:10)

> Now where there is remission of these, **there is no longer an offering for sin.** (Hebrews 10:18)

This doctrine, however, completely contradicts the words of the prophets who clearly foretold that the animal sacrificial system would return in the messianic age.

If, as Paul argues, Jesus was the final sacrifice "once and for all" (Hebrews 10:10, 18), and the animal sacrificial system was merely a temporary "foreshadowing" of Calvary (Hebrews 9-10), why will animal sacrifices be restored in the messianic era? (see Ezekiel 44:27-31, 45:17-25).

# Jews for Jesus Argues that a Blood Sacrifice is Necessary for an Atonement: Here is Our Response

The Jewish scriptures tell us that blood sacrifice, heartfelt repentance, and charity atone for sin – blood sacrifice being the least efficacious of the three. Jews for Jesus disagrees, and they make the following argument:

> **Jews for Jesus argues the following:**
>
> **Is a blood sacrifice necessary for the forgiveness of sin?**
>
> Rabbi Tovia Singer tells us that according to the Tanach (the Hebrew Bible), not only blood but also repentance and charity atone for sin – and atonement by blood is the least important of all of them.
>
> The Tanach does give a few examples in which atonement was procured apart from blood sacrifice. he actions are really to avert God's wrath and not to secure forgiveness There is atonement by a cereal offering designed for poor people (Leviticus 5:11-13); atonement by the burning of incense (Numbers 16:46; Hebrew 17:11); atonement by gold (Numbers 31:50). In the last two cases, for sin; in the first case, an exception is made for a poor person who cannot bring an animal. The general rule remained: atonement came by a blood sacrifice.

# Our response:

In fact, these three verses raised by Jews for Jesus are mentioned nowhere in the audio series. Moreover, these texts do not support their conclusion. Jews for

Jesus' inference "The general rule remained: atonement came by blood sacrifice" is a non-sequitur.

Let's examine these three verses in greater detail: Leviticus 5:11-13, Numbers 17:11,[16] and Numbers 31:50 are examples in the Torah where atonement is procured without the shedding of blood. In Leviticus 5:11-13 the poor man may give a flour offering instead of an animal sacrifice for an atonement. Numbers 17:11[17] describes how Aaron made an atonement for the people with incense, and in Numbers 31:50 the Torah declares that the golden ornaments donated by high officers of the military who successfully defeated the Midianites were offered as an atonement as well.

It is worth mentioning that missionaries often argue that in the case of the poor man's flour offering, the flour was mixed by the priest with the other blood-offerings. Thus, having the flour mixed with the blood of someone else's sacrifice, a partnership was somehow created with another man's blood offering, who has vicariously provided blood for the poor man's sacrifice. The problem with this argument is that it is thoroughly unbiblical. Nowhere does the Torah state that the flour offering was mixed with any other sacrifice. On the contrary, it was equal to any other sacrifice, because it was placed on the altar like any other offering.

Jews for Jesus' statement that the incense and the gold ornaments "are really to avert God's wrath and not to secure forgiveness for sin" is incorrect. The Bible clearly states otherwise. With regard to the incense brought by Aaron, the Torah says:

> So Moses said to Aaron, "Take a censer and put fire in it from the altar, put incense on it, and take it quickly to the congregation and make atonement for them; for wrath has gone out from the Lord. The plague has begun" (Numbers 17:11).

Here the Torah clearly states that the incense both averted God's wrath and provided an atonement for the people. Jews for Jesus' statement with regard to the case of the golden ornaments is even more puzzling because nowhere does scripture ever state that the golden ornaments were to avert God's wrath. The Torah only declares that the purpose of this donation was to procure an atonement.

It is interesting to note that the Hebrew word כפר *kapar* (atonement) used in Leviticus 17:11 – the verse Jews for Jesus uses to "prove" that only blood can be used as an atonement – is the identical word used in all three verses that Jews for Jesus insists did "not secure forgiveness for sin." Well, which is it? Does כפר

*kapar* mean an atonement or not? You can't have it both ways.

The Torah explains in Leviticus 17:11 why it is forbidden to consume blood: it has been set aside for the sole purpose of making atonement on the altar. Leviticus 17:11 does not imply that the only method of atonement is the shedding of blood. By ripping Talmudic texts out of context, Jews for Jesus will argue that Jewish sources differ with Rabbi Singer. Let us examine Jews for Jesus' argument.

## Jews for Jesus:

In connection with this, Rabbi Singer questions the use of Leviticus 17:11 to demonstrate that a blood sacrifice was necessary. The verse reads, "For the life of the flesh is in the blood; and I have given it to you upon the altar to make atonement for your souls; for it is the blood that maketh atonement by reason of the life" (Jewish Publication Society translation). Because the context of Lev. 17:11 is the prohibition against consuming blood, Rabbi Singer argues that the point of the verse is: blood is prohibited because it is used to atone – but not that the verse teaches that blood is the main or only way of atonement.

Traditional Jewish sources differ with Rabbi Singer:

**Babylonian Talmud, Yoma 5a, citing Leviticus 17:11**
Does the laying on of the hand make atonement for one? Does not atonement come through the blood, as it is said: For it is the blood that maketh atonement by reason of the life!.... Does the waving make atonement? Is it not the blood which makes atonement, as it is written, 'For it is the blood that maketh atonement by reason of the life'? (Soncino Talmud edition)

**Babylonian Talmud, Zevahim 6a, citing Leviticus 17:11**
Surely atonement can be made only with the blood, as it says, For it is the blood that maketh atonement by reason of the life! (Soncino Talmud edition)

# Our response:

These traditional sources do not disagree with us at all. Jews for Jesus is again taking these Talmudic texts completely out of context. If these Talmudic quotes texts were indeed sited in context, it would be clear that our sages have nothing at all to do with the point that Jews for Jesus is trying to prove. Let us examine these Talmudic texts further.

Both the Talmud in Tractate Yoma 5a and Zevachim 6a are addressing the same aspect of animal sacrifices, and are therefore quoting from the identical statement in a *Baraisa*.[18] More specifically, both of these sections of the Talmud examining the same question: What specific error might occur during a sacrifice offering that would invalidate it? As noted earlier, there are many rituals that are performed during a sacrificial ceremony, including the leaning of the hands on the animal, the four actions relating to the blood (slaughtering, collecting the blood in a service vessel, carrying the blood to the altar, and the sprinkling of the blood on the altar), and the burning of the entrails and fats, etc. This *Baraisa*, quoted in both Yoma 5a and Zevachim 6a, questions whether when a sacrifice is offered, the does the act of leaning of the sinner's hands on the animal brings about the atonement. The *Baraisa* insists that this could not be the case when we consider that Leviticus 17:11 explicitly states that it is the blood on the altar that makes the atonement for one's soul. Therefore, "there is no atonement other than the blood" (Jews for Jesus), and the leaning would not effect the atonement.

The essential principle of sacrifice and atonement is that atonement can only occur after the blood of the sinner's sacrificed animal has been sprinkled on the altar. The other rituals relating to sacrifice, such as the leaning of the hands, are secondary and do not effect the atonement. The Talmud's quote in Yoma 5a and Zevachim 6a of the *Baraisa* is speaking within the narrow context of the sacrificial offering; and within that slender context, it is only the blood of the animal sprinkled on the altar that brings about the atonement. This section of the Talmud is not addressing atonement in general, but rather sacrificial atonement alone. Our sages do not contradict the words of the Bible which explicitly state that there are other methods of atonement that are superior to ritual sacrifice.[19]

The biblical principle that repentance and charity atone for sin is taught and explained in countless places throughout the entire corpus of the Talmud. In fact, later on in Tractate Yoma – the same tractate that Jews for Jesus uses as support for their claim – the Talmud says that when a person repents of his transgressions out of love, not only are his sins forgiven, but his premeditated transgressions are accounted as merits![20] **(See also Baruch Levine's commentary below on Leviticus 17:11)**

Jews for Jesus also cites the modern Jewish commentator, Baruch Levine, trying to substantiate the Christian doctrine that atonement is only achieved through the shedding of blood. Let us examine their argument.

## Jews for Jesus:

Similarly, modern Jewish commentator Baruch Levine

Expiation by means of sacrificial blood-rites is a prerequisite for securing God's forgiveness. As the rabbis expressed it, '*ein kapparah 'ella' be-dam*, "There is no ritual expiation except by means of blood."

– Baruch Levine, The JPS Torah Commentary: Leviticus; The Traditional Hebrew Text with the New JPS Translation (Philadelphia: Jewish Publication Society, 1989), p. 23, referring to Yoma 5a cited above.

# Our response:

What Jews for Jesus neglects to mention is the context in which Baruch Levine's statement appears. The above quote of Baruch Levine appears in his commentary on Leviticus 4:20, which concludes with the Torah's explanation of how the blood is ceremonially sprinkled on the curtain of the Tent of the Meeting by the priest. Jews for Jesus does not offer an explanation as to which sin the Torah is referencing, and therefore their choice of using Baruch Levine's quote is irrelevant, since not all sins require the offering of an animal, i.e. the shedding of blood, for sacrifice.

Let's now quote Baruch Levine in context, so we get a sense of his commentary on the overall picture of atonement and blood sacrifice. Does Baruch Levine agree with Jews for Jesus?

> "It should be emphasized here, as the workings of the sacrificial system are introduced to the reader, that the laws of the Torah did not permit Israelites to expiate intentional or premeditated offenses by means of sacrifice. There was no vicarious, ritual remedy – substitution of one's property or wealth – for such violations, whether they were perpetrated against other individuals or against God Himself. In those cases, the law dealt directly with the offender, imposing real punishments and acting to prevent recurrences. The entire expiatory system ordained in the Torah must be understood in this light. Ritual expiation was restricted to situations where a reasonable doubt existed as to the willfulness of the offense. Even then, restitution was always required where loss or injury to another person had occurred. The mistaken notion that ritual worship could atone for criminality or intentional religious desecration was persistently attacked by the prophets of Israel, who considered it a major threat to the entire covenantal relationship between Israel and God."

Baruch Levine, *The JPS Torah Commentary: Leviticus; The Traditional Hebrew Text with the New JPS Translation* (Philadelphia: *Jewish Publication Society*, 1989), p. 3, under the heading, The Principal Types of Sacrifice (1:1-7:38)

Below is another quote from Baruch Levine on Leviticus 17:11. Jews for Jesus insists that this verse proves that atonement can only be procured through the shedding of blood. Baruch Levine disagrees.

> "Substitution was allowed only in cases of inadvertence. Where the offense against God had been intentional, ritual expiation did not apply."

– Baruch Levine, The JPS Torah Commentary: Leviticus; The Traditional Hebrew Text with the New JPS Translation (Philadelphia: Jewish Publication Society, 1989), p. 115, on Leviticus 17:11.

To summarize, the Jewish scriptures clearly teach that blood sacrifice is not necessary for the forgiveness of sin. Comments from traditional Jewish sources and the modern commentator Baruch Levine examined critically, in context, lend no support whatsoever to Jews for Jesus' statements.

The Jewish scriptures clearly state that sacrifice was used to atone for man's least grievous transgressions, essentially unintentional sins and therefore the prophets did not dignify the blood sacrificial system. On the contrary, as if with one voice, these men of God declared that repentance and charity were more pleasing to God than a blood sacrifice.[21] Jews for Jesus, however, maintains that Jesus' death was sacrificial in nature, and his death atones for all sins. They obscure the clear words of the Jewish scriptures by quoting modern Jewish commentators out of context who are discussing peripheral issues. Let us look at their argument.

## Jews for Jesus:

Rabbi Singer maintains that sacrifice was only meant for unintentional sins. For example, he cites Leviticus 4 which says that the sin offering (the hattat) was for unintentional sins. Numbers 15 says that the person who sins "with a high hand" will be cut off. The intentional murderer must be put to death; only the man slaughterer who killed someone accidentally can have atonement. How then, Rabbi Singer asks, could Jesus be a sacrifice for all sins, including intentional ones?

The sin offering was only one kind of sacrifice. Though it was specified for inadvertent sins, other sacrifices were not restricted in that way. The full evidence includes the following:

**Exhibit A: Modern Jewish commentators:**

**Jacob Milgrom:**
The function of the burnt offering as exemplified by the Hittite sources, cited above, is clearly propitiatory and expiatory (for "wrath," "guilt," "offense," "sin"), a fact that accords with the purpose assigned to the burnt offering in this chapter [Lev. 1].... "to expiate" (v 4)....

> Some medieval commentators suggest the entire range of unwitting sins (Bekhor Shor; cf. Shadal) and even brazen sins, if their punishment is not specified (Ramban).

– Jacob Milgrom, Leviticus 1-16: A New Translation With Introduction and Commentary (Anchor Bible; New York: Doubleday, 1991), p. 175.

# Our response:

Once again, Jews for Jesus is quoting out of context. The above commentary by Jacob Milgrom appears within the context of the *Olah* offering. This sacrifice which was burnt entirely on the altar had the distinction of being a voluntary offering. It was brought when the individual felt a sense of personal guilt and wished to express his penitence by offering this free-will sacrifice. The unrepentant brazen sinner, however, was barred from the sacrificial system.

Let us now listen to the words of Jacob Milgrom as he speaks about sacrifices in general, and see if he agrees with Jews for Jesus.

> "Inadvertence is a key criterion in all expiatory sacrifice. A deliberate, brazen sinner is barred from the sanctuary (Numbers 15:30-31)."
>
> Jacob Milgrom, *Leviticus 1-16: A New Translation With Introduction and Commentary* (Anchor Bible; New York: Doubleday, 1991), p. 228.

Once again, let's read Jacob Milgrom's own words on the matter of why in the case of the *Asham*, does the Torah place the repentant transgressor in the class of the inadvertent sinner:

> "The witness's defiance of the imprecation is indisputably a deliberate, if not a brazen, misdemeanor. Ibn Ezra would add the element of a memory lapse, which plays a role in the following cases (vv 2-4), but its absence here is hardly accidental. Then, why is his sin expiable by sacrifice? The answer lies in his subsequent remorse, a factor that is not stated in the case itself but in the general protasis governing all four cases (vv 4b, 5a); it is his subsequent guilt אשם (*asem*) that is responsible for converting his deliberate sin into an inadvertence, expiable by sacrifice."
>
> Jacob Milgrom, *Leviticus 1-16: A New Translation With Introduction and Commentary* (Anchor Bible; New York: Doubleday, 1991), p. 295.

## Jews for Jesus:

Baruch Levine

The offenses outlined here [in Lev. 5:20-26] were quite definitely intentional! A person misappropriated property or funds entrusted to his safekeeping, or defrauded another, or failed to restore lost property he had located.... If, subsequently, the accused came forth on his own and admitted to having lied under oath – thus assuming liability for the unrecovered property – he was given the opportunity to clear himself by making restitution and by paying a fine of 20 percent to the aggrieved party. Having lied under oath, he had also offended God and was obliged to offer an *asham* sacrifice in expiation.... God accepts the expiation even of one who swears falsely in His name because the guilty person is willing to make restitution to the victim of his crime....

Baruch Levine, *JPS Torah Commentary*, pp. 32-33. Note: *asham* means a "guilt offering."

Baruch Levine, again

> [In Lev. 5:20-26], an *asham* is offered in expiation of any of a series of deceitful acts involving an oath and the loss of property to others.

Levine, *JPS Torah Commentary*, pp. 25-26.

# Our response:

The Asham sacrifice gives us great insight into the biblical principle where in certain cases, such the breaking of an oath, a willful sinner's transgression may be placed into the unique category of an unintentional sinner, solely due to temporary loss of memory. This occurs in circumstances outlined in the fifth chapter of Leviticus where the transgressor has diminished his iniquity by voluntarily confessing his sin. This individual may therefore bring an *Asham* sacrifice.

> When a person utters an oath to bad or good purpose – whatever a man may utter in an oath – and, though he has known it, the fact has escaped him, but later he realizes his guilt in any of these matters – When he realizes his guilt in any of these matters, he shall confess that

wherein he has sinned. (Leviticus 5:4)

This *Asham* sacrifice offers us a perfect example of how the above principle is demonstrated in the Torah. For example, in Leviticus 5:20-26 (in a Christian Bible these verses appear as Leviticus 6:1-7) the Torah declares that a person who acts deceitfully by causing a loss of property to another, must pay the victim the principal plus a fifth and in addition must bring an *Asham* offering.

> The Lord spoke to Moses, saying: [21] "When a person sins and commits a trespass against the Lord by dealing deceitfully with his fellow in the matter of a deposit or a pledge, or through robbery, or by defrauding his fellow, [22] or by finding something lost and lying about it; if he swears falsely regarding any one of the various things that one may do and sin thereby – [23] when one has thus sinned and, realizing his guilt, would restore that which he got through robbery or fraud, or the deposit that was entrusted to him, or the lost thing that he found, [24] or anything else about which he swore falsely, he shall repay the principal amount and add a fifth part to it. He shall pay it to its owner when he realizes his guilt. [25] Then he shall bring to the priest, as his penalty to the Lord, a ram without blemish from the flock, or the equivalent, as a guilt offering. [26] The priest shall make expiation on his behalf before the LORD, and he shall be forgiven for whatever he may have done to draw blame thereby." (Leviticus 5:20-26 – Leviticus 6:1-7 in a Christian Bible)

So why revisit the issue of theft when it was already addressed by the Torah in Exodus 22, where scripture declares that a thief has to pay the victim double, and in the case of a sheep or an ox, he must repay four and five times, respectfully? Well, which is it? Is it two, four or five times the theft as prescribed by Exodus 22, or is it one and a fifth plus an *Asham* sacrifice, as commanded in Leviticus 5:20-26? Is this a contradiction in the Torah?

Actually, there is no contradiction here at all. In Exodus 22, the thief was caught, and he therefore must repay an exorbitant fine for his transgression. For the brazen sinner, no blood offering is sufficient to make himself right with God, and he is barred from the sacrificial system. In Leviticus 5, on the other hand, the thief was not caught. Rather, after originally swearing falsely that he was innocent, he came forward on his own, admitted his guilt, and amended his crime. In this unique case, the Torah teaches us that in a number of unique cases, the person who confessed his sin is perceived an unwitting sinner in that he may bring a sacrifice to atone, albite his original transgression was deliberate. In the case of the unrepentant sinner who was caught stealing in Exodus 22, however, no sacrifice can undo his iniquity. An animal offering simply was not enough to atone for his deliberate sin.

## Jews for Jesus:

What then about the intentional sin in Numbers 15:30-31 (the sin "with a high hand") which is apparently unforgivable? That verse reads "But the soul that doeth aught with a high hand, whether he be home-born or a stranger, the same blasphemeth the LORD; and that soul shall be cut off from among his people. Because he hath despised the word of the LORD, and hath broken His commandment; that soul shall utterly be cut off, his iniquity shall be upon him."

**We present Exhibit B**, the Talmudic and medieval commentators. According to the sages, repentance could turn an intentional sin into an unintentional sin and so be eligible for sacrifice. This is explained by the original sources and by modern commentators on those sources: Babylonian Talmud, Yoma 86b

> R. Simeon b. Lakish said: Great is repentance, which converts intentional sins into unintentional ones.

As cited by Milgrom, Leviticus, p. 373. The Soncino Talmud edition translates: "Resh Lakish said: Great is repentance, for because of it premeditated sins are accounted as errors."

---

Rashi (11th c.), on Numbers 15:31, explaining the phrase "his iniquity is upon him."

> Only at the time when (under the circumstances that) his iniquity is upon him shall he be cut off, i.e., in the case that he has not repented (Sanh. 90b).

*Rosenbaum-Silbermann* edition (New York: Hebrew Publishing Company)

*Cont.*

## Jews for Jesus continued from the previous page:

Jacob Milgrom

> This literary image [of the "high hand"] is most apposite for the brazen sinner who commits his acts in open defiance of the Lord (cf. Job. 38:15). The essence of this sin is that it is committed flauntingly. However, sins performed in secret, even deliberately, can be commuted to the status of inadvertencies by means of repentance....

Jacob Milgrom, *The JPS Commentary: Numbers; The Traditional Hebrew Text with the New JPS Translation* (Philadelphia: Jewish Publication Society, 1990), p. 125. See also J. Milgrom, *"The Priestly Doctrine of Repentance,"* Revue Biblique 82 (1975): 186-205.

> ...I submit that the repentance of the sinner, through his remorse...and confession..., reduces his intentional sin to an inadvertence, thereby rendering it eligible for sacrificial expiation....

Milgrom, Leviticus, p. 373.

> ...The early rabbis...raise the question of how the high priest's bull is capable of atoning for his deliberate sins, and they reply, "Because he has confessed his brazen and rebellious deeds it is as if they become as unintentional ones before him" (*Sipra, Ahare* par. 2:4,6; cf. t. Yoma 2:1). Thus it is clear that the *Tannaites* attribute to repentance – strikingly, in a sacrificial ritual – the power to transform a presumptuous sin against God, punishable by death, into an act of inadvertence, expiable by sacrifice.

Milgrom, Leviticus, p. 373.

*Cont.*

## Jews for Jesus continued from the previous page:

Is unintentional sin the least significant kind of sin?

Rabbi Singer maintains that unintentional sin is the least significant kind, implying that the sacrifices offered in the Tenach were for insignificant transgressions; real sins would be atoned for in other ways.

In fact, the very opposite was true in Biblical times: unintentional sin was if anything considered more grave than intentional sin, simply because one could never know if one had transgressed in such a case.

We summon to the stand:

Jacob Milgrom

> Unwitting sin as the cause of disaster is widely attested in the ancient world. The sin of unwitting sacrilege against the deity is especially feared....In the early rabbinic period, the "suspended 'asham" (5:17-19) played a more central role. It was brought frequently by the pious, who were certain that they could deter conscious sins but were in dread over the possibility of committing sins unconsciously.

*Milgrom, Leviticus*, pp. 361-362.

**THIS COURT IS IN RECESS...TO BE CONTINUED**

# Our response:

It is difficult to begin our response, because the above statements furnished by Jews for Jesus so perfectly support our point. In fact, if I had not restricted myself to using the Bible alone in the audio series, I could have cited any of Jews for Jesus' quotes to further strengthen my teachings in my presentation on *Sin and Atonement.*

Let's examine this profound statement of this great Amorah[22] Resh Lakish. "Great is repentance, which converts intentional sins into unintentional ones."[23] What does this mean? Why is repentance great? Because it transforms an intentional sin into an unintentional sin. Does this mean that intentional sins are greater or weaker than unintentional sins? Obviously, if unintentional sins were more grievous this statement would make no sense. Clearly, this statement by Resh Lakish is telling us that a sin committed intentionally is far more grave than a transgression committed unwittingly.

Despite the clear provisions of the Jewish scriptures that heartfelt repentance, charity, as well as blood sacrifice atone for sin, Jews for Jesus continues to insist that sin can only be forgiven through the sacrificial shedding of blood.

Moreover, we have shown that Ezekiel, speaking in the name of God, condemns the notion of human vicarious atonement. He therefore encourages his nation to turn to God through repentance alone for a complete atonement. Through this bloodless atonement, he promises, all sin would be forgotten. Throughout his sermon on atonement, Ezekiel never mentions the sacrificial system. The prophet only assures the Jewish people that the Almighty does not wish to punish the wicked, but rather "that they turn from their ways, so they might live."[24]

Furthermore, the prophet Hosea predicted that the children of Israel would spend their bitter exile without the sacrificial system,[25] and encourages his beloved nation to use their lips filled with words of penitence for their atonement so that the lips of the sinner would become as bulls of the sin offerings.[26]

In conclusion, every source cited by Jews for Jesus is taken completely out of context and does nothing to support the Christian doctrines they seek to sustain or the Jewish mind they are trying to satisfy. It is therefore no surprise that not one of the individuals quoted by Jews for Jesus has ever spent a moment of their Jewish lives believing in Jesus.

# CASE IS REALLY CLOSED

## Footnotes:

1. Hebrews 9:22

2. Romans 3:9-18; Ephesians 4:18; I Corinthians 2:14

3. Hebrews 9:22

4. Chapter III

5. Leviticus 4:1-35

6. Deuteronomy 4:26-31; I Kings 8:46-50; Isaiah 55:6-9; Jeremiah 7:3-23; Ezekiel 18:1-23; Hosea 6:6; 14:2-3; Micah 6:6; Psalm 40:7-9 (6-8); 51:16-19;

7. Proverbs 10:2; 11:4; 16:6; Daniel 4:24; II Chronicles 6:36-39

8. This biblical principle is laid out in Leviticus 4:1-35 and Numbers 15:27-31. As will be discussed below, there is a unique case when the Torah tells us that, under certain circumstances, an individual who sinned intentionally is accorded the benefit of the unintentional sinner's ritual blood expiation with an Asham (guilt) offering.

9. The Torah therefore commands us in Leviticus 17:13 – only three verses later – that when the animal is slaughtered, the blood must be poured on to the floor and covered with earth, rendering it useless. See also Deuteronomy 12:16, "You shall not eat the blood; you shall pour it on the earth like water."

10. I Samuel 15:22; Micah 6:6-8; Psalms 40:7 (6); Hosea 6:6, 14:2-3 Proverbs; 10:2 Proverbs 11:4; Proverbs 16:6; Proverbs 21:3

11. In a Christian Bible this verse appears as Psalm 40:6

12. Exodus 20:2-3; Deuteronomy 4:35; 6:14; 32:39; Hosea 13:4

13. Exodus 32:33; Ezekiel 18:1-23

14. Hebrews 10:4 insists that the animal sacrificial system had no lasting value.

"For it is not possible that the blood of bulls and goats could take away sins." This was a necessary assertion for the author of Hebrews because if the animal sacrifices really worked, why was Jesus' death necessary? It should have been sufficient to keep bringing animal offerings.

15 Hebrews 10:1

16 Romans 6:10; Hebrews 9:12; 10:10; 10:18

17. Jeremiah 33:17-18; Zachariah 14:21; Ezekiel 43-44. Missionaries often try to excuse this problem by claiming that the reason animal sacrifices will return is to point back to Jesus. This response, however, is a rationalization that is not even used in the New Testament, and thoroughly contradicts the statements in Romans and Hebrews. Moreover, this response makes little sense. Why would there be any need to point back to anything?

18. In a Christian Bible this verse appears as 16:46

19. A *Baraisa* is a statement made by a *Tanna* which was not included by Rabbi Yehudah Ha'nasi (Approximately 200 C.E.) in the *Mishnah*.

20 Deuteronomy 4:26-31; I Samuel 15:22; I Kings 8:46-50; Isaiah 55:6-9; Jeremiah 7:3-23; Ezekiel 18:1-23; Hosea 6:6; 14:2-3; Micah 6:6; Psalm 40:7-9 (6-8); 51:16-19; Proverbs 10:2; 11:4; 16:6

21 Yoma 86b discusses the greatness and efficacy of repentance. Resh Lakish states that for those who repent out of fear, "Great is repentance, which converts intentional sins into unintentional ones." For those who repent out of love, "Great is repentance which converts intentional sins into merits."

22. The term *Amora* refers to those sages that were contributors to the Talmud. Rabbi Shimon Ben Lakish, or Resh Lakish as he was better known, lived in the land of Israel during the third century C.E.

23. Ezekiel 18:1-23

24. Hosea 3:4-5

25. Hosea 14:2-3

# Index of Scripture References

*Parenthesis ( ) indicates scripture location in a Christian Bible*

## Jewish Scriptures

### Genesis



### Exodus

## Leviticus



## Numbers



## Deuteronomy

## I Samuel



## II Samuel



## I Kings



## II Kings



## Isaiah

## Jeremiah



## Ezekiel



## Joel

## Amos



## Hosea



## Obadiah



## Jonah



## Micah



## Zephaniah



## Habakkuk



## Zechariah



## Malachi



## Psalms

## Proverbs



## Job



## Song of Songs



## Ruth



## Lamentations



## Ecclesiastes



## Daniel



## Ezra

### Nehemiah



### I Chronicles



### II Chronicles



## Christian Scriptures

### Matthew



### Mark



### Luke

## John



## Acts



## Romans